SONOMA VALLEY

The Secret Wine Country

Help Us Keep This Guide Up to Date

Every effort has been made by the authors and editors to make this guide as accurate and useful as possible. However, many things can change after a guide is published—establishments close, phone numbers change, facilities come under new management, etc.

We would love to hear from you concerning your experiences with this guide and how you feel it could be improved and kept up to date. While we may not be able to respond to all comments and suggestions, we'll take them to heart and we'll also make certain to share them with the authors. Please send your comments and suggestions to the following address:

The Globe Pequot Press
Reader Response/Editorial Department
P.O. Box 480
Guilford, CT 06437

Or you may e-mail us at:

editorial@globe-pequot.com

Thanks for your input, and happy travels!

HILL GUIDES™ SERIES

SONOMA VALLEY

The Secret Wine Country

THIRD EDITION

by Kathleen Thompson Hill
&
Gerald Hill

The Globe Pequot Press

Guilford, Connecticut

Cover painting entitled *Sonoma: Valley of the Moon* by Judy Theo Lehner, M.F.A. Studio address: 134 Church Street, Sonoma, CA 95476.
(707) 996–5111. Medium: monotype.
Cover and text design by Lana Mullen
Maps by Jeffrey Holman
Illustrations by Mauro Magellan
Photos by Kathleen & Gerald Hill and Gary R. Beem (Sears Point Raceway)
Historical photos courtesy of Lolita McKinney, CalFed Bank, and
Theresa Janbaz

Library of Congress Cataloging-in-Publication Data

Hill, Kathleen, 1941–
    Sonoma Valley : the secret wine country / by Kathleen Thompson Hill
    & Gerald Hill.—3rd ed.
        p. cm.—(Hill guides)
    Includes index.
    ISBN 0-7627-0653-8
    1. Sonoma Valley (Calif.)—Guidebooks.   2. Wine and wine making—
California—Sonoma Valley—Guidebooks. I. Title: Sonoma Valley,
the secret wine country.   II. Hill, Gerald N.   III. Title.

F868.S7 H56 2000
917.94'180453—dc21   00-022012

Manufactured in the United States of America
Third Edition/First Printing

CONTENTS

PREFACE

We wrote our first guide to Sonoma Valley in 1996 for fun and love of our home and because there was no book that fully described this beautiful place, its people, attractions, wineries, accommodations, businesses, history, and public facilities. The valley was so under-discovered, we subtitled the first Hill Guide The Secret Wine Country.

Now after two editions and several reprintings, there have been so many changes that we agreed with our publishers that a third edition was appropriate. The dynamics of the valley resulted in new restaurants, innovative cuisine, different owners, retirements, new blood, more wines and wineries, many structures rebuilt or renovated, and increased interest in the "Valley of the Moon" as a destination. Thankfully, the essential beauty of the valley lives on.

We hope you will join us in exploring Sonoma Valley, first on the printed page and then as we take you step by step through the not-so-secret wine country.

—Kathleen Thompson Hill
—Gerald Hill

ACKNOWLEDGMENTS

*F*rom the time we first got the idea for a much-needed guide to Sonoma Valley, we received much-appreciated advice, encouragement, and assistance in gathering information, and on occasion a meal or a glass of wine.

In defining what people would want in a guide, we received invaluable advice from friends Mary Evelyn Arnold (who taught us that we own the computer, and it does not own us), travel agent–supreme Sandy Snorey, and Sonoma Valley Visitors Bureau officials Chris Finlay and Jeanne Markson.

Hal Beck, Executive Director of the Sonoma Valley Chamber of Commerce, Lolita McKinnery of CalFed Bank, and Theresa Janbaz of the Pinelli family provided valuable materials and historic photos. Vallejo descendant Earl Douglas generously shared historic data and suggestions, as did knowledgeable Sonomans Rose Millerick and Carmella Vella Benedetto.

Our thanks go to friends Susan Weeks and Sue Holman, who were always available to provide good humor and were willing to sacrifice themselves by testing restaurants upon request. Cartographer Jeffrey Holman gave patient attention to his excellent job on the maps.

One of our great discoveries was the noted Sonoma artist Judy Theo Lehner, whose remarkable paintings now grace the covers of all the Hill Guides series. We love her work and thank her for letting us be the beneficiaries of her talent.

Especially we thank owners, managers, and employees of the Sonoma Valley restaurants, accommodations, wineries, and businesses who were so generous with their time and help. We are particularly appreciative of the Sonoma Valley chefs who were willing to share their secrets and recipes so that the readers can enjoy Sonoma Cuisine at home.

Finally our appreciation to the staff of Globe Pequot Press for their professional and personal care in helping us produce the second and third editions of *Sonoma Valley: The Secret Wine Country,* and a special thanks to Executive Editor Laura Strom for her faith in us.

"Heaven, a place that is said to resemble Sonoma in the spring...."

—Herb Caen, *San Francisco Chronicle*

INTRODUCTION

*A*s we reexplored Sonoma Valley to complete this third edition, more than ever we realized that Sonoma Valley--our home for a quarter of a century–is one of the most beautiful natural locations in the world. A smallish agricultural and commuter community centered on the luxuriant plaza in the heart of the historic town of Sonoma, it is little wonder it had previously been memorialized by Jack London and Luther Burbank.

Author M. F. K. Fisher, our late dear friend with whom we spent many days in her last six years, told us she built her house on what is now the Pleydell-Bouverie Audubon Preserve because the gently rolling hills, the green and then golden-brown grass, the oak trees, the light winter rains and summer heat, and even the aromas of the flowers and the grape crush reminded her so much of France's Provence.

The valley is a peaceful, quiet, and romantic place with little unemployment and a low crime rate. Vineyards, wineries, parks, hiking trails, restaurants, and tourist attractions form a rich mosaic of valley life.

There is a constant struggle to protect the valley from development that might destroy its rural and small-town nature or damage its historic heritage, which dates back to 1823. It is not that Sonomans want to "pull up the drawbridge" to keep out newcomers, but most are adamant in their efforts to preserve its beauty, its peace and pace, and the human scale of this unique valley.

In the summer of 1999, the proposal by out-of-town developers to build a superluxury resort on the backdrop hills overlooking the center of Sonoma was defeated by a vote of more than three to one, with a record-high voter turnout. Rejecting the blandishments of large hotel tax income for the city treasury, the people organized a stunning grassroots campaign to save the hills from development, despite being outspent by the corporate sponsors by almost twenty to one. It was a defining moment, in which the people clearly stated they did not mind some growth and tourism, but not at the expense of the natural beauty of the Sonoma Valley.

THE MEANING OF SONOMA

Sonoma Valley's legendary author Jack London claimed that Valley of the Moon was a loose translation of the Miwok Indian word Sonoma, *because the local Native Americans believed that, as one travels through the valley, one can see the moon rise seven times from behind the hills. The full moon lighting up the Sonoma Valley is a stunning sight, but it would take a horse much speedier than any the local Huichica Indians had to race 15 miles past seven hills as the moon made its way into the evening sky. It also seems hard to believe that three brief syllables could translate into Valley of the Moon.*

Just before he died, Jack London told an interviewer from the literary magazine Bookman: *"I was tired of cities and city people, and I was looking about for a home in the country when I discovered this hillside place in The Valley of the Moon. I observed that some of the professors at the University of California question that translation of Sonoma, but it is The Valley of the Moon to me."*

The usually reliable Illustrated Dictionary of Place Names *says that Sonoma means "nose," from a Wintun Indian word,* Soninmak, *"but the reason is unknown." The entry adds that the Valley of the Moon interpretation is "fanciful." But one problem with the "nose" theory is that the Wintun resided principally in the Sacramento Valley; the closest they ever lived to Sonoma was in the Napa Valley. The Sonoma Valley natives from whom the Spanish first heard the word* Sonoma *were Coast Miwok and Pomo.*

Dr. Alfred L. Kroeber, noted anthropologist and student of Indian culture and language for whom the anthropology building at University of California at Berkeley is named, stated in his Handbook of Indians of California *(1925) that Sonoma is made up of two words used by the Wappo (Pomo) and several other tribes. Dr. Kroeber believed that it combined* noma, *meaning "town rather than people," and* tso, *which meant "earth." He concluded that "Tso0noma" meant "a village of the place," to which you could add your tribe's name. Dr. Kroeber is most likely correct.*

Slownoma is what locals call their town to explain why certain things don't get done quickly, why stores open and close at such civilized (late) times, why no one gets too upset about big-city problems, and why they love to live here. Like Jack London and all the others who looked for a home in the country with romance in their hearts, Sonoma will always be The Valley of the Moon. Nose? No way!

Sonoma Valley is 7 miles wide—like San Francisco—and stretches from Sears Point Raceway, at its southern end, to the northern edge of the village of Kenwood. A string of individual mountains forms its eastern border, while the Sonoma Mountains define its western lines. Sonoma is usually about a forty-five-minute drive north of the Marin County (northern) end of the Golden Gate Bridge. If the traffic is bad, however, plan twice as long to get here.

Sonoma Plaza is a square of lush, green park in the center of town, with rose gardens, fountains, an amphitheater, feedable ducks in and out of the duck pond, chickens, new playground equipment, tied-down picnic tables and benches, new rest rooms (let's take care of them, friends), and loads of trees, from imported palms to native oaks.

The Plaza was laid out as a parade ground by General Mariano Vallejo in 1834 and was made a National Historic Landmark in 1961. Sonoma welcomes use of the Plaza by individuals, mothers' clubs, service clubs, and children galore. Every year the Salute to the Arts, Red and White Ball, Valley of the Moon Vintage Festival, Fourth of July, Kiwanis Turkey Barbecue, Community Center's Ox Roast, Native Sons' Chicken Barbecue, and Cinco de Mayo celebrations take place in the Plaza and are open to the public.

The population in Sonoma's city limits is under 9,000, with more than 80 percent over age thirty. Nearly 50 percent of Sonomans are over fifty-five, and one third more adults are registered Democrat than Republican. The population of Sonoma Valley is about 35,000.

Along with families of Italian, Swiss, French, Irish, and German backgrounds who have lived in Sonoma Valley for generations, many newcomers commute to San Francisco and Marin County or operate businesses here. Several famous people have lived in Sonoma: poets Maya Angelou and Pulitzer Prize–winner Carolyn Kizer, Sam Keen, Jack London, M. F. K. Fisher, Tommy Smothers, Robin Williams, and Academy Award–winners including *Toy Story* director John Lasseter and documentary director Bert Salzman, as well as Emmy Award–winning writer Beth Thompson. Danny Glover and Sharon Stone own homes here now, and both circulate downtown undisturbed by local residents (who usually don't recognize them anyway, which is one of the reasons they like it here). Many other well-known residents live normal lives along with the rest of the locals, participating in community projects and school affairs without publicity or autograph hounds.

Wineries are important to the local culture, lifestyle, and economy. In Sonoma Valley, thirty-six wineries produce thirty types of wines, totaling more than five million cases per year. Fifteen thousand acres of premium wine grapes grow in the Valley, including the first European varietals planted in America in 1857. Sonoma Valley includes three distinct wine appellations: Sonoma Valley,

Sonoma Mountain, and Carneros. Sonoma County actually has more acreage planted in wine grapes than has Napa County. (Blue-stem glasses, the signature wine glasses of the Sonoma Valley appellation, are used in most restaurants and are available for sale at the Robin's Nest, 116 East Napa Street, Sonoma; phone 707–996–4169.)

While most visitors come to the Sonoma Valley wine country during summer, we encourage you to try it in winter or off months. There is little on this earth more beautiful than the Sonoma Valley on a sunny winter day between rains. Lichen dangle from the outlines of leafless oak trees. Sparkling green grass looks like velvet on the grounds of the vineyards and hillsides. Another reason is that winemakers are not as busy as they are the rest of the year, and your chances of tasting wine and actually talking with a winemaker at your favorite winery are very high. Usually all they want is a call to let them know that you are on your way. And finally, before- and after-holiday bargain sales abound at wineries as well as at local shops.

Sonoma's weather is colder in winter and hotter in summer than San Francisco. Temperatures average about 50° F in winter and 82° F in summer, with annual extreme spells of winter lows in the 20s and summer highs in the 100s. Winter fogs and rains never seem to last very long—the 1998 El Niño season excepted—and summer hot spells are always relieved in a few days by fog blowing in from the Pacific Ocean. Summer nights cool off for comfortable sleeping.

Some of the finest foods and wines in the world are grown in Sonoma Valley. Sonoma restaurants combine the best of these local products. While one might try variously to describe the refreshing cooking here as California Nouvelle, California Italian, California Country, or California French, none of those labels is truly accurate or appropriate. Cooking here has evolved into its very own appellation: Sonoma Cuisine.

Sonoma has a prize-winning bakery for every 1,000 people, a winery for every 250 people, and two of the finest cheese producers in the world. Most people who move here gain weight; it's just a fact. This is one place in the United States where indulging in local cheeses and breads and wines is an acceptable as well as expected activity. The products created here are often sold in markets elsewhere with the reverence accorded imports, and appropriately so.

Sonoma also boasts the most northern and last-built California mission, San Francisco de Solano, preserved and restored buildings from Mexico's ownership of the territory, and lots of food and history from the seven national flags that have flown over Sonoma County. Visitors can enjoy exploring this history as well as more modern-day pursuits, like hot-air ballooning and spa wraps.

If you think you can handle all this enjoyment, read on!

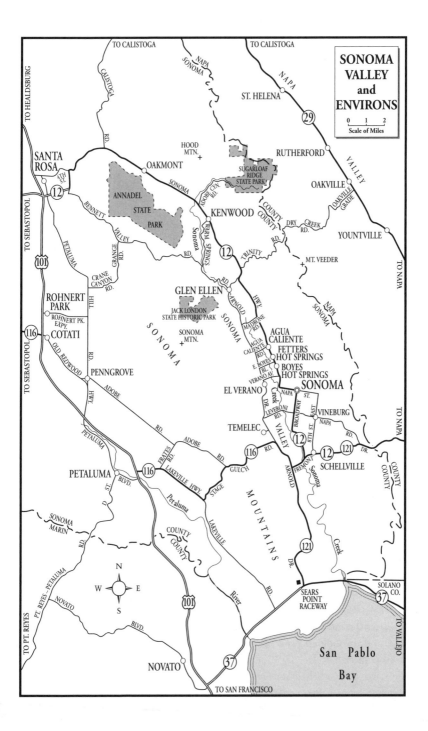

SONOMA
VALLEY
and
ENVIRONS

0   1   2
Scale of Miles

How to Get Here

You really can't get to Sonoma unless you mean to. It isn't on the way to any-where else, and it isn't on a major highway or transportation corridor. (Public transportation is fair to lousy.) You'll find only beautiful two-lane roads in and out of town, in all directions. This fact is what keeps down development and deters crime. Occasionally you might get stuck on a two-lane "highway" behind a local vintner or farmer moving his plow or backhoe from one property to another. There's no point in getting worked up over the delay, so just sit back and enjoy the countryside.

Approaching Sonoma from any direction, you will notice the absence of some huge trees along the road and more new vineyards than even last year. It's called "progress," and many of us are just happy that the land remains in agricultural use.

On the Road from San Francisco

By car: Take Lombard and Doyle Drive or Geary to Park Presidio to the Golden Gate Bridge. Cross the Golden Gate and continue north on Highway 101 past San Rafael in Marin County to the turnoff to Highway 37, going east. This exit is marked SONOMA, SACRAMENTO and NAPA, VALLEJO on different signs. Turn east (right) onto Highway 37. Continue through the traffic signal at Lakeville Highway and proceed over the hill (7.7 miles). Just over the hill at the signal, turn north (left) onto Highway 121 toward Sonoma. (The right-hand lane of the two turning left merges dangerously into the left-hand one. Careful!)

Sears Point Raceway is on the left. You are now on Highway 121, which some wineries and dineries along the way prefer to call Arnold Drive, although you won't find it marked.

You will pass The Fruit Basket vegetable stand on the left. A little farther on, across from the Unocal station on the left, turn right to follow Highway 121, cross a bridge, and turn left onto Highway 12 at the Schell Vista Fire Station and Ford's Cafe toward Sonoma. You're almost here. Highway 12 becomes Broadway and leads you right to the Plaza and City Hall. Sears Point to Sonoma Plaza: 10.6 miles.

By Golden Gate Transit (bus): Route 90 leaves San Francisco Financial District (Fremont between Howard and Mission Streets) at 7:38 A.M. and 5:23 P.M. and the Golden Gate Bridge Toll Plaza at 8:04 A.M. and 5:38 P.M. There is a stop in San Rafael (8:25 A.M. and 6:07 P.M.). The bus arrives at the first Sonoma stop in Schellville (Highway 116 at 121) at 8:57 A.M. and 6:38 P.M. It reaches Sonoma Plaza at 9:09 A.M. and 6:50 P.M. It costs $4.00 each way.

To return to San Francisco, the bus leaves Sonoma Plaza (the duck-pond side of the U in front of City Hall) at 6:28 and 9:55 A.M., from Schellville at 6:42 and 10:09 A.M., and arrives in San Francisco Financial District (First and Mission Streets) at 7:50 and 11:43 A.M. It reaches Folsom and Main at 7:58 and 11:46 A.M. In other words, you can't take the bus to Sonoma in the morning and return to San Francisco later the same day. You have to stay in Sonoma overnight if traveling by bus.

From San Francisco Airport (SFO)

Sonoma Airporter: The burgundy-and-cream vans leave the designated van-line posts on the traffic island outside the baggage level of SFO at 8:05 and 9:45 A.M. and at 12:20, 2:45, 5:40, and 9:40 P.M. (except Saturday). They leave Sonoma for the airport at 5:35, 7:30, and 10:00 A.M. and 12:30, 3:00, and 7:50 P.M. (except Saturday). Plan a good hour and forty minutes for the trip each way. Fares are $20 each way per person at four locations: Sonoma City Hall, Sonoma Airporter Offices at 524 West Napa Street (Sonoma Center shopping center), Ferrando's Plumbing (Airporter's old offices) at 18495 Sonoma Highway in Boyes Hot Springs or the BP Station in Schellville at Highway 121 and Arnold Drive. Door-to-door service is available at your accommodation or home for $25 each way per person. Call (707) 938–4246.

From Napa

Drive south on Highway 29, turn west (right) on Highways 12/121, and travel 8.2 miles. Follow Highway 121 through the signal at Napa Road and past Laura Chenel's Chevre (formerly Stornetta's Dairy), past Babe's Burgers and The Cherry Tree. (This is the way the road signs direct you.) Follow signs to Sonoma. Turn north (right) at Schell Vista Fire Station and Ford's Cafe to Highway 12 toward Sonoma; Highway 12 becomes Broadway and leads you straight to the Plaza and City Hall. Ford's Cafe to Sonoma Plaza: 3.6 miles.

An alternative route is to turn right at the Napa Road signal, follow Napa Road all the way to Broadway, turn right at the signal, and follow Broadway to Sonoma Plaza.

From Oakland Airport

Rent a car and follow the directions given below.

From Oakland/Berkeley and East Bay

Take I–80 east (which seems like north, because it is). Stay in left lanes past

Berkeley (University Avenue Exit) and take I–580 toward Richmond–San Rafael Bridge. Cross San Francisco Bay on bridge, then merge into Highway 101 at San Rafael, continue north about 9.5 miles, and then turn east (right) onto Highway 37 toward SONOMA AND NAPA (signs also say VALLEJO AND SACRAMENTO). Continue on Highway 37 through the signal at Lakeville Road and go over the hill (7.7 miles); turn north (left) onto Highway 121. Sears Point Raceway entrance is on the left. Continue on Highway 121 for 6.1 miles. Turn east (right) with Highway 121 across from the Unocal station. In 0.8 mile turn north (left) onto Highway 12 toward Sonoma, past Ford's Cafe. Highway 12 becomes Broadway somewhere undefined and will take you straight into downtown and Sonoma Plaza and City Hall.

The only way to get to Sonoma from the East Bay by public transportation is to take Bay Area Rapid Transit (BART) to San Francisco and then Golden Gate Transit to Sonoma. Sears Point to Sonoma Plaza: 10.6 miles.

From Santa Rosa and North

Drive east on Fourth Street, which becomes Highway 12, and continue for about 20 miles (30 minutes) through Kenwood, the outskirts of Glen Ellen, Agua Caliente, and Boyes Hot Springs. Turn left either on Spain Street or Napa Street (follow signs) into Sonoma and the Plaza.

Caution: This route is so beautiful that we must caution you to remember to watch the road. Many accidents occur on Highway 12 through Oakmont, Kenwood, and Glen Ellen, partly because of overzealous wine sampling and partly because of the distraction of the romantic natural surroundings that stimulate senses.

By Helicopter

San Francisco Helicopter Tours offer "A Taste of the Wine Country," with a scheduled dramatic stop, tour, and lunch at Vicky and Sam Sebastiani's Viansa Winery, for $240 per person. Individualized tours are available by contacting John J. McClelland at P.O. Box 280776, San Francisco, CA 94128-0776; phone (800) 400–2404 or (510) 635–4500; fax (510) 769–0520.

Private Aircraft: Sonoma Skypark (OQ9)

Three miles SE of Sonoma. Coordinates: N38-15.5 W122-26.0 Waypoint: SGD-112.1 311 5. Open sunrise to sunset. Elevation 20. Pattern altitudes: 1020 MSL light aircraft runways: 8-26 2,500 x 30 asphalt; trees each end. Overnight parking fees $3.00. Approaches: (VFR). FSS: Oakland (800) 345–4546. Frequencies: UNICOM 122.8; CTAF 122.8; FSS 122.5, 122.2. Charts: San Francisco Sectional. Noise abatement procedures in effect—contact airport manager; avoid low approaches; perform predeparture runup W end. Note: light traffic runway 8; night ops prohibited; runway 26 is calm wind runway.

Taxi service from airport: Bear Flag Cab, (707) 996–6733. *Rental cars:* Sonoma Truck and Auto Center, 870 Broadway, Sonoma; phone (707) 996–4521. Open 8:00 A.M.–7:00 P.M. Monday–Friday; 8:00 A.M.–5:00 P.M. Saturday–Sunday; will pick up passenger at airport with prior reservation. Curtice Auto Rental, 23002 Arnold Drive, Sonoma; phone (707) 935–9115. Open 8:00 A.M.–5:00 P.M. Monday–Friday; 8:00 A.M.–3:00 P.M. Saturday; Sunday by appointment. *Fuel:* Chevron 80, 100 LL.

Call Sonoma Skypark Inc. at (707) 996–2100. Open 9:00 A.M.–5:00 P.M. daily. Frequency: 122.8.

Heavy Aircraft

Use Napa County Airport (APC). Location 25 minutes east Sonoma; Coordinates N38-12.8; W 122-16.8. Waypoint: SGD-112.1 048 degrees 4.8. Telephone: (707) 253–4300. Open 8:00 A.M.–9:00 P.M. Elevation 33. Pattern altitude 1033 MSL light aircraft; 1533 MSL heavy aircraft. Runways: 18L-36R 2,500 x 75 asphalt/18R-36L 5,931 x 150 concrete; lights PCL; post and hill rwy 36L/6-24 5,007 x 150 concrete lights PCL. Lights: transmitter activated 8:00 P.M.–7:00 A.M.; 118.7 (3 clicks in 5 seconds, low intensity; 5 clicks in 5 seconds, medium intensity; 7 clicks in 5 seconds, high intensity) beacon dusk to dawn. Obstructions: gulls and numerous birds in vicinity. Fees: parking overnight. Approaches LOC, VOR. FSS: Oakland (800) 345–4546. Frequencies: Tower 118.7 (7:00 A.M.–8:00 P.M.); Ground 121.7; ATIS 124.05; Approach Oakland Center/127.8; CTAF 118.7; FSS 122.1R, 112. 1T. Chart: San Francisco Sectional; Low-altitude L2. Notes: Right traffic runways 18R and 36R. Asphalt taxiway & Apron S-30. Please verify all airport particulars with the appropriate facilities prior to arrival.

Rental cars: Budget (707) 224–7845; Hertz (707) 226–2037; National (707) 257–2585. *Limo service:* Crown Limo (707) 226–9500; Evans Airporter (707) 255–1559; Grape Vine Limo (800) 327–7790. *Food:* Jonsey's Restaurant, located in the airport terminal, (707) 255–2003.

You can call the air terminal at (707) 253–4300. Open 8:00 A.M.–9:00 P.M. Fuel: Chevron 100LL, JET. Helicopter Network International Inc., (707)

255–0809 or (800) 662–6886. Open twenty-four hours; nationwide helicopter reservation system.

GETTING AROUND ONCE YOU'RE HERE

Local transportation is somewhat limited in the Sonoma Valley. The Sonoma County Transit bus service throughout the county brings buses occasionally and regularly, but they are of little use around the valley.

BEAR FLAG TAXI offers twenty-four-hour service; $2.80 base rate, $2.00 per mile, 10 percent senior discounts. Tours or airport runs by special arrangement and rates. Phone (707) 996–6733.

SONOMA VALLEY TAXI drives gray cars for local service. Phone (707) 996–6733. (Yes, the same phone number as for Bear Flag Taxi.)

ALL OCCASION LIMOUSINE AND CALIFORNIA WINE TOURS does just what the name says. Michael Marino recently purchased Sonoma's Chardonnay Limousine and provides hourly limousine service as well as five-hour wine tours ($39 per person), airport service, weddings, and graduation parties in sedans, vans, van buses, and limousines from the headquarters at 22455 Broadway in Sonoma. Phone (707) 939–7225.

Valley Wine Tours offers personalized tours of the Sonoma, Napa, and Alexander valleys, pickup and delivery to San Francisco, terrific picnic lunches, and the most entertaining educational tours you could want.

Co-owner Kate Kennedy is a Shakespearean actress and director of Sonoma's Avalon Players, while her partner, Jake Martin, is a co-founder of the Valley of the Moon Petanque Club. Kate has also worked for Sonoma's best restaurants and caterers and really knows the valleys' food, agriculture, and wine histories.

Valley Wine Tours offers a historical tour of Sonoma Valley to four wineries and picnic lunch for $60 and a five-hour tour of Napa Valley for $75. They will also create specialty tours to suit your interests, including following your favorite varietal, art and wine tours, visits to family wineries, and winemaker luncheons. Address: 1208 Los Robles Drive, Sonoma; phone (707) 975–6462; Web site www.valleywinetours.com.

VIVIANI WINE COUNTRY TOURS–EVENT SPECIALISTS will pick you up in a limousine in San Francisco and/or create your own private and individualized tour of the wine country. If you get yourself to Sonoma or Napa, they offer a wide range of the finest tours, including gourmet local foods, winery visits including conversations with owners and winemakers, shopping, visiting artists' studios and galleries, and professional tour directors. Translators into most languages are available with advance notice.

Viviani's Individual Tours of the Wine Country begin at $750, with lunch extra. Private Wine Tours are customized to fit your group's background and interests including all wines, gourmet catered luncheon based on ten clients, beginning at $70 per person. Half-Day Wine Tours begin at $45 without lunch. Sightseeing begins at $45 based on ten clients; Historic/Viticultural Tours begin at $40; horseback riding through acres of Valley of the Moon history from $85; a private dinner party at an exclusive estate, winery, or winemaker's home from $125 per person; and a cheese/wine pairing by Linda Viviani from $500. Viviani also makes arrangements for hot-air ballooning and gliding and appointments at local spas. Phone (707) 938–2100; fax (707) 938–4924; e-mail lvtcinc@aol.com; Web site www.viviani.com.

SONOMA COUNTY TRANSIT's Bus Routes 32 and 34 travel around Sonoma Valley at regular intervals. The buses stop at places such as City Hall, medical buildings, and shopping centers. Designed primarily for local use, they do not go to wineries or particular points of historic interest. Route 30 travels between Sonoma and Santa Rosa. Its primary stop in Sonoma is in front of City Hall, but you can board it wherever you see a green-and-white Sonoma County Transit sign on Highway 12. The trip takes from an hour to an hour and a half, which may be its drawback, although you can get to almost anywhere in the Sonoma Valley this way. Route 30 also connects to Route 20 out the Russian River. Phone (707) 576–RIDE, (707) 576–7433, or (800) 345–7433.

HOW TO BE A VISITOR AND NOT A TOURIST IN SONOMA

Sonomans are emotionally and intellectually torn between those who believe their valley should be better publicized to increase business and those who prefer to keep Sonoma Valley's glories hidden to keep more outsiders from moving here. Some Sonomans are envious of Napa's greater publicity, reputation for wines, and famous residents. Now that more of you come to visit and more movie stars have moved here, however, Sonomans are a little less sensitive about this competition from Napa.

Your best way to see Sonoma is from a local's perspective, which is the only way you will really find out what this unique, secret valley is all about. When you come to Sonoma and use this Hill Guide to find the secrets of Sonoma Valley, you will experience it as the locals see and live it. That's what we try to do wherever we find ourselves.

Sonoma locals prefer to think that visitors are not tourists. Somehow they resent tourists and love visitors. Thus, a little advice: Don't wear a Sonoma T-shirt or sweatshirt until *after* you leave town—buy all you want and wear them at your next stop. The only ones that locals wear are shirts they have earned by running or walking in either the "Hit the Road Jack" run/walk benefiting Valley of the Moon Hospice and the Boys and Girls Club or the Vintage Festival's Vintage Run. Perhaps you'll pass for a native wearing the shirt using comedian and Kenwood resident Tommy Smothers's line that "Sonoma makes wine, Napa makes auto parts," but you're still taking your chances.

Clean jeans are dress-up in Sonoma, except perhaps at the Red and White Ball and occasionally at the Sonoma Mission Inn. Ties are never required.

Don't take up the whole sidewalk. Leave some space for the locals, who need to walk on the sidewalk to go about their business and move a little faster than visitors. And observe the stop signs; Sonomans always know that it's the out-of-towners who drive through stop signs. Courtesy prevails here, and we usually take turns at four-way stops. Avoid these telltale pitfalls, follow this local secrets guide, and you're sure to enjoy Sonoma Valley to the hilt.

CHAPTER 1

SOUTH SONOMA

*S*outh Sonoma—an area stretching from the junction of Highways 37 and 121 toward Sonoma Plaza—is the part of Sonoma that most visitors first encounter. The total distance from this turnoff to Sonoma Plaza is just 10.6 miles. Don't hurry. You might miss some of Sonoma Valley's most unusual people, terrain, foods, and wineries.

SEARS POINT RACEWAY is one such spot. Admittedly, a racetrack is a rather odd establishment to welcome you to Sonoma's renowned quietude! But it is the first attraction that you will pass on this route to Sonoma Plaza. (As you turn from Highway 37 onto 121, the Sears Point facilities lie immediately to your left.) And, as raceways go, Sears Point is unusual. Its identity hinges on its winding racetrack and its setting among Sonoma's honey-colored, rolling hills.

Speedway Motor Sports, Inc., of Charlotte, North Carolina, bought Sears Point in 1997. Since then, the company has moved quickly to upgrade the entire raceway, tearing down old buildings, building new ones, and straightening the racecourse slightly. While many locals welcome the professional improvements, they also bemoan any new building—and the influx of people they draw. But Sears Point has made an effort to be a positive presence in the community and co-sponsors many events to benefit Sonoma Valley charities.

The Chrysler Wine Country Classic Vintage Races, held in early June, benefit local Sonoma charities. This event features vintage cars, which roar around the track at a breathtaking 20 to 25 miles per hour. The Vintage Races end with a display of thirty roadsters at the Sebastiani Winery parking lot on Fourth Street East (downtown Sonoma) and wine and food tasting.

Sears Point annually hosts the Save Mart Supermarkets 300 NASCAR Winston Cup during the first weekend in May (some 175,000 fans attend!); winter drag races in January; vintage races in March; motorcycle and drag races in April and May; and the June 1 Outdoor Sports Festival, featuring nonmotorized events for the Sonoma Valley community, including bicycling, rollerblading, roller hockey, running, and human-powered drag races.

The NHRA Budweiser Festival of Fire blows up the skies during the last weekend in June. Some 100,000 people attend the Kragen Autolite Nationals, featuring well-known country performers, over the last weekend in July.

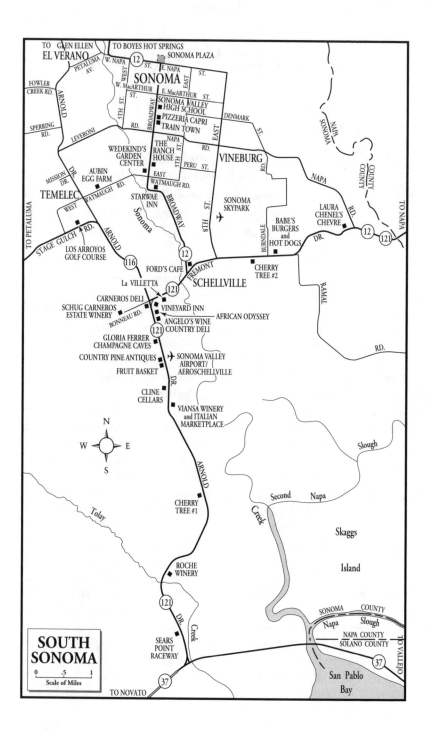

TO GLEN ELLEN   TO BOYES HOT SPRINGS
EL VERANO
12   SONOMA PLAZA
W. NAPA   ST.   E. NAPA   ST.
PETALUMA
FOWLER   AV.   SONOMA
CREEK RD.
W. MacARTHUR   E. MacARTHUR   ST.
ST.
ARNOLD   SONOMA VALLEY
5TH ST.   HIGH SCHOOL   NAPA
WEST   PIZZERIA CAPRI   SONOMA
SPERRING   TRAIN TOWN   DENMARK   COUNTY
RD.   BROADWAY   ST.   COUNTY
RD.   EAST ST.
LEVERONI   THE   NAPA   RD.
RD.   WEDEKIND'S   RANCH   RD.   VINEBURG   NAPA
GARDEN   HOUSE   5TH ST.   PERU   ST.
MISSION DR.   CENTER
AUBIN   EAST
EGG FARM   WATMAUGH RD.
TEMELEC   WATMAUGH RD.   STARWAE   SONOMA   LAURA
WEST   INN   SKYPARK   CHENEL'S
RD.   CHEVRE
STAGE GULCH RD.   Sonoma   BROADWAY   BABE'S
ARNOLD   8TH ST.   BURGERS
LOS ARROYOS   BURNDALE   and   12   121
GOLF COURSE   116   HOT DOGS   DR.
12
FORD'S CAFE   FREMONT   RAMAL
La VILLETTA   SCHELLVILLE
121   CHERRY
CARNEROS DELI   TREE #2
SCHUG CARNEROS   VINEYARD INN
ESTATE WINERY   BONNEAU RD.   AFRICAN ODYSSEY
ANGELO'S WINE
121   COUNTRY DELI
GLORIA FERRER
CHAMPAGNE CAVES   RD.
COUNTRY PINE ANTIQUES   SONOMA VALLEY
FRUIT BASKET   AIRPORT/
AEROSCHELLVILLE
DR.
CLINE
CELLARS   VIANSA WINERY
and ITALIAN
MARKETPLACE

N   Slough
W   E
S   Second   Napa
Creek
Skaggs
ARNOLD
CHERRY   Island
TREE #1
Tolay

ROCHE
WINERY

121   SONOMA   COUNTY
DR.   Napa   Slough
Creek   NAPA COUNTY
SEARS   SOLANO COUNTY
SOUTH   POINT
SONOMA   RACEWAY   TO VALLEJO
0   .5   1   37
Scale of Miles   37   San Pablo
TO NOVATO   Bay

McGraw Insurance California Superbike Challenge highlights August, Good
Guys Nostalgia Drags, Vintage Races and Road Racing Championships are held
in September, and Sears Point finishes off its year with a SuperTruck (pickups)
the first Saturday in October.

RUSSELL RACING SCHOOL (707–939–7600) recently replaced the Skip Barber
Racing School at Sears Point and offers lessons to amateurs who want to sample
the quick thrills of learning safe driving and amateur racing skills. Pros hang out
here and are often available to chat and trade driving and crashing stories.

Fine points: Ticket prices for major events range from $10 to
$130. Be warned: Many ticket holders arrive at events as early as
6:00 A.M. to park their vehicles on favorite hillsides for viewing the
races. And we advise that you avoid the 37/121 junction on the
weekends of those huge events at Sears Point, unless you plan to attend.

❧ *Sears Point Raceway, Highways 37 and 121, Sonoma 95476; phone (800)
870–RACE or (707) 938–8448. Credit cards: Visa, MasterCard, and Discover.
Wheelchair-accessible.*

SEARS POINT RACEWAY

From Sears Point, go north on Highway 121 just over a mile to ROCHE
WINERY. (Take a right at the white ranch fence with yellow roses. You'll recognize the winery by the "R" hedge on the hillside.)

Genevieve and Joe Roche, both M.D.s and pathologists, bought their ranch in
1977, planted their first vineyard in 1982, and opened the tasting room in 1989.

ROCHE WINERY AND FRIENDS

Designed by Sonoma architect Victor Conforti, the winery looks a lot like the barn on the Roches' adjacent cattle ranch, thereby keeping the enterprise compatible with its surroundings. Tasting-room decor features huge French wine posters. The garden is inviting and the ambience low-key and comfortable, as are the Roches themselves.

Picnickers are welcome here. Table views feature a duck pond (migration), rice fields, San Pablo Bay, Vallejo, and the Sears Point Raceway. You'll find mustards, biscotti, and Roche glasses and shirts for sale. Roche also produces personal wine labels on request.

Tasting-room manager Mara Roche is extremely well-informed and offers mostly wines available only here at the winery or in the Bay Area's better restaurants. You will also find an unusually tasteful collection of 100 gifts under $20 and 80 wines made by other producers. We especially like finding Mary's Pizza Shack Italian salad dressing, Très Classique oils, Pometta's spreads and sauces, and M-G Bees honey products.

 Fine points: Featured wines: Carneros Chardonnay, Pinot Noir, Tamarix (Pinot Noir blush wine), Muscat Canelli, Merlot. Owners: Genevieve and Joe Roche. Winemaker: John Ferrington. Cases: 6,000. Acres: 170 planted of 2,000.

Roche Winery, 28700 Arnold Drive (Highway 121), Sonoma 95476; phone (707) 935–7115, or (800) 825–9475; Web site: www.rochewinery.com. Open 10:00 A.M.-5:00 P.M. daily, winter, 10:00 A.M.–6:00 P.M., summer. Tasting fee for reserve wines only on weekends, $3.00. Credit cards: MasterCard, Visa, American Express, and Discover. Wheelchair-accessible.

As you leave Roche, turn right (north) onto Highway 121. Just after the dangerous curves and over the hill (1.7 miles), you'll see the little Cherry Tree #1, the first retail outlet of the now-famous Cherry Tree pure juices and stuffed olives. Owners Rena Lehnert and her husband, the infamous and hilarious Napoli, make cherry juice from a treasured family recipe that originated in Germany more than one hundred years ago. (The Cherry Tree staff will give you an article on cherry juice's powers to cure gout and arthritis by counteracting uric acid.)

CHERRY TREE #1 sells most of the Lehnerts' products, including their famous Black Bing Cherry Juice and Black Bing Cherry Cider, pure apple juices and ciders, juice blends, Napoli Cellars wines and T-shirts, wine-juice jams, honeys, fruit spreads, apple sauce, stuffed olives and shirts, pistachios and unsalted almonds, and picnic supplies.

Fine points: Cherry Tree #1 also sells sandwiches, but they are made by someone else and are not very good. At Cherry Tree Country Store, on Highway 121 east of Eighth Street East (1901 Fremont Drive), you can buy the Lehnerts' made-on-site deli sandwiches, which are much better.

❧ *Cherry Tree #1, P.O. Box 361, Sonoma 95476; phone (707) 938–3480. Open 9:00 A.M.–5:30 P.M. daily, winter; 8:00 A.M.–8:00 P.M. daily, summer. MasterCard and Visa. Not wheelchair-accessible.*

CHERRY TREE #1

APPLE BUTTER UPSIDE DOWN CAKE
from the Cherry Tree

1 package white cake mix
½ cup butter
1 cup Cherry Tree Apple Butter
½ cup brown sugar
½ cup chopped walnuts
Cherry Tree apple cider

Melt the butter at low heat in a heavy baking pan, adding brown sugar until they form a syrup. Remove the mixture from the stove, spread the apple butter over the syrup, and sprinkle with nuts.

Mix the cake mix according to package directions, but substitute apple cider for the water that you would normally add to the mix. Pour cake batter over the apple butter–syrup topping in the pan. Bake 40–50 minutes at 375°F, or until the cake springs back when lightly touched. Let cool 5–10 minutes, then carefully turn over onto the serving plate. Serve with a generous helping of whipped cream, ice cream, or yogurt.

Turn left back onto the highway with great care; cars fly by here a lot faster than it seems. New vineyards are sprouting along here faster than weeds, as cattle pastures give way to more lucrative and romantic pursuits. In about 1.5 miles you will see Vicki and Sam Sebastiani's VIANSA WINERY AND ITALIAN MARKETPLACE at 25200 Arnold Drive (Highway 121), atop this little hill and its dangerous curves. Turn right (east) at a tan cement wall marked VIANSA and signs advertising the Visitors Bureau, the southern office of which is located on Viansa property.

After a somewhat typical wine country family feud, in which he was removed as president of the family's Sebastiani Vineyards, Sam Sebastiani sold the Sebastiani Theater on Sonoma Plaza and his and Vicki's home on the east side of Sonoma. They purchased the then-bare hillside that is now the site of Viansa.

Sam and Vicki moved a mobile home onto the property and put all of their emotional and monetary resources into building their wine and foods business, which they opened in February 1990. Viansa comes from Vi(cki) an(d) Sa(m). At first the Italian flag flew alone over the building site, but it has now been replaced by the American flag.

Some of their children have joined in the business and, for a few years, grew several acres of pumpkins for Halloween picking. In 1997, the kids' enterprise was replaced by the now-grown-up children's new Viansa vineyards. The Sebastianis also grow many of the vegetables and herbs used in their Viansa and Cucina Viansa (formerly Lo Spuntino) kitchens.

As you turn right off Highway 121, either circle Viansa's fountain and go to the Visitors Bureau for more information, or turn a hard right to wind your way

VIANSA WINERY & ITALIAN MARKETPLACE

up the little hill to Viansa. Sam and Vicki recently planted several acres of Italian varietals in cooperation with Jordan Smith on property extending from Viansa south to just across from the Cherry Tree.

Try to park in the parking lot closest to the buildings, because any place closer is reserved for limousines and tour buses. San Francisco Helicopter Tours dramatically land their chartered helicopters between the two parking lots. Rest rooms for customers only are on the entry or first level along with the actual winery (we mention them first because they are what you see first). While there is a bit of a slope up to the marketplace and tasting room, it is all wheelchair-accessible.

As you wind your way up to the fun stuff, you might get your first confusing feeling and wonder whether you are in Italy or Sonoma. Mesquite barbecue aromas make your mouth water before you reach the top of the steps.

The Sebastianis imported large specimen olive trees and decorative plants from Italy, which now look as if they've been there for decades. Viansa's architecture is sort of nouveau-Italian, as are the Tuscan-style lawn, garden paths, and tables. You can imagine beautiful people with big hats and swinging dresses at a lawn party or a few older men playing boccie (as they used to do in Sonoma Plaza).

While fine wines are Viansa's primary products, visitors are struck on entering the tall-ceilinged and vast but cozy Marketplace by the abundance, smells, and stunning displays of creative Californian/Italian foods. The fabulous aromas

BISTECCA ALLA FIORENTINA ALLA SAM
(Sam's Marinated Steak)
from Vicki and Sam Sebastiani of Viansa Winery and Italian Marketplace

1 cup fresh thyme leaves stripped from twigs
1 ½ cups fresh rosemary stripped from twigs
¼ cup olive oil
¼ cup Viansa Cabernet Sauvignon vinegar
½ cup dry red wine
2 Tbs Viansa Hot Sweet Mustard
3 cloves garlic
8 to 10 pounds rib market or New York steaks

Puree all the marinade ingredients in a food processor or blender until creamy. Marinade is best if made 24 hours ahead of use to marry flavors.

Trim any excess fat from the steaks and cover both sides with the marinade. Place steaks in a shallow glass baking dish. Cover with plastic wrap and refrigerate for 2–4 hours before barbecuing. Serves 8–10.

Be sure to see Vicki Sebastiani's new cookbook *Cucina Viansa*.

of basil, garlic, rosemary, and other herbs come from opened jars and bottles tastefully displayed at every turn, offering ample samples of Viansa products for you to dip locally baked breads or pretzels in. This is the ultimate food- and wine-tasting room.

The tasteables include blood-orange vinegar, balsamic country mustard, rosemary or hot sweet mustards, mustard caper sauce, sun-dried tomato pesto, red- or yellow-pepper pesto, olive-anchovy pesto, basil pesto aioli, rosemary peach conserve, raspberry chardonnay di cioccolato, and orange cranberry preserves. We especially like the new olive caper pesto, spinach thyme pesto, and Sam's Gorgonzola Dressing. Much of this romantic and aromatic food is also available at Cucina Viansa, the family's restaurant on Sonoma Plaza's northeast corner, across from the mission.

Vicki and her kitchen staff have developed unusual and spectacular California/Italian specialties such as focaccia sandwiches, pâtés, tortas, salads, and fine desserts available at the food counter. Espresso drinks are also available. The servers loan you a woven basket to load with your picnic purchases, served on a paper plate with plastic utensils for enjoying here.

Plenty of picnic tables overlook the southern end of Sonoma Valley and the wildlife preserve, Sam Sebastiani's pride and joy. The Sebastianis have even dedicated a corner of the Marketplace to Ducks Unlimited merchandise, the profits of which go to the preservation organization.

Viansa prepares and packages some of the most elegant gift baskets anywhere, combining olive oils, dried fruits, condiments and sauces, miniature Roman artichokes, roasted pork loin, white truffle oil, arborio rice, balsamic vinegar, and even radicchio in oil and handmade pasta.

Fine points: Many of Viansa's best wines are sold exclusively at the winery or to members of their Tuscan Club. They also import Italian wines that they deem to fit into Viansa's gustatory and physical ambience. Featured wines: Sauvignon Blanc, Arneis, Chardonnay, Muscat Canelli, Barbera Blanc, Anatra Bianco, and reds Piccolo Poscano, Nebbiolo, Di Pacomio, Prindelo, Riserva Anatra Rosso, Pacomio Aleatico, Athena Dolcetto, Zinfandel, Piccolo Toscano Sangiovese, Fresia, Muscat Canelli, Tocai Fiulano, Cabernet Franc, Augusto Barbera, Ossidiana, and Cabernet Sauvignon; $9.00–$22.00. Winemakers: Sam and Michael Sebastiani. Cases: 20,000. Acres: 85–100.

ᕈᕈ *Viansa Winery and Italian Marketplace, P.O. Box 35, Vineburg 95487–0035; phone (707) 935–4700 or (800) 995–4740; fax (707) 935–7306; Web site www.viansa.com. Open 10:00 A.M.–5:00 P.M. daily. Rest rooms for customers only. No outside foods. MasterCard, Visa, American Express, and Discover. Wheelchair-accessible.*

Practically across the road is the large metal gate to Cline Cellars (0.2 mile north of Viansa Winery, left (west) side of Highway 121, 4.5 miles from the 37/121 junction). Be careful of traffic coming too fast from both directions.

Cline Cellars' ambience differs dramatically from Viansa's. More than 1,000 colorful and well-tended rose plants line Cline's vineyards. Most of the Cline property on both sides of the highway is defined by low local-rock walls built recently and carefully by Mexican laborers. As you go up the driveway, the most beautiful winery gardens in the valley greet you. The 1850s farmhouse serves as tasting room and office for the winery. The Cline family, the front porch, and the surrounding grounds all invite you to spend as much time with them as you would like. Fred and Nancy Cline, their children, and Nancy's father, Ed Bunting, all live on the winery property. They encourage you to bring your own picnic, or they can provide personalized tours and catered luncheon or dinner paired with their wines. Nancy Cline has added some old railroad cars in which you can explore and relax.

According to Cline Cellars president Fred Cline, the Pulpuli, a subtribe of the Miwok Indians, inhabited this property, known as the Rancheria Pulpuli, when Father Jose Altimira came through to find the mission site. Attracted by the warm, natural mineral springs, Altimira planted a cross for the first site of Mission San Francisco de Solano and his encampment on the land on July 4, 1823, and eventually moved on to what is now Sonoma. German immigrant Julius Poppe bought 640 acres from the Rancho Petaluma and grew carp in ponds on the property. (The story goes that all carp now grown in the United States come from the three that Poppe began with here.) The Yenni family, still next-door neighbors to the south, bought the property from Poppe and later sold it to Haddon Salt, formerly of the fish-and-chips chain.

The Clines recently purchased a collection of California Mission replicas, which are now on display at the winery.

Fred Cline began his winery in Oakley, Contra Costa County, with $12,000 inherited from his grandfather, Valeriano Jacuzzi (yes, pumps and spas). Fred Cline loves to joke that he successfully turned that inheritance into a $3–million debt. The Clines quickly became well-known specialists in Zinfandel and California Rhone-style wines. Relocating the winery to Sonoma in 1991, they grow Syrah, Merlot, and white Viognier, Marsanne, and Roussanne grapes in the both hot and cool Carneros climate.

 Fine points: Having sponsored the Oakley Wine and Jazz Festival, Cline Cellars now stages a marvelous Chocolate Festival at its Sonoma winery over the first weekend in November (11:00 A.M.–5:00 P.M. both days). Premium confectioners create specialties for chocoholics, and you sip Cline's Rhone-style wines along with chocolate tastes. Heaven! Cline also offers winemaker dinners with music and dancing ($65 per person) and loads of other catchy events. Its slightly illegal portable sign on the highway informs passersby of the latest events, releases, and winery births. *Featured wines:* Zinfandels from one–hundred-year-old vines, Semillon, white Rhone-style wines such as Viognier, Marsanne, and Roussanne (both fruity flavors), and red Rhone-style wines including Côtes D'Oakley (blend of Carignane, Mourvèdre, Syrah, Zinfandel, and Alicante Bouschet and similar to Côtes de Rhone), Muscat Canelli, Zinfandel. Carignane, and Mourvedre. Winemaker: Matt Cline. Cases: 100,000. Acres: 850.

❧ *Cline Cellars, 24737 Arnold Drive (Highway 121), Sonoma 95475; phone (707) 935–4310; fax (707) 935–4319. Open 10:00 A.M.–6:00 P.M. daily. MasterCard, Visa, and American Express. Wheelchair-accessible.*

Nearly a half-mile north on the same side of Highway 12—be careful turning in and out!—is the F RUIT B ASKET (4.9 miles from the 37/121 junction). The Fruit Basket has been a staple of Sonoma Valley for several decades, primarily owned by Greek-American families. Gus and Karen Dalakiaris continue to maintain the traditional quality.

While the Fruit Basket does not sell locally grown vegetables (it shops at the San Francisco Produce Market, as most stores do), it does feature its own excellent pastas, legumes, nuts, candies, and grains, as well as locally produced wine, Cherry Tree juices, and Mezzetta capers, pickles, and salsas.

Fine points: The best thing about the Fruit Basket is the prices. While its Petaluma mushrooms are rarely popping-white fresh, they are also a dollar less per pound than at most other stores. Lettuce, bananas, zucchini, tomatoes, parsley, and lemons and limes are usually much less expensive here.

➳ *Fruit Basket, 24101 Arnold Drive (Highway 121), Sonoma 95475; phone (707) 938–4332. There is also a branch at 18474 Sonoma Highway, Sonoma 95475; phone (707) 996–7433. Open daily, daylight hours. MasterCard, Visa, and American Express. Wheelchair-accessible.*

Now, for a true oasis in this windswept neighborhood, head next door to COUNTRY PINE ANTIQUES (4.9 miles north of the 37/121 junction). In this former highway restaurant, Selma and Howard Aslin welcome you into their home away from home: a warm, cozy array of English and Irish antiques and replica and pine furniture and collectibles. Their pine beds are particularly inviting. Prices range from $45 to $6,000. Be sure to check out their new barn and "soft furniture." You will also find lovely candles, placemats, interesting European kitchen accessories, and walking sticks.

Country Pine hosts new shipment openings every other month, with signs and balloons on the highway announcing special shipments. The Aslins also present elegant local charity benefits, which may feature well-known floral artist Valerie Arelt and caterer Elaine Bell.

➳ *Country Pine Antiques, 23999 Arnold Drive (Highway 121), Sonoma 95475; phone (707) 938–8315. Open 10:00 A.M.–5:30 P.M. Monday–Saturday, 11:00 A.M.–5:30 P.M. Sunday. MasterCard and Visa. Wheelchair-accessible.*

Across the road—and the cause of your looking up at the sky, wondering where that noise is coming from—is Sonoma Valley Airport/Vintage Aircraft. While this is not the transportation airport for Sonoma Valley, it is home to Vintage Aircraft (formerly known as Aeroschellville) and 150 antique and classic aircraft. (Sonoma Valley Airport also hosts the biannual "Wings Over Schellville" dinner to benefit the Sonoma Valley Hospital Foundation.)

Christopher Prevost offers rides seven days a week in his fleet of authentic 1940 Boeing-built Stearman biplanes, gliders, and a North American–built

World War II Navy SNJ-4 war plane designed and built to train pilot candidates for the Air Force and Navy. These meticulously restored and maintained legendary planes and gliders provide you with a once-in-a-lifetime flying experience. This is a must for thrill-seekers. Rates range from $60 to $135. You can also take flying lessons at the primary level ($25 per hour) and commercial, aerobatic levels ($30 per hour), or arrange for skywriting, banner-towing, and aerial advertising.

✈ *Sonoma Valley Airport/Vintage Aircraft, 23982 Arnold Drive (Highway 121), Sonoma 95475; phone (707) 938-2444. Open weekdays by appointment, 9:00 A.M.–5:00 P.M. weekends. MasterCard and Visa. Wheelchair-accessible.*

On the left side of Arnold Drive heading north, the Spanish structure at the foot of the hills to the west is Gloria Ferrer Champagne Caves (5.4 miles north of 121/37 junction). As you turn left (west) off Highway 121 coming north, you swing onto the narrow road across the Gloria Ferrer Chardonnay and Pinot Noir vineyards, the expanse of which makes many foolhardy drivers take a deep breath and rev their cars up to a low flying speed. Don't (even though we can attest to it being a wee thrill).

This acreage used to look like a barren rattlesnake haven that no one wanted—until José and Gloria Ferrer came along. To them, the bleak land looked like a gold mine. As owners of Freixenet, which produces the renowned Cordon Negro near Barcelona, Spain, the Ferrers also own wineries in France and Mexico. Freixenet/Ferrer is the largest producer in the world of méthode champenoise wines.

Recognizing the traditional importance of women in the history of the family company, José named the Sonoma winery for his wife, Gloria, and the winery in Mexico for his mother, Doña Dolores (who, after being widowed in the Spanish Civil War, directed Freixenet for more than forty years).

As you get closer to the winery and caves, you'll notice the Spanish and Catalan influence in the building design, arches, and, of course, the Catalan flag flying in front. After parking, you will see a picnic area at the east end of the building. Picnic tables are available only with purchase of Gloria Ferrer wines. Bring your own picnic (we suggest trying Angelo's Wine Country Deli across the road or Carneros Deli $1/4$ mile north for supplies), as Gloria Ferrer does not sell foods.

Steep, almost imposing stairs lead you to the Visitor Center (an elevator is also available). Once inside the door, you experience a bit of Catalonia: dark tiles on the floors; warm, comforting arches and Spanish tapestries; cookbooks specializing in Catalan and Spanish cookery; a luxurious but informal tasting area and bar; and the Vista Terrace, where you can relax, enjoy sparkling wines and your picnic in good weather, or snuggle by the fireplace in winter. Enjoy white truffle oil, grapeseed oils, wine bottles dipped in dark and light chocolate, Scottish-plaid boxer-shorts, and even throw-away cameras to memorialize the occasion.

Fine points: Gloria Ferrer puts on several Catalan food fests annually, as well as Catalan cooking classes and Fireside concerts. The winery and its entire romantic setting are available for private parties and weddings. Try to see the new caves holding the still wines.

Featured wines: Sonoma Brut, Blanc de Noirs, Royal Cuvée, Carneros Cuvée Brut Rose, Chardonnay, Pinot Noir. Winemaker: Robert Iantosca. Cases: 80,000 sparkling wine. Acres: 315. Eighty percent of the grapes used by Gloria Ferrer are grown on the Sonoma Carneros property. It buys additional grapes from Carneros grower Sangiacomo Vineyards of Sonoma.

Gloria Ferrer Champagne Caves, 23555 Carneros Highway (Highway 121 or Arnold Drive); phone (707) 996–7256; fax (707) 996–0720; Web site www.gloriaferrer.com. Open 10:30 A.M.–5:30 P.M. daily; tours hourly. Call 9:30–10:30 morning of visit for schedule. Tasting fee: Sparkling wines $3.50–$6.25, still wines $2.00, full glass $4.00. MasterCard, Visa, American Express, and Discover. Wheelchair-accessible.

Across from Gloria Ferrer is a Sonoma and Petaluma treasure, ANGELO'S WINE COUNTRY DELI (5.7 miles north of the 121/37 junction; you can spot Angelo's between the eucalyptus trees because of the wooden cow on the roof). Soon after arriving from Genoa, Italy, thirty years ago, Angelo opened his meat market and started smoking meats (not cigarettes) at 2700 Adobe Road, on the way to Petaluma.

A few years ago, Angelo took over the site on Arnold Drive (or Carneros Highway or Highway 121, depending on who is calling it) and has been wooing Sonomans and visitors ever since. Hundreds of local workers and highway patrol personnel stop by daily to pick up their lunches. Bill Mandel of the *San Francisco Examiner* called Angelo's "jerky to die for." Our favorites are garlic beef and turkey jerky, somehow rationalizing the latter as not as bad for us.

Angelo makes all his own sausages. In addition to the flavors you would expect, he also offers Hawaiian Portuguese, turkey and broccoli, and chicken and basil, all favorites of ours. Smoked hams, bacon, pork chops, turkey, and game hens are all highly recommended. You will also find smoked trout, smoked New York steak, smoked duck legs, and seasoned tri-tips.

Angelo and his helpers make the best sandwiches anywhere, featuring his prime, cooked-on-site meats. All salads are made here daily; none comes in a plastic container from the deli-salad-in-the-sky place.

Angelo's Theory: "The best way to eat garlic is to get your friends to eat it

ANGELO'S WINE COUNTRY DELI

too!" He recently won four gold medals at The Sonoma County Harvest Fair, and he also makes don't-miss-it honey from his own bees.

Oh yes, don't forget to try one of his frozen products: white-bean chicken chili. It's more like a chicken stew with white beans. You hardly even need tortillas or other accompaniment. He also makes wild garlic salsas, marinara sauces, and stuffed olives.

Angelo's Wine Country Deli, 23400 Arnold Drive (Highway 121), Sonoma 95475; phone (707) 938–3688 or (800) 631–4796; fax (707) 763–0841; e-mail moregarlic@aol.com. Open 9:00 A.M.–5:00 P.M., Sunday–Thursday, 9:00 A.M.–6:00 P.M. Friday–Saturday. Visa, Mastercard, and American Express. No public rest rooms. Wheelchair-accessible.

On the right (east) side of the road, you will be pleasantly distracted by marvelously whimsical metal sculptures that live on the grounds of Hossain Amjadi's home and studio, called Art Forms. We used to think these were made from car parts gathered from accidents along the highway until they began to make even more serious statements.

Sculptor and designer Amjadi welcomes browsers but asks that you not take photographs. Prices range from $1,400 to $16,000.

Art Forms, 23150 Arnold Drive (Highway 121), Sonoma 95475; phone

ITALIAN CHICKEN CHILI
ANGELO'S FAVORITE

¾ cup chopped turkey or chicken or
   ground turkey
1 lb. white northern beans, cooked
   per package instructions
2 Tbs. olive oil
1 jar Angelo's Garlic Salsa
2 small yellow onions, diced
½ cup red wine
Angelo's Italian Spice, to taste

Sauté onions in olive oil until transparent in color. Add chicken and Angelo's Italian Spice and cook until chicken is done throughout, stirring often so that chicken does not burn. Add wine and cook 2 minutes longer. Add Angelo's Garlic Salsa and simmer for 5 minutes. Stir to blend ingredients. Add cooked beans and more Angelo's Italian Spice to taste. Simmer 20 minutes. Serve with green salad and crusty Italian bread. Serves 4.

(707) 935–0126. Open during daylight hours. MasterCard and Visa. Wheelchair-accessible.

AFRICAN ODYSSEY is a new enterprise in an old building. Owners Sheila Sharman and Don Lindsay met in Kenya, and Don had a dairy farm outside Johannesburg, where he recycled railroad ties to make furniture for friends. When a local government required the water he used at the dairy, he transferred the workforce to making furniture from gorgeous local woods. If you recognize the furniture and many other imported products, some of them used to be available in Sonoma's Zimbabwe Trading Co., then part of the Shona Gallery group.

Here you will also find Putamayo world music, African candles and rugs, figurines, masks, picture frames, lamps, jewelry, Penzo Zimbabwe ceramics, and an interesting, mellow atmosphere. African Odyssey also offers a fenced yard in back with water for your dog. You can also visit their stores in Carmel, Colorado, New Mexico, and Texas.

❧ *African Odyssey, 23002 Arnold Drive (Highway 121), Sonoma 95476; phone (707) 933–9199; fax (707) 933–9242; Web site www.africanodyssey.com. Open 10 A.M.–6:00 P.M. Monday–Saturday, 11:00 A.M.–5:00 P.M. Sunday. MasterCard, Visa, and American Express. Wheelchair-accessible. Dog friendly.*

As you follow Highway 121 around to the right (straight ahead, Arnold Drive goes north to Glen Ellen), Vineyard Inn Bed and Breakfast pops up. It is a classic California motor court with updated conveniences, formerly known as El Bend Grande. The landscaping and bright flowers were designed by the late Robert Earnest of Sonoma.

Right across the road at this junction is a favorite hangout, CARNEROS DELI (intersection of Highway 121 and Arnold Drive, 6.1 miles from 121/37 junction), handily located next to the Unocal station (formerly known as Bonneau's Shell) and owned by the same family.

The former site of Ford's Cafe (which is now located east of this intersection), Carneros Deli caters to local workers, farmers, visitors, and anyone needing a caffeine fix. The sandwiches are made to order and reliable—albeit average—and the salads are made somewhere else, usually with an overdose of acid preserves. The espresso machine is the push-button kind, but you get to push the buttons yourself, adding extra shots, chocolate, and other goodies to your personal taste. Bottles of flavored syrups are kept right by the machine so that you can add any exotic sugar flavor you desire.

As you walk in the front door, you immediately run into the sandwich line. To your left is a case loaded with soft drinks and beer, and around the corner to the right is a vast case with an ice-cream novelty selection unequaled in these parts. More ice cream waits along the window to the left of the espresso machine. Some local wines are also available.

While the whole place is a bit cluttered with well-used fixtures, clean and attractive tables and chairs invite you to eat your picnic at the back of this establishment, which also has a few redwood picnic tables on the south (gas station) side of the building (smokers' delight).

Carneros Deli, *23003 Arnold Drive, Sonoma 95475; phone (707) 939–1646. Open about 7:00 A.M. to 7:00 P.M. daily. MasterCard and Visa. Wheelchair-accessible.*

Beside the Carneros Deli is Bonneau Road, which leads to SCHUG CARNEROS ESTATE WINERY. Schug is technically not allowed to have a sign on the highway (Arnold Drive) because its property is not adjacent to the road, but on weekends the staff props a portable sign against a fence to alert visitors. Persevering to find this hidden treasure is well worth the effort and adventure.

Former Joseph Phelps Winery vice president and cellarmaster Walter Schug and his wife, Gertrud, bought "the old Meier Place," overlooking the prime, sought-after Sangiacomo family Carneros vineyards, and turned it into a storybook, Germanesque winery. Both Schugs come from distinguished winemaking families in Germany and have spent decades in California winemaking. The two traditions blend at Schug, where their primary products come from the fragile Pinot Noir grape. Walter Schug left Joseph Phelps solely to pursue his dream to produce the best Pinot Noirs possible. After much research, the Schugs selected their fifty-acre site as the most capable of yielding character similar to the finest French Burgundies.

The Rhine River Valley–style post-and-beam construction gives the winery a romantic German ambience, with gorgeous caves built into the natural

ASPARAGUS AND SNOW PEA SOUP
WITH LEMON-TARRAGON CREAM
FROM SCHUG CARNEROS ESTATE WINERY

4 Tbs butter

2 large onions, peeled, quartered, and sliced

½ cup very thinly sliced celery

½ tsp. salt

2 quarts vegetable or chicken stock

1 lb snow peas, trimmed, strings removed

1 lb asparagus, trimmed, cut in 1-inch lengths, tips set aside

freshly ground black pepper

lemon-tarragon cream (see below)

Blanch asparagus tips in salted boiling water until tender. Rinse in cold water to stop cooking; set aside. In a large soup pot over medium heat, melt the butter and add the onions, celery, and salt. Gently sauté until the onions and celery are limp. Add the stock and bring mixture to a boil. Simmer approximately 20 minutes or until onions and celery are completely cooked through.

Now add the asparagus (except for the tips). One minute later add the snow peas and simmer for 7–8 minutes or until peas and asparagus are tender but still bright green.

Quickly puree soup and strain out vegetable fibers. Return strained soup to pot and reheat, but do not boil or the pretty bright green color will be lost. Correct seasonings and ladle hot soup into warm serving bowls. Garnish with an asparagus tip or two and 1 Tbs of tarragon cream. Serve immediately. Serves 10.

LEMON-TARRAGON CREAM
FROM SCHUG CARNEROS ESTATE WINERY

½ cup sour cream

½ tsp lemon zest, minced

1 tsp fresh lemon juice

1 Tbs fresh chives, chopped

1 Tbs fresh tarragon, chopped

salt and pepper to taste

Mix all ingredients together in a small bowl. Set aside for soup garnish or refrigerate up to two days.

hillsides under the winery. Enjoy the refreshing duck pond, complete with reeds and friendly ducks that may follow you around.

Schug exports 25 percent of its Chardonnays and Pinot Noirs. Its Pinot Noirs are fermented in rotary fermenters, then proceed to a secondary, malolactic fermentation in large German oak casks, and then age in French oak barrels.

SCHUG CARNEROS ESTATE WINERY

Son Axel Schug serves as director of marketing. Daughter-in-law Kristine Schug serves as hospitality director; she hosts and cooks unparalleled meals served in Schug's caves and throughout the United States. Daughter Claudia Schug handles marketing in Europe, from Dusseldorf, Germany.

 Fine points: Schug celebrates the harvest with an Oktoberfest from Gertrud Schug's home region, the Palatinate, featuring still-bubbling wine direct from the cask, traditional onion bread, and German-style sausages, all for only $5.00. Get on the mailing list for exact dates.

Featured wines: Carneros Chardonnays, Pinot Noir, Merlot, Cabernet Sauvignon, and Rouge de Noir sparkling wine. Winemaker: Michael Cox. Cases: 20,000. Acres: 42. Hours: 10:00 A.M.–5:00 P.M. daily. MasterCard and Visa.

⋆↳ *Schug Carneros Estate Winery, 602 Bonneau Road, Sonoma 95475; phone (707) 939–9363 or (800) 966–9365; fax (707) 939–9364; e-mail schug@schugwinery.com; Web site www.schugwinery.com. Open 10:00 A.M.–5:00 P.M. daily. MasterCard and Visa. Wheelchair-accessible.*

Now, to get to Sonoma, turn right opposite the Unocal station, heading east on Highway 121. In 0.8 mile turn left onto Highway 12 at the Schellvista Fire Station. Once you make this turn, you are on Broadway.

As you round the bend to your right and pass Vineyard Inn (formerly called El Bend Grande) and head east on Highway 121, you immediately come to LA VILLETA DE SONOMA, a wild and crazy place dedicated to Mexican and Italian ceramics, the passion of Armenian-American Mando Sarkissian, who once had an art gallery in Jerusalem. Sarkissian got turned onto Mexican pottery during his life phase when he was a consultant to Mexican farmers.

Here you will experience thousands of pieces of finite and gigantic hand-painted pottery, landmark-sized pots, ornaments from around the world, huge bird cages for finches, replicas of archaeological treasures, Majolica painted ceramic ware, carved stone and metal, and handcrafted terra cotta. Just stop in for the heck of it.

La Villeta de Sonoma, 27 Fremont Drive, Sonoma 95476; phone (707) 939–9392, fax (707) 939–3693, Web site www.lavilleta.com. Open 10:00 A.M.–6:00 P.M. daily. MasterCard, Visa, American Express, and Discover. Wheelchair-accessible.

After you leave La Villeta and continue eastward, just after you cross the bridge over Sonoma Creek, turn right carefully across from the Schellvista Fire Station to SONOMA CREEK WINERY, a hilariously fun place about good wine. Besides its wines, Sonoma Creek is known for its bright and cheerful graphics, which exemplify owners Tom and Becky Larson's attitudes.

What is now Sonoma Creek Winery was once the Embarcadero, the farthest navigable point up Sonoma Creek from San Francisco Bay, where European visitors landed in small craft as early as 1823. From 1847, steamboats docked here, and a steamboat captain built the Civil War–era farmhouse some lucky visitors get to stay in and in which Tom and Becky lived for several years. Tom's great-grandfather, Michael Millerick, bought the house and 120 acres in 1899.

From 1929 to the early 1950s, the Sonoma Rodeo was held nearby on the Millerick Ranch and was the largest and longest-running rodeo in the Bay Area, annually feeding thousands of attendees on beef roasted in underground pits. One year even August Sebastiani won a roping trophy!

With a degree in fermentation science from the University of California, Davis, Tom says, "When we made more wine than we could drink ourselves, we got serious." Now you taste wines at a bar in the barrel barn, usually entertained by host Jim Kelley.

Fine points: Featured wines: Gewürztraminer, Chardonnay, Merlot, Pinot Noir, Cabernet Sauvignon, Zinfandel, Meritage. Owners: Tom and Becky Larson. Winemakers: Tom Larson and Scott Peterson. Cases: 80,000. Acres: 150 and buy from others, including Sangiacomo Vineyards.

❧ *Sonoma Creek Winery, 23355 Millerick Road, Sonoma   95476; phone (707) 938–3031; fax (707) 938–3424. Tasting fee: none. Open 10:30 A.M.–4:30 P.M. weekends April–harvest. MasterCard, Visa, American Express, and Discover. Wheelchair-accessible.*

FORD'S CAFE, is a must-stop for local color (0.1 mile north of 121/12 junction, next door to the Schellvista Fire Station). Since we last wrote about Ford's, it has fallen into the no-one-goes-there-anymore-it's-too-crowded category. But we suggest that you go there anyway.

William Ford Cook moved his wonderful greasy spoon from its original site, now occupied by Carneros Deli, after the owners forced him out. He simply moved all his funk and junk up the road a tiny piece, and his legions of loyal customers followed right along, never missing a beat or a cup of coffee.

The walls tilt slightly, the people tilt slightly, the American flag gets stolen, and the building floods when Sonoma Creek overflows, but hundreds of people pass through this place every day. A big sign at the end of the kitchen warns: BEWARE. MEAN JUNK YARD DOGS. WILL BITE. A Chicklets machine and an empty chewing-tobacco dispenser hang from the wall. Truckers line up at 6:30 A.M., local ranchers meet here every morning, and downtown Sonomans make their way out here for fabulously drippy hamburgers, eggs, and country fries (deep). It's by far the best greasy breakfast around.

FORD'S CAFE

The daily special may include an ostrich patty with eggs, potatoes, and toast for $6.50. The regular breakfast menu features The Hay Bailer, with two huge pieces of French toast and two eggs on a slice of ham with jack cheese; Going Fishing, with three eggs, two sausages, country potatoes, and two golden cakes; chicken-fried steak; and linguica and eggs. The rest room is filthy, so plan accordingly. Breakfast is served until 11:30 A.M., a new policy, and greasy lunch follows until 2:00 P.M.

The walls are covered with old signs, photos, and bad jokes—a side of Sonoma history unhung in the museums. Tiny Christmas-tree lights flicker constantly, while the busgirl comes by serving coffee occasionally, chewing gum and wearing a Petaluma Speedway T-shirt. The waitresses are local and appropriately surly, and everyone knows them and loves them. Visiting this place is a must experience to know Sonoma. Take the kids!

Ford's Cafe, 22900 Broadway, Sonoma 95475; phone (707) 938–9811. Open 5:00 A.M.–2:00 P.M., Monday–Friday; 6:00 A.M.–2:00 P.M., Saturday and Sunday; although locals hang around for a beer later. No credit cards. Wheelchair-accessible.

Again driving toward Sonoma, carefully negotiate the sharp curves by the superb Sangiacomo Vineyards (left, or west) lined with climbing red roses along the fence. The Sangiacomo family does not make wine, but they sell their fine grapes to the best wineries in California.

Next you'll see STARWAE INN on the right (north), a unique vacation rental that includes an octagonal house, owned by artists John Curry and Janice Crow. This is a favorite and unlikely hideaway of several famous people, including Bill Moyers and his family.

Just after the road straightens out and you cross Watmaugh Road, WEDEKIND'S GARDEN CENTER—WHERE GARDENING IS AN ART is on the left (west). Although the nursery property was sold to the Sangiacomo family and founder Frank Wedekind died in 1995, owner Janet Rude continues the nursery with the highest quality and knowledge available about local and native plants. A walk through the color aisles and gardens brings joy, whether or not you buy something. Many varieties of specialty organic seeds and indoor plants are in the room to the right as you enter.

Wedekind's Garden Center, 21095 Broadway, Sonoma 95475; phone (707) 938–2727. Open 9:00 A.M.–5:30 P.M. daily. MasterCard, Visa, and American Express. Wheelchair-accessible.

One of our favorite Mexican restaurants, THE RANCH HOUSE, lies just beyond Wedekind's, on the right (east) side of Broadway, 1.1 miles south of

Sonoma Plaza. The Avila family, originally from the Yucatán town of Merida, cook and serve their own delectable versions of their native Mayan and Yucatán specialties in this small but charming and fun restaurant. Having worked for years for the Guerra's Sonoma French Bakery, the Avilas dared to dream, and their dream certainly has come true. The Avilas are well known in the community, and locals dine here frequently.

Called "the "best Mexican food in the North Bay" by the *San Francisco Examiner's* Bill Mandel, The Ranch House offers a perfect chicken mole; blackened sea bass; prawns sautéed five ways; carne asada; beefsteak fried with potatoes; flautas, Yucatán or machaca; and exceptional tostadas, enchiladas, and chimichangas. All beef and chicken used in the dishes is cooked to perfection and hand shredded or pulled. The Ranch House uses white beans, even when "refried." Prices range from $5.95 to $12.50 for lunch or dinner.

The atmosphere is funky Mexican, with formica tabletops and vinyl chairs. There is an outdoor dining area on a deck enclosed with latticework and grapevines. On Sunday afternoons in summer, you may enjoy Mexican bands playing romantic music outdoors. On Sundays the Avilas make their very special menudo, known to be a sobering experience.

✢ The Ranch House, 20872 Broadway (Highway 12), Sonoma 95475; phone (707) 938–0454. Open 11:00 A.M.–9:00 P.M., Tuesday–Saturday; 8:00 A.M.–9:00 P.M., Sunday. MasterCard, Visa, American Express, and Discover. ATM. Wheelchair-accessible.

At the intersection of Broadway (Highway 12) and Napa Road, there are two new businesses collectors might enjoy. The most obvious, Salsa Trading Company, is on the northeast corner. Three Sisters Antiques recently moved to the southwest corner next to Broadway market.

SALSA TRADING COMPANY is the most exciting new addition to Sonoma's substantial import scene. Owners Bruce and Edna Hayes Needleman took over a dilapidated building and turned it into the third outpost of their growing network. Sonoma's Salsa is larger and slightly more pizzazzy than their Larkspur and Berkeley stores and a must-visit for lovers of natural furniture and personal accessories.

Born of the Needlemans' desire to furnish their own home with Mexican imports better than those they could already find in California, the first Salsa Trading Company is still in old Larkspur under the Highway 101 trestle, on a western-motif block used by Clint Eastwood in *Dirty Harry.*

Here you can browse through vast rooms and rooms of always tasteful Mexican furniture; tooled leather table place mats, belts, bags, and luggage; blue glassware; exquisite turquoise and silver jewelry; $80 Native throw rugs;

Mexican architecture and art books; hand-tooled leather photo albumns at $199; milagros crosses at only $35; and even reasonably priced armoires. Check out the new, huge black pink-pebble patio full of wrought-iron furniture. Take your dark glasses and try not to trip over colorful pots!

❧ *Salsa Trading Company, 20940 Broadway, Sonoma, 95476; phone (707) 939–1710. Open 10:00 A.M.–6:00 P.M. Monday–Saturday, noon–6:00 P.M. Sunday. MasterCard, Visa, and American Express. Wheelchair-accessible.*

Make your way across the intersection to THREE SISTERS ANTIQUES, which used to be just north of Ford's Cafe. Sisters Linda Hunter, Robin Kingsley, and Christina Kingsley made the smart move of their lives to this location, which has loads of parking for antiques and collectibles fans. You can find almost anything you might collect here, so it warrants frequent stops since the stock varies constantly. They also offer craft classes and supplies.

❧ *Three Sisters Antiques, 20525 Broadway (Highway 12), Sonoma, 95476; phone (707) 996–7173. Open 10:00 A.M.–5:30 P.M. Tuesday–Sunday. MasterCard, Visa, and American Express. Wheelchair-accessible.*

The landmark store at Four Corners is BROADWAY MARKET, a handy grocery store that has now developed excellent deli and meat departments. They feature Harris Ranch beef, if you don't mind feedlots, Basque Boulangerie breads, and terrific sandwiches ranging from tuna or egg salad at only $2.99 to meats at $3.69 with cheese an extra 30 cents and avocado 75 cents. Right next to the microwave for customer use is a refrigerated box of fishing bait including mealy worms at $1.25 and frozen mud shrimp at $4.99. Don't get confused and warm the mud shrimp in the microwave.

Broadway Market's surprising wine section stocks Ravenswood Château Cache$ Fl'eau, Freixenet's Millennium Special Champagne, and Domaine Ste. Michelle Cuvée Brut.

❧ *Broadway Market, 20511 Broadway, Sonoma 95476; phone (707) 938–2685. Open 6:00 A.M.–8:00 P.M. Monday–Saturday, 7:00 A.M.–7:00 P.M. Sunday. MasterCard, Visa, ATM. Wheelchair-accessible.*

Visitors drive from all over the west to ride the rails at TRAIN TOWN RAILROAD AND PETTING ZOO (9.7 miles from 121/37 junction). A miniature steam railroad for kids of all ages, Train Town has given many Sonoma children their first railroad experience. Enjoy the carousel and miniature Old West town, feed goats, and feast on sweet snacks. A very special place to experience.

❧ *Train Town Railroad and Petting Zoo, 20264 Broadway, Sonoma 95475; phone (707) 938–3912. Open 10:00 A.M.–5:00 P.M. daily, June –September; same*

TRAIN TOWN RAILROAD AND PETTING ZOO

hours October–May, but open only Friday–Sunday and holidays. No credit cards. Wheelchair-accessible except trains. (See "Train Riding," page 217.)

At PIZZERIA CAPRI, next door to Train Town on Broadway, Jacob Tuncay presents his own brand of non-Italian pizza and pasta. Many locals swear by his pizza, particularly to-go, although we favor his pastas. He does a big business with high school students (Sonoma Valley High School is just up Broadway) and Train Town patrons with his $2.50 "big slice" every day but Sunday. Tuncay also offers family pizza and pasta specials at about $28, including family salad, half a loaf of garlic bread, and a pitcher of soda. The Caesar salad is respectable.

 Fine points: Pizzeria Capri has been so successful in serving the pizza cravings on this end of Sonoma that it has added two large dining rooms and offers live music on weekend evenings. Solid local wines and microbrews. Public telephone at sidewalk.

✦ *Pizzeria Capri, 1266 Broadway, Sonoma 95475; phone (707) 935–6805. Open 10:00 A.M.–9:30 P.M. daily. MasterCard, Visa, and American Express. Wheelchair-accessible.*

MACARTHUR PLACE (at the corner of Broadway and East MacArthur, just around the corner from Sonoma Valley High School) is renovation goddess

Suzanne Brangham's latest gift to Sonoma and the visiting public—and to her investors, of course.

Known for years as the Goode house, this is Sonoma's second-oldest Victorian (second only to General Mariano Vallejo's home). Suzanne bought the property in 1997 and completely restored the house and developed the perfect wine-country inn and executive retreat. The century-old barn has become a 4,200-square-foot conference center (desperately needed in Sonoma), and the house and additions offer thirty-three individually decorated guest rooms, a gorgeous swimming pool, pétanque courts, horseshoes, and a resident chef. Suzanne is adding thirty-three more rooms.

 Fine points: Suzanne has won the hearts of city mothers and fathers and other residents by founding the Red & White Ball and raising a cool half million for Broadway and Plaza beautification projects, to say nothing of her renovation of Vallejo's daughter's home into the General's Daughter restaurant and her new Ramekins cooking school (next door to the General's Daughter on West Spain Street).

❧ *MacArthur Place, 29 East MacArthur, Sonoma 95475; phone (707) 938-2929; fax (707) 933-9833. MasterCard, Visa, and American Express. Wheelchair-accessible.*

In fall of 1999, Suzanne opened her new SADDLES STEAKHOUSE and TACK ROOM bar in the one-hundred-year-old barn of her MacArthur Place. What started out to be an "Executive Retreat" has evolved into a whole "country inn and spa." Saddles features a sophisticated equestrian decor with restored hardwood floors, vaulted ceilings, wood-topped tables, and local artists' work on the walls. Urban cowboys will feel right at home with cowboy boots, hats, ropes, and bridles hanging around the walls, with a brown leather couch and chairs in the bar.

Chef Seth Thornton, formerly of Suzanne's General's Daughter, has created a menu of steaks cooked on an outdoor wood-burning grill combined with spa conscience foods. One of the appetizers at the "Starting Gate" we look forward to is the red cornmeal haystack onion rings with blue cheese, aioli, or chipotle ketchup ($3.95). Salads include a classic American wedge of iceberg lettuce with either thousand island or blue cheese dressing ($4.50) or the heirloom tomato and onion salad with Maytag blue cheese and vinaigrette dressing ($6.95).

Things get more serious in the steak department, which range from an 8-ounce petit filet mignon at $21.95 to the 16-ounce T-bone steak at $26.95. Sautéed mushrooms or caramelized onions cost an extra $2.00. Other entrees include Saddles "falling off the bone" baby back ribs (half rack $12.95, full rack $17.95), half roasted chicken finished on the wood-burning grill ($13.50), pasta or fish of the day, and a healthy burger with fries ($8.95). Try special "Side Saddles" of creamed spinach, mashed or baked potatoes, steak fries, potatoes au gratin, and even coleslaw, all under $4.00.

ᴥ *Saddles Steakhouse, 29 East MacArthur, Sonoma 95476; phone (707) 938–2929. Open 5:30–9:30 P.M. nightly, weekend brunch 10:00 A.M.–noon. Full bar. MasterCard, Visa, and American Express. Wheelchair-accessible.*

On your way into town, you might want to stop at the Flag Store or at two art galleries and frameries on Broadway. Artworks (at 20075 Broadway, on the left side coming into town) features large, modern works. The Framery (762 Broadway) shows a variety of local art and features Sonoma events and art posters as well as whimsical paintings and drawings of owner and framer Scott Sherman.

DETOUR OPTIONAL

If you're dying for a huge greasy cheeseburger with enough fresh local veggies on it to rationalize as your salad course, loaded French fries, local color, and ticklish abuse, take a detour east on Highway 12/121 toward Napa. BABE'S BURGERS AND HOT DOGS is a local monument to the cattle industry's one-time prominence and dominance in the American diet. At this true concrete-block diner, park in front (if you can find a place) and enter through the east-side swinging door. Walk by several duct-taped, virgin vinyl-benched booths and formica tables, turn right around the post, and get in line. The place is packed with locals, drooling in anticipation of their dose of grease, red-meat juice, and thick fries made to order.

Babe himself cooks the hamburgers when the horses aren't running anywhere in the San Francisco Bay Area. He looks like a guy who has smoked Camels or Lucky Strikes most of his life. The bouffant Mrs. Babe runs the cash register and takes the orders—and gives a few back. If you dare to order a veggie burger (which they have), she will laugh at you robustly. We inquired about the grilled chicken-breast sandwich, and she and Babe both sneered that they were frozen and from out of town. Their only new concession to food fads, as they see them, is a turkey burger.

While you wait for your order, check out the signs and stuff for sale along the walls. One advises: GOOD FOOD TAKES TIME, IF YOU CAN'T WAIT, LEAVE. And ANY SOFT DRINK WITHOUT ICE IS 20 CENTS EXTRA. (What they don't tell you is that there are free refills if you have ice.)

The right-hand wall facing the counter sports a faded handwritten sign for Babe's Toyland, which refers to the pink Barbie Porsche; wooden banana holder; and 59-cent baskets for sale on the shelves below. A public telephone hangs on the north wall, and Babe's uses it to receive phone orders. No faxes or e-mail here! Supposedly they serve espresso drinks, but no customer I know has ever seen one beyond the excellent coffee milkshake.

Babe's Burgers and Hot Dogs, 2660 Fremont Drive (Highways 12/121), Sonoma 95475; phone (707) 938–9714. Open 7:00–11:30 A.M.; lunchtime 11:00 A.M.–3:00 P.M.; closed Wednesday. No credit cards. Rest rooms for customers only. Wheelchair-accessible.

There's an option to Babe's along this route, and that's the CHERRY TREE COUNTRY STORE, which offers the same Cherry Tree juices and stuffed olives and nuts as Cherry Tree #1, but this one is the home base. This full deli of fresh sandwiches and prepared-elsewhere salads, made-here soups and chilis, makes a slightly more healthy stop. Picnic tables and a "grass" area offer accessible "dining"—with one problem: The location is surrounded by Mulas Ranch cattle and manure piles, which waft an interesting odor in most directions. To some people cattle smells are mouth-watering, to others repulsive. If you are in the latter group, purchase your juices and sandwiches and take the picnic elsewhere, perhaps to a winery.

The Lehnert family recently sold The Cherry Tree Stores to H. Bosch & Proulx, Inc. You will now also find a wine-tasting bar featuring family wineries' products, Häagen-Dazs and other ice cream, and Maraska Cherry Wine from Croatia.

Cherry Tree Country Store, 1901 Fremont Drive (Highways 12 and 121), Sonoma 95475; phone (707) 938–3480. Open 6:00 A.M.–6:30 P.M. daily, winter; 6:00 A.M.–9:00 P.M. daily, in season. No credit cards. Rest rooms are wheelchair-inaccessible portapotties. Store and picnic area are accessible.

Although she does not give tours or welcome visitors, LAURA CHENEL'S CHÈVRE is now located at what was Stornetta's Dairy at the intersection of Highways 12/121 and Napa Road. You can see her goats tenderly enjoying the Sonoma grasses on the hill behind the dairy. Laura Chenel's carefully crafted goat cheeses are available in Sonoma at most of the cheese factories, Sonoma Market, and Glen Ellen Village Market.

Laura Chenel's Chèvre, 4310 Fremont Drive (Highways 12/121), Sonoma 95475; phone (707) 996–4477.

NON-DETOUR DIRECTIONS

Follow Broadway straight into Sonoma Plaza, facing Sonoma City Hall. Deuce Restaurant and Magliulo's Pensione is on the west side of Broadway at France Street, in a deceptively small-looking Victorian house. Rin's new Noodle House and On Trays On Broadway are just north of the Post Office, and Sonoma's new dining sensation Freestyle! is on the east side of the street just south of the Plaza.

Now we will start you on a walking, shopping, and eating tour of the Sonoma Plaza area.

THE SEVEN FLAGS
OF SONOMA

Throughout Sonoma Valley there are references to seven flags. They fly from tall poles at Sebastiani Winery and from the balcony at the El Dorado Hotel. These are the seven flags that have been unfurled over Sonoma County (although only five have been raised in Sonoma Valley):

- The flag of St. George, a simple cross on white, which was the English flag raised by Sir Francis Drake while his ship the *Golden Hind* was being repaired and cleaned on shore in 1578. He claimed the land for Queen Elizabeth and named it New Albion.
- The Spainish flag, which was carried by a squad of Spanish soldiers who marched from Bodega Bay on the coast down through Sonoma Valley in 1810 but believed the valley too wet for settlement. Spain claimed California until Mexico gained independence, announced in California in April 1822.
- The Russian flag, which flew over the trading post established in 1812 on the Sonoma coast at what is known as Fort Ross, which lasted until 1841, when the land was sold to John Sutter.
- The Mexican Empire flag of the short-lived Mexican government following independence from Spain. A leader of the rebellion proclaimed himself Emperor Agustin the First (and also the last). He was ousted in 1824, and a republic was declared.
- The flag of the Mexican Republic, distinguished by an eagle holding a serpent, from 1824 to the present. It was brought to Sonoma shortly after the founding of the mission in 1823 and flew until June 14, 1846, when it was pulled down by the Bear Flag rebels.
- The Bear Flag, raised by the American Bear Flaggers who invaded Sonoma from Sacramento and Napa Valleys on June 14, 1846. It stayed up on the pole in the Plaza for twenty-five days.
- The American flag was raised in the Plaza on July 9, 1846, by Navy Lieutenant Joseph Warren Revere, after taking down the Bear Flag. He was under orders to do so, but official reports of the war with Mexico did not arrive for another month.

CHAPTER 2

SONOMA PLAZA

*W*e now take you around the beautiful Sonoma Plaza, providing descriptions of all the shops, galleries, eateries, and wine-tasting
possibilities that you may encounter so that so you can arrive at each spot
with the latest information possible or select those you want to visit ahead
of time. We lead you down East Napa Street, up First Street East, east of
the Plaza on East Spain Street as far as Vella's Cheese on Second Street
East and Sebastiani Sonoma Cask Cellars on Fourth Street East, back on
Spain across the Plaza, and west on Spain as far as The General's
Daughter and Ramekins Cooking School and Bed & Breakfast. Then we
lead you down First Street West, Napa Street, and Broadway.

As you drive into town on Broadway, you can drive smack into City Hall.
Completed in 1908 of Sonoma basalt stone, the City Hall was designed by
architect A. C. Lutgens so that each side was identical, in order not to favor any
commercial areas on the streets around the plaza.

Until 1980 the City Council, city commissions, and sessions of the munic-
ipal court were held on the second floor, though the only access was via two
flights of steep stairs. These functions were then moved to the new police
station/courtroom at the top of First Street West, partly to meet wheelchair-
accessibility requirements.

In the mid-1980s City Hall was rebuilt on the inside, the offices were
remodeled, and an elevator was installed. The city manager, clerk, treasurer,
and the planning, water, and building departments are all located here. At the
top of the stairs is an interesting exhibit of memorabilia from Sonoma's four
sister cities: Chambolle-Musigny, France; Greve, Italy; Kanev, Ukraine; and
Patzcuaro, Mexico.

❧ *City Hall, 1 The Plaza, Sonoma 95476; phone (707) 938–3681. Open 8:30
A.M.–noon and 1:00–5:00 P.M. daily.*

The CARNEGIE PUBLIC LIBRARY/SONOMA VALLEY VISITORS BUREAU faces
First Street East. With a boost of a $6,000 gift from the Andrew Carnegie

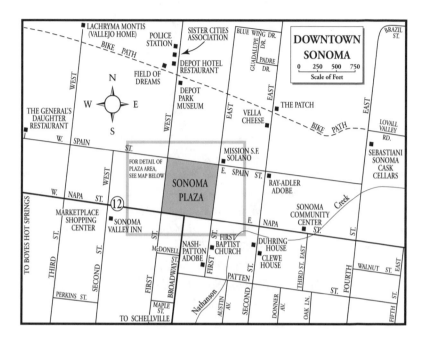

DOWNTOWN SONOMA

0 250 500 750
Scale of Feet

LACHRYMA MONTIS (VALLEJO HOME)
POLICE STATION
SISTER CITIES ASSOCIATION
BLUE WING DR.
GUADALUPE DR.
PADRE DR.
BRAZIL ST.
BIKE PATH
DEPOT HOTEL RESTAURANT
FIELD OF DREAMS
DEPOT PARK MUSEUM
THE PATCH
WEST
WEST
THE GENERAL'S DAUGHTER RESTAURANT
W. SPAIN ST.
EAST
EAST
VELLA CHEESE
BIKE PATH
LOVALL VALLEY RD.
N
W E
S
FOR DETAIL OF PLAZA AREA, SEE MAP BELOW
MISSION S.F. SOLANO
E. SPAIN ST.
SONOMA PLAZA
RAY-ADLER ADOBE
SEBASTIANI SONOMA CASK CELLARS
WEST
W. NAPA ST.
12
SONOMA VALLEY INN
E. NAPA ST.
SONOMA COMMUNITY CENTER
Creek
TO BOYES HOT SPRINGS
MARKETPLACE SHOPPING CENTER
THIRD ST.
SECOND ST.
McDONELL ST.
FIRST ST.
BROADWAY
NASH-PATTON ADOBE
FIRST ST.
FIRST BAPTIST CHURCH
DUHRING HOUSE
CLEWE HOUSE
THIRD ST. EAST
FOURTH ST.
WALNUT ST. EAST
PERKINS ST.
MAPLE ST.
PATTEN ST.
Nathanson
AUSTIN AV.
SECOND ST.
DONNER AV.
OAK LN.
FIFTH ST.
TO SCHELLVILLE

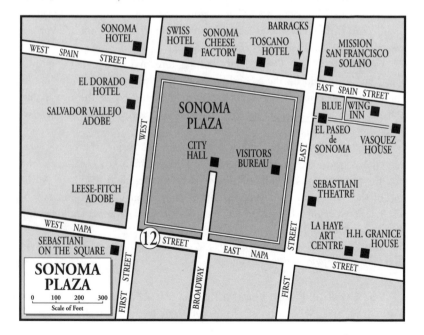

SONOMA HOTEL
SWISS HOTEL
SONOMA CHEESE FACTORY
BARRACKS
TOSCANO HOTEL
MISSION SAN FRANCISCO SOLANO
WEST SPAIN STREET
EL DORADO HOTEL
SALVADOR VALLEJO ADOBE
WEST
SONOMA PLAZA
EAST SPAIN STREET
BLUE WING INN
EL PASEO de SONOMA
VASQUEZ HOUSE
CITY HALL
VISITORS BUREAU
EAST
SEBASTIANI THEATRE
LEESE-FITCH ADOBE
WEST NAPA
SEBASTIANI ON THE SQUARE
12
STREET
EAST NAPA STREET
LA HAYE ART CENTRE
H.H. GRANICE HOUSE
FIRST STREET
BROADWAY
FIRST STREET

SONOMA PLAZA

0 100 200 300
Scale of Feet

SONOMA CITY HALL

Foundation, this Palladian-style library was built for the City Trustees between 1911 and 1913.

This building served as the city's public library until 1978, when a regional library was built on West Napa Street (beyond Seventh Street). For several years the building housed the Sonoma Valley Chamber of Commerce. It now is headquarters for the Sonoma Valley Visitors Bureau and some city offices. Both had to move out temporarily for earthquake retrofitting, completed in June 1998.

❧ *Sonoma Valley Visitors Bureau, 453 First Street East, Sonoma 95476; phone (707) 996–1090. Open 9:00 A.M.–5:00 P.M. daily. Not wheelchair-accessible.*

SOUTH SIDE OF EAST NAPA STREET

Now let's continue from the southeastern corner of the Plaza, at East Napa Street and First Street East.

Right at the corner is the new MAYA RESTAURANT, which opened the summer of 1999 to the warm embrace of Sonomans. Owners Craig and P. J. Clark, who have fabulous backgrounds of Mustard's in the Napa Valley and opening the Sonoma Piatti and the General's Daughter, now are living out their dream at Maya.

CAMARONES A LA DIABLO
from Craig and P. J. Clark
of Maya Restaurant

10 large (16–20 count) prawns,
    peeled and deveined

3 oz ham, julienned

1/2 medium yellow onion, sliced

1 red bell pepper, sliced

6 oz Maya ranchero sauce or
    prepared red enchilada sauces
    such as Las Palmas

4 oz sour cream

5 cloves garlic, minced

2 Tbs olive oil

salt and pepper to taste

cayenne to taste

chili powder to taste

Marinate prawns in olive oil and 1/2 of garlic for 1 hour. In a large sauté pan heat remaining oil until hot but not smoking. Add onion and cook for 1 minute. Add bell pepper, ham, and garlic and cook for 1 more minute. Add enchilada sauce and sour cream, stir to incorporate, then lower heat to prevent curdling. Season with salt, pepper, cayenne, and chili powder. Serve with cilantro rice, whole black beans, and roasted butternut or acorn squash. Serves 2.

As you enter the door at the corner, your eyes will affix on Sonoma artist Steffan Gold's dramatically colorful mural, beautiful carved furniture, a small, friendly bar, and the best of Yucatán artifacts. Even the chairs, which look slightly daunting, seem to be carved for both the boniest and cushioniest bottoms possible. Craig made all of the interesting pine tables himself, believe it or not, and Bev Prevost, whose pottery studio is just down the block at La Haye Art Center, made the salsa trays! This place makes you smile, even before you taste the food.

Freshly made chips and salsas with chopped onions, peppers, and cilantro come to your table automatically, but you may want to try the appetizers, including the Tlacoyaos, which are Maya chicken and mole verde in natural tortillas de masa ($6.50), or the camarones a la Parrilla, which are grilled tiger prawns with sweet pepper and corn salad and chili and guayaba salsa ($7.75). One of our favorite salads is the grilled hearts of romaine with green Caesar dressing, which reminds us of good old Green Goddess dressing, pico de gallo, and dry Jack masa croutons ($5.50), to which you can add perfect shredded Maya chicken ($4.00) or grilled tiger prawns ($5.50).

Among the platos grandes, everything is terrific, and we favor the pan-seared plantain crusted salmon ($15.95), the pan-seared Chilean sea bass ($17.50), and the grilled lamb rack filled with spinach and peppers ($17.95). Always listen to the specials, because the seafood on broccoli risotto is outstanding. The dessert flan is larger and more textured than you may be used to, but be sure to try it for a taste treat ($4.95). Maybe also order the rollito con leche, which are rolled dough with fresh fruit, whipped cream, and chocolate cinnamon ganache to die for ($4.95).

A must try!

❧ *Maya Restaurant*, 101 East Napa Street, Sonoma 95476; phone (707) 935–3500, fax (707) 935–3529. Full Bar. Open 11:45 A.M. on. MasterCard, Visa, local checks. Wheelchair-accessible.

FILIGREE moved here from West Napa Street in 1999 and specializes in estate jewelry, including restorations, sales, and purchases amidst blue-sky ceilings, rose textured walls, and old-style patterned carpeting.

❧ *Filigree*, 107 East Napa Street, Sonoma 95476; phone (707) 935–0383. Open 10:30 A.M.–5:00 P.M. Wednesday–Saturday, 11:00 A.M.–5:00 P.M. Sunday.

Andre Mansour closed his EXCEL PHOTOGRAPHICS shop in Fairfield and opened one in Sonoma, where he and his family live. Excel does full color and black-and-white development, printing, enlargement, and excellent professional photography. We applaud Andre for starting a business on this block. He joins Readers' Books in offering services and products locals might actually use.

❧ *Excel Photographics*, 109 East Napa Street, Sonoma; phone (707) 996-5100. Open 10:00 A.M.–6:00 P.M. Monday–Friday, 10:00 A.M.–5:00 P.M. Saturday. MasterCard and Visa. Wheelchair-accessible.

The HAT GENERATION is a northern branch of hat shops featuring hats by Sonni and others.

❧ *The Hat Generation*, 111 East Napa Street, Sonoma 95476; phone (707) 939–1772. Open 11:00 A.M.–5:30 P.M. Sunday–Friday, 10:00 A.M.–6:00 P.M. Saturday. MasterCard, Visa, and American Express. Wheelchair-accessible.

We love J. SUMNER GALLERY's optical-illusion oblong sign, which declares that the gallery is "slightly off square," a reference to its ambience as well as its location. Della Ziegler and John Sumner offer bright, whimsical paintings and contemporary useful objects, primarily featuring cats and other animals. Every time we walk into this gallery/shop, we just grin and giggle. Sumner's paintings hang in collections throughout the country, and we happen to enjoy the ones at the Sunnyside Cafe in Mill Valley. The zany work includes John's and that of fifteen other nationally known artists. Some of our favorites are the hand-painted shoes, crazy clocks, and metalwork, and papier-mâché moon lamps. Ziegler correctly describes what she sells as "stuff with a twist." The price range is quite reasonable, almost affordable.

❧ *J. Sumner Gallery*, 111 East Napa Street, Sonoma 95476; phone (707) 939–8272. *Open noon–6:00 P.M., more or less. MasterCard, Visa, and Discover. Wheelchair-accessible. Live pets welcome!*

Next door, Michelle Erbs has opened a new gallery, ALTA CALIFORNIA, where the avant-garde Gallery Gae Shulman was located for several years. (Locals miss Gae Shulman's flare and pizzazz.) Alta California features fine crafts from California and beyond, including a few local artists (some of whom also exhibit across the street at the Arts Guild of Sonoma Gallery). We were pleased to find Jackie Hipkiss working at Alta California. Jackie learned hilarious ceramic sculpture from her mother, Cynthia Hipkiss, whose work can also be viewed and purchased.

❧ *Alta California*, 115 East Napa Street, Sonoma 95476; phone (707) 938–9188; fax (707) 938–9190. *Open 11:00 A.M.–5:00 P.M. Wednesday–Monday. MasterCard and Visa. Wheelchair-accessible.*

SONOMA DESIGN JEWELERS' goldsmith and owners Bob and Carolyn Raciti specialize in designing and making jewelry, particularly recasting your gold, diamonds, or gems; making family-crest rings; repairing all kinds of jewelry; replacing watch batteries on the spot, and showing local artists' work on the walls. Bab Raciti is a third-generation California jeweler and has created a solid gold Sonoma charm ($165). Check out the cases of lost-wax patterns for rings from which they will make you a ring.

❧ *Sonoma Design Jewelers*, 115 East Napa Street, Sonoma 95476; phone (707) 939–9334. *Open 10:00 A.M.–5:30 P.M. Monday–Saturday. MasterCard, Visa, and American Express. Wheelchair-accessible.*

At BEAR MOON CLOTHING's new location here, Robin Pitts and Denise Murray provide a truly idealistic and pure stock of "quality clothing in natural fabrics with fashion and the environment in mind." You will find organic cottons, clothes by City Lights, Eileen Fisher wool coats, Ojai jackets made of recycled plastic bottles, Putupayo, Riki, Teva shoes, Hot Sox, jewelry, Royal Robbins, Miski, and True Grit specialty labels. Check out the hemp rugs ($25).

❧ *Bear Moon Clothing*, 117 East Napa Street, Sonoma 95476; phone (707) 935–3392. *Open 10:00 A.M.–5:30 P.M. Monday–Saturday, 11:00 A.M.–5:00 P.M. Sunday. MasterCard, Visa, American Express, and Discover. Wheelchair-accessible.*

READERS' BOOKS happens to be our favorite hangout in town. In the charming stone building that used to house the Castex French Bakery, Lilla and Andy Weinberger began with a little one-room store, which has grown rapidly into three storefronts, including a wonderfully cozy back room for children and their books. The Weinbergers feature fine literature but carry everything from best-sellers to philosophy.

In their nine years as a community bookstore, Andy and Lilla have become friends to thousands and mentors to many. They have made Sonoma the northern outpost on many well-known authors' book tours, enhancing the intellectual and cultural life of locals. (Readers' Books' 1995 Sonoma Valley Poetry Festival won the national contest for a community event inspired by Bill Moyers' "Language as Life," resulting in an inspiring weekend of presentations by Moyers in Sonoma.) This wonderful place about books has become a positive gathering focus for teenagers, younger children, and those who claim to be adults. What is unusual about this fiercely and lovingly independent bookstore is that, no matter what book you request, it seems as though someone on the staff has actually read it or is familiar with it. They probably even have it in stock.

Across the street check out Readers' used and rare books, audio rentals, and cozy patio in back. The super local Second Sunday Company performs dramatic readings on—you guessed it—the second Sunday evening of each month.

🦋 *Readers' Books, 127 and 130 East Napa Street, Sonoma 95476; phone (707) 939–1779; Web site www.readersbooks.com. Open 10:00 A.M.–9:00 P.M. Monday–Saturday, 10:00 A.M.–6:00 P.M. Sunday. MasterCard, Visa, American Express, Discover, Diners, and Carte Blanche. Wheelchair-accessible through adjoining path to back door (a rest room is accessible the same way).*

The Stone Buildings, at 101–129 East Napa Street, were erected between 1896 and 1911 by three local gentlemen. Grocer Pete Boccoli added the second story to what had been the Post Office (101 and 103). Barber Charles Dal Poggetto built 107–115, and French baker Andre Castex built 129 as a restaurant in 1911. His huge bread-baking oven was in the room behind where Readers' Books' children's books room is today.

DELLA SANTINA'S TRATTORIA, ROSTICCERIA AND PASTICCERIA moved here from the corner of East Napa and First Street East when the Peterson Building had to be retrofitted to withstand earthquakes. The last great restaurant here was Charles Saunders' Eastside Oyster Bar and Grill.

The Della Santina family—former longtime owners of Marin Joe's in Corte Madera—have brought the finest of true Italian cuisine to Sonoma. There's no California cutesy to this place. Della Santina's is an intimate bistro with a casually elegant ambience indoors and loads of tables in the flower-festooned restored patio in back and in the walkway next to Readers' Books. White-tile floors add to the romantic old Italian look. Windows on the north and west sides of the restaurant look out on the Plaza.

Many locals go here repeatedly, some just for special occasions like birthdays and anniversaries. Local vintners, particularly those of Italian descent, eat here regularly. The Tuscan/Sonoma food is always fresh, exciting, prepared to perfection, and reliable—and at reasonable prices. The roaster dominates the corner window, with chickens, rabbits, pork roasts, and turkey cooking right out in public. Handmade pastas, including melt-in-your-mouth gnocchi with special daily sauces and daily ravioli, penne, and cannelloni specials, draw a crowd at both lunch and dinner.

The Della Santinas and their staff graciously accommodate requests to split their nearly perfect Caesar salad to accompany two entrees. Try the tiramisù, chocolate amaretto mousse tart, or a torta di frutta fresca to finish. This restaurant is the only one in Sonoma that offers a Chianti from Sonoma's Italian sister city, Greve in Chianti, in addition to an excellent Sonoma Valley and Italian wine list.

 Fine points: All food is also prepared to go, including a special Italian picnic box for two ($15.95–$23.95), which makes for an elegant picnic in the Plaza. Prices range from $8.95 to $25.00 for entrees at dinner; lunch is slightly less, with sandwiches added to the menu. Reservations are highly recommended at dinner. Beer and wine are served.

✒ *Della Santina's Trattoria, Rosticceria and Pasticceria, 133 East Napa Street, Sonoma 95476; phone (707) 935–0576. Open 11:00 A.M.–3:00 P.M., 5:30–9:30 P.M. daily. MasterCard, Visa, and American Express. Wheelchair-accessible.*

CLEWE HOUSE (1876)—NOW CEDAR MANSION

You might walk to the end of the block and turn right on Second Street East to see two of Sonoma's most charming classic homes. Just around the corner and across Nathanson Creek is the Clewe House (531 Second Street East), an Italianate mansion built in 1876 for Dorothea Clewe Duhring's brother Frederick and his wife. The house and grounds were well maintained and preserved with historic accuracy until recently. In the early 1990s, a buyer from Germany removed the old tennis court and some of the old trees to "modernize" the structure for a bed and breakfast inn. After much construction and destruction, a fire, and more construction, adverse community reaction moved the new owners to abandon the project. The property was for sale for several years, with an asking price of more than $1 million. Recently new owners opened it as Cedar Mansion, an elegant bed and breakfast. (see pg. 196)

The Duhring House is across the street, at 532 Second Street East. Only four years after their arrival in Sonoma, with just a small loan from friends to start a general store, merchant Frederick Duhring and his music-teacher wife, Dorothea, built this Greek Revival home on three acres, which they called Pine Lodge. The west wing was built in 1890, and the house was remodeled in 1928. The interior includes grand rooms, a former ballroom, and fabulous inlay hardwood floors.

NORTH SIDE OF EAST NAPA STREET

Take the time to walk a block farther east on East Napa and cross the street. It's worth it. Donna Lewis's Victorian Garden Inn, three doors past the Sonoma Community Center, has the most beautiful setting of any bed and breakfast or quasi-public establishment in downtown Sonoma. Pansies, primroses, or petunias always decorate the white picket fence in front of this elegant property. Built in 1870 as a Greek Revival farmhouse, the house was saved initially by Marge Eliassen, whose son Garth later sold it to Donna Lewis. Lewis, a well-known interior designer who worked in Vail, Colorado, and Park City, Utah, has completed the restoration and redecoration to tasteful perfection.

The SONOMA COMMUNITY CENTER building was Sonoma's elementary school for many years. When it was condemned in 1949, Dr. Carroll Andrews purchased it from the school district and saved it. Dr. Andrews created a nonprofit corporation and then donated the building to the board of directors. In 1982 Kathleen Hill, then president of the board of directors, got the building listed in the National Register of Historic Places. Since then it has been completely "earthquaked," preserving the brick facade and fine woods and character of the interior.

The Community Center strives to provide a meeting place and a cultural

SONOMA COMMUNITY CENTER

arts center with a full pottery school, featuring nationally recognized instructors, a strong arts program, local theatrical and operatic productions, Jazzercise, yoga, and a music library all living happily here together.

🍃 *Sonoma Community Center, 276 East Napa Street, Sonoma 95476; phone (707) 938–4626. Open 8:00 A.M.–9:00 P.M. daily. Wheelchair-accessible.*

Near the corner of East Napa and Second Street East is the casually elegant Hidden Oak Bed and Breakfast. Valerie and Don Patterson run a most comfortable, quiet and friendly English-style bed and breakfast with a few updates in this 1913 brown-shingled house that once served as a parsonage and then as a home for women teachers during World War II.

Just west, Moona O'Toole presides over her VIVA SONOMA. Moona's home and heart are in both Sonoma and in Mexico. Fortunately, she has reopened her classic historic house to the public, selling exquisite Mexican, Italian, and French imports and what we call "Moona clothes." This partial adobe was built in 1850 and served as the Bates family home. It was restored substantially in the 1970s, suffered a fire, and was rebuilt with care and historical accuracy.

When we cross the threshold of this womblike building, we feel as if we have stepped back in time and love. Be sure you don't miss a room. The parlor is to the left of the front door. Straight ahead, the hallway opens into a large room, where the antique bed is so enticingly decorated (with the quilt and sheets turned down) that we want to jump in, and probably not alone. Moona has made the back garden even more appealing by adding a fountain and an expansive lush green lawn that you can walk around on your way to sucking figs and plums right off her trees.

Everything you need and don't need is here: pitchers and bowls, wrought-iron planters, padded Mexican woven-leather furniture, tables and chairs, faucets, pillows, blankets, clothes, and reproductions of old dish-display racks of painted wood with door knobs attached for hanging coats. Moona, who is fluent in Spanish and has worked with migrant populations for years, is an expert scene-setter. So give in to her experience and enjoy.

Viva Sonoma, 180 East Napa Street, Sonoma 95476; phone (707) 939–1904. Open 10:00 A.M.–6:00 P.M. Monday, Wednesday–Saturday, closed Tuesday. 11:00 A.M.–6:00 P.M. Sunday. MasterCard and Visa. Wheelchair-accessible.

The H. H. Granice House (156 East Napa Street) was built in the 1880s and has been called "the best example of modest Victorian stick style" in Sonoma. It was the first home in town of publisher H. H. Granice when he began printing the *Sonoma Index*, later to become the *Index-Tribune*, in the back room of the house. In 1998 the house was sold for nearly $500,000.

Just west of the Granice House is LA HAYE ART CENTRE. La Haye was built originally as Gottenberg's Garage around 1910, and later it became a foundry. An unusual feature of the building is the pressed metal siding made to resemble cut stone. Sally and Frank La Haye now own this historic foundry, which ceased to function as such in 1973. As a symbol and example of their beliefs in supporting the arts, they have converted the family's building to six spacious art studios surrounding an enclosed peaceful and rustic garden, Cafe La Haye restaurant, and the gallery and headquarters of the Arts Guild of Sonoma.

The artists work in their studios daily, and you are welcome to come in and visit them. Their cast-bronze sculptures, ceramics, and paintings, all for sale, are on display in the hallways and alcoves of the building. Local artists include Beverly Prevost, James Callahan, Tehra Braren, David Dale Diamond, Diana Lee Craig, and another fine artist yet to be selected. Jim Callahan creates large iron sculptures and currently uses the front gallery, formerly the Works gallery, as a work and display space. La Haye Art Centre exemplifies the ideal of a supportive, cooperative, and fun place to create. We wish writing were a "fine art" so we could move in.

GRILLED ASPARAGUS WITH BLOOD ORANGE VINAIGRETTE, ROASTED BEETS, AND MINT
from Chef/Co-owner John McReynolds of Cafe la Haye

1 lb. fresh asparagus
½ lb chioggia or golden beets
chopped fresh spearmint
shaved dry Jack or Parmesan cheese (optional)
blood orange vinaigrette (see below)

Cut off lower quarter of asparagus stalk and discard. Peel any remaining tough or white part with sharp vegetable peeler. Blanch 2½ minutes in boiling salted water. Cool in ice water and drain.

Lightly oil beets and roast in 375 ° oven on sheet pan for 1 hour. When cool, peel and cut in thin (⅛-inch) slices. Lightly oil asparagus and season with salt and pepper. Grill 1 minute on each side over hot charcoal fire. Arrange slices of beets in circle on 10-inch plate. Lay asparagus spears on top of beets. Drizzle with vinaigrette and sprinkle with mint.

VINAIGRETTE

1 Tbs lemon juice
2 Tbs blood orange juice
2 Tbs champagne vinegar
4 Tbs canola oil
2 Tbs olive oil
½ tsp grated lemon zest
½ tsp grated orange zest
1 shallot, finely chopped
salt and pepper to taste

Put ingredients all together in bowl and mix until well blended.

❧ *La Haye Art Centre, 148 East Napa Street, Sonoma 95476; phone (707) 996–9665. Open when the door is unlocked. Wheelchair-accessible.*

CAFE LA HAYE is the artful culinary creation of Sol Gropman and John McReynolds, who cooked for several years at George Lucas's Industrial Light and Magic. John expertly blends comfort foods with original twists and Sonoma products, including local vegetables, poultry, and meats. Many locals and visitors gravitated to Cafe La Haye for refreshing lunches, but John and Sol decided to concentrate on producing perfect dinners. John's wife, Brigitte, provided the unusual hand-painted sign and table displays, and her original work hangs on the walls in rotation with John Curry's and the art of other successful Sonoma artists. In 1998, *San Francisco Chronicle* Food Editor Michael Bauer called Cafe La Haye "the find of the year."

Sunday brunch usually includes potato pancakes, while dinner includes spectacular specials and regulars such as seared black pepper–lavender filet of beef with gorgonzola potato gratin ($17.95), melt-in-your-mouth risotto, and perfect fish. *Cafe La Haye, 140 East Napa Street, Sonoma 95476; phone (707) 935–5994; Web site www.cafelahaye.com. Open 5:30–9:00 P.M. Tuesday–Saturday; from 9:00 A.M. brunch Sunday. Visa and MasterCard. Wheelchair-accessible. Beer and wine.*

ARTS GUILD OF SONOMA is the gallery of a unique, nonprofit organization run by member artists since 1977. Fifty artists belong, and twenty to thirty of them exhibit at a time. Here you will find local artwork and jewelry of remarkably high quality at affordable prices. Ask for their schedule of East Napa Street galleries' occasional open houses. *Arts Guild of Sonoma, 140 East Napa Street, Sonoma 95476; phone (707) 996–3115. Open 11:00 A.M.–5:00 P.M. daily. MasterCard and Visa. Wheelchair-accessible.*

READERS' BOOKS' annex enlarges the comfort zone across the street with used and rare books, air conditioning, and a cool, breezy browsing patio. Enjoy! *Reader's Books' bookstore annex, 130 East Napa Street, Sonoma 95476; phone (707) 996–0966. Open 10:00 A.M.–9:00 P.M. Monday–Saturday,.10:00 A.M.–6:00 P.M. Sunday. MasterCard, Visa, and American Express. Wheelchair-accessible.*

Jo-Ellen Wilson's J. WILSON GALLERY features whimsical, lighthearted art and gifts aimed at women executives looking for fun stuff on their desks, clocks, metal sculpture and wall pieces, particularly our cover artist Judy Theo Lehner's monographs and Judie Bomberger's elegantly funny work. Not a repetitive groovy gallery, this one also includes work of Julie Higgins, Mylette Welch, and twenty-four other local artists. This one is exceptional! Go for it. *J. Wilson Gallery, 124 East Napa Street, Sonoma 95476; phone (707) 935–7376. Open 11:00 A.M.–5:00 P.M. Wednesday–Monday, 11:00 A.M.–6:00 P.M. Saturday–Sunday. MasterCard and Visa. Wheelchair-accessible.*

Walking into the recently enlarged FRAMING ON THE SQUARE is like walking into a women's comedy routine. Linda Semple, the self-proclaimed "Queen of Framing," specializes in framing memorabilia of any kind, wine-country posters, particularly Vintage Festival and Sebastiani Theater art, and fabulous French and Italian poster reproductions. A stuffed mobile is their "baby whiner," as in "Sonoma Whine Country," and they deliver on an old fat-tire bicycle. Go in for the fun of it at least.

❧ *Framing on the Square, 122 East Napa Street, Sonoma 95476; phone (707) 935–6611. Open 10:00 A.M.–6:00 P.M. Wednesday–Saturday, noon–5:00 P.M. Sunday; closed Monday and Tuesday. MasterCard and Visa. Wheelchair-accessible.*

At the ROBIN'S NEST, Debra Friedman and her father, Larry Friedman, sell kitchenware and tabletop gifts at discount prices. You can spot the Robin's Nest from a distance, since it is the only shop on the block with an old Frigidaire door on the sidewalk leaning against the outside wall. Originally the receiving building for Duhring's General Store and then Mission Hardware, this was built in the 1870s. The current building is an exact replica built after the disastrous fire of 1990.

Theirs is the kind of store where it pays to go in often because discontinued, closeout, or seconds bargains show up unannounced. Brightly colored ceramic teapots or cream-and-sugar sets, ramekins, trivets, cooking utensils, platters, and more for the professional or amateur chef can be found here. Among the Friedmans' hot items are Italian and Portuguese ceramic pitchers and platters in bright earth colors, pop-up sponges at only $1.99 (compared to $6.99 at Williams-Sonoma), full sets of cookware, reversible griddles, chef's jackets at $19.95, and Messermeister (sounds like us in the kitchen) utensils to use with nonstick pans. The Friedmans also feature local artists' ceramic plates and dishes, handcrafted cutting boards, crumb boxes, spice racks, wooden recipe boxes ($2.29), ceramic and wood seconds, elegant locally hand-painted butter trays ($24.99), as well as the Sonoma Valley Appellation blue-stem wine glasses ($2.99). We always find great gifts here.

❧ *Robin's Nest, 116 East Napa Street, Sonoma 95476; phone (707) 996–4169. Open 10:00 A.M.–6:00 P.M. daily. MasterCard, Visa, and Discover. Wheelchair-accessible.*

PARDON MY GARDEN is a beautiful shop for home accessories wedged in behind The Corner Store, which was once Pinelli's Mission Hardware. Sandra Shanahan Haddad carries delightful Italian house numbers, squirrel bafflers, ceramic wall birdfeeders, recycled metal garden faucets, culinary herb seeds, painted furniture, birdhouses, gorgeous books on tea service, and painted mailboxes. Sandra has done Sonoma a grand favor by placing enormous planters with small trees and lots of colorful flowers along the brick wall adjacent to her store. Get your hats and *Bird Watching for Dummies* books here, if they're out at Readers' Books.

❧ ***Pardon My Garden,*** *112 East Napa Street, Sonoma 95476; phone (707) 939–9282, fax (707) 939–8361. Open 10:30 A.M.–5:00 P.M. Wednesday–Monday, noon–5:00 P.M. Sunday. MasterCard and Visa. Wheelchair-accessible.*

First Street East

On the west side of First Street East, near the end of the block and just up from the Sonoma Fire Department, you'll find the Nash-Patton Adobe, 579 First Street East. Lumberman Henry A. Green built this house in 1847 on a land grant owned by Alcalde John H. Nash, a Bear Flagger. In July 1847 Nash was arrested here by Lieutenant William Tecumseh Sherman (who later marched through Georgia in the Civil War) to force Nash to resign as alcalde in favor of the army's choice for the leadership position, former Missouri governor Lilburn Boggs.

Donner Party survivor Nancy Bones Patton and her husband bought the adobe in 1848. After her husband died, she married wealthy Sonoma merchant

NASH-PATTON ADOBE

Lewis Adler. In 1866 it was purchased by a butcher, who cured sausages and hams in the attic. Eventually title to the property was reacquired by Nancy's descendants; and in 1931 her great-granddaughter, schoolteacher Zolita Bates, began a gradual and full restoration on her meager salary. The building remains a fine example of a Monterey-style adobe, including walls that are not straight. It is now a private residence.

Now, cross First Street East and walk back toward Napa Street a few steps.

The Julius Poppe House, at 564 First Street East, is Sonoma's only Gothic cottage. It is decorated with the gingerbread wooden filigree popular in the late 1850s, when it was built. The kitchen in the back northeast corner was built several years after the original three rooms.

Sonoma's First Baptist Church, at 542 First Street East (just down the street from the Napa Street intersection), currently occupies this Gothic Revival church built in 1854. As Ames Chapel (William Ames had "acquired" the lumber), it was a Methodist Church on Napa Street, before it was moved, and one of the first Protestant churches in Northern California. In 1868 the Methodists moved it to this site, on land donated by James McMackin, and added the classic steeple. The church also served as the town's public school until 1870. One of the first teachers was fired for beating a boy accused of stealing a bottle of whiskey from the teacher's desk! In 1950 the Methodists sold the church to the Baptists. It was used for scenes in the Ron Howard movie *Bitter Harvest* in the 1980s.

THE CORNER STORE occupies the corner building at Napa Street and First Street East. It has evolved over the last few years from Mission Hardware and then Pinelli's Mission Hardware. (As the principal downtown hardware, carpeting, and appliance store for generations of Sonomans, the store was run by August Pinelli Jr., the undisputed town leader for decades.)

Sam Morrows established a dry-goods store and Express Office here in 1848. In 1853 Frederick Duhring and his bride, Dorothea, came from Germany to California, after which Mrs. Duhring was hired as a music teacher at Dr. Ver Mehrs' Academy in Sonoma. A San Francisco merchant loaned Mrs. Duhring $1,000 to set her husband up in a store. During a 1889 fire, which threatened to reach the store, Mr. Duhring dropped dead on the sidewalk while watching, and his son Frederick Jr. took over the business. In 1891 the adobe building was replaced with the first brick building. In 1911 most of the east side of the Plaza burned again. The fire was finally extinguished with wine stored by Augustino Pinelli Sr. at the Blue Wing Inn.

August Pinelli Jr. was hired to work at the store five years later, at age fourteen. Eventually he opened his own store. When Mr. Duhring died, his widow asked Pinelli to come back and take over the store, beginning in 1932. Somehow the Pinelli family and their store survived several floods, underground streams, and fires, the last of which blew out the southern brick wall and wiped out next-door neighbor Brundage's, a favorite ice-cream emporium. The building was restored to perfection, according to drawings by local architect Reiner Keller, and with funds raised in the community with the help of the League for Historic Preservation. August Pinelli, who served as mayor, constable, draft-board chairman, and many other trusted positions, never returned to his store.

 Fine points: In the back left corner of the store you can see the original safe. You can no longer buy loose nails, coffee, or doormats, but you will find umbrellas, rain boots, film, Adamson's jams and preserves, pillows, Smokey Cheddar Bread Spread, soaps, Tuscan Hills Champagne Vinegars, and work of our cover artist, Judy Theo Lehner, water, and other "just what I need"s here. Buena Vista Winery now serves tastes of its wines at an elegant mahogany bar along the north wall, and the murals alone are worth the visit. You can also sip Haywood, Robert Stemmler, Viola, and Pionero wines.

❧ *The Corner Store, 498 First Street East, Sonoma 95476; phone (707) 996–2211. Open 10:00 A.M.–6:00 P.M. Monday–Saturday, 10:00 A.M.–5:30 P.M. Sunday. MasterCard, Visa, and American Express. Wheelchair-accessible.*

SUNSHINE JEWELERS—THE ORIGINAL really isn't. The original was actually around the corner and across Napa Street. Naomi Konkoff, who sounds like a knowledgeable New Yorker but is local (she says she was conceived under a tree in Agua Caliente), returned after a few years in Hawaii and reopened her store in the Mission Hardware building after its post-fire restoration in 1992.

A favorite with locals, you can always find reasonably priced decorative jewelry in silver and gold, much of it made expressly for Sunshine Jewelers. Naomi and Curt Radtke also offer exquisite leather bags and purses, handmade vests, wooden boxes, and Stanley Mouse T-shirts. (Stanley Mouse, a Sonoma resident best known for his Grateful Dead and Jefferson Airplane posters, recently received a liver transplant, and the community tries to help with his medical expenses.) The Sonomans who work here are always knowledgeable and good at answering questions. Sunshine also sells those magical jewelers' polishing rags for a mere $3.00. Deal!

❧ *Sunshine Jewelers—The Original, 496 First Street East, Sonoma 95476; phone (707) 996–6710, fax (707) 996–7610. Open 10:00 A.M.–6:00 P.M. daily. MasterCard, Visa, American Express, and Discover. Wheelchair-accessible.*

Right next to Sunshine Jewelers, i-elle has opened a new boutique, SIMPLICITY, to appeal to more casual younger somethings. You will find lots of linen ladies' clothing and jeans in sizes 4–14, Big Star denims, Garron, Custo mod designs, Z Cavaricci, Tessuto, and Michael Stars designs.

Simplicity by i-elle, 492 First Street East, Sonoma 95476; phone (707) 938–5422. Open 11:30 A.M.–5:30 P.M. daily in summer, noon–5:00 P.M. in winter. MasterCard, Visa, and Discover. Wheelchair-accessible.

Sonoma Shirt Gallery and Shirt Stompers, the best possible of T-shirt shops, had to move their stock from the now-vacant lot just north of Vincent Sports to Steve and Heidi Pond's other enterprise, The Chocolate Cow, in the Mercado, a half-block north on First Street East. Building owners Kenneth and Patricia McTaggart sold the property to developer Steve Ledson, who plans to build a small hotel and wine bar here.

Just north of the vacant lot, the TOWN SQUARE is a real bar, with television; good, stiff, not-too-expensive drinks; and lots of local color in the Sebastiani Theatre Building. At least one former mayor hangs out here as well as other regulars, partly because of the friendly, warm atmosphere. No smoking.

❦ Town Square, 482 First Street East, Sonoma 95476; phone (707) 996–2922. Open 8:00 A.M. until people are gone, but usually closed tight before 2:00 A.M. MasterCard, Visa, American Express, and Discover. Wheelchair-accessible.

Samuele Sebastiani built the grand rococo-style SEBASTIANI THEATRE for the Sonoma community to view films. He opened it April 7, 1934. It

OPENING NIGHT AT THE FIRST SONOMA VALLEY
FILM FESTIVAL, 1997

remains a historic period theater, with one screen showing old and new release movies. The upstairs has housed the Moose Hall, offices, nightclubs, and an exercise gym.

In 1985, after the Sebastiani family removed Sam Jr. from the presidency of its winery, Sam sold the theater, almost secretly, to a group headed by Oakland developer Neil Goodhue, to raise funds to start Sam's own winery (now Viansa Winery and Italian Marketplace). Goodhue then leased the theater to the City of Sonoma for $3,000 a month for twenty-five years. The City currently subleases it to Roger Rhoten. Rhoten, as well as the Friends of Sebastiani Theatre, is dedicated to preserving and renovating the historic theater and to running it successfully for the community. With no help from Goodhue, the community works slowly to completely restore the theater. In a recent project, Sonoma Sister Cities Association and Sonoma Plaza Kiwanis removed the old seats, which were then reupholstered. The first annual Sonoma Valley Film Festival (1997) attracted Danny Glover and Timothy Robbins to sold-out events, helping to fund the restoration completion.

Rhoten and a cardboard cutout of Humphrey Bogart greet customers at the ticket booth, and a local crooner sings before each weekend screening. Roger strives to present the best mainstream and artistic films available and offers almost-healthy foods at the antique counter. Check the theater's billboards for live shows and movie schedules. Diana and Roger Rhoten perform Witchie Poo and magic acts, respectively, on mostly appropriate occasions.

 Fine points: Most shows start at 6:00 and 8:15 P.M. Movie tickets for adults cost $6.00, for juniors ages twelve to seventeen, $4.50, and for children and seniors, $3.75. Tuesday bargain seats $3.50.

❧ *Sebastiani Theatre, 476 First Street East, Sonoma 95476; phone (707) 996–2020 for show information, (707) 996–9756 for business. Wheelchair-accessible.*

Lili and Gratien Guerra brought the SONOMA FRENCH BAKERY to its international reputation and sold it in 1987 to Charlie and Frances Cho, who learned his fine baking techniques from Gratien Guerra. The Chos in turn sold the bakery to Alan Ong, who learned to bake from the Chos, and now offers almost the same French bread, Danish pastries, cookies, and other breads and fine sweets, as well as coffee, soft drinks, and waters. The Guerras' daughter, Françoise Hodges, and her husband opened the Basque Boulangerie and Cafe two doors up the street, so try it, too.

❧ *Sonoma French Bakery, 470 First Street East, Sonoma 95476; phone (707) 996–2691. Open 6:55 A.M.–2:00 P.M. Monday–Friday, 7:00 A.M.–5:00 P.M. Saturday, 7:00 A.M.–4:00 P.M. Sunday. Wheelchair-accessible.*

Between the law office and the Basque Boulangerie and Cafe, you must wander down the alley through Lili and Gratien Guerra's Place des Pyrénées. On the right you'll come first to the Parmelee Art Company, where retired lawyer Robert Parmelee buys and sells Oriental rugs and sells quilts made by his wife, former mayor Nancy.

On the right side of the alley you then come to the BRIAR PATCH AND JEANINE'S COFFEE AND TEA COMPANY, where Bruce and Jeanine Masonek sell imported teas and coffees, tobaccos, pipes, cigars and cigarettes, and coffee beans and roasters, and make a full range of espresso drinks to go. They have a couple of tables outside, and you can often share one or take your espresso across from Murphy's Irish Pub. In the summer Jeanine's stays open late, so you can enjoy an espresso after or instead of your Irish brew.

> ### IRISH POTATO SOUP
> from Melody Field of Murphy's Irish Pub
>
> ---
>
> *1 lb potatoes, cubed*
> *2 yellow onions, chopped*
> *4 stalks celery, chopped*
> *¼ tsp salt*
> *¼ tsp pepper*
> *3 cups chicken broth*
> *¼ head cabbage, chopped*
> *half & half*
>
> *Sauté onions and celery with salt and pepper in large pot. Pour chicken broth into onion and celery mixture. Add potatoes and cabbage to broth. Cook until everything is soft. Add half & half until soup is creamy before serving. Serves 2–4.*

✤ *Briar Patch and Jeanine's Coffee and Tea Company, 464 First Street East, Suite H, Sonoma 95476; phone (707) 996–7573. Open 10:00 A.M.– 5:00 P.M. Monday–Thursday, 10:00 A.M.–7:00 P.M. Friday–Saturday, 11:00 A.M.–4:00 P.M. Sunday. MasterCard, Visa, and American Express. Wheelchair-accessible.*

MURPHY'S IRISH PUB is a true local favorite among City Hall staffers, Celtic fans, and the general Sonoma populace. Rose and Larry Murphy took over a former English pub and turned it Irish overnight. Murphy's has become so popular with locals and visitors that it recently moved across the way when Babette's Restaurant left.

Larry's beer-bottle collection lines the walls, with wires holding them on their shelf to protect customers in the event of an earthquake! Their memorabilia from Ireland, Murphy's pubs, and Catholic universities everywhere combine for a warm, cozy, and convivial atmosphere, and Rose and Larry pin on the wall any and all beer coasters you bring them from afar. Murphy's features Irish music and Irish stouts and beers and has a beer of the month, wine and hard ciders, and a few local brews.

Here you can indulge in the best fish and hand-cut thick chips anywhere, soups, light salads, veggie burgers, great hamburgers, chicken-breast sandwiches, wine-country sausage, Cornish beef pie, shepherd's pie, Irish stew, and curried vegetarian pie. Side orders include mushy peas and some of the best coleslaw and garlic bread around. Prices range from $3.50 to $8.95 for lunch and dinner.

The Murphys' personal popularity contributes to their success. Larry is a former commercial and government pilot, art teacher, and mayor of Sonoma. Rose ran their Kate Murphy's Cottage Bed and Breakfast for years and has become a travel writer and a scholar and teacher of Irish literature.

 Fine points: Murphy's presents Bloomsday readings by local actors, Irish poetry and literature nights, a grandiose St. Patrick's Day (and night) celebration, and pedro nights to benefit Sonoma's La Luz Bilingual Center.

❧ *Murphy's Irish Pub, 464 First Street East, Sonoma 95476; phone (707) 935–0660. Open 11:00 A.M.–11:00 P.M. daily. No credit cards. Pub wheelchair-accessible; rest room not accessible. Children encouraged.*

THE IRISH SHOP may be the prettiest, most elegant Irish shop you will ever find. Kathy Barnett got the idea to open the ultimate Irish shop and actually went on to make it happen, opening March 10, 1995. She later sold it to Will Roll. Here you will find a most appealing and practical stock of Irish foods, including flour, sausages, chutneys, chivers, jams and jellies, and Batchelors Baked Beans; Irish linens; Aran sweaters and caps; and Galway crystal. There are books, perfumes, Claddagh jewelry, Celtic music, teas, Clona Craft jewelry, posters, and calendars. The family-crest mugs, caps, T-shirts, and sweatshirts all make great gifts. Buy yourself a treasure, wander back a few steps to Murphy's, and sit down and enjoy.

❧ *The Irish Shop, 464 First Street East, Sonoma 95476; phone (707) 935–3455. Open noon–5:00 P.M. Sunday–Thursday, noon–6:00 P.M. Friday–Saturday. Master-Card, Visa, American Express, and Discover. Wheelchair-accessible.*

Next to Murphy's is DAWN'S CHANSON D'AMOUR, a substantial jewelry store featuring handcrafted romantic silver jewelry. Definitely worth a long look.

❧ *Dawn's Chanson D'Amour, 464 First Street East, Sonoma 95476; phone (707) 935–1359. Open 11:00 A.M.–5:30 P.M. Tuesday–Saturday, 11:00 A.M.–5:00 P.M. Sunday. MasterCard, Visa, American Express, and Novus. Wheelchair-accessible.*

The rest of the storefronts in the Place des Pyrénées have been taken over by Françoise Guerra Hodges' hugely successful **Basque Boulangerie Cafe**, which faces First Street East. Yes, you do remember the Guerra name from the Sonoma French Bakery. When Françoise Guerra had her Cafe Pilou, people used to refer to her as "the French baker's daughter." Locals missed her personality and fine cooking during her try-other-professions years and were delighted and excited when she and her husband opened the Basque.

Jack Montaldo, longtime "apprentice" to Françoise's father, Gratien Guerra, joined Françoise and her husband as a partner in the Basque Boulangerie. He is now the baker known as "Jack in the back." The breads seem even better than at their Sonoma French Bakery: less air and more there. In addition to Basque sourdoughs, country wheats, and sweet and sourdough rolls, the Basque Boulangerie now offers sandwich loaves of wheat and white, both of which are sourdough, and the staff willingly slices on request.

This place is packed from the minute it opens until it closes. Locals come in early for coffee, tea, rolls, apricot scones (which sell out fast), granola, fruit bowls, or simply newspapers and conversation. "The Basque" or "Françoise's" has become the early morning hangout where almost all the world's local problems are solved. Some clusters of retired men sip several refills of coffee, slowing things down ever so slightly.

Lunch is predictably crowded, with Sonomans and visitors intrigued by the

Basque Boulangerie Cafe

Basque Potato Omelette
from Françoise Guerra Hodges, Basque Boulangerie Cafe

2 lbs red potatoes

12 whole large eggs

1 green bell pepper, sliced coarsely, discarding seeds and stem

1 red bell pepper, sliced coarsely, discarding seeds and stem

1 large yellow onion, peeled and sliced coarsely

2–3 Tbs chopped garlic

salt and pepper

olive oil

You will also need a 10-inch oven-proof sauté pan and food-release spray.

Preheat oven to 350 °. In a pot big enough to hold all the potatoes, add them and cover with water. Add 1 Tbs salt and bring to a boil over high heat, uncovered. Reduce to a simmer and gently cook the potatoes until a knife inserted into the thickest one comes out easily. Drain and reserve. Do the rest as the potatoes are cooking.

Spray or oil your 10-inch sauté pan really well and set aside.

Crack the eggs and beat together well, but don't get them all foamy. You don't want a lot of air in them, just well mixed. Set aside.

Put about 2 Tbs of olive oil in the sauté pan and heat. When oil is hot, add the sliced onions and both bell peppers. Sauté for about 5 minutes till the onions begin to caramelize or take on a golden color and the peppers are softened. While the onions and peppers are cooking, shake them occasionally and slice the cooked potatoes into thick slices, cubes, or wedges. Reserve.

Add the chopped garlic to the onion mixture and sauté for 2 more minutes. Pour the drained and sliced potatoes into the sauté pan with the onions and immediately pour the beaten eggs over the top. The mixture should come right up to the top of the pan. If it doesn't, quickly crack a few more eggs and add them. Sprinkle with ¾ tsp salt and ½ tsp black pepper. Don't shake the pan, but allow the ingredients and eggs to set for about 3 or 4 minutes over medium heat. Put the pan into the preheated oven and cook for approximately 45 minutes or until a knife inserted in the middle comes out clean.

Let "omelette" come to room temperature before placing your serving platter on top of the sauté pan and flipping it over to invert it for presentation. Serve as a luncheon entree warm with a green salad, as a dinner appetizer, or slice up when it's cold and use as a filling for a torta or sandwich. Serves 8–10 as a luncheon entree or an appetizer.

Basque potato omelet, sweet onion tarte, fabulous Caesar salads with or without grilled chicken, Niçoise or roasted-chicken salads, daily special pasta salads, reuben and grilled cheese and tomato sandwiches, soup and salad, and mouth-watering prosciutto and brie sandwich at only $5.50, and quiche. There are great and different sandwiches, such as a Niçoise or the best grilled ham and cheese anywhere. We often rationalize that the Niçoise salad is healthy, even though it combines French and Caesar dressings on tuna, egg, carrot, and potato salads. Friday's clam chowder is lowish fat and thick with real clams and potatoes. Many soups are made without cream.

How to work this place: You order and pay at the counter, the leftish line more or less majors in baked goods, the rightish one in other foods, but don't worry about it. Then you sit down at tables or at the counter and wait for some-one to shout your name and then you go pick up your food. There are a few tables in front facing the Plaza and the Sonoma Valley Visitors Bureau. Children friendly—great hot dogs and cookies. Run, don't walk.

 Fine points: The holidays always bring in locals for everything from day-old bread for stuffing to *bûches de Nöel* and an espresso while you wait. The holiday line often goes from the counter all the way out to the street. Local wines are sold by the glass, start-ing at $2.75. Lunch entrees range from $3.00 to $5.00, another reason why this favorite hangout is so popular. Espresso drinks are priced reasonably. Ghirardelli chocolate is used in mochas.

❧ *Basque Boulangerie Cafe, 460 First Street East, Sonoma 95476; phone (707) 935–SOUR (7687). Open 7:00 A.M.–6:00 P.M. daily. No credit cards. Wheelchair-accessible. Rest room for customers only.*

SPIRITS IN STONE ZIMBABWE SHONA SCULPTURE is a remarkable gallery. Laura and Tony Ponter live their belief that "art is the shortest distance between two cultures." They demonstrate that "the spirit in stone, as revealed in the pro-found sculpture that comes from Zimbabwe . . . has much to teach us all . . . about dignity, compassion and peace." Special exhibits here include work by women sculptors from Zimbabwe. The Ponters' staff say these galleries possess the largest Shona sculpture collection outside Zimbabwe.

The Ponters' personal mission is to stimulate creativity and to purchase, import, and present the best in elegant, simple sculpture from the Shona tribe, "The People of the Mist." Less than forty years ago, Shona artists resumed their ancient tradition of carving from natural materials and objects. After becoming independent from the British in 1980, Zimbabwe (formerly Rhodesia) passed its Equal Rights for Women, a declaration that gave women a new confidence to explore working in stone. The Spirits in Stone Gallery provides an exceptional experience for adults and children to witness unusual beauty and learn important lessons from another culture. We have watched children oohing and aahing and begging parents to go into this gallery with them.

Fine points: Once you become a Shona collector, you receive invitations to private uncratings at the Ponters' monstrous and elegant warehouse in Glen Ellen, where you are treated to Benziger wines and Gatsbyesque lunches. Visit the Ponters' other galleries in the St. Helena Outlets, Sausalito, and Carlsbad.

❧ *Spirits in Stone Zimbabwe Shona Sculpture, 452 First Street East, Sonoma 95476; phone (707) 938–2200 or (800) 474–6624; Web site www.spiritsin-stone.com. Open 10:00 A.M.–6:00 P.M. daily. MasterCard, Visa, American Express, and Discover. Wheelchair-accessible.*

To the north of the Basque is the PAPYRUS specialty shop, featuring cards and calendars for all persuasions and religions. Great after-Christmas sales.

❧ *Papyrus, 452 First Street East, Sonoma 95476; phone (707) 935–6707. Open 10:00 A.M.–6:00 P.M. Monday–Saturday, 10:30 A.M.–6:00 P.M. Sunday. MasterCard and Visa. Wheelchair-accessible.*

At the WINE EXCHANGE OF SONOMA, you can wander among a vast collection of wines and beers from around the world, presented in the atmosphere of a comfy old book store. Every day the Wine Exchange offers tastes or drinks of fourteen special wines that you can't find at winery tasting rooms, as well as six draft beers, including local microbrews. As you walk in the door, you find yourself surrounded by boxes and racks of wine bottles, mostly from small, hard-to-get wineries. Along the right wall are 265 different bottled beers from which to choose.

The tasting bar is at the back of the shop. After 5:00 P.M. it is usually lined with local vintners and winemakers, who come in for a good beer after work to compare notes. You are welcome to join them. Get on the mailing list to get the latest catalogs. This is one of the best places anywhere to buy and ship wine in a single stop. You can also get cigars and grapeseed oils here.

❧ *Wine Exchange of Sonoma, 452 First Street East, Sonoma 95476; phone (707) or (800) 938–1794; fax (707) 938–0969. Open 10:00 A.M.–6:00 P.M. Monday–Thursday and Saturday–Sunday, 10:00 A.M.–6:30 P.M. Friday. MasterCard and Visa. Wheelchair-accessible.*

SOUTH SIDE OF THE MERCATO

Around the corner of the Wine Exchange you enter the alleyway known as the MERCATO, designed by Sonoma architect Reiner Keller. A few years ago the building to your right was a roller rink and locals' then-favorite grocery store, Food City, and the gray building to the left was a parking lot. The water fountain, built recently, worked until a child fell into it and insurance concerns forced the developers to turn it off. Too bad.

At LEGACY GIFT SHOP Barbara Stern presents an attractive home gift shop with wine-country trinkets, Crabtree & Evelyn products, books on elegant tea service in several countries, and products to pamper yourself. Delivery is free within the Sonoma city limits. Unfortunately we have an allergic reaction to the eucalyptus and other scents and can't stay here as long as we would like!

❦ *Legacy Gift Shop, 452 First Street East, Sonoma 95476; phone (707) 935–9447. Open 10:00 A.M.–6:00 P.M. MasterCard and Visa. Wheelchair-accessible.*

Everyone loves the CHOCOLATE COW. And why not—almost everything in here is chocolate and decorated like cows. You can watch Steve Pond and his staff make chocolate and fudge, either from the window or inside. Then drink an excellent espresso or enjoy custom-made gelato and ice cream, Joseph Smith or Steve's truffles, Jelly Bellys, chocolate pasta and sauces, Hawaiian shaved ice, Italian sodas, and sugar-free candies. Far Side T-shirts hang everywhere. A definite yes for children. The Chocolate Cow welcomes tours or field trips if you call ahead.

We know local women who walk and diet daily and then sneak into the Chocolate Cow to buy a handful of fresh caramels. The store also carries candy for diabetics, and T-shirts and other humorous souvenirs that Heidi Pond featured at her T-shirt shops on the Plaza before the building was torn down.

❦ *Chocolate Cow, 452 First Street East, Sonoma 95476; phone (707) 935– 3564. Open 9:30 A.M.–8:00 P.M. weekdays, 9:30 A.M.–10:00 P.M. weekends. MasterCard, Visa, and American Express. Wheelchair-accessible.*

MARY'S PIZZA SHACK offers the best inexpensive lunches and dinners in town. Mary Fazio started her first pizza restaurant in 1959, in a small house on Highway 12 in Boyes Hot Springs, in answer to friends' requests that she cook for them. While the original building still looks a bit like a shack, Mary's has moved on and now has "stores" (that's what happens when you grow to two or more) throughout Sonoma and Napa Counties.

While this new Mary's Pizza is a little more plastic-looking than some, it's still lots of fun. Local high school kids always work and hang out here, and people of all ages come back and back for more pizza, breadsticks, garlic bread covered with garlic butter and mozzarella cheese, salads (the best!), wonderfully drippy hot Italian sandwiches, and heavenly pasta with weekly and daily specials. Don't miss the garlicky pesto breadsticks and crunchy bruschetta. Our now-adult children always "have to go to Mary's" their first night home for a visit. Many locals eat lunch here every day.

Pizzas start at $6.95, sandwiches with salad and soft drink or coffee at about $6.00. Lunch specials begin at about $5.50.

❧ *Mary's Pizza Shack, 452 First Street East, Sonoma 95476; phone (707) 938–8300. Open 11:00 A.M.–10:00 P.M. Sunday–Thursday, 11:00 A.M.–11:00 P.M. Friday–Saturday. MasterCard and Visa. Wheelchair-accessible. Rest room for customers only.*

In case you're looking for Vintage Game and Hobby Shop, it's gone and moved back down First Street East to Vintage Sports. Mrs. Grossman's sells stickers (yes, stickers) in this large shop facing the parking lot.

Just across the walkway from Mary's is RODEO SONOMA, the ultimate elegant Western boutique featuring cowboy couture. Marcy Edelstein had similar shops in resort towns and now focuses on Sonoma. She carries handmade and tooled leather cowboy/girl boots, O'Farrell hats, Double D ranch wear, huge turquoise and stone belt buckles, fringed leather jackets, and Westward Ho china.

❧ *Rodeo Sonoma, 452 First Street East, Sonoma 95476; phone (707) 939–7992. Open 10:00 A.M.–6:00 P.M. Monday–Saturday, 11:00 A.M.–5:00 P.M. Sunday. MasterCard and Visa. Wheelchair-accessible.*

NATURE, ETC. is a kids' paradise of animal puppets, glow-in-the-dark planets to hang in your room, geography place mats, historical puzzles, nature rubber-stamp sets, fake snakes and reptiles, books, walking sticks, stuffed animals, wind chimes, Koosh stuff, and Beanies.

❧ *Nature, Etc., 450 First Street East, Sonoma 95476; phone (707) 938–5662. Open 10:00 A.M.–5:30 or 6:00 P.M. MasterCard and Visa. Wheelchair-accessible.*

THE TOTAL LOOK, a boutique of contemporary women's clothing, features cottons, rayons, resort wear, and items in natural fibers. Owner Barbara Mezzetta has long experience in the clothing business and extends every courtesy, including a glass of wine for her guests on weekends. Barbara just remodeled the store and painted it in warmer colors, making the whole place look larger and more welcoming. She has expanded the inventory with some new lines: Color Me Cotton and Mill Valley Cotton. We especially like their new Flax line.

❧ *The Total Look, 450 First Street East, Sonoma 95476; phone (707) 996–8103. Open 10:00 A.M.–5:30 P.M. Monday–Saturday, noon–5:00 p.m. Sunday. MasterCard, Visa, American Express, and Discover. Wheelchair-accessible.*

HALFPINT is a grandparent's paradise. You can enter this dreamy children's clothing store from either the Mercato or First Street East. Owner Pam Howard's motto is, "Great clothes for great kids … hats and shoes too!" And is she right! You'll find Doc Martens for kids at $65, distinctive play clothes, gorgeous velvet dresses, stuffed animals, Fairytale Fashions and fairy equipment, "u-make" wooden-bead name bracelets, and mannequins of several skin tones. The clothes (and prices) are elegant and both European and American. Bring grandmother.

❧ *Halfpint, 450 First Street East, Sonoma 95476; phone (707) 938–1722. Open 10:00 A.M.–5:45 P.M. Monday–Saturday, 11:00 A.M.–5:00 P.M. Sunday. Closed Mothers' Day! MasterCard, Visa, and American Express. Wheelchair-accessible.*

Walking into ARTIFAX INTERNATIONAL GALLERY AND GIFTS is like entering another world. Artifax is a gallery of rare African and Asian artifacts, from Chinese tea services to African masks, baskets, scarves, tribal jewelry, boxes, incense burners, rare woven textiles, wood and stone carvings, iron garden bells, bamboo and slate water features, ethnic collector beads, musical and ceremonial instruments, and Ikebana supplies. It's also a great place to pick up that Republic of Tea gift you meant to take to your brother. Candice Tisch and Thomas Rubel offer the finest of imports and have arranged their stock so sensitively that you feel like moving in.

❧ *Artifax International Gallery and Gifts, 450 First Street East, Sonoma 95476; phone (707) 996–9494. Open 11:00 A.M.–5:00 P.M. winter, 10:00 A.M.–6:00 P.M. summer. Visa, MasterCard, and American Express. Wheelchair-accessible.*

After you cross the driveway north of Artifax, you see a law office with a square arch over its driveway marked THE ICE HOUSE. Yes, this used to be the local ice house. The ice hook hung over the arch, for loading and unloading.

ZINO'S RISTORANTE is the first business you encounter that is part of Betty Gordon's El Paseo de Sonoma, a historic and modernized courtyard of shops, galleries, and restaurants. Built with historic local stones from a nearby quarry, as the Old City Bakery, Zino's appears to be a small Italian bistro, with a dining room on the right and a peaceful bar to the left.

Zino Mezoui, a native of Algeria, began his Sonoma career as chef for what was then Jerry Rosenberg's Gino's Restaurant and Bar on this site. Soon Zino cooked and ran the restaurant as his own. He eventually bought out Rosenberg completely—lock, stock, bar, and restaurant. Since then, Zino has been so successful with locals and visitors alike that he has expanded his restaurant into four additional storefronts, all the way to the back of El Paseo. His Sonoma-Italian

CELERY ROOT SALAD
from Françoise Guerra Hodges, Basque Boulangerie & Cafe

1–2 bulbs of celery root, peeled
1–1½ cups Best Foods mayonnaise or homemade mayo
2–3 Tbs Dijon mustard
juice of one lemon
salt and pepper to taste (you can use white pepper or cayenne)

Squeeze the lemon juice into a bowl and fill it with cool water, enough to hold both celery bulbs once they are peeled (see below). Put aside.

Mix the mayonnaise with the mustard in a medium-sized mixing bowl. Put aside.

Peel the celery root bulbs with a paring knife or really good and strong vegetable peeler, making sure to get all the brown skin off. Put the first peeled bulb into the lemon-water bath so that it won't discolor while you're peeling the second bulb. Once peeled, take one bulb out of the lemon-water at a time and run it through your food processor with the julienne blade. (See note below if you don't have a food processor.)

If you use a shredder, it sometimes makes the celery taste like "mush." If your juliennes are too thick (more than ¼-inch thick), you will have to blanch them in boiling salted water for 2 minutes only. Quickly drain and refresh the ice water. Drain.

Fold the julienned celery root into the mayonnaise mixture. Correct seasoning with salt and pepper. Chill and then serve on top of some fresh butter lettuce.

Note: If you don't have a processor, slice a thin piece off one side of the bulb so that it will lay flat on your cutting board without rocking. Continue to slice down through the bulb, making big slices, about ⅛–¼-inch thick. Then stack all the slices together (or a few at a time so that they don't slip under your knife's pressure) flat, and cut long, thin strips the same width as before.

Serves 5–8 as an appetizer, or fewer for lunch.

specialties include a giant hamburger, linguine con vongole (an absolute orgy of fresh clams, broth, garlic, and cream), and turkey piccata.

The ambience varies slightly by room, from intimate bistro in the front to a larger Italian family-style restaurant feeling in the back. Outdoor seating is available during warm months.

Fine points: Prices range from $8.50 to $16.50 for entrees. A take-out menu is also available.

❧ *Zino's Ristorante, 420 First Street East, Sonoma 95476; phone (707) 996–4466. Open 11:00 A.M.–10:00 P.M. daily. MasterCard, Visa, American Express, and JCB. Wheelchair-accessible.*

Gemologist John Zarembski has been importing and making fine jewelry at his **CORNERSTONE JEWELERS** since 1979. He moved from the El Paseo courtyard to his current Plaza location in 1995, in case you remember his previous cubbyhole. A true artist, Zarembski also resets jewels, makes repairs, imports diamonds, does appraisals, and has monumental sales.

❧ *Cornerstone Jewelers, 416 First Street East, Sonoma 95476; phone (707) 996–6635. Open 10:00 A.M.–5:00 P.M. daily. MasterCard, Visa, American Express, Discover, and Sonoma Express. Not wheelchair-accessible.*

Just north of Cornerstone Jewelers, turn into the covered passageway of **EL PASEO DE SONOMA**. A colorful vineyard scene mural leads you back to El Paseo Courtyard and its several shops and restaurants. A Renaissance Revival–style complex built in 1891 for stonemason Augustino Pinelli, and originally called the Pinelli Building, it was built of local, hand-hewn plum stone—a beautiful material aptly named for its color.

Living quarters (now offices) were on the second floor, and commercial shops were on the ground floor. The interior was burned out in the fire that swept the block in 1911. Wine from Pinelli's wine cellar in The Blue Wing was used to douse the fire, so the stone shell survived and the insides could be reconstructed. Al and Betty Gordon purchased the buildings in 1967 and renovated them with great success and taste. They also provided the land within their complex for the Sonoma League for Historic Preservation to put the Vasquez House (General Hooker House).

Earlier in the 1990s the City of Sonoma required buildings to have earthquake retrofitting, which necessitated tearing down the back part of the structure. With the designs and help of Sonoma architect Adrian Martinez, Betty Gordon built the complex that stands today. Note the textured mural down the passageway.

MILAGROS is one of our favorites. *Milagros* means "miracle," and this is one. Louise Salvador and Kenny Clayton share their unusually fabulous array of affordable fine Mexican folk-art imports, from 3-inch Day of the Dead Devil Ladies ($6.95) to Mayan masks, blankets, silver treasures, papier-mâché objects, candelabra, Christmas ornaments, earrings, *milagros* (sacrificial silver charms),

EL PASEO DE SONOMA (FORMERLY THE PINELLI BUILDING)

and *retablos* (paintings on metal). One of Milagros's all-time bargains are the striped Mexican double-bed blankets, at $19.95. Enjoy the rare works by Louise and Kenny's good friends in Mexico, artists Martin Melacher, Josephine and Irena Aguilar, and the well-known Lineras family. If you can't go shopping in Mexico, this is the next best thing.

❧ *Milagros, 414 First Street East, Sonoma 95476; phone (707) 939–0834; fax (707) 935–8566; Web site www.milagrosgallery.com. Open 10:00 A.M.–5:00 P.M. Wednesday–Monday. MasterCard, Visa, and American Express. Wheelchair-accessible.*

SONOMA ROCK & MINERAL GALLERY, is a new addition to El Paseo and features elegant but reasonably priced rock specimens, crystals, fossils, and carvings for decoration and collections; inexpensive gifts from jade and carnelian rings, $15–$20; and rare pieces valued in the thousands of dollars. Ko Abe manages the gallery and is kind and gentle with naïve questioners exploring the rock world for the first time.

❧ *Sonoma Rock & Mineral Gallery, 414 First Street East, Sonoma 95476; phone (707) 996–7200; fax (707) 996–2137. Open 10:00 A.M.–5:00 P.M. daily. MasterCard and Visa. Wheelchair-accessible.*

The Sonoma League for Historic Preservation owns and maintains VASQUEZ HOUSE, the former Joseph Hooker House (built about 1856) as its headquarters, library, and Tea Room. (The League for Historic Preservation can supply you with detailed history of all Sonoma buildings of historic interest.) This is one of six houses shipped in 1851 from Sweden around Cape Horn to Sonoma in numbered, pre-cut parts. Its assembly was completed in 1852 for Colonel Joseph Hooker near the southwest corner of First Street West and Napa Street. Two years later Hooker sold the house to the Vasquez family. In the early 1970s Robert and Jean Lynch, owners of the *Sonoma Index-Tribune*, purchased the house to save it from the wrecking ball. The Lynches then donated it to the Sonoma League for Historic Preservation. The League's founder, Margaret Eliassen, spearheaded relocation of the house within El Paseo in 1974. El Paseo owners Al and Betty Gordon granted the League a thirty-year lease with optional extension without charge.

The Tea Room is the town bargain. A cup of coffee or tea costs a whopping 25 cents, and a whole pot of tea is 50 cents, as is iced tea or coffee. Outstanding cake slices or muffins are just $1.00.

❧ *Vasquez House, El Paseo Courtyard, Sonoma 95476; phone (707) 938–0510. Open 1:30–4:30 P.M. Wednesday–Sunday. No credit cards. Wheelchair-accessible.*

Just up the street from the El Paseo passageway and still in its historic building is the SONOMA WINE SHOP, whose tasting room faces El Paseo courtyard. Here Peter and Joan Robichaud offer a collection of fine and exclusive wines from Sonoma, Napa, Mendocino, and Lake and Monterey Counties, and wine accoutrements—T-shirts, corks, trivets, literature, glasses, and other attractive knickknacks.

❧ *Sonoma Wine Shop, 412 First Street East, Sonoma 95476; phone (707) 996–1230; fax (707) 944–2710. Open 10:00 A.M.–6:00 P.M. daily. Tasting fee: $2.00 Friday–Monday. MasterCard, Visa, American Express, and Discover. Wheelchair-accessible.*

At the corner of First Street East and Spain Street, directly across from the Mission San Francisco de Solano, Vicki and Sam Sebastiani and their children serve scrumptious Viansa foods and wines at CUCINA VIANSA. For decades this space was The Creamery, an old-fashioned ice-cream fountain and local civic center. Recent owners turned it into a sort of delicatessen and sold it to the Sebastianis in late 1995. After extensive remodeling, the Sebastianis opened Lo Spuntino ("light lunch," according to our Italian–English dictionary) in March 1996 and renamed it Cucina Viansa in 2000.

VASQUEZ HOUSE IN THE EL PASEO COURTYARD

The Sebastianis's goal is to honor and offer Sonoma's Italian immigrant heritage in food and history. Served deli style (you order at the counter), there is a rotisserie cooking chickens, rabbits, and ducks; a pasta machine; sandwiches; gelato; espresso drinks; and a wine bar, with daily tastings. The gift shop in the back features pottery, kitchen tools, and Viansa products. Rare historical photographs, contributed by several old-time families, line the walls.

Try the homemade tiramisù (funny we mention that first), the shrimp and pea pasta, spinach ravioli with corn and fennel salad, the pork loin or lamb panino, or your own side portion of garlic mashed potatoes, wild rice and riso salad with grilled tangerine chicken, or grilled corn fennel and potato salad. At the wine bar you might want to taste Viansa's new sparkling wine, Bisol. Best sandwiches and salads anywhere.

Fine points: Seating is limited, but fortunately, this food is perfect for picnics. An immediate success with curious locals and visitors, Cucina Viansa is a must-try, with jazz on summer weekend nights.

🍂 *Cucina Viansa, 400 First Street East, Sonoma 95476; phone (707) 938–2938. Open 10:00 A.M.–7:00 P.M. Sunday–Thursday, 10:00 A.M.–11:00 P.M. Friday–Saturday, 8:00 A.M.–11:00 P.M. Friday–Saturday in summer. MasterCard, Visa, American Express, and Discover. Wheelchair-accessible.*

As you turn right on East Spain Street, Mission San Francisco Solano is across the street.

LA CASA RESTAURANT, right across from the Mission and next door to Lo Spuntino, was founded by the late writer and scholar Al Gordon, with consultations by Trader Vic's son Joe Bergeron. La Casa is currently on its fourth owner.

The nachos are sensational here, and we found surprisingly good gringo additions to the old menu: a decent Caesar salad with sautéed chicken, and a hamburger supreme. There are daily specials, both Mexican and gringo-esque. Margaritas have always been good here; they still sneak up on you. La Casa makes the best tortilla chips; they are sold not only here but also at Sonoma Market and some chain grocery stores.

The bar is fun as well as charming in itself. As close to authentic architectural design as was possible, the whole ambience, including Mexican woven-leather chairs, makes you feel as if you will hear the local mariachi approaching from a distance especially to serenade you. Occasionally one does. For some reason, recently the bar has turned into a San Francisco '49er sports bar, with team flags, a wall-banner schedule, a new CD juke box, and video games for kids of all ages.

 Fine points: If you want to people-watch, sit in the bar lobby or, if the weather is good, outside in back. For the best, most relaxing view of historic Sonoma, the Mission, and the Barracks, ask for a window table upstairs. As is true in all Sonoma restaurants, smoking is allowed only in the bar.

✿✿ *La Casa Restaurant, 121 East Spain Street, Sonoma 95476; phone (707) 996–3406. Open 11:30 A.M.–12:00 midnight daily, dinner until 10:00 P.M., bar food until midnight. MasterCard, Visa, American Express, Discover, and Diners. Wheelchair-accessible.*

Just east of La Casa on Spain is the Blue Wing Inn. This large, pure adobe has the most colorful history of any building in Sonoma. It was built in two stages, beginning in 1840. The first part originally housed some of General Vallejo's soldiers. The building grew gradually, and by the Gold Rush it was a hotel with rooms upstairs and a saloon that featured gambling.

In August 1849, James Cooper and Thomas Spriggs took it over and called it Sonoma House—an inn and bar. It was *the* place to stay, carouse, or gamble. Its clientele ranged from future generals Ulysses S. Grant, John C. Frémont, and William Tecumseh Sherman to horse thieves and killers "Three Fingers" Garcia and (as legend has it) Joaquin Murietta, as well as a host of miners who paid their bills in gold dust.

Cooper and his wife, Sara, lived on the premises for three years. They changed the name to The Blue Wing sometime between 1853 and 1856, the year that

Spriggs died and Cooper was stabbed to death by his son's schoolmaster. The Widow Cooper sold the place to General Vallejo's attorney, Martin Cooke, who made the second floor a residence. The Blue Wing passed through several owners' hands and became a grocery store.

Augustino Pinelli bought The Blue Wing near the turn of the century and turned it into a winery, storing wine in the cellar. Pinelli's wine was poured on the El Paseo buildings during the 1911 fire, thereby saving the exterior.

In the 1930s Walter and Celeste Murphy, owners of the *Index-Tribune*, bought The Blue Wing (and the Barracks). The Murphys then sold the building to William and Polly Black, who rescued the structure, which was near collapse, and completely renovated it. The Blue Wing is unusual in that the exterior adobe surfaces, roughly covered verandas, and hand-hewn posts have been retained in their natural state.

In 1964 The Blue Wing was sold to the State of California, which has allowed ground-floor shops and second-story apartment living to continue. When long-term shopkeepers have retired or died, their spaces have been rented as apartments to other local characters. Lucky them! In addition to its regular tenants, the second floor is inhabited by a ghost, whose appearances many responsible people have witnessed on several occasions.

ANN APPLEMAN FLOWERS & PLANTS is a welcomed addition to Spain Street, having replaced Sloan & Jones, which moved to the northwest corner of

BLUE WING INN (CIRCA 1840)

the Plaza. Ann aptly describes her lovely, peaceful shop as "a unique botanical experience." Give it a try. Check out the building while you're there. Known as the Pinni House, this little hip-roof house was built in 1906 by a stoneworker named Pinni from stone rubble he "acquired" at the Schocken Quarry, where he was employed. He applied plaster over the stone, but it has eroded, leaving an appealing Old World look. Eventually purchased by William Black, it served for years as Taylor's Florist until Sloan & Jones moved in, in 1995.

❧ *Ann Appleman Flowers & Plants, 147 East Spain Street, Sonoma 95476; phone (707) 938–3571. Open 11:00 A.M.–5:00 P.M. Wednesday–Saturday, 12:00 noon–4:00 P.M. Sunday. MasterCard and Visa. Not wheelchair-accessible.*

If you have time, walk to the next corner for a look at the outside of the Ray-Adler Adobe (205 East Spain Street). Pioneer John Ray built this Monterey Colonial house in two stages. He built the eastern wood-frame part in 1847 for his wife and five children. Then, after making a strike during the Gold Rush, he completed the dominant adobe section with 22-inch-thick walls and veranda in 1850. Ray used the downstairs of the new part as a mess hall for American Army officers stationed in Sonoma.

Merchant Lewis Adler, who had amassed even more gold dust by selling supplies to '49ers, bought the house from Ray in 1851. Adler rented the upper floor to the newly formed Masonic Lodge. Fortunately, subsequent residents preserved its historic style. It is inhabited by a ghost, a woman in a blue dress, who appears to unsuspecting guests on the second floor.

In the next block, on the north side of Spain, view the Cook-Hope House (245 East Spain Street). One of the earliest wood-frame houses built in Sonoma in the mid-1850s, it is named for the first and second families to own it. The redwood siding has proved durable.

The Lewis Adler Store and Pioneer Saloon (256 East Spain Street) was built in 1848. Now a two-story, gabled-roof residence, it was built as a one-story, lean-to store for Lewis Adler and Charles Meyer. Eventually they moved this commercial building closer to the Plaza, across the street from the Blue Wing. In 1856 Adler and Meyer moved the building again, this time to the corner of First Street East and Napa Street, as Adler's Pioneer Saloon. The second story was added in 1878. In 1902 Henry Castagnasso bought the building and had it rolled back down Spain Street to its present location, where it has remained, thankfully, for nearly a century.

Turn north on Second Street East to look at the Castagnasso's Clydesdale horses, and walk the half-block up to VELLA'S CHEESE, where you will be welcomed at the door by a new doormat acknowledging Vella's as the National Cheese Champions for 1995–1996.

RAY-ADLER ADOBE (1846–1851)

Vella's Cheese has been proclaimed one of the finest cheese makers in the world. While it does not have the tourism exposure on the Plaza that the Viviani family's Cheese Factory does, it makes fine handmade cheeses. It wins the most international prizes for the Dry Jack, which can vary from firm to hard; and the Bleu Cheese, made at its factory in Oregon. Vella's also offers Laura Chenel's Chèvre, Rouge et Noir's brie, and some dry sausages for your picnic.

Vella's is small, so the minute you walk in the swinging door, you'll find yourself at the counter. Take the time to back up and read letters and history on the walls. Ignazio Vella, who served as county supervisor from this district and director of the Sonoma County Fair, runs the cheese operation. He is usually on the premises and will gladly chat with you about cheese or local politics.

The old Sonoma cheese families are somewhat intertwined. In 1915 Joseph Vella and John Iacono of San Francisco began the Sonoma Mission Creamery, in the then-Pinelli property that is now El Paseo. (They already had cheese plants in Tomales, Nicasio, Half Moon Bay, and Lake County.) Trucks delivered cream and milk from Sonoma dairies to the plant in San Francisco, where it was processed into butter and sold under the brand "Valley of the Moon." They also made cheese in what is now La Casa Restaurant and stored it in the Blue Wing building.

In 1930 Joseph Vella built the Spanish-style building on the corner of First Street East and Spain, across from Mission San Francisco de Solano, known for decades as Vella's Fountain and Ice Cream Manufacturing Plant. Many old-time local residents remember having their first jobs at Vella's Fountain, as those in this generation do at Mary's Pizza Shack.

Tom Vella, Joseph's younger brother, came to America in 1924, and in 1931 he and Celso Viviani removed the brewery equipment from the fine stone building where Vella's is today, on Second Street East, and brought in cheese-making machines. At the end of World War II, Rocco Benedetto and his wife, Carmela, niece of Tom Vella and cousin of Ig Vella, took over the yummy business and ran it as a Sonoma social center and creamery for thirty-five years. In 1977 the Benedettos sold the building, and it began its cycle as a deli of various tastes to its current state as Lo Spuntino.

Meanwhile, the Viviani family split off from the Vella cheese plant and started their own on the Plaza, now known as The Sonoma Cheese Factory. Italian-American splits and spats are legendary in cheese and wine families, and many have been well publicized. Happily, this one was patched up long ago, and both families continue to make fine cheeses sold throughout the world.

Here you can get Columbus Salamini Secchi, Monet crackers, and other locally produced special cheeses.

Fine points: Vella's staff will cheerfully cut you a slice of any cheese you would like to taste. Be sure to take home a little of their almost-salt-free butter; it's unparalleled anywhere. Vella's has the only apprentice cheesemaker in California. Try their new Toma soft ripened cheese.

❧ *Vella's Cheese, 315 Second Street East, Sonoma 95476; phone (707) 938–3232. Open 9:00 A.M.–6:00 P.M. Monday–Saturday, 10:00 A.M.–5:00 P.M. Sunday. MasterCard and Visa. Wheelchair-accessible.*

The assistant head cheesemaker, Roger Ranniker, and his wife, Claudia, live across the street from Vella's. In back of their house, at Claudia's Perennial Heaven, Claudia grows and sells exquisite perennials for the gardening addict. These people have the tidiest garden on earth. Ring the red bell for service. Locals drop off plastic plant containers for Claudia to recycle.

Just a few steps farther up Second Street, Bette Kolstad runs THE PATCH, a one-woman organic-vegetable farm on property owned by the Castagnasso family, whose Clydesdale horses entertain throngs back down at the corner of Second Street East and East Spain Street.

The Patch posts a sign on Second Street East announcing what is for sale each day, but there is often much more available. Bette grows many kinds of squashes, tomatoes including yellow pears and romas, potatoes, and the absolute local favorite, sweet corn. Lots of her vegetables wind up served at restaurants on Sonoma Plaza. Corn is available July 4–Thanksgiving.

☙ *The Patch, 260 Second Street East, Sonoma 95476; phone (707) 939–9054. Open 10:00 A.M.–5:00 P.M., and Bette means it. No credit cards. Wheelchair-accessible.*

If you are interested in cemeteries, continue the long block up Second Street East to the City Cemetery. (Access is easier from First Street West.) St. Francisco Solano Cemetery, on the north side of East Napa Street, just past Fifth Street East, is another historical site where many of the old Catholic Italian and French family members are buried, as well as town founder General Mariano G. Vallejo—whose birth date is wrong on his tombstone.

The only winery actually located "downtown" is SEBASTIANI SONOMA CASK CELLARS. It is on Fourth Street East, just 3 blocks from the Plaza or 2 short blocks from Second Street East. It was known as Sebastiani Vineyards until 1997, when the name was changed to signal that only Sebastiani's finest wines

THE PATCH VEGETABLE GARDEN

are made here, while the rest are made in California's Central Valley. Sebastiani's history is tied to Sonoma and always will be, hopefully.

Sebastiani Vineyards includes two acres across from the winery on Fourth Street East, on which the Franciscan fathers planted the first vineyard north of San Francisco (1825) to make sacramental wines (State Historical Landmark #739). In the 1980s the Sebastianis pulled out those original vines and now use the land as their experimental vineyard. To learn more about the fascinating history of Sebastiani Vineyards and its important contributions to California wine-making, see page 253 in the History chapter.

To get to Sebastiani, you can walk over from Vella's Cheese on Second Street East by following the paved Bike Path through The Patch vegetable fields and the original historic vineyard, or you can just follow Spain Street East. Where Spain Street ends, you are facing the home of Pat and Kenneth McTaggart, son of Sabina Sebastiani McTaggart, sister of August and daughter of Samuele Sebastiani. You can also ride the new Sebastiani trolley, a San Francisco cable-car reproduction, from its stop behind the Toscano Hotel and the Barracks. Then turn left and you will immediately see Sebastiani and its colorful flags.

FACADE OF SEBASTIANI WAREHOUSE (1905), UNCOVERED
DURING RECENT EARTHQUAKE RETROFITTING

RISOTTO WITH MUSHROOMS
from Sylvia Sebastiani, Sebastiani Sonoma Cask Cellars

$1/2$ cup butter

1 medium onion, minced

$1^1/_2$ cups uncooked rice

$1/2$ thinly sliced mushrooms

$1/8$ tsp powdered saffron (optional)

$1/2$ cup Chardonnay

4–5 cups boiling chicken broth

$1/2$ cup grated Parmesan cheese

$1/2$ cup shredded Swiss cheese

salt and white pepper to taste

Melt butter in a large, heavy skillet. Add onions and sauté very slowly, stirring frequently. Do not let them brown. Add rice, then mushrooms, and stir gently for 1–2 minutes. Add salt and pepper to taste and stir frequently for about 10 minutes.

Dissolve saffron in 1 Tbs heated wine, then add to rice with remaining wine. Add chicken broth a little at a time, stirring for about 25 minutes until rice is tender and all the liquid is absorbed. Stir in cheeses just before serving. Serves 6.

Sebastiani gives tours hourly, the last tour leaving the tasting room at 4:30 P.M. This is an excellent educational tour, and it gives you the chance to see the unusual carved casks by artist Earle Brown. Sebastiani offers some of its best and rarest wines only in the tasting room. You get the real feeling of old Sonoma's wine business here, and for good reason.

You might want to stay at the charming Stone Cottage, Mary Ann Sebastiani Cuneo's newly renovated historic bed & breakfast right across the street from the winery. (See page 207.)

Fine points: You can watch the grape-crushing operation here from a balcony in the back of the main winery building from early September into October. By the way, check out Sylvia Sebastiani's excellent cookbook *Mangiamo* ("Let's eat"). Many locals swear by her simple Italian recipes. Featured wines: Estate Cherry Block Cabernet Sauvignon, Nouveau Beaujolais, Talus Cabernet Sauvignon and Chardonnay, Sonoma Cask Barbera, Merlot, Syrah, Zinfandel, Mourvèdre, Sangiovese, and

Dutton Ranch Chardonnay, and Vendange Pinot Noir, Sauvignon Blanc, Chardonnay, Cabernet, Zinfandel and Merlot, and Grappa di Sebastiani. Head winemakers: Mary Sullivan and Mark Lyon. Cases: 7,000,000 (yes!). Acres: lots. ❧ *Sebastiani Sonoma Cask Cellars, 389 Fourth Street East, Sonoma 95476; phone (707) 938–5532. Open 10:00 A.M.–5:00 P.M. daily. MasterCard, Visa, and American Express. The winery is wheelchair-accessible; there is also wheelchair access to the employee rest room across the street (inquire in tasting room).*

Now walk back downtown along Spain Street, and look again for Castagnasso's famous Clydesdale horses. They like carrots and apples, but a new sign begs you not to feed them. As you pass the horse field, note the three saltbox-design houses ahead toward the Mission. The Solomon Schocken Houses (130, 138, and 146 East Spain Street) were built by said Solomon between 1886 and 1890 on former Mission property that he bought, along with the Mission itself, in 1881.

MISSION SAN FRANCISCO SOLANO occupies the northeast corner of the Plaza at First Street East and Spain Street. The last built and most northern of the California missions, this was the only one founded under Mexican rule. The original mission's construction, under the direction of Father José Altimira, began in 1823. The Mission was dedicated on April 23, 1824. The original Mission comprised a large compound, with the chapel built of wood and thatch where the church stands today. This chapel burned down in 1827 and was replaced by a larger church, built of adobe and completed in 1833, at the eastern end of the compound.

Although the Sonoma Mission was larger and more active than most, it was reduced to the function of a parish church after the Mexican government

MISSION SAN FRANCISCO SOLANO

secularized all the California missions in 1834. Captain Salvador Vallejo, brother of Commandante General Mariano Vallejo, cannibalized the chapel's tile roof, and subsequent rains wreaked havoc on the adobe walls. In 1840 General Vallejo, at his own expense, had a new chapel built by local Indians at its current location (also the site of the 1824 church) and let the damaged chapel fall into ruin.

The long, low building fronted by an arcade currently facing East Spain Street is the surviving section of the *convento* (priest's residence), constructed in the 1830s under the direction of Father Buenaventura Fortuny. The belfry was added in about 1850. In 1858 General Vallejo, who had become an American citizen, had the mission remodeled, with the basic walls as they stand today. Vallejo abandoned the pure Mexican Colonial

THE MOST NORTHERLY MISSION BELL ALONG EL CAMINO REAL

style and "Americanized" the buildings with arched window casements built of wood.

Deterioration of the Mission buildings accelerated due to trains passing on tracks laid on East Spain Street in 1879. The next year the Catholic Church won a long legal battle to have the Mission property returned to the Church. This triumph enabled the Church to sell the Mission for $3,000 to a local merchant, Solomon Schocken. Schocken used the Mission variously as a hay barn, warehouse, and blacksmith shop, and built a saloon in front of the chapel.

In 1900 the Sonoma Valley Woman's Club took an interest in restoration of the Mission. With the help of a fundraising campaign headed by William Randolph Hearst, publisher of the *San Francisco Examiner*, the California Historic Landmarks League bought the property from Schocken for $3,000 in 1903.

Before restoration could be completed, the April 1906 earthquake shook the Mission, along with the rest of the area. During the next three years, weakened walls and roof of the Mission gave way. As money was raised again, more improvements were made, and finally the California legislature appropriated $5,000 in 1913 so that the work could be completed. The reconstruction of the chapel and the *convento* strengthened and beautified the Mission and returned it to the Mexican Colonial style. The *convento,* however, encompasses only four of the original twenty-seven rooms.

The large bell that hangs in front of the Mission was most likely cast in Peru and is dated 1829. It was stolen in the 1850s but was discovered in 1910 in San Francisco's Sutro Museum. The bell was restored to the Mission in 1920. The smaller bell hanging in front of the chapel was the last of the El Camino Real bells hung by the Native Sons of the Golden West every few miles along the route taken by mission padres from San Diego to Sonoma. Another small bell, erected in the same manner, hangs in front of Sonoma City Hall. These are two of the few remaining such bells, because most of them have been stolen from along El Camino Real.

The Mission was deeded to the State of California in 1926 and became a state park in 1927. A few marriages are performed here, occasionally one of the historical organizations hosts an event here—and both events are usually beautiful and romantic. (But since the Mission now belongs to the state and not to the Catholic Church, few Catholic priests will marry people here.)

SONOMA BARRACKS, at the northwest corner of First Street East and East Spain Street, was built between 1837 and 1840 by Indian labor for the Mexican troops under General Vallejo. The Sonoma Barracks is a classic, two-story adobe of Monterey Colonial style. For the four weeks between the raising of the Bear Flag over Sonoma on June 14, 1846, and the raising of the American flag over Sonoma on July 9, 1846, the Barracks was the capitol building of the California Republic.

Between July 9, 1846, and January 1852, various American military units occupied the Barracks, as the U.S. Army made Sonoma the military headquarters for the Pacific states. During 1847 the New York Volunteers improved the building and completed flooring on the second story. Starting in 1852, the Barracks also served many commercial uses, including General Vallejo's own winery.

Solomon Schocken bought the Barracks in 1878, two years before he bought the Mission. Schocken turned the Barracks into a general store with apartments upstairs, including his own. He also covered the adobe with wood to create a Victorian look that had no relationship to its origin.

Walter and Celeste Murphy, owners of the *Index-Tribune,* bought the Barracks in 1934 and saved it from destruction. The Murphys removed the gingerbread facade and returned the building to close to its Colonial roots. They installed offices and their own spacious apartment on the second floor, and stores on the ground floor. In 1958 the Murphys deeded the Barracks to the State of California, retaining a life estate in their apartment, which allowed them to continue living there. The state ended the commercial uses of the building and restored and reinforced the adobe with steel beams in the late 1970s, adding new stucco on the exterior of the adobe bricks to preserve them.

The State Parks store in the Barracks deserves a good look. The book area is loaded with great, if obscure, books for both children and adults on all the California missions, Native Americans, and California history in general. There are coloring books in English and Spanish, games, and historic costume-making.

 Fine points: Every year on the Friday of Vintage Festival weekend (the last weekend in September), sponsors (that is, anyone who will pay for the tickets) attend a wine tasting in the Mission or Barracks courtyard, with nearly all Sonoma Valley wineries pouring their finest wines. The Sonoma State Historic Park Association provides three docent-led walking tours of the state-owned historic sites in Sonoma on Saturday and Sunday. A $2.00 admission fee for adults and $1.00 for children six to twelve years old gives you entry to all three buildings and the Petaluma Adobe. At noon there is a tour of Mission San Francisco de Solano. At 1:00 P.M. there is a tour starting at Mission San Francisco de Solano (meet in the courtyard), El Cuartel de Sonoma (soldiers' barracks), Casa Grande Area including the Toscano Hotel, and the Casa de los Criados (servants quarters). At 2:00 P.M. there is a tour of the Vallejo Home.

❧ *Sonoma Mission and Barracks, 20 East Spain Street, Sonoma 95476; phone (707) 938–1519. Open 10:00 A.M.–4:00 P.M. daily. Admission: adults $3.00; children six to twelve $2.00, under six free, bookstore free. Same ticket good for Vallejo Home, Petaluma Adobe, and Mission San Francisco de Solano. MasterCard and Visa. Wheelchair-accessible.*

The Toscano Hotel, on East Spain Street, was built in the 1850s for Mrs. Dorothea Nathanson as a general store and lending library. The building housed a variety of businesses until it became the Toscano Hotel in 1886. A kitchen and dining room were added in the rear of the building in 1902. After the State of California gained ownership of the Toscano in 1957, the state restored the building between 1967 and 1972. Since then, the Sonoma League for Historic Preservation has collected period furniture for the interior and provides docents to explain the building's history. It is now part of the Sonoma State Historic Park.

The Hotel Annex (20 East Spain Street) is now the State of California Department of Parks and Recreation office for the Sonoma area. This wood structure was built in the 1870s as a one-story saloon in front of General Vallejo's Indian Servants' Quarters. Settimo Ciucci bought the Hotel Annex in 1903; built a new first floor about 40 feet east (current location) of the original; and then had the old saloon lifted up and placed on top to form a two-story, nine-room hotel.

Beside the Sonoma Cheese Factory, don't miss the Casa Grande Indian Servants' Quarters (20 East Spain Street). Located on the western side of the

T OSCANO H OTEL A NNEX (C ALIFORNIA S TATE H ISTORIC P ARK
OFFICES AT SONOMA)

open courtyard, the Servants' Quarters building was built in 1835 as a wing of
General Vallejo's so-called Casa Grande. (This name and building should not be
confused with Vallejo's other Casa Grande, on Adobe Road southeast of
Petaluma, which served as the center of his agricultural operations and summer
home.) With its thick adobe walls, the Indian Servants' Quarters is an example
of Monterey Colonial–style architecture.

From the parking lot behind these buildings, you can take the Sebastiani
Sonoma Cask Cellars Trolley to the winery.

The large Vallejo home, located just east of the Servants' Quarters, burned
to the ground on April 13, 1867, in a fire that lasted for four hours. A bucket
brigade and a hand pump operated by volunteers saved this building. Soon
afterward the Servants' Quarters became a run-down apartment building and
wine warehouse, eventually falling into disuse and decrepitude. In the 1960s the
State of California restored the deteriorating adobe walls and put on a new shin-
gled roof, but the building remains a shell with little internal structure.

The Viviani family traces the S ONOMA C HEESE F ACTORY's origin to the same
day in 1931 when Celso Viviani and Tom Vella started making cheese on Second
Street East, where Vella's Cheese is now. Certainly the family's passed-down
cheesemaking skills trace to 1931, but this separate business and building date to
1945. Designed by Pero D. Canali, its angular lines and slanting columns out-
raged some locals when it was built and clearly designate it as a period piece.

CASA GRANDE INDIAN SERVANTS' QUARTERS

Directed by Pete Viviani and his son, David Viviani, the Cheese Factory has a full deli serving many favorite sandwiches, with most salads made elsewhere, a wide range of soft drinks, beer, and local wines, and generous plates of cubed cheese to taste with toothpicks. In addition to the traditional Sonoma Jack and cheddars with or without flavors, the Vivianis make excellent "lite" white cheddar and other "lite" cheeses. They sell local breads, including Sonoma French, Brother Juniper's, and Passini Scambria; a whole case of imported cheeses; and an entire wall of imported and local wines. You can even try their new hamburgers (with cheese, of course) barbecued in their patio for only $4.50. Check out the new cooler with ready-made lunches of fruit, cheese, baguette, and salami ($5.49).

 Fine points: A little more modern in presentation than Vella's, the Sonoma Cheese Factory provides a recorded voice telling a brief version of local cheese history and cheesemaking when you press a button by the viewing window at the back of the store. A bulletin board tells you exactly when you can watch the cheesemakers do their thing, usually at almost anytime all day.

❧ *Sonoma Cheese Factory, 2 West Spain Street, Sonoma 95476; phone of retail store (709) 996–1931, of office and factory (707) 996–1000. Open 8:30 A.M.–5:30 P.M. Monday–Friday, 8:30 A.M.–6:00 P.M. Saturday and Sunday. MasterCard, Visa, American Express, and Discover. Rest rooms for customers only. Wheelchair-accessible.*

THE CHEESE FACTORY

MARIONI'S RESTAURANT'S building served for many years as the office of the Sonoma Valley Unified School District until the district bought another restaurant site from the Nicholas turkey-growing family. Parts of the Marioni family own both this building and the Swiss Hotel next door. Jim Marioni owns Marioni's Restaurant, and his brother Hank is co-owner of the Swiss Hotel.

Following David Pleydell-Bouverie's design, the remodeling to create the restaurant left no traces of drab school-district offices. Instead you now enjoy a clubby atmosphere in a somewhat abstract design with the bar a couple of steps below the entry floor and dining on three other levels. Each interior terrace presents a different ambience. The "outdoor" area in front of the restaurant is a great place to sip or nibble and watch the world go by, and it is heated in winter with a built-in fireplace.

Marioni's has a whole new menu with huge salads, Niçoise salad with grilled Ahi tuna ($9.75), New York steak and fries ($12.75), filet mignon and prawns ($18.50), a half barbecued chicken ($13.25), or a half roasted duck ($15.25). They still offer their reliable burgers and pastas.

❧ Marioni's Restaurant, 8 West Spain Street, Sonoma 95476; phone (707) 996–6866. Open 11:30 A.M.–2:00 A.M. MasterCard, Visa, and American Express. Front patio is wheelchair-accessible.

BAKSHEESH, an exciting little shop wedged between Marioni's and the Swiss Hotel, is the pride and joy of owner Candi Smucker ("just like jelly"). Baksheesh features truly "handcrafted gifts from the developing world," from thirty countries, to be exact. We have found numerous bargains, including colorful scarves, colorful dangles for babies, rattles for adults, alabaster bookends, baskets and loose-fitting clothes galore, unique musical instruments and masks, bags and purses, candles and candleholders, cards, chess sets, musical instruments, unusual and abstract nativity scenes, and damned good chili and cornbread mixes. Think about the hand-painted river rocks from Vietnam and greeting cards from around the world.

Candi knows her business. She and her husband opened several other stores as their voluntary mission with the Mennonites and are "committed to trading fairly with artisans in the developing world and the U.S." They are "affiliated with alternative trade organizations and guarantee living wages to artisans for their work." Much of their crafts come to them through Ten Thousand Villages Handicrafts, formerly known as Selfhelp Crafts.

Baksheesh, 14 West Spain Street, Sonoma 95476; phone (707) 939–2847; fax (707) 939–3726. Open 10:00 A.M.–6:00 P.M. Monday–Saturday, noon–6:00 P.M. Sunday. MasterCard and Visa. Not wheelchair-accessible.

One of our favorites, THE SWISS HOTEL occupies the great two-story historic adobe restaurant and hotel. Built as a wing of Salvador Vallejo's home in 1850 and operating as a hotel since 1880, it is now a California Historical Landmark and a remarkably well-preserved adobe. It has been in constant use since it was constructed. Notice the angles at which the walls don't meet.

Owned by Helen Marioni Dunlap, the restaurant and hotel are now run by Helen's nephew, Hank Marioni (brother of Jim Marioni next door at Marioni's) and his wife, Lori; Robert and Sylvia Gordenker Bernard; and Roger Roessler. Helen's parents ran the Swiss for years, and she worked right along with them. Upon her mother's death, Helen and her husband, Ted Dunlap, took over the restaurant. You will recognize The Swiss by the Swiss, Italian, and American flags flying from its balcony.

Red-and-white-check tablecloths cover round cafe tables, and standing heaters on the sidewalk in front make for wonderful dining, drinking, and people-watching. Smoking is allowed at the tables in front. The patio in back which has been remodeled to a most pleasurable country state with a fireplace and space heaters. Lunch and dinner are served at all tables, inside and out.

As you walk into the Swiss Hotel bar (there's another entrance to the hotel lobby to the right), you enter Sonoma history. The bar room is lined with Sonoma memorabilia and signed photos of celebrities including Charles Kurault, George Blanda, and Heavyweight Champion of the World Gentleman

OVEN-ROASTED ROSEMARY CHICKEN
from Mary Ellen Oertel of
The Swiss Hotel

3 3–3 ½ lb chickens
6 Tbs garlic, chopped
6 sprigs rosemary, leaves removed from stems and chopped fine
3 tsp cracked black pepper
salt
olive oil

Debone chickens completely. Remove last two joints of the wings. You will have two halves. Mix black pepper, garlic, and rosemary. Sprinkle the mixture on the chicken. Allow to marinate several hours or overnight. In a large, very hot sauté pan, add approximately ¼ cup olive oil (not extra virgin). Salt chickens to taste. Carefully place chicken halves in pan, skin side down. Let sear till golden, then turn. Sear about 3 minutes. Turn back to skin side down and finish in a moderate to hot oven (400–500° F) approximately 8–10 minutes, or until cooked through. Remove from pan, discard oil, and use that pan for the sauce of your choice.

OLIVE-TOMATO SAUCE
6 Roma tomatoes, peeled, seeded, and chopped coarsely
6 oz Calamata olives, chopped coarsely
1 oz extra virgin olive oil
10 oz chicken stock
1 oz butter
salt and pepper

In a hot sauté pan, add the olive oil and sauté tomatoes for 2 minutes. Add the olives, stock, butter, and salt and pepper. Cook until the mixture comes to a boil. Spoon over chicken halves. Serve with garlic mashed potatoes and seasonal vegetables. Serves 6.

Jim Corbett. Beside the doorway entrance to the "Dinning Room" are two walls of old pictures of local characters from the past—mostly Italians like Stornetta, Leveroni, Cereghino, and Marioni. There's even one of Maria de la Luz Carrillo, the estranged wife of Don Salvador Vallejo.

You actually walk from the bar into the lobby, which also has dining tables, and turn left to another doorway and the dining room. For decades the dining-room walls were screaming pink and nearly covered with historic pictures. Now you will find sedate white walls, hung with the cleaned-up photos, light-blue carpet, and white tablecloths. The most romantic room is the old Wine Room, off to the right, with historic tools and racks of wine bottles.

Generations of local families used to eat family-style Italian dinners here weekly. Some still come regularly now that the menu has been updated and injected with a la carte Sonoma Cuisine selections. Innovative wood-burning, brick oven–baked pizzas are especially popular ($13.00), as is the nearly bone-less roasted rosemary chicken with garlic mashed potatoes ($13.50). Pastas are always fresh and al dente. Our favorite is the linguine with prawns ($12.50). The Swiss's famous garlic salad is a must; just make sure everyone you're going home with eats some. Locals definitely hang out here—in fact, the cafe tables in front are usually standing-room-only on weekend evenings.

 Fine points: Call it "The Swiss." The "Swiss Hotel" label house wine is really Gundlach-Bundschu, and a very good deal. Swiss Hotel bartenders make the best Shirley Temples and Roy Rogers our kids ever tasted and host some of the loudest laughter in town. Even famous columnist Herb Caen liked their dry $2.50 martinis, and we have had the hilarious pleasure of joking with Tommy Smothers at the bar. Full bar. By the way—don't forget that this *is* also a hotel!

❧ *The Swiss Hotel, 18 West Spain Street, Sonoma 95476; phone (707) 938–2884; fax (707) 938–3298. Open 11:30 A.M.–10:00 P.M. daily, with a midafter-noon break from food service; the bar is open until it closes. Visa, MasterCard, and American Express. The restaurant is wheelchair-accessible through the back; the hotel is not accessible.*

Susan Allen's UNIQUELY CALIFORNIA occupies the vast space where the Sonoma Valley Hospital Auxiliary once sold recycled goodies and Susan B. later sold her own line of clothes. Uniquely California turns out to be an excellent one-stop shop where you can buy gourmet delicacies, including Sonoman Lesley B. Fay preserves and sauces (Belgian chocolate espresso!), books, paintings, Napa Valley Herbs, personalized gift baskets, microbrews, bath and body products, glassware, and tapestries. New interesting offerings include glass dishes made from recycled bottles made by Fire & Light, a woman-owned company; Sonoma lavender; etched wine bottles, and fabulous ties made by twelve-year-old sisters under the "Kid Stuff" label. Take a peek.

❧ *Uniquely California, 28 West Spain Street, Sonoma 95476; phone (707) 939–6768 or (888) 227–5367; e-mail gifts@uniquelycal.com. Open 10:00 A.M.–6:00 P.M. Wednesday–Monday. MasterCard, Visa, and American Express. Wheelchair-accessible.*

THE CANDLESTICK moved here from the Village Fair in Sausalito and sells wildly shaped candles that look like everything from cartoon characters to roses that float in water.

❧ *The Candlestick, 38 West Spain, Sonoma 95476; phone (707) 933–0700. Open 10:00 A.M.–6:00 P.M. daily. MasterCard, Visa, and American Express. Wheelchair-accessible.*

PLAZA BOOKS is a wonderful, cavernous shop of antiquarian and used books, from old Book of the Month Club selections to rare M. F. K. Fisher editions and old comics. Boris Bruton began with a little stock of Club selections and personal libraries and has put lots back into procuring some interesting and rare volumes, including obscure books on many topics. Primary interests include aesthetics, scholarly works, and Western and California history. Boris continues to show his knowledge and taste by his investments in intriguing collections.

❧ *Plaza Books, 40 West Spain Street, Sonoma 95476; phone (707) 996–8474. Open 11:00 A.M.–6:00 P.M. daily. MasterCard and Visa. Wheelchair-accessible for part of the store.*

Joan Sayler and Linda Corzine recently moved their SUMMER VINE here from Sausalito's Village Fair, where they had been since 1982. We like their home accessories such as beautiful books, woven throws, journal books, Bay Area artists' work, Judy Severson quilt prints, needlepoint pillows, and blue and white dishes with mugs as low as $6.95. Bird lovers will enjoy the birdhouses made of wood recycled from Victorian houses.

❧ *Summer Vine, 100 West Spain Street, Sonoma 95476; phone (707) 933-8810. Open 10:00 A.M.–6:00 P.M. daily. MasterCard and Visa. Wheelchair-accessible.*

Across First Street East is the Sonoma Hotel, a historic hotel built in 1880. Originally a two-story structure with stores and a large meeting and a dance hall upstairs, a third story was added in the early 1900s, when it became a twenty-one-room hotel. Neglected in the 1960s and 1970s, it was completely restored by owners Dorene and John Musilli, who bought it in 1980.

Recently the Musillis sold the whole works to Craig Miller and Tim Farfan, who also have a large home-accessories shop, Harvest, next to Sebastiani on the Square on West Napa Street. Craig and Tim completely redid the hotel in French country decor and added private baths, televisions, phones, and air-conditioning in all rooms—great improvements!

Craig and Tim's new HEIRLOOM RESTAURANT took off like a shot under the deft culinary hand of Chef Michael Dotson, recently of the popular Slow Club in San Francisco and PlumpJack at Lake Tahoe. *San Francisco Chronicle* Food Editor Michael Bauer says Dotson "clearly is one of the Bay Area's stars."

Try his comfort cuisine in the historic bar, outside in the shady patio, or in the adjoining cozy rooms. At lunch Kathleen likes the romaine hearts with Gala apples and Maytag blue cheese ($6.50); juicy flank-steak salad with French green beans, cherry tomatoes, and lemon Balsamic vinaigrette ($9.75); and the grilled swordfish club sandwich with applewood smoked bacon, tomatoes, watercress, and basil aioli ($9.75).

Dinner offers quail fumet soup ($5.00) or grilled Wolfe Ranch quail with Quinoa tabbouleh and Meyer lemon oil ($9.50) for appetizers. Entrees may include lemon-pepper noodles with rock shrimp and toasted garlic ($12.75), roasted wild salmon with whole grain mustard mashed potatoes ($16.75), or a grilled Niman Ranch pork chop ($17.25). Give it a try!

❧ *Heirloom Restaurant, 110 West Spain Street, Sonoma 95476; phone (707) 939-6955. Open 11:30 A.M.-2:30 P.M., 5:30–9:30 P.M. daily. Full bar. MasterCard, Visa, and American Express. Wheelchair-accessible. Friendly dog in patio; entrance from First Street West.*

General Vallejo's home, LACHRYMA MONTIS, stands opposite Third Street West at West Spain Street. General Mariano G. Vallejo built this Gothic Revival

SONOMA HOTEL (1880)

LACHRYMA MONTIS, GENERAL VALLEJO'S HOME (1851)

home in 1851–1852, at the impressive cost of $50,000. Vallejo named the residence Lachryma Montis ("Tears of the Mountain") because of a spring on the property. Vallejo had redwood lumber hauled in from the port at Vallejo, while bricks and marble mantels were shipped from Hawaii to supplement a pre-cut Victorian house package shipped around the Horn from the East Coast. Landscaping, a glass pavilion (now gone), and every convenience of the era were included. The Vallejos' fifteenth and sixteenth children were born here.

Vallejo's once-great holdings eventually were reduced to the acreage around this home. He died in 1890, and the property passed to his daughter, Luisa Emparan, who stayed on and lived in the house. Luisa married a Mexican consular official, Richard Emparan, gave birth to three children, and then found herself a widow. She supported herself by continuing her father's water company and was a popular civic and social leader. In 1933 she sold the property to the State of California and contributed much of the Vallejo family furniture and relics that were in the house. Much of the furniture you see in the house today was acquired from other sources. Until her death in 1943, Mrs. Emparan stayed on as official custodian of the house. The old wine and olive storehouse is now a museum.

❧ *Lachryma Montis, Third Street West and West Spain Street; phone (707)*

THE GENERAL'S DAUGHTER RESTAURANT

938–1519. Open 10:00 A.M.–5:00 P.M. daily. Admission $2.00; group-tickets and tour information at the Barracks. Partially wheelchair-accessible.

A short block west from the driveway entrance to Vallejo's home, the yellow THE GENERAL'S DAUGHTER RESTAURANT rises from the field. *Gourmet* magazine's readers voted The General's Daughter their seventh-favorite "Top Table" in the San Francisco Wine Country in 1997, following the prestigious culinary Meccas The French Laundry, Domaine Chandon, Terra, Auberge du Soleil, Tra Vigne, and Cafe Beaujolais.

Built as a house in 1864 by General Mariano Vallejo for his daughter Natalia and her husband Atilla Haraszthy, the building was purchased, renovated, and added on to in 1994 by well-known housing renovator and contractor Suzanne Brangham. Natalia's penchant for entertaining and hospitality have been revived. Locals have known this house for years as "The Pink House," which it no longer is. The bar served as Natalia's bedroom when she was trying to escape the second-floor ghost. It is now decorated with contemporary paintings by Rod Knutson and with mosaic tables.

As you drive into the circular driveway or into the parking lots on either side of the house, you begin to get a glimpse of the century-old climbing roses that seem to branch out from the yellow exterior walls and shade patio dining and the half-acre garden. While the decor is primarily French Country, bits of

BABY SPINACH AND FRISÉE SALAD
from Michael Dotson, Craig Miller, and Tim Farfan of Heirloom

4 cups baby spinach
2 medium-sized heads of frisée
2 red Anjou pears
½ lb bellwether Carmody cheese
½ cup sliced natural almonds
1 oz white balsamic vinegar
3 oz virgin olive oil
1 small shallot, minced
salt, freshly ground pepper, and sugar

Before you begin, remove cheese from refrigerator and place in a cool spot to begin coming to room temperature. Wash and dry spinach and frisée and keep refrigerated. To toast almonds, place on a cookie sheet in a preheated 400 ° oven and bake for 7 minutes or until they just begin to turn light brown around the edges.

While this is happening, brown 1 tsp of butter in a sauté pan large enough to hold the almonds. When almonds are ready, add to sauté pan and toss with salt, pepper, and sugar in equal portions until well seasoned. Spread on cookie sheet to cool.

For vinaigrette, whisk together vinegar, virgin olive oil, and shallot and season with salt and pepper to taste.

To assemble salad, put spinach and frisée in a large bowl. Cut pears into wedges, remove cores, and thinly slice, adding to salad. Gently toss with vinaigrette. Taste and season with salt and pepper if needed. Divide salad evenly among four 10-inch salad plates and garnish with the almonds and thinly sliced triangles of the cheese. Serves 4.

Suzanne's humor creep in, like the dog footprints painted on the hardwood floors leading into the kitchen door. (Note that Suzanne has built Sonoma's first cooking school, Ramekins, a rammed-earth building, just west of the General's Daughter.)

Chef Joe Vitale, formerly at the Madrona Manor, presents organically grown local produce, the finest naturally grown local meats and fish, and Sonoma cheeses in his Sonoma Cuisine, obviously influenced by Mediterranean and Southwest flairs. The menu changes daily and ranges from salmon-corn cakes or crisp buttermilk and cornmeal onion rings with lemon-pepper aioli to grilled filet mignon with alderwood-smoked tomatoes, rack of lamb, artichoke mashed potatoes, risotto with grilled salmon, or a simple and bountiful hamburger. Prices range from $8.50 for the grilled Bradley Ranch hamburger to $23.00 for the grilled filet mignon. A large Caesar salad with killer croutons and Reggiano Parmesan cheese is a bargain at $7.50, with a smaller version at $4.75. No wonder locals hang out here.

Fine points: Reservations are advised. Although the restaurant seats 200 inside the various old parlors and out on the patios, you always feel as if you are part of an intimate occasion. Full bar. Nearly ninety wines, many from Sonoma, complete the wine list, and fourteen are available by the glass.

❧ *The General's Daughter Restaurant, 400 West Spain Street, Sonoma 95476; phone (707) 938–4004; fax (707) 938–4099. Open 11:30 A.M.–2:30 P.M. for lunch Monday–Saturday, 5:30–10:00 P.M. daily for dinner, and 11:00 A.M.–2:30 P.M. for Sunday brunch. MasterCard and Visa. Wheelchair-accessible up ramp on east side.*

RAMEKINS brings nationally known chefs to Sonoma to teach home chefs in the most pleasant surroundings possible. Suzanne Brangham's Ramekins Cooking School invites anyone who wants to add to their culinary skills to come visit and learn. The new rammed-earth building includes an elegant bed and breakfast, as well as kitchens, dining rooms, and special-events space. Culinary classes cost from $30 to $50, or $65 for classes that include dinner. Ramekins B&B rates range from $125 to $195 and include a fabulous breakfast created by the resident chef. Ask for a new class catalog.

❧ *Ramekins, 450 West Spain Street, Sonoma 95476; phone (707) 933–0450; fax (707) 933–0451; e-mail info@ramekins.com; Web site www.ramekins.com. MasterCard, Visa, and American Express.*

On the south side of West Spain Street and across from On a Lark, notice La Casita Adobe, at 143 West Spain Street. Also known as the Jones Adobe, La Casita is the lone survivor of several modest adobe residences built by Salvador Vallejo in the 1840s.

In 1948 Gregory and Harriet Jones bought the run-down adobe and meticulously restored the building, removing the wood sheathing over the adobe by hand and laying the floor tiles themselves. After Mr. Jones's death, Mrs. Jones deeded La Casita to the Sonoma League for Historic Preservation in 1980, with the right to live there until her death. Harriet Jones died in January 1996, at age ninety-six. La Casita, as it stands today with the American flag flying, has been called "a lasting tribute to Greg and Harriet's love affair with Sonoma."

At 171 West Spain Street, you will notice the beautiful Thistle Dew Inn, magnificently located for those looking for pleasant accommodations close to the Plaza. The back of the house was built in 1869 and the front in 1905. Norma and Larry Barnett added on and redecorated this classic Sonoma Victorian in 1990 and reopened it as a bed and breakfast with fabulous food. (See Chapter 6, Where to Stay in Sonoma Valley.)

FIRST STREET WEST

One block up First Street West from Spain Street is the DEPOT PARK MUSEUM, in Depot Park and across from Depot Hotel Restaurant. Originally the Depot was located in the Plaza, where the Sonoma Valley Railroad terminated—much to the chagrin of many Sonomans who felt the Plaza had been turned into a railroad yard, turntable and all. So in 1890 the Depot was moved here. It served as the depot for what became the Northwestern Pacific Railway until the railroad stopped serving Sonoma, when the City of Sonoma acquired the property.

The Sonoma Valley Historical Society developed plans to restore this classic depot and create a park. In 1976, while the restoration was in progress, the Depot burned, apparently the work of an arsonist. After a successful fundraising campaign, the Depot was completely rebuilt according to the original plans. It opened in 1978 as the Depot Museum. Managed by the Historical Society, the museum and its railroad cars contain a terrific collection of historic Sonoma memorabilia. *❧ Depot Park Museum, 270 First Street West, Sonoma 95476; phone (707) 938–1762. Open 1:00–4:30 P.M. Wednesday–Sunday. Donations welcomed. Wheelchair-accessible.*

The DEPOT HOTEL RESTAURANT was built in 1870 of stone from General Vallejo's quarries as a three-room home and has a colorful history. Owner Giacoma Mazza, one of the first stonemasons to come to Sonoma from Italy, turned the living room into a saloon.

In 1890 the San Francisco and North Pacific Railroad purchased the Sonoma Valley Railroad and extended the tracks adjacent to what was the saloon. When the railroad station was built across the street, the railway company bought the Depot Saloon and added a kitchen to serve passengers. Later it added eight rooms upstairs, calling it the Northwestern Depot Hotel. For seventeen years it served robust Italian dinners to Sonoma residents. Then, in 1923, it again became a private residence.

After some years of restoration, the Depot Hotel was again opened in 1974 as a restaurant. Michael and Gia Ghilarducci purchased it in 1985 and moved in upstairs with their children, in an old Italian tradition. A native of San Francisco's North Beach and Little Italy, Master Chef Ghilarducci began cooking at age eleven in his father's restaurant and has been cooking ever since. His menu of Northern Italian cuisine highlights locally produced meats and poultry, seafood, bread, cheeses, and vegetables; it also reflects his classic French and Italian training.

Gia usually greets you as you enter the charming barroom, decorated in white and blue. Even locals are struck on each visit by the view through the large windows of the classic Italian garden and pool with Roman fountain. The dining rooms are one step up to the right. The Main Dining Room suggests comfortable formality in burgundy and rose, and the Garden Room opens onto the garden and pool—ask for a window table here.

Now that you are here, you can tell by the aromas that Chef Ghilarducci has talent. While his Northern Italian food bears a California flair, the food is always reliable and filling. No cutesy cuisine tastes here. The menu includes heart-healthy choices. Lunch choices range from a huge hamburger or cured Italian ham and Sonoma Jack cheese on French bread, $6.75, to hand-stuffed tortellini, $8.25, and green-peppercorn steak of filet mignon sautéed with cream and white wine, $16.00. Pastas cost from $8.50 to $9.25. Our favorite is the vongole-clams (it is occasionally offered as a special) and Ravioli al Bosco (round ravioli stuffed with shiitake mushrooms, herbs, and spices, and sautéed with white wine, shallots, garlic, and fresh mushrooms), each at $9.95. Salads and desserts range from $3.50 to $4.50—$8.00 for a large Caesar. Ducktrap River salmon and completely vegetarian dishes are also available.

Check out the sidebars for a few tempting recipes from Chef Ghilarducci. He is especially generous with his recipes, and he presented them to us in highly usable form for the home cook. It was very hard to choose from the many he supplied. Our two top choices are in the sidebars on pages 90 and 91.

 Fine points: The Depot Hotel's wine list received the *Wine Spectator* magazine's Award of Excellence in 1992, 1993, and 1994. It features Sonoma Valley and Carneros wines by the glass or bottle. The Depot Hotel has a very special dinner and party on July 4, which also assures you prime viewing of Sonoma's unusually good fireworks. Get on the newsletter mailing list. Wine and beer only.

Depot Hotel Restaurant, 241 First Street West, Sonoma 95476; phone (707) 938–2980. Open for lunch 11:30 A.M.–2:00 P.M. Monday–Friday, open for dinner 5:00–9:30 P.M. Wednesday–Sunday. MasterCard and Visa. Only barroom and patio are wheelchair-accessible. No hotel rooms here!

FRITTATA ALLA VERDURA
from Chef Ghilarducci, Depot Hotel Restaurant

3 Tbs extra-virgin olive oil	*6 oz fresh mushrooms, sliced*
6 eggs, beaten	*2 bell peppers, seeded and diced*
½ lb zucchini, diced	*½ lb fresh spinach, blanched and chopped*
salt and pepper	*4 oz Sonoma Jack cheese, grated*

Heat oil in 14-inch skillet over high heat. Sauté the first three vegetables until cooked, but still firm. Add the spinach and sauté to warm through. Add salt, pepper, and the beaten eggs. Stir and cook mixture over medium heat until firm enough to loosen from the pan, and flip over. After turning, top with the cheese. Cook 2–3 minutes more, until the center is done, but still slightly soft. Cut into six wedges and serve at once. Serves 6. (This recipe is already rather low in cholesterol, since it is only one egg per person; but to reduce cholesterol further, two of the six eggs may be replaced with four egg whites.)

Now come back down First Street West, pass the Sonoma Hotel, and cross Spain Street to **RISTORANTE PIATTI**, inside El Dorado Hotel. This restaurant is one of the several Piatti created by Claude Rouas and Group (L'Etoile, Auberge du Soleil). What distinguishes this Piatti from others is the gorgeous patio courtyard off the dining room—and its nestling within the El Dorado Hotel. On many occasions we have wished that we could just move in here or that someone would take care of our interior patio this well. When Chili Kohlenberg owned the El Dorado, she added a lovely swimming pool and poolside rooms. Since she sold the building to the Rouas Group, the care and atmosphere have continued to improve toward perfection.

You may enter Ristorante Piatti either through the El Dorado lobby door on First Street West (two steps up) or by the doorway on Spain Street (wheelchair-accessible). The dining room is open and light, with California/Southwest decor built upon the Mexican floor tiles and stucco barricades. Most of the flashy cooking and pizza baking are done at the kitchen end of the dining room. The service is exceptionally friendly, even comical sometimes.

As soon as you are seated, fresh breads appear with a saucer of the best olive oil–garlic dipping mixture we have tasted. We would be happy with just it and a salad. Guests rave about Chef Jude Wilmoth's saltimbocca alla Romana, veal scallopini with prosciutto, mozzarella, polenta, sage, and lemon. The soup is always interesting, the daily pizza specials are unusual for their fresh vegetables and meats, and the Raviolone di Zucca con Burro e Salvia are filled with butternut squash and fontina. Some locals order the Risotto del Giorno, no matter what it is. Recently we had the best salmon salad anywhere for $12.50.

Fine points: Any table is a good one at Piatti. But, while the tables near the patio windows are most attractive, they tend to get overly warm in hot summer weather. The restaurant has a full bar with television.

Ꟑ *Ristorante Piatti, 405 First Street West, Sonoma 95476; phone (707) 996–2351; fax (707) 996– 3148. Open 11:30 A.M.–10:00 P.M. Sunday–Thursday, 11:30 A.M.– 11:00 P.M. Friday–Saturday. MasterCard, Visa, and American Express. Wheelchair-accessible, through Spain Street entrance.*

> ## RED PEPPER AIOLI
> ### *from Chef Ghilarducci, Depot Hotel Restaurant*
>
> *2 egg yolks*
> *6 cloves garlic*
> *¼ tsp cayenne*
> *1 tsp paprika*
> *1½ cups extra-virgin olive oil*
> *salt and white pepper*
>
> Beat the egg yolks until smooth and lemon-colored. Then add the garlic, cayenne, and paprika. Slowly beat in the olive oil, a trickle at a time, until a smooth, shiny emulsion has formed. Add the salt and white pepper to taste. Serve at room temperature.
>
> This aioli is great for dipping Sonoma French or Basque bread, or on crab cakes or sandwiches.

Originally the building in which Ristorante Piatti is located was part of a one-story adobe built with Indian labor for Salvador Vallejo in the mid-1840s. Salvador ran into his usual financial troubles, never completed the interior, and had to sell it at a sheriff's sale to pay his debts in 1850. Mayor George Miller bought the building and used it briefly as a city hall. Then he turned it into the EL DORADO HOTEL and built a second story over the adobe ground floor. In 1858 Miller sold the building to Cumberland College, a Presbyterian boarding school for nice young men and women from around the West and some Sonoma day students. Cumberland stayed at this site until 1866.

Camille Aguillon, a French vintner and Sonoma winemaker, purchased the building, lived upstairs, and ran part of his business from the first floor. In 1890 it was reestablished as a hotel, first called the City Hotel and then again the El Dorado, under the ownership of Mr. and Mrs. Leonido

> ## LEMON CREAM SAUCE
> ### *from Ristorante Piatti*
>
> 13 oz heavy cream
> 1 lemon, zest and juice
> ½ cup grated parmesan cheese
> ⅛ tsp white pepper
> ½ tsp kosher salt
>
> Bring all ingredients to a boil and strain through a fine strainer. Pour immediately over ravioli or other pasta.

Quartaroli. The Italian country cuisine was extremely popular with Sonomans and San Francicans under both the Quartarolis and their successors, John and Theresa Merlo, and, in turn, their daughter-in-law Marie Merlo.

Following the 1906 earthquake, the badly damaged El Dorado was restored with a stucco facade without the grace of the original style. Sonoma building historian James Beauchamp ("Beach") Alexander has called it "an architectural disaster." The Spain Street side of the El Dorado was an open breezeway until Marie Merlo enclosed it to accommodate the Sonoma Kiwanis, who held dinner meetings there from the 1920s through 1981.

Upon Marie Merlo's death, a local developer purchased the building. Sonoma architect Remo Patri used an 1875 rendering of the building to draw plans for reconstruction to its near-original look. The restoration included a new kitchen, the landscaped patio garden, and modern hotel rooms upstairs. The owner was ordered not to remove the remaining historic adobe wall, but he tore it down anyway, claiming that the original adobe bricks were stolen.

That developer went bankrupt, and the hotel was sold to Chili Kohlenberg and then to Claude Rouas and his group of investors. The El Dorado is now a gem on the Plaza with romantic, luxurious, yet reasonably priced hotel rooms upstairs, a swimming pool, and Piatti Restaurant.

Jeannie Dixon just loves being at her EARTHWORKS at the El Dorado corner, both "to make friends" and to offer "things we would love to wear or give." Specializing in the most elegant Sonoma County and Berkeley designers' work, Earthworks has quickly become popular with visitors and locals alike who search for high quality, and full price range, pottery, jewelry, blown glass, and paintings. Artists whose "uncommon" work is represented include jewelry makers Britta Schomer, Anne Hellman, John Bagley, Shay Harris, Mylette Welch, Zak Zaikine, Kris Patzlaft, and Sticks' hand-painted wood-framed mirrors and accessories.

❦ *Earthworks, 403 First Street West, Sonoma 95476; phone (707) 935-0290. Open 10:00 A.M.–9:00 P.M. daily summer; 10:00 A.M.–6:00 P.M. Sunday–Thursday, 10:00 A.M.–9:00 P.M. Friday–Saturday winter. MasterCard, Visa, and American Express. Wheelchair-accessible.*

Another place you might want to visit in this building is WINE COUNTRY GIFTS. After running the La Quinta Hotel gift shop in Palm Desert for three years, England native Shirley Broughton returned to Sonoma and took over this shop in 1992. Wine Country Gifts carries an attractive supply of wine-related gifts for your home or for presents. Hot-air balloon ornaments are very popular, as are wine-bottle collars, party napkins, silver corks, and ceramic teapots. And, while they aren't exactly wine-country products, we can always rely upon Shirley to have a good supply of English Christmas Crackers at reasonable prices.

✤✧ *Wine Country Gifts, 407 First Street West, Sonoma 95476; phone (707) 996–3453; Web site www.winecountry-gifts.com. Open 10:00 A.M.–6:00 P.M. daily. MasterCard, Visa, American Express, and Diners Club. Wheelchair-accessible, through Ristorante Piatti and then through the El Dorado Hotel lobby.*

THE COFFEE GARDEN is an early-morning gathering place for locals and visitors alike, primarily because it is the only local cafe whose outdoor tables face the morning sun. While the interior part of this cafe in the Salvador Vallejo building is small, the sumptuous garden of 400 native and other flowering plants in the back of the building is where locals like to gather. One of the oldest (160 years) fig trees in California shades the patio. When you walk through the gift-shop part of the cafe, notice the heavy beams above and adobe brick walls in what once served as a throughway for the horses and carriages heading for the stables that were located in the rear of the adobe. Local teenagers and young adults love to hang out at the tables on the sidewalk in front, sipping coffee and watching the human parade go by.

While most people agree the espresso could be better, generous canisters of interesting, freshly brewed coffees are free for you to refill your cup. The sandwiches and salads are good and reliable. Our favorite edibles here are the exceptional scones in the bakery case. Daily soups are available with a mini-baguette or served in a French-bread bowl. Prices range from $3.25 for a bowl of soup, $3.95 for a house green salad, and $5.95 for an albacore-tuna salad to $6.50 for a smoked-salmon-fillet sandwich. A bagel and cream cheese is just $1.50 and Italian sodas cost $1.95. Try the cheese melts with chicken, tuna, or the Reuben ($5.50–$6.50). All this and you can take whatever you order to the tables in front or in back among the most colorful flowers in town.

✤✧ *The Coffee Garden, 421 First Street West, Sonoma 95476; phone (707) 996–6645. Open 7:00 A.M.–10:00 P.M. Friday–Saturday, 7:00 A.M.–9:00 P.M. Sunday–Thursday. MasterCard, Visa, and Diners Club. Wheelchair-accessible.*

Captain Salvador Vallejo, brother of Mexican commander Mariano G. Vallejo, built this adobe-brick building in the 1840s. The redwood upstairs was added in 1851 by the Masons.

French winemaker Camille Aguillon bought the building and turned the rear into a winery with sales in the front. He prospered until his death in 1906. Since then the building has housed many different businesses and families, from saloons to liquor stores (until Prohibition) and Adobe Drug (now on West Napa Street).

A Sonoma must-see is located in another famous site, the Ruggles Building. Dick Foorman and Gene Quindt originally established SIGN OF THE BEAR and built it into a dignified kitchen store, similar to but much more personal than Williams-Sonoma. M. F. K. Fisher was a dear friend of Dick and Gene and relied upon them to supply her with kitchen goodies in emergencies. The popular but untrue rumor still has it that Chuck Williams actually began his first store at this site.

The Ruggles Building was originally known as the Camille Aguillon Building, because it was built by Aguillon to store wine from his winery located in the Salvador Vallejo adobe (described above). The false front to the building was added in the early 1900s, and a loft was built later.

Daniel Ruggles Sr. started a five-and-dime store in the building in 1931 and bought it in the early 1940s. Daniel Ruggles Jr., longtime city councilman, continued the dime store with all the little glass trays full of goodies. He added sheet music and instruments (which he also rented). Eventually Ruggles switched places with Sign of the Bear, and later he turned over all the stores to the successful Havleks.

Steve Havlek bought Sign of the Bear from Dick and Gene in 1991 and quickly created an even better "general store" for gourmets. Having grown up in Sonoma (his mother, Beth LaBelle, owns The Kaboodle down the street), Steve worked for Cost Plus for several years and brings modern display, wares, and systems to the store, to say nothing of his enthusiasm and love for what he is doing. Now Steve and his wife, Laura, have expanded Sign of the Bear into all of the Ruggles Building storefronts—but no matter how much space they have, it isn't enough. You always feel as if you're there just as the cartons of merchandise arrive. And you are.

Here you will find the perfect garlic press, extra interesting designs of kitchen utensils you are going to use anyway, Emile Henry and Italian ceramic cookware, oddball German ice trays, decorative placemats, paella pans, ceramic cookie molds, madeleine pans, aprons, and a marvelous selection of cookbooks. Perhaps an iron wine cage will do, or iron pot racks, or French tablecloths. Of course there's lots of fantastic cookware and bakeware. You'll find even more treasures, from charlotte molds and leftse sticks to larding needles and napkin rings. Many locals rely on Sign of the Bear. We do.

❧ *Sign of the Bear, 435 First Street West, Sonoma 95476; phone (707) 996–3722. Open 10:00 A.M.–6:00 P.M. daily. MasterCard, Visa, and Discover. Wheelchair-accessible.*

JUDY THEO LEHNER, our Hill Guides cover artist, has moved her RED WOLF STUDIO closer to the plaza. Just walk down the alley between Sign of the Bear and Fairmont Gallery to 134 Church Street. We promise a visual and emotional treat as you experience Judy's bold expressions.

❧ *Judy Theo Lehner's Red Wolf Studio, 134 Church Street, Sonoma 95476; phone (707) 996–5111. Open weekends or by appointment. MasterCard, Visa, and American Express. Wheelchair-accessible.*

Just south of Sign of the Bear, Manette Fairmont's most pleasant FAIRMONT GALLERY of "nationally respected local artists" sports a sign in the door window: WELCOME TO RELAX AND BROWSE. How refreshing! This is a highly respected gallery featuring watercolors, oils, pastels, and works of mixed media, and an inviting green wooden rocking chair on the sidewalk in front.

❧ *Fairmont Gallery, 447 First Street West, Sonoma 95476; phone (707) 996–2667. Open noon–5:00 P.M. daily. MasterCard and Visa. Wheelchair-accessible.*

The first story of the Fairmont Gallery building was built in the 1860s and, like the El Dorado and the Ruggles Building, was owned by Camille Aguillon and then by his daughter and son-in-law Leonard Heggie. The second story was actually another house moved from a nearby lot and lifted to a position on top of the first story. For more than forty years, it was called the Hi-Lo House and served as a laundry as well as an employment office for Chinese labor (used to plant early vineyards). Those businesses were founded by Hop Wo and later run by popular Charley Hoy.

One evening in the 1890s, a man named Marion Patrick argued with the elderly Chinese manager over laundry and began hitting the old man. Patrick was shot dead by a young guest who fired from the back room and then vanished. The Chinese manager was removed to Santa Rosa to prevent a lynching, but was soon cleared of any crime.

During World War I the building served as a boardinghouse and restaurant. In 1933 Daniel Ruggles Sr. and his family moved into the building, as their residence. They bought it from the Heggies during World War II. It is now owned by Charles and Margaret Ruggles, who live on the upper floor. The duplex behind the building is owned by Larry and Judy Theo Lehner.

In the next shop down First Street West, THE KABOODLE, Beth LaBelle presides over the most incredible emporium of stuffed animals, dolls, dried flowers, carved Italian ornaments, birdcages, and other fabulous things you will ever encounter. For San Francisco travelers of a certain age, this is the Podesta Baldocchi of dried stuff. And then there are the stacks of Jimmy Durante tapes on the counter. Be sure to check out Beth's new outdoor garden section along the Kaboodle's north side.

This is one store that has genuinely grown to meet its popularity. It is jam-packed with goods. There's just more and more of everything every year. Beth simply loves what she does, and you will, too.

The New Brunswick native's mother believed that her daughters should be schooled in the "home arts." "We were all supposed to be Martha Stewarts," LaBelle says. Beth overdid it, to the pleasure of everyone who crosses The Kaboodle's threshold.

The Batto Building, in which The Kaboodle is located, was built of glazed bricks by Fred Batto in 1919 on the lot in front of the adobe that housed the original Swiss Hotel. One of the first tenants in this part of the three-section building was the First National Bank of Sonoma, of which Batto was president, and Batto & Sons Grocery. Beth LaBelle says the bank's vault is still under her floor, and you can see the early bank's tin ceiling in The Kaboodle.

Fine points: The Kaboodle has been praised and recommended by newspapers and magazines all over the United States. You simply have to experience it yourself. We suggest that you plan a little time to browse—but you still won't see everything. (One thing you do see is a lot of men out in front waiting for their wives. Beth has graciously put chairs and benches out in front to accommodate such deserted visitors.) And remember that the general theme of romantic, eclectic merchandise changes, and the whole store takes on a new personality, by the season. So if you are here in the summer, come back to see The Kaboodle at Thanksgiving and Christmas.
❧ *The Kaboodle, 453 First Street West, Sonoma 95476; phone (707) 996–9500. Open 10:30 A.M.–5:30 P.M. daily. MasterCard and Visa. Wheelchair-accessible.*

SONOMA SPA is Sonoma's downtown spa (as opposed to the Sonoma Mission Inn Spa in Boyes Hot Springs and the Kenwood Inn and Spa in Kenwood). As a self-billed "Oasis of Tranquillity on the Sonoma Plaza," Sonoma Spa features a complete range of natural and rejuvenating spa treatments including body mud treatments, herbal facials, full body massages, and spa packages. When you go into Sonoma Spa, the employees explain everything to you in a nonselling, friendly way and cheerfully give you brochures and prices.
❧ *Sonoma Spa, 457 First Street West, Sonoma 95476; phone (707) 939–8770.*

Open 9:00 A.M.–9:00 P.M. daily. MasterCard, Visa, and American Express. Wheelchair-accessible.

Between Sonoma Spa and Eraldi's, the Masonic Building retrofit for earthquake protection was completed in 1997, and Glendale Federal Bank, which sponsors the Sonoma Film Festival, moved its office. This building was built by the Masons in 1909 in Italian Renaissance Revival style and is now the home of Steiner's Tavern.

STEINERS TAVERN is one of the few real Sonoma bars left over from the old days. Its green swinging doors make it look like a shootout might happen at high noon and everyone inside should be wearing spurs. Steiners has actually been cleaned up a bit and is popular with several generations of patrons. This is a good place to go for local gossip and a good, stiff drink.

Fine points: Be sure to follow the new arrow on the street and turn your car right onto Napa Street after you come out of Steiners. The police watch here.

🍇 *Steiners Tavern, 465 First Street West, Sonoma 95476; phone (707) 996–3812. Open all hours except from 2:00 to 6:00 A.M. No credit cards. Wheelchair-accessible.*

Next you come to **ERALDI'S MEN'S WEAR**, the only place in Sonoma for classic Sonoma men's clothing, from good old Levi's and overalls to patterned sweaters, boots, and shoes. Eraldi's has outfitted several generations of Sonomans, beginning in 1922 at the current site of The Kaboodle, from 1928 in the Duhring building, and since 1960 in this location. Don Eraldi and his son Dan both work in the store every day, know the old-timers' preferences and sizes, and treat everyone with great respect and hospitality. They actually carry Levi's up to size 50-inch waist with 30-inch inseam.

The Eraldis carry Ben Davis shirts and pants in more colors than our son ever saw in Los Angeles. While they know which farmers always get which shirts, they were amazed when kids picked up the fad. Among the staples the Eraldis keep in stock for the community are Pendleton shirts; Clark's, Rockport, Ecco, Teva, Birkenstock, Red Wings, Florsheim, and Timberland shoes; and Ducks Unlimited caps, shirts, and sweatshirts. You can also pick up Tommy Bahama and other quality Hawaiian shirts, and, if you absolutely have to, a shirt, tie, and sports coat.

🍇 *Eraldi's Men's Wear, 475 First Street West, Sonoma 95476; phone (707) 996–2013. Open 9:00 A.M.–6:00 P.M. Monday–Saturday, 11:00 A.M.–5:00 P.M. Sunday, April–December 31. MasterCard, Visa, American Express, and Discover. Wheelchair-accessible.*

Next door to Eraldi's, Jill Lury and Josh Massie's BATH FACTORY is an out-growth of their quickly successful bath-products catalog business. Jill served as manager of the Sonoma Mission Inn and Spa and at the Greenhouse in Dallas, Texas. So they know baths.

Josh delights passersby by clicking his bubble maker and sending lovely bubbles drifting over the sidewalk and street whenever he feels the whim. Everyone walks in this shop smiling.

Try their famous Fango Mud Bath Powder, olive oil soaps you can cut to the size you want, Fairy Dust from the Utah Desert, Exotic Soaks, Sea Salt Soaks, bubble bath salts, and Vegetable Mud Mousse. You, too, can join their Frequent Bathers Club.

✤☙ *The Bath Factory, 481 First Street West, Sonoma 95476; phone (707) 935–5903. Open 10:00 A.M.–6:00 P.M. daily. MasterCard, Visa, American Express, and Discover. Not wheelchair-accessible.*

SANTA FE TRADING COMPANY is the tiniest store in Sonoma and sells inter-esting American Indian and Southwestern jewelry and artifacts, "wholesale to the public." Kaye Rosenthal features the work of Zuni, Hopi, and Zia Indians, hand-painted tiles, headdresses, and Acoma pottery. You will also see bows and arrows, tomahawks, carvings, Hopi kachinas, and fetishes. The big news here is: Everything is always wholesale and half the marked price. (In this case, that does *not* mean that it's overpriced and then marked down.)

✤☙ *Santa Fe Trading Company, 481 First Street West, Sonoma 95476; phone (707) 996–7523. Open 11:00 A.M.–5:00 P.M. daily, March–December, Friday–Monday January–February. MasterCard, Visa, and American Express. Not wheelchair-accessible.*

LEGENDS, "A gallery of American Artisans," was founded by Michael and Diane Michlig, whose departures from corporate America in preference to doing exactly what they want to do has been publicized in the media through-out the country. Both former Sears executives, they took early buyouts and turned their lives to wood carving and finding artists for their gallery. Legends is a family business, with two kids in college and a golden retriever, Kurby, who regularly does tricks in the store and has her own fan club. Many locals love the Michligs's story—and their gallery. The sign on the door warns: OPEN—COZY AND DANGEROUS PLACE TO SHOP.

Legends offers the finest in handmade leather bags, hand-carved wooden puzzles and boxes, unusual laminated cutting boards, taxi wallets, copper wind chimes, ornate nightlights, birdhouses, Barking Dog Wind Machines, Urban Art handcrafted "Watch Craft" watches, and a variety of cheerful paintings.

Whimsical metal dogs greet you along with the live one and the Raku clay cats (no live one).

᠕᠗ *Legends, 483 First Street West, Sonoma 95476; phone (707) 939–8100. Open 10:00 A.M.–6:00 P.M. Monday–Saturday, 11:00 A.M.–5:30 P.M. Sunday. MasterCard and Visa. Wheelchair-accessible.*

The LEESE-FITCH ADOBE was built in 1841–42 by Jacob Leese as the east wing of a U-shaped trading post and upstairs residence then facing on West Napa Street. This building was the second building on Sonoma Plaza, following General Vallejo's billiard parlor on the east side. The house was looted while Leese was imprisoned at Sutter's Fort during the Bear Flag Revolt. To finance a trading trip to China, Leese sold the building to Vallejo in 1848. Vallejo promptly sold it to his sister-in-law, Josefa Carrillo de Fitch, who in turn rented it to General Persifer Smith (the American military governor of California) and his wife. Smith's second-in-command, Colonel Joseph Hooker, had the building painted, the roof reshingled, and a fireplace added.

After the army left in 1852, the building served as St. Mary's Academy, a young ladies' boarding school, and then became a hotel, the Fitch House. Much

LEESE-FITCH ADOBE (1840)

of the building was eventually torn down to make room for new buildings. Like many buildings around the Plaza, the Leese-Fitch Adobe was purchased in the 1970s by the Leonard Deterts.

MISSION BELLES ladies' apparel store on the corner is a wonderfully comforting addition to Sonoma. Owners Claire Samaras and Linda Gavron used their health-care backgrounds of concern and support to bring us feminine and soft clothing for "mature women" along with '40s retro suits, Cape Cod designs, and Taryn DeChellis and Tina Davis creations. Don't miss Sonoma artist Don Nix's jewelry.

Most important, Claire, Linda, and Jennifer, who has worked here ever since Champagne Taste occupied the space, provide truly old-fashioned personal service in a nonpushy way. Remember when store owners and their staff actually helped us? Well, folks, you can relive that luxury here.

🌺 *Mission Belles, 497 First Street West, Sonoma 95476; phone (707) 938–8880; fax (707) 938–8891. Open 10:00 A.M.–6:00 P.M. daily. MasterCard, Visa, American Express. Wheelchair- accessible.*

Now, turn right around the corner of Mission Belles onto Napa Street, and walk a few steps to some more charming shops.

The ANTIQUES CENTER COLLECTIVE is truly a collective, not just in name only, managed by collectors and dealers who have their own displays and partake in sharing knowledge and helping you find what you are looking for. Many of these dealers have had independent shops and have found that working together and sharing responsibility is better than going it alone. You can find almost anything here, at a wide range of prices.

🌺 *Antiques Center Collective, 120 West Napa Street, Sonoma 95476; phone (707) 996–9947. Open 11:00 A.M.–5:00 P.M. daily. MasterCard and Visa. Wheelchair-accessible entry, but the aisles are a little narrow.*

This FIRE HOUSE uses controlled heat, and no red engines show up. This is a great pottery center where you paint cups, vases, plates, and loads of other objects, and they fire it for you. In the back-of-the-shop loft, you can select nude furniture to paint with your own designs. It's fun and reasonable, at $6.00 an hour plus the cost of the piece you choose. There are also special birthday-party, tea-party, and girls'-night-out rates. Great idea.

🌺 *Fire House, 124 West Napa Street, Sonoma 95476; phone (707) 935–6507. Open mostly 10:00 A.M.–6:00 P.M., later Thursday–Friday. MasterCard, Visa, and American Express. Wheelchair-accessible.*

Now walk back to the corner and cross Napa Street—in the crosswalk, please! Even in this smallish town, crossing this main thoroughfare can be dangerous.

The building that takes up the whole southwest corner of First Street West and Napa Street was called the Feed Store, and before that the Griffith Block. Fifteen years ago it really was a country feed store, where you could buy straw and hay for your horses, alfalfa for whomever, and baby chicks for your kids. A cold breeze usually blew through from one street to the other. Now the building has been "developed" into interesting boutiques and restaurants.

On the south side of Napa Street just west of the Plaza, walk a few extra steps to HARVEST, an emporium of "affordably priced" American country style furniture and home accessories. Craig Miller and Karsten Iwers, whose Harvest on Sacramento Street in San Francisco's Pacific Heights has been tremendously sucessful, bring country to the country, in a space many visitors frequented in its previous incarnation as Zambezi Trading Company.

You will find lamps, rugs, tea towels, interesting wood furniture, feather beds, candles, silhouette hooks, a wide choice of picture frames, and an ever-changing array of little decorative novelties. Be sure to visit their Sonoma Hotel and Heirloom Restaurant a block up First Street West.

❧ *Harvest, 107 West Napa Street, Sonoma 95476; phone (707) 933–9044. Open 10:00 A.M.–6:00 P.M. daily. MasterCard, Visa, American Express, and Discover. Wheelchair-accessible.*

Right on the corner of West Napa Street and First Street West is newish SEBASTIANI ON THE SQUARE, the retail shop and wine bar of Sylvia Sebastiani and her daughter, Maryann Sebastiani Cuneo. This elegant room sells high-end Mediterranean heritage linens, ceramics, and collectibles, and the wine bar serves, surprise, Sebastiani Sonoma Cask wines. You will also find Lesley Fay Fine Foods with Sebastiani labels, olive oil with blood oranges, and the best of local hand-painted pottery . Don't miss the interesting oak bar, terra-cotta walls, and green slate tile floors, all presenting a calming, cooling, elegant ambience.

You can even take the Sebastiani Trolley from here to Sebastiani Sonoma Cask Cellars or just taste and purchase wine here. Sebastiani wines to taste here include Chardonnay, Sangiovese, Merlot, Barbera, Mourvèdre, Zinfandel, Syrah, and Cabernet Sauvignon.

❧ *Sebastiani on the Square, 103 West Napa Street, Sonoma 95476; phone (707) 933–3290; Web site www.Sebastiani.com. Open 10:00 A.M.–5:00 P.M. daily. Tasting fee: $3.50 includes souvenir glass. MasterCard, Visa, and American Express. Wheelchair-accessible.*

Just around the corner from Sebastiani on the Square in this old Feed Store Building is SIENA RED BREWERY & BISTRO, the latest effort to bring micro-brewing to the Sonoma wine country. Formerly the Feed Store, where our children bought baby chicks and feed for them, this spot evolved into the Feed Store Café, another brewery that never quite opened, and now this tasteful sight popular with twenty-thirty-somethings.

Brewmaster and Managing Partner R. J. Trent has completely renovated the restaurant and beer tasting/drinking rooms to look like a cavernous living room with deep leather chairs, rich, dark colors, three large televisions, and free pool tables. Brews range on the light end from Plaza Pale Ale, Hefe-Wheat, and Pale Oatmeal Honey Wheat to Siena Red Ale, I Apologize India Pale Ale, gold medal–winning Breakfast Toasted Ale, and Seven Ring Stout.

Chef Albert Chitwood, formerly of the Mendocino Hotel and Antelope Valley Country Club, has created upscale pub food ranging from Andouille sausage or artichoke and asparagus frittata, eggs Benedict, fondue, and fries with aioli (all under $8.00) to seared Ahi tuna salad ($9.27), Caesar salads ($5.88–$7.88), Mediterranean chopped salad ($6.18), burgers, fish and chips, macaroni and cheese with extra sharp Sonoma cheddar cheese, and a great grilled Ahi tuna sandwich. All this with live music Thursday–Saturday nights.

✥✥ *Siena Red Brewery & Bistro, 529 First Street West, Sonoma 95476; phone (707) 938–1313; fax (707) 939–7147. Open 11:30 A.M.–1:30 A.M. daily, with food served until 11:00 P.M. MasterCard and Visa. Wheelchair-accessible.*

Just down First Street West from the Napa Street corner, don't miss SILVER MOON TRADING COMPANY (formerly Restless Natives), which looks like a Berkeley store in Sonoma, and Kathleen says that as a Berkeley native. Racks of tie-dye clothes line a wall, along with Mexican crinkle clothing, Nepalese and Indian jackets, Balinese and hemp clothing, reusable and scented candles galore, crystals and rocks, incense, jewelry, milagros, lava lamps, angels, tarot cards, and beaded curtains. Silver Moon also carries lots of women's sizes fourteen to twenty.

✥✥ *Silver Moon Trading Company, 539 First Street West, Sonoma 95476; phone (707) 939–6993. Open 11:00 A.M.–6:00 P.M. (until 7:00 P.M. summer) Friday–Saturday. MasterCard and Visa. Wheelchair-accessible.*

Now walk back up to Napa Street and turn right, toward the east. You'll pass the Bank of America, where Sonoma's one deadly holdup occurred in 1995, and arrive at PLAZA LIQUORS. Co-owner Dick Gregory played professional football for the Green Bay Packers before coming to Slownoma. Plaza Liquors is a well-

AHI TUNA SANDWICH WITH
PINEAPPLE MANGO RELISH
from Chef Albert Chitwood and Brewmaster R. J. Trent,
Siena Red Brewery & Bistro

6 poppy seed rolls

¼ cup garlic-lemon aioli

1 beefsteak tomato, sliced into 6 pieces

1 cup baby greens

1¼ lb Ahi tuna loin

2 Tbs cracked black pepper

2 Tbs coriander seed

4 Tbs olive oil

1 cup pineapple mango relish (see below)

Roll tuna loin in mixture of black pepper and coriander seed. Sear tuna loin in olive oil and then cool. Slice tuna loin into 3.5-oz portions. Slice rolls and spread the aioli on the bun bottoms. Place ⅙ cup greens on each bottom, then 1 slice of tomato. Add the tuna slice and top with 2 Tbs of pineapple mango relish. Serves 6.

PINEAPPLE MANGO RELISH

1 cup mango, finely diced

1 cup pineapple, finely diced

2 Tbs red onion, finely diced

½ Tbs jalapeño pepper, finely diced

1 Tbs cilantro, chopped

2 Tbs fresh lime juice

salt and pepper to taste

Combine all ingredients.

known quick stop for many locals, if only to buy a newspaper and say "hi." Local characters work here. Kids love the candy and chip supplies and the sodas in the case next to the cash register. Grown-ups like the good wine selection and prices, the full liquor inventory—including twenty tequilas, seventeen single-malt Scotches, and sixteen different Ravenswood wines—Broadway Market sandwiches, and the friendly chitchat and local stories.

VEGETARIAN POT STICKERS
from Yupa Garrett of Rin's Thai Food

(Yupa and Kathleen sat together at Rin's and worked out this recipe, since Rin's Thai cooks do not cook from recipes. Still try it.)

Ingredients for pot stickers:

½ small cabbage, diced
¼ lb garlic chives, diced finely
1 cup taro root, diced finely
¼ cup dry black mushrooms, soaked and then diced finely
1 clove garlic, finely chopped
½ tsp sugar
½ tsp ground white pepper
1 tsp "lite" soy sauce
1–2 Tbs oil
pinch salt
8 medium-thick square won ton wrappers
4 egg whites

Ingredients for dipping sauce:

1 Tbs Kikkoman soy sauce
1 Tbs flavored vinegar (jalapeño pepper)
1 Tbs dried chili oil
parsley sprigs chopped with onion

Preparation of pot stickers:

Sauté cabbage, garlic chives, taro root, dry black mushrooms, pinch of salt, and garlic in oil until soft. Set aside in bowl and add sugar and white pepper. Lay won ton wrapper flat in the palm of your hand. Paint all 4 edges of wrapper with egg white. Place 1 heaping tsp filling in middle of wrapper. Bring won ton corners together and pinch so that egg white can seal and stick it all together, making a pillow with stuffing. In nonstick pan with tiny bit of oil, place pot sticker upside down so that sealed side is down and rounded side is up. Brown and then put in already steaming steamer until soft to avoid adding oil.

Preparation of dipping sauce:

Mix ingredients.

☙ *Plaza Liquors, 19 West Napa Street, Sonoma 95476; phone (707) 996– 2828. Open 8:30 A.M.–8:30 P.M. Monday–Thursday, 8:30 A.M.–10:00 P.M. Friday–Saturday, 8:30 A.M.–7:30 P.M. Sunday. MasterCard and Visa. Wheelchair-accessible.*

WEST SIDE OF BROADWAY

Turn the corner to the right and head down Broadway, past Great Western Savings and on to KLEIN'S SONOMA MUSIC INC. Local guitar maker Steve Klein and Ed Dufault completely revamped this large store and carefully formed a creative, acoustically sound space for musical instruments and performances in their seventy-seat theater. Cat Austin produces the Women's Performing Arts Series at Klein's.

Following Ruggles Music's final closure in 1997, Steve and Ed have become Sonoma's community music-supply center, renting band instruments and selling guitars, drumsticks, and sheet music. Klein's sells handmade and vintage guitars, as well as beginners' guitars, Irvin Somogyi wood cuttings and guitars, and instrument reeds to stand-up bases.

One of Sonoma's underpublicized treasures, Steve makes about ten guitars a year for musicians such as Joni Mitchell, David Tom, Michael Hedges, Bill Frizell, Joe Walsh, and Lou Reed.

☙ *Klein's Sonoma Music Inc., 521 Broadway, Sonoma 95476; phone (707) 996–2196; fax (707) 935–6665. Open 10:00 A.M.–6:00 P.M. Monday–Saturday. MasterCard, Visa, and American Express. Wheelchair-accessible.*

Don't miss J. POWERS & CO. AMISH FURNISHINGS where longtime Sonomans Jack and Karen Powers offer genuine hand-crafted Amish oak and cherry furniture. Jack says, "We are an outlet for the Amish." It all started on a driving trip through Amish country when the Powers bought a table and chairs and shipped them back to Sonoma. The couple later sold their ornament business and convinced the Amish farmers that they could make enough furniture to sell through a store off the farm. It's our good fortune.

☙ *J. Powers & Co. Amish Furnishing, 529 Broadway, Sonoma 95476; phone (707) 996–0819; fax (707) 996–6798. Open 10:00 A.M.–5:00 P.M. Tuesday–Saturday, or by appointment Sunday–Monday and evenings. MasterCard and Visa. Wheelchair-accessible.*

It's worth it to walk another half-block past Realty World and Morgan Lane Real Estate to get to the next food places and poster store.

RIN'S OF SONOMA THAI FOOD is a Sonoma favorite, located right next to the Post Office. Yupa and Bob Garrett's first Thai restaurant was in San Francisco's Noe Valley. This is their second one, and is Sonoma lucky! Yupa now teaches Thai cooking at Napa Valley College and in private homes.

This tiny restaurant has only seven tables inside (and a few outside in good weather). Large windows look out on Broadway and toward the Sonoma Plaza. The three other small walls are lined with Thai artwork and tapestries and all of Gundlach-Bundschu's hilarious wine posters. Many locals dine here. At lunch the conversation sometimes becomes a group one, including everyone in the place. The tempo is a little hectic but lots of fun. Check out the full-color poster in the window entitled "Eat it or go to bed hungry."

Rin's usually features four or five daily specials, and the Pad Thai is excellent ($5.50). Lunch or dinner specials might include garlic eggplant with pork, onion cakes, varied chicken curries, garlic squid, drunken noodles, or Thai chicken salad. Try the vegetarian pot stickers, so popular on Mondays that locals forced Yupa to make them available every day. There are excellent local wine selections and beers to accompany the food. Be sure to try Rin's convenient new restaurant scheduled to open in 2000 on East Napa Street in the Victorian next to Della Santina's and across from Cafe La Haye.

❧ *Rin's of Sonoma Thai Food, 599 Broadway, Sonoma 95476; phone (707) 938–1462. Open 11:00 A.M.–9:00 P.M. Monday–Saturday, closed Sunday. MasterCard, Visa, American Express, Diners Club, Carte Blanche, and JCB. Wheelchair-accessible.*

ON TRAYS ON BROADWAY replaced DiGioia Catering and Good to Go Take Out Cuisine, where Jim DeJoy headquartered his successful catering business from one storefront and a popular take-out right next door with Charlotte Meyn. (DeJoy was hired by M. F. K. Fisher to cater dinner for Julia Child a few years before Fisher's death, and his ginger snaps were served at her memorial party. He is now purchasing director for the Culinary Institute of America Greystone Restaurant in St. Helena.) Tom Romano and Chef Linda Gilbert bought the business from Jim and continue the high quality.

Linda cooked at the Ross Garden Restaurant for several years and creates fabulous soups and salads. She makes innovative deli sandwiches, including foccacia with turkey or chicken breast and veggie wraps; and caters parties of all sizes, including box lunches, all colorful and playful in character. Linda and Tom raise all their vegetables and herbs in the garden in back of the store. They also offer microbrews and local wines.

❧ *On Trays On Broadway, 603 Broadway, Sonoma 95476; phone (707)*

938–0301; fax (707) 938–9627. Open 7:30 A.M.–6:00 P.M., Monday–Friday, 7:30 A.M.–3:00 P.M. Saturday. MasterCard and Visa. Wheelchair-accessible.

Next door, at SONOMA POSTER CO. AND THE FRAME FACTORY, Chris Mullany sells posters and calendars and will frame anything on the spot. He primarily sells through catalogs but also deals in obscure posters and "will find any poster made in the world."

❧ *Sonoma Poster Co. and The Frame Factory, 605 Broadway, Sonoma 95476; phone (707) 996–2253. Open 9:00 A.M.–5:30 P.M. Monday, 9:00 A.M.–6:00 P.M. Tuesday–Friday, noon–3:00 P.M. Saturday. MasterCard and Visa. Wheelchair-accessible.*

One block south you will find a local favorite, DEUCE, the new creation of Kristin and Peter Stewart of Bear Flag Cafe. The popular Stewarts took over Magliulo's in spring 1998. They hit the road running and have continued to build their following and that of Chef Richard Whipple. Richard features American bistro cuisine, serving lunch appetizers like asparagus salad with creamy shallot vinaigrette or smoked salmon carpaccio with avocado and cream cheese, moving on to entrees such as duck confit with balsamic-scented lentils, grilled salmon with artichoke, fennel, olives, and sliced garlic in a basil broth, or simply a perfect hamburger. Dinner entrees may include onion-crusted chicken with roasted polenta. Prices range from $8 to $12 at lunch and $13 to $18 at dinner. The special, brief bar menu offers burgers, fries, salads, and other light or substantial and sobering fare.

The patio on the south side of Deuce is a delight, and you will find Peter's personally selected wine list to be local and interesting.

Fine points: Excellent parking behind restaurant (around the corner). Full bar.

❧ *Deuce Restaurant, 691 Broadway, Sonoma 95476; phone (707) 996–1031. Open for lunch 11:30 A.M.–2:30 P.M., for dinner 5:00–9:00 P.M. daily. MasterCard, Visa, and Discover. Wheelchair-accessible from back parking lot.*

No matter where you cross Broadway, do it carefully!

EAST SIDE OF BROADWAY

THE WINE RACK SHOP amazes us to imagine that a shop with all this wine stuff and no wine could make it, but Don Whetstone, who has served as cellar master for Gallo, Benziger, and Sebastiani and certainly knows his stuff, does. Don offers every form of wine rack imaginable. A great place for wine chat. You will also find tables made from grapevines, refrigerated wine cabinets, wine-cork trivets and bulletin boards, and any wine accessories he can find.

🌿 *The Wine Rack Shop, 536 Broadway, Sonoma 95476; phone (707) 996–3497. Open 10:00 A.M.–6:00 P.M. Sunday–Wednesday, 10:00 A.M.–8:00 P.M. Thursday–Saturday. MasterCard, Visa, American Express, and Discover. Wheelchair-accessible.*

AVE (ahvay, as in Maria) is a rare gallery of ancient Asian temple carvings and other unusual art works that Sedona, Arizona, transplant Gordon Hall opened here in 1999. A corporate motivational speaker who survived a near-death experience after being hit by a car, Gordon offers elegant and authentic Han, Song, and Ming pieces to help with your home's Feng Shui. Perhaps you will find treasures to awaken your spiritual nature. Gordon's procurer and mentor in the field was a professor of antiquities at Beijing University. Don't miss the stuffed red slipper (as in Dorothy's) at the desk.

🌿 *Ave, 530 Broadway, Sonoma 95476; phone (707) 938–1400; fax (413) 451–6644; e-mail sanada@pacbell.net. Open 9:00 A.M.–5:00 P.M. Thursday– Monday. MasterCard, Visa, and American Express. Wheelchair-accessible.*

We always find a comfort zone at CHANTICLEER BOOKS, which has an excellent collection of used and out-of-print books in all subjects but specializes in art, history, literature, mythology, gardening, and cooking. On inquiring we discovered some rare, signed first editions by M. F. K. Fisher. Stephen Blackmer moved from his charming store down Broadway into this one. Blackmer makes everyone feel comfortable and welcome and encourages browsers. He also buys books. There's always a 50-cent to $5.00 table outside the door that demonstrates the wide range available inside.

This is the Marcy Building, a false-front building dating from the 1880s, when it was built by Gus Marcy to house his plumbing business. The Sonoma League for Historic Preservation worked to preserve these false fronts, and now they cannot be altered, thank heavens.

🌿 *Chanticleer Books, 526 Broadway, Sonoma 95476; phone (707) 996–5364. Open 11:00 A.M.–6:00 P.M. Monday, Wednesday–Saturday, 11:00 A.M.–5:00 P.M. Sunday, "Tuesday by chance." MasterCard, Visa, American Express, and Discover. Wheelchair-accessible.*

MERITAGE is Sonoma's newest hot restaurant in the space formerly occupied by Freestyle! Owner/chef Carlo Cavallo has both community attitude and prices appealing to locals, the mainstay of any wine country restaurant that wants to make it year round. He has made the decor warmer and more welcoming, and the acoustics are greatly improved so you can actually converse. Carlo comes from good places: Il Fornaio, Armani, and Angelo's in Mill Valley.

And then there's the menu: Lunch is quite reasonable in price with a range of wonderful salads, including one of organic greens, grilled Angus hanger steak, roasted corn and almonds, and French goat cheese. Burger of burgers is the Durham ranch buffalo burger with herb Sonoma goat cheese and hand-cut fries ($7.00). The grilled salmon on dill bread with tartar sauce, potato, and mixed greens ($8.00) is also recommended.

Dinner appetizers range from crostini topped with eggplant ratatouille, cannelini, and roasted garlic ($5.00), to seared ostrich carpaccio with porto-bello mushroom and lemon white truffle dressing ($7.00), or try the vodka-and-anise cured salmon and sturgeon gravlox with Ostera caviar sauce ($8.00), or the semolina battered calamari, tiger prawns, zucchini sticks, and fennel ($9.00).

Pastas are gorgeous and only $9.00–$13.00 with a chef's sampler platter at $14 each person. Carlo also offers his Chef's Five Course Prix Fix dinner featuring seafood, meat, vegetarian, or surf and turf for $30 to $45, a deal if you were going to order a few courses anyway.

Seafood lovers will go to heaven with fresh Sterling salmon with asparagus, artichokes, heirloom tomatoes, Yukon potatoes, garlic, and thyme baked in parchment ($15), or fresh halibut encrusted with crispy potato strings ($15), while carnivores should try the New York strip steak ($19).

Don't miss the rotating exhibit of local artists' work on the walls.

❧ *Meritage, 522 Broadway, Sonoma 95476; phone (707) 938–9430. Open 11:30 A.M.–2:30 P.M. for lunch, and 5:30–9:30 P.M. for dinner. Wine and beer. MasterCard, Visa, and American Express. Wheelchair-accessible.*

Just east of Morgan Lane Real Estate on Napa Street you will find TOTAL LIVING COMPANY (TLC) with products that make life easier to live, such as Good Grip kitchen utensils, reading magnifiers, magnetic and copper jewelry, massagers, and magnifying mirrors. Check out the huge television remote controls!

❧ *Total Living Company, 5 East Napa Street, Sonoma 95476; phone (707) 939– 3900; Web site www.totalliving.com. Open 10:00 A.M.–5:30 P.M. Monday– Saturday, noon–5:00 P.M. Sunday. MasterCard and Visa. Wheelchair-accessible.*

THOMAS KINKADE recently moved his "painter of light" gallery to this new location from El Paseo. Thomas Kinkade galleries are found in most tourist meccas, sometimes with more than one in the same town. Kinkade claims to have painted all of the works available in his many galleries, which are usually fairly formal scenes exhibited in fairly formal surroundings.

❧ *Thomas Kinkade—Painter of Light, 11 East Napa Street, Sonoma 95476; phone (707) 996–2994. Open 11:00 A.M.–5:00 P.M. Tuesday–Sunday. MasterCard, Visa, American Express, and Discover. Wheelchair-accessible.*

St. Francis Solano Catholic Church runs the CHURCH MOUSE as "The Thrift Shop with a Difference" and benefits the parish's school. The Church Mouse has three stores in the Sonoma Valley, and this is the "downtown" or "upscale" one. Run by volunteers, it really is different, in that it has a substantial year-round costume loft. Here you can find bargain-heaven, high-quality (sometimes major designer) women's, men's, and children's clothes, and even lots of new things.

You will find carefully selected new woven baskets, Lumber Jack wool shirts, bargain luggage (after you see these prices, you won't buy suitcases anywhere else), religious jewelry, dolls, and Christmas stuff of all sorts. The Church Mouse claims accurately that it is "the busiest store on the Plaza."

❧ *Church Mouse, 15 East Napa Street, Sonoma 95476; phone (707) 938–9797. Open 9:00 A.M.–6:00 P.M. daily, no matter what the sign says. No credit cards. Wheelchair-accessible.*

I-ELLE is a boutique of women's clothing and accessories featuring "wine country clothes" and fabulous leather bags and satchels. This is another Melissa Detert building, remodeled and rebuilt with an attractive courtyard and passageway, weeds, and her private parking lot.

❧ *I-elle, 25 East Napa Street, Sonoma 95476; phone (707) 938–2282. Open 10:00 A.M.–5:30 P.M. Monday–Saturday, 11:00 A.M.–5:00 P.M. Sunday. MasterCard, Visa, American Express, and Discover. Wheelchair-accessible.*

CHICO'S is a Florida 190-store clothing chain selling clothing for working women up to size 20 and from 0–4 European sizes. They offer lovely washable silks and linens, although many locals boycott the chain's alterations to the historic Simmons Drug Store.

❧ *Chico's, 29 East Napa Street, Sonoma 95476; phone (707) 933–0100. Open 10:00 A.M.–6:00 P.M. Monday–Thursday, Saturday, 10:00 A.M.–8:00 P.M. Friday, noon–5:00 P.M. Sunday. MasterCard, Visa, American Express, and Discover. Wheelchair-accessible.*

On to your next stop: MELANIE'S CLOSEOUT EMPORIUM. Here Melanie Laybourn sells eclectic clothes and stuffed animals from other stores' and factories' closeouts, jewelry, and gifts. This is one of those stores you have to wander through occasionally because on one of these trips you'll find something you absolutely must have. On a recent trip we found red and black leather jackets for $85, Gap sweats, Banana Republic windbreakers, Lands' End and Coach bags, and Anne Taylor, Eddie Bauer, and Liz Claiborne clothes. Try this place for fun wild ties, cool T-shirts, walking sticks, swimsuits, sequined vests, and just plain weird stuff, including Beanie Babies.

Melanie brings an interesting background to her shop: time at Nordstrom in San Francisco and stints as a limousine driver and tour director.

➳ *Melanie's Closeout Emporium, 31 East Napa Street, Sonoma 95476; phone (707) 996–7856; Web site www.melaniesemporium.com. Open 10:00 A.M.–6:00 P.M. Sunday–Thursday, 10:00 A.M.–8:00 P.M. Friday–Saturday. April–December, 10:00 A.M.–6:00 P.M. daily January–March. MasterCard, Visa, American Express, and Discover. Wheelchair-accessible.*

MODERN EVE presents quite a contrast to Melanie's. It's an elegant women's clothing store with pizazz and sequins, featuring leather jackets in many colors, camelhair jackets and skirts, decorated denim, and belts and jewelry.

➳ *Modern Eve, 35 East Napa Street, Sonoma 95476; phone (707) 938–0645. Open 9:30 A.M.–5:30 P.M. Monday–Saturday, noon–5:00 P.M. Sunday. MasterCard, Visa, and American Express. Wheelchair-accessible.*

SIGNIFICANT OTHERS:
WORTHWHILE SIDE STEPS BEYOND THE PLAZA

While not precisely on the well-beaten Sonoma Plaza path, the following shops and restaurants are worth checking out.

WILD THYME CAFÉ is the new baby of Joanne and Keith Filipello, owners of well-known Wild Thyme Catering, and building owner Ann Thornton. Wild Thyme has one of the most beautiful patios and some of the best cafe food anywhere. We first met the Filipellos at the Glen Ellen home of our mutual friend, the late M.F.K. Fisher.

At Wild Thyme you can sample and purchase French cheeses aged perfectly by "Cheese Queen" Virginie Berger or dine casually and inexpensively on salads such as grilled vegetable pasta, aromatic French green beans, roasted root vegetables (Kathleen's favorite), ratatouille, and red, yellow, and purple roasted potatoes, or a combination plate for about $6.00. Jerry's favorite sandwich is roast beef with caramelized onions on a Basque roll au jus ($6.50), and there are loads of other

MARINATED GRILLED VEGETABLES
WITH TAPENADE TOASTS
from Chef Keith Filipello, Wild Thyme Café: A Food Library

mini-toasts

For the marinade:

1 lb summer (zucchini) squash

1 eggplant or other favorite vegetables

1 Tbs garlic paste

1 cup ginger-flavored soy sauce

$^1/_4$ cup extra virgin olive oil

$^1/_2$ cup Gloria Ferrer Champagne

For the tapenade:

2 cups Niçoise olives, pitted

1 Tbs capers

1 6 oz can of tuna

1 Tbs herbs of Provence

6 anchovy fillets

Clean and slice lengthwise in $^1/_4$-inch thick slices squash, eggplant, and other veggies. Dip in the following marinade and drain before grilling. Grill.

For the marinade: Combine marinade ingredients.

For the tapenade: Combine tapenade ingredients.

Spread tapenade on mini-toasts. Top with grilled vegetables cut to fit toast. Garnish with roasted pepper.

GLORIA'S GLORIOUS CHAMPAGNE CAVIAR PASTA SAUCE
from Chef Keith Filipello, Wild Thyme Café: A Food Library

2 cups Gloria Ferrer Champagne

1 Tbs shallots, diced

1 lb softened butter

2 oz Sevruga Sturgeon Caviar or other caviar

angel hair pasta

Heat champagne and reduce to $^1/_4$ cup, adding 1 Tbs shallots to reducing wine. Whip butter into reduced wine with a whisk. Add caviar to sauce just before serving over cooked angel hair pasta. Wow! Serves 4.

sandwiches. Go ahead and pig out on a whole plate of garlic mashed potatoes ($2.50), herb-roasted free-range chicken plate with mashed potatoes ($7.99), or baby back ribs with coleslaw ($9.50). The poached eggs and thick toast at breakfast are perfect, as are the thin, crisp waffles and hot syrup. The espresso helps.

You can also avoid grocery shopping elsewhere by purchasing Paul's Organic Veggies from the bins against the western wall.

❧ *Wild Thyme Café, 165 West Napa Street, Sonoma 95476; phone (707) 996–0900, fax (707) 996–0925, Web site wildthymecafe.com. Open 7:00 A.M.– 9:00 P.M. daily. Beer and wine. MasterCard, Visa, American Express, and Discover. Wheelchair-accessible.*

June Edelman's **BOOK NOOK** is Sonoma's newest bookstore, featuring used hardcover and paperbacks. We found a real treasure on making cheeses at home, a book we've never found anywhere else.

❧ *Book Nook, 255 West Napa Street, Sonoma 95476; phone (707) 938–3280. Open 10:00 A.M.–6:00 P.M. Monday–Saturday. No credit cards. Checks okay. Wheelchair-accessible.*

At **THE TOY SHOP**, in the Marketplace Shopping Center just off West Napa Street and Second Street West, Dee Mathews has assembled the best toy shop we know of anywhere. Stocking toys for people of all ages, Dee's motto is "from the womb to the tomb." She began her store by consulting her own children on what to stock. Even though her children are now adults, Dee's buying is still sensitive, with-it, environmentally sound, and popular. Parents and kids alike love to shop here because it is so much fun.

Dee also provides extremely personal service. She keeps track of kids' personal favorites and hordes them until they can come in.

❧ *The Toy Shop, 201 West Napa Street, Sonoma 95476; phone (707) 938– 1197. Open 10:00 A.M.–5:30 P.M. Monday–Saturday, 11:00 A.M.–4:00 P.M. Sunday, extended hours in December. MasterCard, Visa, and Discover. Wheelchair-accessible.*

DOWN TO EARTH NATURAL MARKET AND CAFE is also located in the Marketplace. This excellent natural-foods store features natural vitamins, packaged foods, and an expanded organic local-produce section. New owner Christopher Kysar, who operates big-time in the natural-foods business statewide, really knows his stuff, and he has updated the store's offerings tremendously. Unique to Sonoma Valley, Down to Earth also features organically grown wines.

❧ *Down to Earth Natural Market and Cafe, 201 West Napa Street, Sonoma 95476; phone (707) 996–9898. Open 8:00 A.M.–8:00 P.M. Monday–Saturday; 9:00 A.M.–6:00 P.M. Sunday. MasterCard, Visa, American Express, and Discover. Wheelchair-accessible.*

HOMEGROWN BAKING COMPANY is known locally and simply as "The Bagel Shop." Stuart Teitelbaum's bagels are worth walking down the street a ways. Hundreds of locals do so every day. Again, it's worth it. (Which is probably why there is another Homegrown shop, in Maxwell Village Center on Sonoma Highway.) Carol Bertolini reigns here as "the Bagel Goddess," despite her Italian heritage, and keeps customers and staff in good humor. The walls are lined with huge frames of pictures Carol has taken of customers grinning and bearing it. Formality was never introduced here.

The Bagel Shop offers economical fare from a plain bagel for 50 cents to great lox, Vella's cream cheese, onions, etc. for $4.50. We have never spent more than $5.00 for two at breakfast here. Soups are made daily, and there are special-of-the-day coffees and espresso drinks.

❧ *Homegrown Baking Company, 201 West Napa Street, Sonoma 95476; phone (707) 996–0166. Open 6:15 A.M.–2:00 P.M. Monday–Friday, 7:00 A.M.–2:00 P.M. Saturday–Sunday. No credit cards. Restaurant wheelchair-accessible, rest room questionable.*

THE SHANGHAI RESTAURANT, in a small shopping center across from Safeway on Fifth Street West, is a clean and somewhat amusing Chinese restaurant that features foods from Shanghai, plus southern and northern specialties. No MSG is used in this restaurant. Jimmy Ling's Sizzling Iron Platters with prawns, beef, or chicken and especially garlic are aromatic, exciting, and delicious, as is the sizzling rice soup. The hot iron platters and fresh foods are brought to your table and quickly sautéed before your eyes. The chicken in garlic sauce, crab and asparagus soup, and Peking Spareribs are also exceptional.

The Shanghai offers a good deal for lunch: a choice of a full range of entrees with steamed or fried rice, soup of the day, fried won ton or egg rolls, tea, and fortune cookies, all for just $3.50!

❧ *The Shanghai Restaurant, 563–567 Fifth Street West, Sonoma 95476; phone (707) 938–3346. Open 11:00 A.M.–9:00 P.M. daily. MasterCard, Visa, and American Express. Wheelchair-accessible. Beer and wine.*

THE FLAG STORE is the ultimate flag store in the western United States. Owner Dallas Dutson has tripled his supply of fun flags and banners, already sells the new Hong Kong flag, has more books on flags than anyone else, and can (and will happily) answer any legitimate question you might have about flags and history.

The Flag Store carries flags of several sizes from all U.S. states and territories, most countries of the world, banners of many fraternal organizations, car window decals, lapel pins, and T-shirts. Dutson even has two trunks of "Discontinued

Country" flags, which are lots of fun to rummage through and find a treasure for a wall at home. This store is usually fairly cluttered, because Dutson is almost constantly in motion showing an interesting flag or book to visitors. Enjoy!

❧ *The Flag Store, 20089 Broadway, Sonoma 95476; phone (707) 996–8140; fax (707) 996–8171; e-mail flags@vom.com. Open 10:00 A.M.–5:00 P.M. Monday–Saturday, 12:30–4:30 P.M. Sunday. MasterCard, Visa, American Express, and Discover. Wheelchair-accessible.*

SONOMA MARKET is Sonoma's gourmet grocery store and is expanding to include more specialty foods and its own sushi bar. Here you can find cheeses, mustards, and pâtés from several countries, five local bakeries' breads, as well as local Willie Bird free-range turkeys, local free-range chickens and eggs, chemical-free beef, and even the basics like recycled toilet tissue! Many locals shop here daily. We do. Most days a food maven offers tastes of barbecued marinated meats, sausages, mustards, or pastries.

The deli makes excellent sandwiches ($3.50–$5.25), with excellent hot specials daily. It uses local turkey and beef, cooked in the store's kitchen, and offers excellent, tangy, eggless Caesar salad. The hot foods are very popular with busy people; and there is usually a healthy choice, such as artichoke ravioli with sun-dried tomatoes, rotisseried chicken with garlic mashed potatoes and greens, braised salmon, and—oh yes—that Sonoma Market meatloaf.

Sonoma Market also owns Glen Ellen Village Market, a newish building with the most up-to-date healthy and gourmet foods available. If you're in Glen Ellen, it's the perfect place to get your picnic supplies.

❧ *Sonoma Market, 520 West Napa Street (at Fifth Street West), Sonoma 95476; phone (707) 996–3411. Open 7:00 A.M.–9:00 P.M. MasterCard and Visa. Wheelchair-accessible.*

AMY'S PEKING PALACE, next to Sonoma Market, offers the best quick Asian food in town, with entrees as low as $1.00 (yes!) and several lunch selections at $4.25. It's cafeteria-style, but with extremely fresh food and absolutely no MSG.

❧ *Amy's Peking Palace, 520 West Napa Street (at Fifth Street West), Sonoma 95476; phone (707) 938–8886. Open 11:00 A.M.–9:00 P.M. No credit cards. Wheelchair-accessible.*

SUSHINOMA is Sonoma's best and only sushi bar, and are we lucky! While one should never watch sausage being made (Kathleen has), watching the fine art of sushi making here is a delightful pleasure. Enjoy a dozen rolls from California to Rock 'n' Roll, Alaska Roll, Kamikaze, spicy tuna, Tekka maki, and

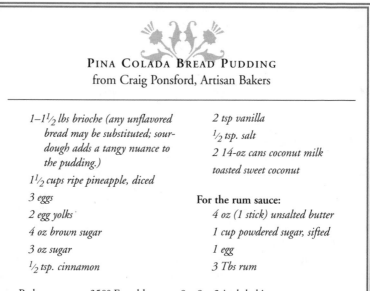

PINA COLADA BREAD PUDDING
from Craig Ponsford, Artisan Bakers

1–1½ lbs brioche (any unflavored bread may be substituted; sourdough adds a tangy nuance to the pudding.)

1½ cups ripe pineapple, diced

3 eggs

2 egg yolks

4 oz brown sugar

3 oz sugar

½ tsp. cinnamon

2 tsp vanilla

½ tsp. salt

2 14-oz cans coconut milk

toasted sweet coconut

For the rum sauce:

4 oz (1 stick) unsalted butter

1 cup powdered sugar, sifted

1 egg

3 Tbs rum

Preheat oven to 350° F and butter a 9 x 9 x 2-inch baking pan.

Cut brioche or bread into 1-inch cubes and combine with pineapple in a large bowl. If you cut the crust from the bread, make sure that the total weight of the cubes is at least 1 pound.

Whisk the eggs and then add the next six ingredients. Pour egg mixture over the bread and pineapple, mix gently, and let sit for 20–30 minutes, stirring occasionally. When most of the liquid has been absorbed, place mixture in the prepared pan and bake for 45 minutes or until the custard has just set. Place under broiler for a few minutes until the crust is golden.

Garnish with toasted coconut. Serve warm with rum sauce. Serves 6–8.

For the rum sauce: This sauce cannot be reused or reheated, so make it just before serving.

Melt butter in a small saucepan and heat until bubbly. Turn heat to low and whisk in the powdered sugar all at once. By whisking rapidly, a fragile emulsion is formed between the sugar and the butter, and the mixture thickens. Whisk the egg into this warm mixture, then the rum, and heat through over low heat, stirring constantly until the sauce is thick enough to coat the back of a spoon.

combinations, all under $6.00 There are another eight vegetable rolls and a wide variety of Nigiri sushi, temaki, and sashimi, most in the $3.00–$4.00 range.

Miso soup is only $2.00, with seaweed salad at $3.50.

❧ *Sushinoma, 512 West Napa Street in the Sonoma Market shopping center (Sonoma Center), Sonoma 95476; phone (707) 935–0956. Beer and wine. MasterCard and Visa. Wheelchair-accessible.*

Highly acclaimed caterer Elaine Bell headquarters her food operations at LAINIE'S CUISINE TO GO, on West Napa Street just beyond Jack-In-The-Box, and presents her fine cuisine retail at this store adjacent to her kitchens. Many locals call ahead or stop here on their way home for dinner-to-go.

Lainie changes the menu weekly and offers Lainie's Lean Cuisine every day. The week's menu might include soy-baked red snapper at $8.98 per pound, Japanese eggplant stuffed with fontina cheese at $5.98 per pound, and herb-roasted new potatoes with garlic at $4.98 per pound, in addition to salads of spinach, carrot, or orzo pasta with pesto and oven-dried tomatoes.

Lainie also makes box lunches to go for your party or picnic. It's best to call or fax your order ahead. The six box-lunch menus begin at $3.00. You might opt for the homemade Italian focaccia bread sandwiches layered with sliced meats, fontina cheese, and roasted vegetables; oven-dried tomato salad with young greens; marinated green beans and mushrooms with herb dressing; fresh fruit; and lemon biscotti dipped in white chocolate, $10.00 per person.

The Heart Healthy Menu, with poached fillet of salmon served on a bed of baby lettuces with julienne of carrots, baby red potatoes, and celery root with fat-free Wine Country Herb Dressing, roasted-garlic red-pepper olive oil, whole-wheat roll, and fresh fruit, is $14.00 per person.

Local favorites include Lainie's unequaled chocolate chip cookies, her veggie sushi on Thursdays, and her baby red potatoes stuffed with asiago soufflé. Lainie's also sells Artisan Bakers breads after their closing at 3:00 P.M.

❧ *Lainie's Cuisine to Go, 678 West Napa Street, Sonoma 95476; phone (707) 996–5226; fax (707) 996–5773. Open 11:00 A.M.–7:00 P.M. Tuesday–Friday, 11:00 A.M.–5:00 P.M. Saturday. MasterCard and Visa. Wheelchair-accessible.*

Just west of Lainie's on West Napa you'll find ARTISAN BAKERS, an outstanding and ever-growing bakery featuring crunchy-crust peasant breads, some with walnuts and olives, and one of the most popular: a garlic–Jack cheese blend. Artisan also features huge biscotti, scones, focaccia, croissants, globe-sized morning buns, and muffins; and seasonable breads such as Irish soda bread, pumpkin bread, and holiday favorites. They make good, strong, espresso drinks, elegant sandwiches, and pizza slices that come out of the oven at 11:00 A.M.

Partner/baker Craig Ponsford won the 1996 Coupe du Monde world baking contest in Paris, France. You can also enjoy Artisan at San Francisco's Stars,

BREAKAWAY BREAKFAST COFFEE CAKE
from Bob Rice, Breakaway Cafe

1 lb. sweet butter, room temperature

4 cups sugar

4 whole eggs

2 tsp. vanilla

2 cups sour cream

4 cups flour, plus extra for dusting the pan

2 Tbs baking powder

1$\frac{1}{2}$ tsp salt

For the topping:

3 cups chopped walnuts

$\frac{1}{2}$ cup sugar

$\frac{1}{2}$ cup cinnamon

Preheat oven to 350° F. Cream butter and sugar with an electric mixer. Add beaten egg, vanilla, and sour cream and mix well.

In a separate bowl, sift together flour, baking powder, and salt. Mix into above mixture until the batter is smooth.

Mix topping ingredients in a separate bowl.

Butter and dust with flour a 10-inch angel-food-cake pan. Pour in half of the batter. Sprinkle with half of the topping. Pour in the remaining batter and cover the top with the rest of the topping mixture. Bake approximately 1 hour or until toothpick comes out clean. Enjoy with cold milk or hot coffee! Makes 10–12 servings.

Millenium, and Rose Pistola, Napa's Auberge du Soleil, Bistro Jeanty, and The Grill at Meadowood, as well as Sonoma reliables Swiss Hotel, Della Santina's, and Cafe LaHaye. All daily breads are sold half-off from 5:00 to 6:00 P.M.
Artisan Bakers, 750 West Napa Street, Sonoma 95476; phone (707) 939–1765. Open 6:30 A.M.–6:00 P.M. Monday–Saturday, 7:00 A.M.–2:00 P.M. Sunday. No credit cards. Wheelchair-accessible from sidewalk, but be careful.

Our good friend Bob Rice moved the BREAKAWAY CAFE from behind the Sonoma Mission Inn in Boyes Hot Springs to the old Lyons Restaurant site at Maxwell Village Shopping Center in the fall of 1999. Bob had "inherited" the Breakaway from its founder, Jenny Bushnell, who married a customer, had two more adorable children, and lived happily ever after. Prior to this major life change, Bob had founded the Glen Ellen Inn Restaurant, had a liver transplant, and developed the Breakaway to even greater success.

Bob moved the Breakaway to this high-traffic location to give Sonomans a place to eat good food at good, local prices, and locals have responded overwhelmingly, overwhelming Bob and his delightful staff. We hesitate to tell you how good it is, how reasonably priced it is, and what fine paintings by Dennis Zieminski decorate the walls. Go see for yourself!

In addition to great, big breakfasts, kids' menus, and lunchtime salads and sandwiches, Bob now offers Breakaway Platters after 4:00 P.M., all including soup or salad, French fries, and bread and butter. Feast on Rib Eye steak ($12.50), prawns Veracruz ($9.50), four-cheese ravioli ($8.50), half-roast chicken marinated with lemon and herbs ($9.50), a garden platter of grilled fresh vegetables and yummy potato gratin to die for ($8.50). And there's a whole play corner for the kids!

*❧ **Breakaway Cafe**, *19101 Sonoma Highway, Sonoma 95476; phone (707) 996–5949, Web site www.breakawaycafe.com. Open 7:00 A.M.-9:00 P.M. Sunday–Thursday, 7:00 A.M.–10:00 P.M. Friday–Saturday. Beer and wine. MasterCard and Visa. Wheelchair-accessible.*

CHAPTER 3

EAST SONOMA

*O*ur East Sonoma tour takes you on a 10-mile loop of vine-
yards and wineries, designed for either car or bicycle. On this route you
visit Ravenswood Winery, Bartholomew Park Winery, Buena Vista
Winery, Gundlach-Bundschu Winery, and the Pauline Bond
Community Farm. And you can start it all from Sebastiani Sonoma
Cask Cellars on Fourth Street East.

Many of Sonoma's best, most beautiful, and most intriguing wineries are
hidden in these hills just a few miles from Sonoma Plaza. You will need either a
bicycle or car to get to them all in one day. But at any point along the way, you
can retrace your tracks or improvise to get back to Sonoma Plaza.

Start at the northeast corner of Sonoma Plaza at Mission San Francisco de
Solano. Go east on Spain Street to its end—the equivalent of 3 blocks—at
Fourth Street East. Turn left onto Fourth Street East. There you will find
Sebastiani Sonoma Cask Cellars. (see page 69)

Turn right onto Lovall Valley Road. (Sebastiani winery and picnic tables are
on the right; its newer Cherry Block vineyards are on the left.) Now, turn left
up Gehricke Road. Where Brazil Street meets Gehricke Road, veer to the right
up the hill and go up Gehricke to RAVENSWOOD WINERY. When you pass the
eucalyptus trees on your right, you are almost there. Ravenswood prefers that
you park in the lot across the narrow road and walk up the steps or driveway to
the tasting room. (There's plenty of handicap parking at the top of the driveway
right next to the tasting room.)

Ravenswood, once the site of Peter Haywood's winery, is a small, charming,
and hilarious operation that produces some of the best Zinfandels anywhere.
Joel Peterson and Reed Foster have created this jewel of a winery; they gained a
reputation for highly specialized wines since their first crush, in 1976. Three
years later they produced 327 cases. Now they average 200,000 cases a year,
almost doubling their output in the last two years. Joel believes that wine is a
collaborative business that should emphasize camaraderie instead of competition and that the public likes to enjoy a wine and then try another as their tastes
diversify. If you make good wines, people will come back to yours. It's all

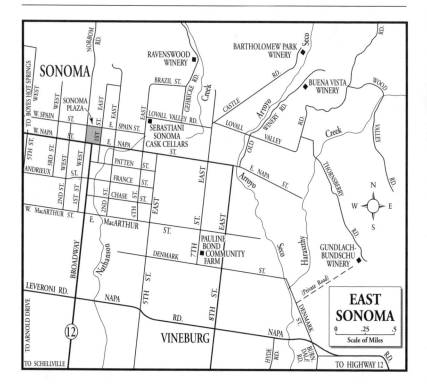

cyclical. Ravenswood's motto is "No Wimpy Wines," which, as you will see on aprons and T-shirts, translates to loose Latin "Nullum Vinum Flaccidum" and even looser French "Pas de Vins Poules Mouillées."

One of the most pleasant parts of visiting Ravenswood is the view from its small patio and picnic area. Turn around with your back to the tasting room for a minute and catch the sunlight on the vineyards in the surrounding hills. You'll understand why people live here.

The tasting room is small, even intimate, and lots of fun. Sonoma architect Adrian Martinez designed the comfortable tasting room and production facility. The people who work in the tasting room are knowledgeable about both food and wine. Each day the staffers write the wines available to taste on a board hanging from the wall behind the counter in the order they recommend you taste them. Usually you can move from a Gewürztraminer through Chardonnays, to a Zinfandel, Merlot, French Colombard, Petit Syrah, and Cabernets. Ravenswood's wines range from an excellent Vintners' Blend Zinfandel from around $10 a bottle to one of their best Merlots at under $25 and Pickberry, a Bordeaux-style blend, at $31.50. Some of these are available only in Ravenswood's tasting room, so come on in.

Ravenswood plans a new winery south of Viansa across from the Cherry Tree at what is now the quarry. But this will always be the tasting room.

 Fine points: In addition to buying the wines made by Ravenswood's "stubborn and impractical Old World oenological practices," you can choose from a good selection of cookbooks, wine posters, and comedic gift cards, shirts, aprons, and caps. And try Ravenswood's reasonably priced weekend barbecues in the summer. Chef Tony Najiola, formerly of New York's River Café, and The Village Green and San Francisco's Ernie's, creates no-muss-no-fuss barbecues on the weekends at Ravenswood's "Cafe Nevermore." Featured wines! Chardonnay, French Colombard, Zinfandel, Merlot, Cabernet Sauvignon, Cabernet Franc, Rosato, Moscato, Leggiero, Late Harvest Gewürztraminer. Winemaker: Joel Peterson. Cases: 200,000. Acres: 16.

✻✿ *Ravenswood Winery, 18701 Gehricke Road, Sonoma 95476; phone (707) 938–1960. Open 10:00 A.M.–4:30 P.M. daily. Tours by appointment. Call before 10:30 A.M. MasterCard, Visa, American Express, and Discover. Wheelchair-accessible.*

Now, come back down Gehricke Road, turn left onto Lovall Valley Road, and turn left onto Seventh Street East. Turn right for a little more Lovall Valley Road; then quickly turn leftish up Castle Road to BARTHOLOMEW PARK WINERY.

You may recognize Bartholomew Park Winery as that of the former Hacienda Winery, which is now owned by Bronco. This is a must-see for several reasons:

RAVENSWOOD WINERY TASTING ROOM AND ANN HADDAD

TINY GREEN BEAN SALAD
WITH SMOKED DUCK
(OR HAM) AND CREAMY
WALNUT VINAIGRETTE
from Chef Tony Najiola,
Ravenswood Winery

For the salad:

1½ lbs haricots verts

*¼ lb smoked duck or ham,
julienned*

¼ lb dried figs, julienned

¼ lb toasted walnuts

For the vinaigrette:

½ cup cold-pressed walnut oil

¼ cup crème fraiche

3 Tbs sherry wine vinegar

4 Tbs Italian parsley, chopped

salt and freshly ground pepper

For the salad: Blanch green beans in boiling salted water until tender but still crisp; refresh under cold water and allow to drain until dry. Toss with remaining components. Add dressing and seasoning to taste.

For the dressing: Place shallots and vinegar to infuse for 10 minutes or so. Whisk in crème fraiche, then the oil. Add parsley and seasoning. This dressing does not age well and should be served immediately. Serves 6.

It has the only History of Wine in America Museum in Sonoma Valley, created by former general manager Meg Scantlebury (Meg's office was once the morgue); it was once a hospital and then a women's prison; and it has an outstanding collection of Ron Zak photographs of its extremely independent grape growers in compromising poses.

Known once as "The Castle," built by Robert and Kate Johnson in about 1880, the building north of the current winery building was sold to the State of California in 1920, which turned it into the "Industrial Workfarm for Women" ("wayward" and "wild" women) as an alternative to prison. While the community opposed such a use, the Woman's Christian Temperance Union supported it, saying "let us remember that the men have made these unfortunate wards of the state outcasts that they are."

The current winery building was built in 1922 as the receiving hospital for the Workfarm. The next year the Castle (Workfarm) burned to the ground "under suspicious circumstances," and the women were moved to the hospital (the current winery), where they rioted. After this incident the sheriff scattered the women to other institutions.

Eventually the property became the State Hospital for the Feeble Minded, housing epileptic boys, and then it served as the local community hospital from 1945 to 1957.

In 1943 Frank and Antonia Bartholomew bought the 435 acres at a state silent auction for $17,050—just $39 per acre. A foreign war correspondent with

United Press, and later its president, Frank left Antonia in Sonoma to run the new property and oversee replanting the historic Buena Vista vineyards. The Bartholomews opened Hacienda Winery in 1973 and sold it (except 15 percent) to Crawford Cooley in 1978, who later closed the doors and sold the Hacienda inventory to Bronco Wine Company. In the meantime, after Frank's death at eighty-six in 1985, Antonia built a reproduction of "Father of the California Wine Industry" Agoston Haraszthy's Pompeiian-style villa on the site of the original he built in the early 1860s. Sonoma architect Victor Conforti designed the reproduction villa from illustrations and photographs, because no original plans existed. Antonia then died, at age ninety, on the evening of the villa's dedication in 1990.

Local newspaper articles recounting all of these unusual incidents are on display in the museum along with authentic old tools, photographs, apparel, a covered wagon, and memorabilia from Frank Bartholomew's days as a foreign correspondent. Now the Bundschu Family (Gundlach-Bundschu) operates the winery for the Bartholomew Trust Foundation.

Bartholomew Park Winery's picnic sites among native oaks are unequaled, giving a feeling of Celtic mysticism along with the views of Sonoma Valley. Its wines are sold only at the winery, so for many reasons it's worth the trip. Guests can register by computer just inside the door.

 Fine points: Bartholomew Park has a very special feature: the Punch Down Club. You can join and get down and dirty and cover yourself with juice as you participate in the stirring and punching of fermenting "must," which floats to the top and must be pushed back down to the bottom four or five times a day, known as punching down. Then you're called when your wine is ready. Featured wines: all single-vineyard designations, Chardonnay, Pinot Noir, Merlot, Cabernet Sauvignon, and Zinfandel. Winemaker: Antoine Favero. Cases: 4,000. Acres: 37.

❧ *Bartholomew Park Winery, 1000 Vineyard Lane (at top of Castle Road), Sonoma 95476; phone (707) 935–9511; fax (707) 935–0549. Winery open 10:00 A.M.–4:30 P.M. daily, villa open Wednesday, Saturday–Sunday by appointment only. MasterCard and Visa. Wheelchair-accessible.*

After leaving Bartholomew Park, head back down Castle Road and then take a sharp left turn up Lovall Valley Road.

Turn left onto Old Winery Road. Old Winery Road winds gracefully toward BUENA VISTA WINERY through eucalyptus trees, vineyards, and charming old homes. With direct ties to Agoston Haraszthy, this winery is one of the oldest in California. It is currently owned by the Racke family of Germany.

Park in the lot and walk ¼ mile to the winery itself. (Vehicles carrying hand-icapped people may drive up the driveway.) Notice that the closer you get to the winery, the larger the native oaks are. In fall and winter, you can see huge sul-fur mushrooms at the base of eucalyptus trees near the winery.

You can taste wines in the Press House, which is the first building you come to on the right, covered with ivy. Every time we open the heavy doors to this building, we gasp at the majesty of the two-story room.

This is probably the most commercial tasting room in Sonoma Valley. Here you can taste Buena Vista wines, learn a little, and buy almost everything to accompany wine that you can imagine. Varieties of Buena Vista food prducts include cheese sauces, fudges, salad dressings, mustards, olives, preserves and jellies, books, napkins, hats, shirts, aprons, bottle corks, dried soups, brie cheese, Marcel & Henri pâtés, French bread, French sausages, and flavored mayonnaises are everywhere. Grapeseed oil seems to be featured here, on the theory that "grape seeds are reportedly fifty times more potent as an antioxidant than either vitamin C or vitamin E." Try the dipping oils and a variety of beautiful related books.

You are welcome to enjoy a repast at one of the winery's many picnic tables on the asphalt. You'll note a large number of gray cats—a holdover from the time when Robert and Kate Johnson lived at what is now Bartholomew Park and Kate had 200 felines.

BUENA VISTA WINERY TASTING ROOM

Buena Vista has an artist-in-residence program, displaying each month's work upstairs in the Press House Gallery. Local theater companies stage Shakespeare productions here in summer, and an annual music series also attracts Sonomans and visitors alike.

Fine points: There is an easy, self-guided tour that you can take by following the display boards around the asphalt. A human-guided historical presentation takes place daily at 2:00 P.M. Featured wines: Gewürztraminer, Pinot Noir, and Cream sherries, which are sold only in the tasting room. Owner: Raacke U.S.A. Winemaker: Judy Matulich-Weitz. Cases: 500,000. Acres: 1,000.

Buena Vista Winery, 18000 Old Winery Road, Sonoma 95476; phone (707) 938–1266; fax (707) 939–0916; Web site www.buenavistawinery.com. Open 10:30 A.M.–5:00 P.M. daily. MasterCard, Visa, and American Express. Wheelchair-accessible.

Back in your vehicle, carefully wind your way back down Old Winery Road. Turn left onto Lovall Valley Road. After about ½ mile, Lovall Valley Road makes an extremely sharp left turn. Careful. Turn right onto Thornsberry Road, a beautiful, narrow country road that meanders through Sonoma's eastern foothills. Follow it to GUNDLACH-BUNDSCHU WINERY, a place where life and wine are fun. You will never find one iota of wine snobbery here, but you will find some unique wines, history, and family pranks.

Founded in 1858 by Jacob Gundlach and Emil Dresel, the winery was selling 150,000 cases of Bacchus Table Wines annually by the 1870s. They produced the wines here at the winery and then stored them in their wine vault in San Francisco. Prosperity continued until the 1906 earthquake destroyed all the family's property in San Francisco, including the vault. During Prohibition, when the winery was closed down, son-in-law Charles Bundschu, and then his son Walter, ran the vineyards. Gundlach-Bundschu's grapes were in great demand by those wineries with licenses to make sacramental and medicinal wines, including Inglenook, where Walter's brother Carl was winemaker and general manager, Almaden, and eventually Sebastiani. Walter's son Towle and his wife,

GUNDLACH-BUNDSCHU
MEXICAN IMMIGRANT WORKERS'
MURALS

GUNDLACH-BUNDSCHU CAVES

Mary, who still lives here at Rhinefarm, returned to the ranch and raised pears, cattle, and wine grapes. In 1967 their son Jim persuaded his father to replant the entire ranch to wine grapes. In 1973 they resurrected and reopened Gundlach-Bundschu Winery, thank heavens.

The winery's tasting room is lined with original Sonoma and San Francisco historic photographs and the complete collection of Gundlach-Bundschu/Ron Zak posters. The Rhinefarm bell has hung behind the left door since 1860; it was rung from 1860 to 1983 to call laborers in from the fields.

Jim Bundschu dedicated the eastern exterior wall of the winery for a mural and commissioned a Mexican laborer/artist to honor Mexican immigrants' importance in California wine business' history, and he has installed a permanent stage for performances of Shakespeare's work every summer. Jim is also founder of the Sonoma Valley Wine Patrol, which holds up the Napa Valley Wine Train whenever they think they should. Every other year he also organizes the outrageous "Marching Vineyard" entry in the Valley of the Moon Vintage Festival Parade.

 Fine points: The winery's caves, to the northwest of the winery building, are dug into the natural hillside, on which the Bundschus maintain a scenic hiking trail and picnic sites. Featured wines: Chardonnays, Gamay, Pinot Noir, Merlot, Petite Syrah, Polar Bearitage, Tempranillo (from Spanish cuttings), and Zinfandel. Winemaker: Linda Trotter. Cases: 55,000. Acres: 560.

✴✶ *Gundlach-Bundschu Winery, 2000 Denmark Street, Sonoma 95476; phone (707) 938–5277. Open 10:00 A.M.–4:30 P.M. daily. MasterCard and Visa. Wheelchair-accessible.*

Now you can either retrace your tracks back to Sonoma Plaza or take the lower road out of Gundlach-Bundschu, which takes you by the Bundschus' Rhinefarm Victorian home up to the left and to Denmark Street. Follow Denmark Street west, and cross Eighth Street East. Turn right onto Seventh Street East, and visit the PAULINE BOND COMMUNITY FARM. This is a working organic community farm, offering educational exhibits, plots for "tenants" to grow their own vegetables, a sales table, and hands-on opportunities to learn how food is grown. Pauline Bond willed her six-acre "ranch" to the City of

Sonoma for a park. The property was saved from a city manager's plan to sub-
divide and sell the parcels for development.

➳ *Pauline Bond Community Farm, 19990 Seventh Street East, Sonoma 95476;
phone (707) 996–9744. Open 9:00 A.M.–5:00 P.M. Monday–Saturday. No credit
cards. Wheelchair-accessible.*

Continue up Seventh Street East, past MacArthur, to Napa Street. Turn left
onto Napa and continue toward Sonoma Plaza. St. Francis Solano Cemetery is
on the north side, just before Fifth Street East.

CHAPTER 4

BOYES HOT SPRINGS, EL VERANO, AND AGUA CALIENTE

*W*elcome to the next stops on our tour through Sonoma Valley. In this chapter, we point out the highlights among the restaurants, shops, and coffeehouses in Boyes Hot Springs, El Verano, and Agua Caliente, the towns you'll pass on your way north to Kenwood and Glen Ellen. While these are important communities unto themselves, they are also Sonoma's "suburbs." (More people actually live outside the Sonoma city limits than within.) Follow Highway 12 (Sonoma Highway) to Kenwood, and then we will bring you back to Sonoma through Glen Ellen.

Follow either West Napa Street until it turns north—as Highway 12—at the El Pueblo and Off Broadway Cleaners, or take West Spain Street through the Fifth Street West stop sign to the signal; then turn right.

The following establishments are part of the MAXWELL VILLAGE SHOPPING CENTER.

Drop into the BREAKAWAY CAFE for wholesome California food. (see pages 118–19)

GOURMET TACO SHOP is the ultimate shopping-center Mexi-California taqueria. While there is a slight assembly-line feeling about the place, it is clean and fast. Locals flock here on their lunch hours for the excellent McDougall menu, with fat-free vegan Mexi-California food, in addition to the regular menu.

Try the marinated chicken with tomatillo sauce at $7.50; crispy or soft tacos at $2.45; wet burritos at $4.95; or full dinners of sizzling fajitas at $7.95, sautéed prawns at $9.75, or crab-meat enchiladas at $9.95. Our friends highly

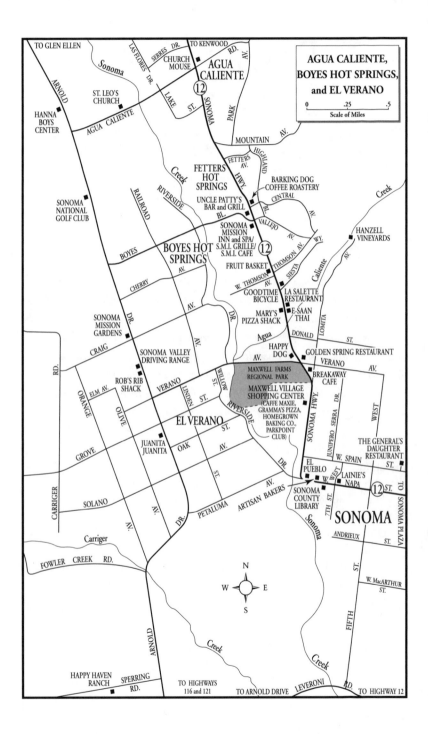

AGUA CALIENTE,
BOYES HOT SPRINGS,
and EL VERANO

0   .25   .5
Scale of Miles

TO GLEN ELLEN

Sonoma

LAS FLORES DR.
SERRES DR.
TO KENWOOD
CHURCH
MOUSE
AGUA
CALIENTE
(12)

ARNOLD

ST. LEO'S
CHURCH

LAKE ST.

SONOMA ST.

PARK AV.

HANNA
BOYS
CENTER

AGUA CALIENTE

MOUNTAIN AV.

FETTERS
AV.

HIGHLAND

HIGHWAY HWY.

Creek

FETTERS
HOT
SPRINGS

RIVERSIDE

RAILROAD

BARKING DOG
COFFEE ROASTERY

CENTRAL AV.

UNCLE PATTY'S
BAR and GRILL
BL.

VALLEJO AV.

Creek

SONOMA
NATIONAL
GOLF CLUB

BOYES

BOYES HOT
SPRINGS
AV.

SONOMA
MISSION
INN and SPA/
S.M.I. GRILLE/
S.M.I. CAFE
(12)

FRUIT BASKET

THOMSON AV.

CALIENTE AV.

WY.

HANZELL
VINEYARDS

CHERRY

AV.

W. THOMSON AV.
GOODTIME
BICYCLE

SIESTA AV.

LA SALETTE
RESTAURANT

DR.

MARY'S
PIZZA SHACK

E-SAAN
THAI

LOMITA AV.

SONOMA
MISSION
GARDENS

CRAIG

AV.

DR.

Agua

HAPPY
DOG

DONALD

ST.

GOLDEN SPRING RESTAURANT

RD.

SONOMA VALLEY
DRIVING RANGE

AV.

WILLOW ST.

MAXWELL FARMS
REGIONAL PARK

VERANO
AV.

VERANO AV.

BREAKAWAY
CAFE

WEST

ELM AV.

ROB'S RIB
SHACK

VERANO AV.

LINDEN ST.

RIVERSIDE

MAXWELL VILLAGE
SHOPPING CENTER
(CAFFE MAXIE,
GRAMMA'S PIZZA,
HOMEGROWN
BAKING CO.,
PARKPOINT
CLUB)

SONOMA HWY.

JUNIPERO SERRA DR.

ORANGE

OLIVE ST.

JUANITA
JUANITA

OAK ST.

EL VERANO

ST. AV.

THE GENERAL'S
DAUGHTER
RESTAURANT

W. SPAIN ST.

GROVE

EL
PUEBLO

7TH ST.

W. ST.

LAINIE'S
NAPA
(12) ST.

TO SONOMA PLAZA

CARRIGER

SOLANO

AV.

DR.

PETALUMA AV.

ARTISAN BAKERS

SONOMA
COUNTY
LIBRARY

Sonoma

SONOMA

ANDRIEUX ST.

Carriger

FOWLER CREEK RD.

FIFTH ST.

W. MacARTHUR
ST.

N
W   E
S

HAPPY HAVEN
RANCH

SPERRING
RD.

TO HIGHWAYS
116 and 121

Creek

TO ARNOLD DRIVE

Creek

LEVERONI RD.

TO HIGHWAY 12

recommend this restaurant as providing excellent, highly flavored food with no lard, artificial ingredients, or preservatives. Even the tortillas are lard-free. Beer and wine are available.

❧ *Gourmet Taco Shop, 19235 Sonoma Highway, Sonoma 95475; phone (707) 935–1045. Open 11:00 A.M.–9:00 P.M. daily. MasterCard and Visa. Wheelchair-accessible.*

BRUNDAGE'S CAFFE MAXIE is right next door in the Maxwell Village Shopping Center. As you turn left at the signal into Maxwell Village, Caffe Maxie is over to the left.

Don Brundage opened Caffe Maxie before the disastrous 1990 fire that wiped out his fabulously eclectic Brundage's in Sonoma Plaza. Having no insurance on the downtown place, the Brundages set up their whole operation at Caffe Maxie. Many customers followed Brundage's out here. The shop has an unmatched supply of chocolate truffles and other sumptuous candies as well as candies for diabetics, coffeemakers, coffee beans, espresso drinks, hot dogs, and even a popcorn cart outside.

It's worth trying out Brundage's just for a conversation with Don. He knows as much about classical music and San Francisco history and politics as he does about Sonoma. Don is always about to add something new to his shop; we're still waiting for his wife, Pan, to bring in that dim sum.

❧ *Brundage's Caffe Maxie, 19231 Sonoma Highway, Sonoma 95476; phone (707) 938–3889. Open 7:00 A.M.–6:00 P.M. Monday–Friday, 7:00 A.M.–7:00 P.M. Saturday, 8:00 A.M.–6:00 P.M. Sunday; or whenever Don is there. Visa, MasterCard, and Discover. Wheelchair-accessible.*

GRAMMA'S PIZZA, located next to the Payless Drugs, flips out some of the best pizza in the world and has won several national awards in its short history. Jim Cahoon (Gramma) and his wife, Angie, took over a take-and-bake pizza shop a few years ago and, with lots of hard work and creativity, developed the tastiest pizza and pasta an Irish American ever made. Now they will bake it for you or make it up for you to bake at home. You can also have it delivered to wherever you are staying for $2.00. Recently Gramma's expanded into the preschool next door (they left) with Gramma's Pizza and Cal-Italia Restaurant, an honest name for a restaurant that sells Shiitake Happens pizza. If you stay for dinner, do not miss the better-than-Gramma's pot roast with wide noodles. The best!

Some of Gramma's finest and most unusual pizzas include The Green Goddess vegetarian; the Mexicali, with marinated grilled chicken, red, green, and gold bell peppers, and fresh cilantro; The Blue Moon, with chicken and bleu

cheese; The Irish, with white sauce, sausage, seasoned potato, green onions, and cheddar cheese; and, last but not least, their "killer pie," The Capone, a deep-dish, Chicago-style pizza with two toppings. Two other highly unusual items at Gramma's are a large fresh green salad for four for only $3.95 and a $2.39 lunch.
*❧ *Gramma's Pizza, 19213 Sonoma Highway, Sonoma 95476; phone (707) 938–1003. Open 11:00 A.M.–9:00 P.M. daily, later in summer. Delivery up to the last minutes. Visa, MasterCard, Diners Club, Carte Blanche, and JCB. Wheelchair-accessible.*

HOMEGROWN BAKING COMPANY'S first outpost of the original Napa Street bagel shop is here in Maxwell Village. This Homegrown features fresh bagels and fillings, excellent daily soups and coffees, and full breakfasts. It draws many locals from its downtown restaurant.
*❧ *Homegrown Baking Company, 19161 Sonoma Highway, Sonoma 95476; phone (707) 996–0177. No credit cards. Open 6:00 A.M.–2:00 P.M. Monday–Friday, 7:00 A.M.–2:00 P.M. Saturday–Sunday. Wheelchair-accessible.*

THE PARKPOINT CLUB is a full health club, gym, and swimming pool, affiliated with many clubs through the United States. It is also located in the Maxwell Village Shopping Center.
*❧ *The Parkpoint Club, 19111 Sonoma Highway, Sonoma 95476; phone (707) 996–3111. Open 5:30 A.M.–10:00 P.M. weekdays, 8:00 A.M.–7:00 P.M. weekends. Wheelchair-accessible.*

Now it's time to continue north. As you leave the shopping center, turn left to reach Boyes Hot Springs, El Verano, Agua Caliente, Glen Ellen, and Kenwood. Soon you come to the corner of Sonoma Highway (12) and Verano Avenue, also known locally as "Fast-Food Gulch." Most of them are here. No more to be said about that; we always encourage you to try the home-grown eateries to experience local foods and cultures.

In the little shopping center on the northeast corner you will find one treasure, GOLDEN SPRING, a Chinese restaurant featuring Mandarin cuisine. Mrs. Wong's menu is similar to that of the Shanghai on Fifth Street West, but a little spicier and more adventurous, and always with a little MSG. If that doesn't bother you, go for it. The Dragon's Delight prawns and scallops sautéed with green peppers and onions in black-bean sauce; Mongolian lamb; Three Princess pork, with three kinds of mushrooms and vegetables; and pepper-fried duck are all exceptional selections. The Golden Spring offers a complete lunch, including appetizers, soup, entree with rice, fortune cookies, and tea for just $3.95. Beer and wine are available.

❧ *Golden Spring, 18991 Sonoma Highway, Sonoma 95476; phone (707) 938–1275. Open for lunch 11:30 A.M.–2:30 P.M. Monday–Saturday, for dinner 4:00–9:30 P.M.; dinner only on Sunday. MasterCard and Visa. Wheelchair-accessible.*

Across Highway 12, **The Happy Dog** is Sonoma's answer to the fast-food joints' hamburgers. The Happy Dog is more like a truck stop, serving huge, drippy hamburgers, an excellent grilled chicken-breast burger, fries, onion rings, chili hot dogs, and corn dogs.

Fine points: To get here safely, turn left (west) at the Verano Avenue signal. Take the first right around the back of McDonald's to the back of the Happy Dog. Park on the west side, because the grease blows to the east and will land in a thousand little droplets on your car if you park on the highway side.

❧ *The Happy Dog, 18962 Sonoma Highway, Sonoma 95476; phone (707) 935–6211. Open 11:00 A.M.–8:30 P.M. daily. No credit cards. Wheelchair-accessible.*

One of our favorites, **Hanzell Vineyards**, is one of the least-known yet finest wineries in California. Familiar to connoisseurs for its "unbeatable," "landmark" Chardonnays and Pinot Noirs, this small winery is worth making the required appointment to see and experience. Hanzell's 1997 crop was so robust that it saved the finest fruit to make its own wines and sold the rest to favorite wineries.

Founded in 1953 by former American ambassador to Italy James Zellerbach, Hanzell lives within its natural limits of estate wine grapes, marketing abilities, and physical means. Zellerbach brought back from France a love of Burgundy and dedicated his land, soul, and sizable lumber fortune to creating vineyards of Chardonnay and Pinot Noir. The first to import French oak barrels from Burgundian coopers, Sirugue, Zellerbach basically "invented" using French oak barrels in California. At a 750-foot elevation, Hanzell is nestled in the hills in a peaceful, rambling compound that makes you want to stay there forever. The facade of the winery itself is the mirror image of Clos de Vougeot in Burgundy, and the house is of the same style and feeling.

After her husband died in 1963, Hana Zellerbach first sold all the wine and then sold the estate vineyards, winery, and family house to Douglas and Mary Day in 1965. In 1975 the Day family sold the property to Barbara de Brye, an Australian heiress who lived in London and married a Parisian banker, Count Jacques de Brye. Later divorced from the count, she died unexpectedly in 1991, leaving the estate and fortune to their son, Alexander.

Fine points: Bob Session runs Hanzell for the young Alexander de Brye. Featured wines: Chardonnay, Pinot Noir. Winemaker: Bob Session. Cases: 3,000+. Acres: 31.

❧ *Hanzell Vineyards,* *18596 Lomita Avenue, Sonoma 95476; phone (707) 996–3860. Open by appointment only. Not wheelchair-accessible.*

A fairly new addition to Sonoma Valley, E-SAAN THAI HOUSE is a peaceful, dignified, and casual Thai restaurant with reasonable prices and excellent service. Less than ½ mile from the Verano Avenue intersection, E-Saan's owners put loads of money and love into upgrading and redecorating what for several years had been the King Hwa Chinese restaurant.

This is one of those places where you see famous, unfamous, and infamous locals. County officials, Bruce Cohn of B. R. Cohn Winery and Doobie Brothers manager, visitors, and volunteer firemen all stop here occasionally for lunch or dinner. The fish cakes, larb, mixed vegetables with tofu, E-Saan curry, and Pad Thai are all great. We have never found anything other than excellent here. No MSG is used in this restaurant, and all spicy dishes may be mild, medium, or hot and spicy, and all dishes can be made vegetarian. E-Saan offers lunch specials on weekdays; at $5.95 to $7.25, they include the soup of the day or an iceberg-lettuce salad with red onions and a light peanut dressing and a wide choice of entrees. Try the Pia Goong (grilled prawns) salad ($7.95) and any and all of the appetizers.

❧ *E-Saan Thai House, 18629 Sonoma Highway, Boyes Hot Springs 95416; phone (707) 939–9077. Open 11:00 A.M.–9:00 P.M. Monday–Friday, 4:00–9:00 P.M. Saturday–Sunday. MasterCard, Visa, and American Express. Wheelchair-accessible.*

Manuel and Kimberly Azevedo launched their LA SALETTE RESTAURANT when Kristin and Peter Stewart left their Bear Flag Cafe and opened Deuce on Broadway south of Sonoma Plaza.

Formerly chef at Kenwood Restaurant, Manuel's superb Portuguese-African cooking takes him back to his mother's roots and offers a welcome addition to Sonoma's cuisine. We especially enjoy the trout escabeche at $7.00; salmon com milho, a roasted salmon served on grilled corn off the cob and braised collard greens ($14.75); Mozambique prawns ($15.00); and Piri-Piri chicken, a crisp grilled boned half range chicken with mashed yams, coconut milk, and grilled asparagus at $13.75. Our favorite dessert is the Basmati rice pudding, plenty for two people to share with two rice cakes topped with cinnamon sauce and sliced figs at $5.00. The hamburger-needy can enjoy a great ½ pound burger with baked (helps the conscience) garlic fries at $7.50. Outdoor seating facing Mary's Pizza Shack across the road in good weather.

❧ *La Salette, 18625 Sonoma Highway, Sonoma 95476; phone (707) 938–1927. Open 5:00–9:00 P.M. Tuesday–Sunday. Beer and wine. MasterCard and Visa. Wheelchair-accessible.*

The Boyes Hot Springs **MARY'S PIZZA SHACK**, right across from La Salette Restaurant, is as close to the original of this local chain as you will get. The first one was actually in Mary Fazio's home, and then she catered to her friends' wishes and opened her first restaurant in a little clapboard "shack" up the road a piece to take her great pizza and pasta public. The community quickly outgrew the shack, and Mary built this "new" restaurant in the late 1970s. The pizza makers still throw every pizza dough into the air, and some splat on the overhead pipes and stay for a while. That was your pizza up there, not ours.

Young and older baseball teams usually end up here after a game, and many Sonoma high school kids work their first jobs here. On Fridays you can drool over the special, steaming polenta with sausage and marinara sauce and see eighty-something Mary holding court at a table against the back wall. Oh yes— '49ers Joe Montana and Brent Jones drop in often, as does basketball star Chris Mullin. See autographed photos and menus on the front wall. Beer and wine are served; smoking is allowed on the patio.

❧ *Mary's Pizza Shack, 18636 Sonoma Highway (12), Boyes Hot Springs 95416; phone (707) 938–3600. Open 11:00 A.M.–11:00 P.M. daily. MasterCard and Visa. Wheelchair-accessible.*

GOODTIME BICYCLE, Sonoma Valley's favorite community bike store, stocks all Schwinns, mountain and racing bikes, exercise bikes, three wheelers, and all necessary and unnecessary equipment. You can rent bikes and take tours from here, too. Owner Doug McKesson has (elevated on the wall behind the cash register) a collection of rare bikes demonstrating bicycle history, one with wooden wheels made in 1900.

Doug and his shop are popular because of his long-term involvement in community efforts, from sports to cooking at Community Center events and raising money for the Valley of the Moon Boys and Girls Club.

Fine points: Also known as "The Bikeman," Doug leads tours for private groups as well as for the Sonoma Mission Inn. You can take his Galloping Gourmet lunch rides, winery tours, or just plain Valley-sites tours up to $55 per person.

❧ *Goodtime Bicycle, 18503 Sonoma Highway, Boyes Hot Springs 95416; phone (707) 938–0453; Web site www.bikemantours.com. Open 9:00 A.M.–5:00 P.M. Monday–Saturday, 10:00 A.M.–4:00 P.M. Sunday. MasterCard, Visa, and American Express.*

THE FRUIT BASKET is Karen and Gus Dalakiaris's northern outpost. While the veggies are not locally grown, they are always a bargain. Mushrooms are often just $1.35 a pound here, and lettuce is about 59 cents, except in winter. Their best buys include pastas, rices, and bulk nuts and candies wrapped in small packages.

❧ *The Fruit Basket, 18474 Sonoma Highway, Boyes Hot Springs 95416; phone (707) 996–7433. Open 9:00 A.M.–7:00 P.M. daily. No credit cards. Wheelchair-accessible.*

SONOMA MISSION INN SPA AND COUNTRY CLUB is a true oasis on the west side of Sonoma Highway in Boyes Hot Springs. Once a resort center based on natural artesian mineral hot springs, "Boyes" and Agua Caliente consisted primarily of small cabins and cottages from an era when San Francisco families came up to the area for baths and a vacation.

Originally built in 1927, the now-expanded and luxurious Sonoma Mission Inn dominates the area and has inspired neighborhood improvements. The Sonoma Mission Inn's public dining restaurants include the Grille in the Inn and the Sonoma Mission Inn Cafe (the least expensive of SMI's restaurants) on the corner of Sonoma Highway and Boyes Boulevard. You can eat, exercise in the gym, swim, play tennis, get a massage, a manicure, or a facial, and simply soak up the luxury and pampering if you wish. And now that SMI has bought Sonoma National Golf Course, you can also play golf on a gorgeous course.

Executive Chef Toni Robertson oversees the excellent food throughout the Sonoma Mission Inn, Spa and Country Club. Her fabulous background includes stints as Executive Chef at Singapore's Pan Pacific Hotel, the Palace Hotel in Sun City, South Africa; she also worked at the Four Seasons Hotel in Beverly Hills and the Ritz-Carlton in Chicago. Toni also writes a weekly restaurant column for the *Sonoma Index-Tribune.*

SONOMA MISSION INN CAFE, once the popular Big 3 grocery store with a sandwich and soda fountain, grew under former SMI owner Ed Safdie to the Big Three Cafe, and under current SMI ownership to the Sonoma Mission Inn Cafe. The really big changes took place between Big 3 and Big Three, when the counter disappeared and white tablecloths and rich blue carpeting appeared.

Fine points: SMI Cafe has a beautiful gift and souvenir shop with the highest-quality shirts and caps and a wide variety of pertinent cookbooks, olive oils, and jams. Service in both the cafe and store are exemplary. Full bar.

❧ *Sonoma Mission Inn Cafe, 18140 Sonoma Highway, Boyes Hot Springs 95416; phone (707) 938–9000. Open 11:30 A.M.–3:00 P.M. for lunch, 3:00–5:30 P.M. bar food, 5:30–9:30 P.M. dinner, 7:00–11:00 A.M. weekend breakfast,*

YUKON GOLD POTATO CANNELLONI WITH BRAISED LEEKS, MUSHROOMS, AND MUSTARD GREENS
from Executive Chef Toni Robertson, Sonoma Mission Inn, Spa & Country Club

2 large baking potatoes	*3 Tbs olive oil*
4–5 Yukon gold potatoes	*1 cup red wine*
2 cups vegetable stock	*2 Tbs shallots, chopped*
1 cup julienned leeks	*2 Tbs herbs (chervil, Italian parsley, chives, etc.), chopped*
1 cup diced leeks	
1/2 lb assorted wild mushrooms	*1 cup assorted fresh herbs, same as above*
1/2 lb mustard greens	*1 lemon*
1/4 cup Strauss Family clabbered cottage cheese	*salt and pepper to taste*

For cannelloni filling: Boil Yukon gold potatoes until soft. Mash potatoes with a ricer. Meanwhile, puree clabbered cottage cheese with 1 cup of vegetable stock and 1 Tbs olive oil. Fold in potato puree. Salt and pepper to taste. Set mixture aside.

Slice baking potatoes into 1/10-inch-thick slices using meat slicer or mandoline. Place potato slices on nonstick baking sheets and bake approximately 2–3 minutes until the starches are out of the potato. Carefully remove potato slices and arrange 3 slices overlapping one another to form a square sheet approximately 4 x 4 inches. Place potato filling on cannelloni sheet and roll them. Continue this process three more times.

Sauté the cannelloni in a nonstick pan until one side is nicely browned. Remove from the pan and place back on the nonstick baking sheets and bake in the oven at 350° for 8 minutes until the outer layer of the potato is cooked.

Sauté wild mushrooms and leeks in a large skillet with chopped shallots. Deglaze the pan with red wine. Continue cooking for 5 more minutes until red wine is reduced to half. Add remaining cup of vegetable stock. Bring to a boil. Add mustard greens and cook for 2–3 minutes. Add chopped herbs and season with salt and pepper.

To Garnish: Toss julienned leeks and remaining scraps of potato with olive oil and bake in oven until brown and crisp.

To Assemble: Place braised leeks and mushrooms in the middle of the pasta bowl. Place cannelloni on the mushroom mixture. Garnish with crisp leeks and potato. Add assorted herbs, which have been tossed with olive oil and juice from lemon. Serves 6.

SPA YOGURT PANNA COTTA WITH FIVE SEASONAL FRUIT COULIS

from Executive Chef Toni Robertson, Sonoma Mission Inn, Spa & Country Club

1½ cups low-fat yogurt (use top quality like Strauss Family)	*½ cup fresh blueberries*
1 cup nonfat milk	*½ cup fresh mango, diced*
½ cup sugar	*½ cup kiwi, diced*
4 sheets gelatin	*½ cup strawberries*
	½ cup blackberries

Soak the gelatin sheets in cold water to soften. Combine the sugar and non-fat milk in a saucepan and bring to a boil. Add the soft gelatin sheets into the saucepan and stir until fully dissolved. Remove the saucepan from the heat and allow to cool down to room temperature. Fold in the yogurt and divide the mixture evenly into five individual flan molds. Place the molds in the refrigerator overnight to cool completely.

To prepare the fruits coulis, puree each of the five fruits individually in the blender and keep separate, aiming for a thick consistency.

Presentation: Place the molded panna cotta in the center of the dessert dish. Garnish the mold with generous dollops of the individual fruit purees around the panna cotta and on top. Finish the garnish with fresh mint and a light sprinkling of powdered sugar. Serve immediately. Serves 4.

and 7:00 A.M.–3:00 P.M. Sunday brunch. MasterCard, Visa, American Express, and Carte Blanche. Wheelchair-accessible.

SONOMA MISSION INN GRILLE has always been a haven of casual elegance, serving both its regular and spa menu selections. Most of the tables face the interior patio and pool. Lunch ranges from divine Dungeness crab dumplings in a spicy lemongrass broth and hearts of romaine Caesar salad to the classic SMI burger with applewood-smoked bacon and cheese to steamed clams and mussels with spinach linguine. Dinner appetizers range from a grilled vegetable Napoleon with Laura Chenel Chèvre at $7.50 to pan-seared Sonoma foie gras at $13.00. Entrees range from fresh orecchiette pasta with portabello mushrooms, baby spinach, and Laura Chenel Chèvre at $17.00 to grilled rack of Sonoma lamb at $26.00.

❧ *Sonoma Mission Inn Grille, 18140 Sonoma Highway, Boyes Hot Springs 95416; phone (707) 938–9000. Open daily 11:30 A.M.–2:30 P.M. for lunch, 6:00–9:30 P.M. dinner. MasterCard, Visa, American Express, and Carte Blanche. Wheelchair-accessible.*

Right across the Boyes Hot Springs triangle from the Sonoma Mission Inn is UNCLE PATTY'S BAR AND GRILL, an old Sonoma country-style restaurant that looks in one room like a San Francisco bar and grill. As you enter, you walk into a popular local bar with good, stiff drinks and local wines. There are dining rooms downstairs to both the right and left, with deep upholstered booths and white tablecloths.

Owners Patrick and Linda Scheiblich are from old Sonoma families and deliver hearty, solid, all-American food with little nonsense. They offer "weekly specials" with soup or salad, such as Monday's BBQ baby back ribs with Aunt Linnie's potato pancakes, pot roast every Wednesday, or Thanksgiving turkey and all the trimmings every Thursday, all for $9.95. Other dinner selections include Chicken Gloria at $12.95, pasta primavera at $10.95, braised lamb shank at $14.95, and roasted Petaluma duck at $13.95. The wide variety of sandwiches ranges from grilled eggplant and roasted red peppers at $6.95 to a good, pre-Nouvelle cuisine steak sandwich at $9.95. The chef is Custodio Colin.

❧ *Uncle Patty's Bar and Grill, 15 Boyes Boulevard, Boyes Hot Springs 95416; phone (707) 996–7979; fax (707) 996–8965. Open daily 11:00 A.M.–3:00 P.M. for lunch, 5:00–9:30 P.M. dinner, bar until 2:00 A.M. MasterCard, Visa, and American Express. Wheelchair-accessible through lower (left) dining room; rest room not accessible.*

A newish and much-needed real coffeehouse, BARKING DOG COFFEE ROASTERS satisfies local coffee cravings in a small space converted from an old laundromat into an attractive and comfortable space. It stands out in Boyes Hot Springs because of its brightly colored petunias and cosmopolitan appearance.

All coffee beans are roasted daily in the only room, so you barely need to do more than inhale—but don't miss the outstanding espresso. Pleasant small tables and lots of free newspapers make you want to come back if you can't stay. Try the back garden. Artisan Bakers' muffins, Homegrown bagels, and crunchy biscotti make this an excellent alternative to larger breakfasts.

❧ *Barking Dog Coffee Roasters, 17999 Sonoma Highway, Boyes Hot Springs 95416; phone (707) 939–1905. Open 6:15 A.M.–5:00 P.M. weekdays, 7:30 A.M.–5:00 P.M. Saturday, 8:00 A.M.–2:00 P.M. Sunday. No credit cards. Wheelchair-accessible.*

JOHNNY & FLO'S APPLIANCES & CLASSIC RANGES is an absolute must-stop for food and kitchens-as-culture fans, which Kathleen is. Had we known this place was here when we built our house fifteen years ago, we would have organized the kitchen around one of Johnny & Flo's '50s Okeefe & Merritt stoves; now we can only wait for our newish one to wear out and die.

You'll know you're there when you see the pink and white Cadillac with huge, pointy fins out in front. Johnny & Flo have been collecting and restoring 1900–1960 ranges for thirty-five years here in Sonoma Valley, just 2 blocks north of the Sonoma Mission Inn. Check out (and plan to take home) fully restored American classics such as Wedgwood, Buck's, Gaffers & Sattler, Roper, Magic Chef, and Quick Meal. You can also pick up (well, not exactly) vintage refrigerators.

Fine points: We particularly enjoy the displays of classic books and antique kitchen utensils, which Kathleen also collects. Flowered terrycloth dish towels hang over oven door handles, and then there's the classic gas pump in case you need one.

❧ *Johnny & Flo's Appliances & Classic Ranges, 17549 Sonoma Highway, Sonoma 95476; phone (707) 996–9730. Open 10:00 A.M.–6:00 P.M. Wednesday–Saturday. MasterCard and Visa. Not wheelchair-accessible.*

JOHNNY & FLO'S APPLIANCES & CLASSIC RANGES: PART OF THEIR COLLECTION

SWEET HEART COOKIES
from Chef Linda G. Kittler,
Valley of the Moon Winery & Vineyard

$1/2$ cup butter	$1^1/_4$ cup flour
$3/4$ cup sugar	$1/4$ tsp. salt
2 egg yolks	$1/4$ tsp. baking powder
$1/2$ tsp vanilla	$1/2$ cup roasted almonds,
$1/2$ tsp almond extract	chopped
$1/2$ tsp orange extract	parchment paper
$1/2$ Tbs lemon zest	$1/2$ cup confection sugar
1 Tbs cream	2 Tbs cream

Preheat oven to 375° F.

Chop almonds, spread on a parchment-lined cookie sheet, and bake for 12–15 minutes until light brown. Cream together the butter and sugar until light and fluffy. Add the egg yolks, one at a time, thoroughly blending after each yolk. Mix in the extracts, zest, and cream. Blend the flour, salt, and baking powder and add to the butter mixture. Finally, add the roasted chopped almonds.

Place the dough between two pieces of parchment paper, roll out to $1/4$-inch thick and chill in the refrigerator for 10 minutes. Remove parchment from both sides, place dough on a cutting board, and cut out cookies, using your favorite cutter. Place on parchment-lined cookie sheet and bake for 12–15 minutes. Decorate with simple icing of $1/2$ cup confectioners' sugar plus 2 Tbs cream and food coloring if you wish.

VALLEY OF THE MOON WINERY, now owned by Korbel, has been through a lot of changes lately, all positive if you like progress. Harry Parducci Sr. sold his baby to Kenwood, who then sold themselves and it to Korbel. While the Parducci family is no longer involved and Valley of the Moon no longer provides label-free table wines to San Francisco's North Beach Italian restaurants, new ownership has brought high-tech, modern techniques and money to expand and improve the local wine scene.

Be sure to visit Valley of the Moon and its new large and gorgeous tasting room, state-of-the-art tanks and systems, and some wonderful wines unusual in the Sonoma Valley. To get here, turn onto Madrone Road from either Highway 12 or Arnold Drive and go about 0.5 mile.

One of the oldest wineries in Sonoma Valley, it was owned in the past by the Spreckels (sugar) family, General Joseph Hooker, Eli T. Sheppard, and U.S. Senator George Hearst. This oldest winery in Glen Ellen fell into disuse during Prohibition. In 1941 the Parducci family began to reactivate it and turned it into an attractive business.

Featured wines: Chardonnay, Pinot Blanc, Syrah, Sangiovese, Zinfandel, and Cuvée della Luna, a Cabernet/Merlot blend. Winemaker: Pat Henderson. Cases: 25,000. Acres: 60.

❧ *Valley of the Moon Winery, 777 Madrone Road, Glen Ellen 95442; phone (707) 996–6941; e-mail luna@vomwinery.com; Web site www.vomwinery.com.*

You can also get to this point in our tour by driving west on West Napa Street or West Spain Street from Sonoma Plaza, turning right onto Highway 12, and following it toward Glen Ellen and Santa Rosa. Following this route, you'll pass Mary's Pizza Shack, La Salette Restaurant, and Sonoma Mission Inn. Continue north. It is 4.7 miles from Sonoma Plaza to Valley of the Moon Winery. Then you can carry on to experience Kenwood and Glen Ellen.

CHAPTER 5

KENWOOD AND GLEN ELLEN

*O*ur tour through Kenwood and Glen Ellen covers about 20 miles round-trip from downtown Sonoma, or 25 miles round-trip if you include downtown Glen Ellen on Arnold Drive. You actually pass through outer Glen Ellen, on Highway 12 on your way to Kenwood. If your time is limited, you can eliminate the Kenwood part and just go to Glen Ellen by turning left on Arnold Drive about 0.5 mile past the Garden Court Cafe and the Secret Garden. Whatever route you choose, you'll find wonderful things to do and see.

The owner of **B. R. COHN WINERY** (5 miles from Sonoma Plaza), Bruce Cohn, made his first reputation and fortune managing rock bands like the Doobie Brothers and Night Ranger, which he still does. Doobie Brothers gold records line the walls of the winery tasting room.

Once a natural-spring watering hole for the stagecoach traveling between Santa Rosa and Sonoma, the winery's California stucco-and-wood ranch house now serves as a watering hole for curious and thirsty travelers who want to see how fine wine and rock music blend. When the Cohns bought this property, it was called Olive Hill Ranch, because of the gracious old olive trees on the property. Never one to let an opportunity slip by, Cohn now makes elegant cold-press olive oils and gourmet vinegars.

Winemaker Mikael Guylash began making wine at Jordan Vineyards, studied chemistry at Sonoma State University and winemaking at Fresno State, and worked at King Estate and with consulting winemaster Mary Edwards.

 Fine points: Bruce also sponsors an annual celebrity golf tournament to benefit local charities at Sonoma National Golf Club on Arnold Drive. Get on his mailing list for these events. Featured wines: Chardonnay. Cabernet Sauvignon, Merlot, Pinot Noir. Winemaker: Mikael Guylash. Cases: 25,000. Acres: 80 in grapes, 8 in olives.

❧ *B. R. Cohn Winery, 15140 Sonoma Highway, Glen Ellen 95442; phone*

OAK HILL FARM'S FALL BOUNTY,
DISPLAYED FOR HALLOWEEN

(707) 938–4064. Open 10:00 A.M.–5:00 P.M. daily. Tasting fee depends on what's left in stock. MasterCard, Visa, and American Express. Wheelchair-accessible.

Near the winery on Sonoma Highway is the OAK HILL FARM, Ann and the late Otto Teller's prize organic vegetable and flower farm. Turn right immediately past the enormous upturned eucalyptus tree stump. Employee Teresa runs the barn and knows everything about vegetables, flowers, garlic, wreaths, and cooking that you may want to know. Her exquisite arrangements delight your senses. Every time we go here we want to live like this.

❧ *Oak Hill Farm, 15101 Sonoma Highway, Glen Ellen 95442; phone (707) 996–6643. Open 10:00 A.M.–4:00 P.M. Friday–Sunday in summer, 10:00 A.M.–3:00 P.M. from fall to Christmas. No credit cards. Barn is wheelchair-accessible.*

When you come out Oak Hill's driveway, turn right to proceed to **ARROWOOD VINEYARD AND WINERY** (0.7 mile from Oak Hill Farm). Built in 1987 to resemble a New England farmhouse, this charming winery brings beauty as well as expertise to the Sonoma Valley. As you turn off Highway 12 into the driveway shared by the winery and brewery, enjoy the colors and backdrop of the Mayacamas Mountains. Park in the parking lot and walk to the exquisite new tasting room with blond wood floors and huge brown wicker chairs in front of the fireplace.

President and Winemaster Richard Arrowood served as winemaster and executive vice president for sixteen years at Château St. Jean in Kenwood and worked as chemist and assistant manager of Korbel Champagne Cellars on the Russian River. The Canadian flag flies next to the American flag at Arrowood because Richard's wife, Alis Demers Arrowood, is Canadian and an equal partner in the winery. When they first opened their dream winery, Richard continued to work at Château St. Jean for three years, and Alis held down the fort during the week, doing all the grunt work such as topping barrels, dragging hoses, and running the bottling line. Having lived through that down-and-dirty phase of creating a new winery, she now concentrates on sales and marketing. Richard also serves as winemaker for Remick Ridge/Smothers Brothers winery.

 Featured wines: Chardonnay, Pinot Blanc, Viognier, Syrah, Merlot, Malbec, Cabernet Sauvignon, Late Harvest White Riesling. Winemaster: Richard Arrowood. Winemaker: Mike Berthoud. Cases: 27,000. Acres: 10.

❧ *Arrowood Vineyard and Winery, 14347 Sonoma Highway, Glen Ellen 95442; phone (707) 938–5170; fax (707) 938–5947. Web site www.arrowood-vineyards.com. Open 10:00 A.M.–4:30 P.M. daily. Tasting fee: $3.00 for three tastes. Visa, MasterCard, and American Express. Wheelchair-accessible.*

Turn right when you leave Arrowood, pass Sunny Slope Ranch, and on the right you'll find the Bouverie Audubon Preserve. The small house against the hills with the arch over the porch is where M. F. K. Fisher lived the last twenty years of her life, and where she died.

David Pleydell-Bouverie gave his large ranch and home to the Bouverie Audubon Preserve, which he created with the Audubon Society. Tours of the grounds, library, and birding may be arranged.

❧ *Bouverie Audubon Preserve, P.O. Box 1195, Glen Ellen 95442; phone (707) 938–4554.*

Nestled into the Bouverie Ranch property along Sonoma Highway and across from the county park is a small, heavenly oasis containing **THE SECRET**

GARDEN and The Garden Court Cafe. The Secret Garden is a den of bliss for craftspeople and those who would like to make a little something but don't know how to get started. Everything you could possibly need is here and inexpensive. Owner Penny Burns reveals some precious secrets through a full calendar of classes, in everything from paper making to embroidery and stenciling. Get on the mailing list.

🌺 *The Secret Garden, 13885 Sonoma Highway, Glen Ellen 95442; phone (707) 996–7531. Open 10:00 A.M.–5:00 P.M. daily. MasterCard, Visa, American Express, Discover, and Novus. Wheelchair-accessible from back.*

Peter and Lesley B. Fay bought THE GARDEN COURT CAFE AND BAKERY, a successful breakfast and lunch cafe, from Peter and Kirsten Stewart (now at Deuce Restaurant in Sonoma) and made it even better. Now Rich and Stacy Treglia have, in turn, bought it from the Fays and somehow improved it yet again. This diner has sold and resold simply because it is extremely successful. All three couples have worked their cinnamon buns off to deliver the best, most entertaining service around. Spiffed up with new, brighter paint, the Garden Court is small, cozy, and intimate, with a few tables on the enclosed patio.

As you drive up, ease off the highway carefully, and don't be put off by the people hanging out in front. First go in and put your name on a list just to the right and inside the front door. Then come back out and pour yourself a cup of the highest-quality (and complimentary) coffee available, including decaf, from the table outside to the right of the door. Every few minutes Stacy or Rich

LAST HOUSE OF WRITER M. F. K. FISHER

comes out with a tray of irresistible scones or coffeecake for you to nibble on while you wait. Don't leave; that's not fair.

Breakfast ranges from $4.25 to $9.95, and from scones to intricate, personalized omelets. (You can have any number of eggs you want, and if the omelet of your dreams isn't on the menu, they will make it.) Pancakes come in medium or large and often bear little taste twists like orange, strawberry, or wheat, and come with heaps of perfectly ripened fresh fruit. Eggs Benedict and cinnamon buns are extremely popular. Rich has added non-health-food favorites, such as pork chops or chicken-fried steak and eggs, for which Stacy has a list of sixty fans to call for their chicken-fried steak alert.

When you order tea, they bring you the whole can of the Republic of Teas flavors and allow you to use all the little round baggies you wish.

At lunch the rosemary-grilled chicken breast with cranberry ginger relish is mouthwatering ($8.75). The grilled artichoke sandwich ($8.75) is a surprising new experience, as is the albacore-tuna and cheddar-cheese melt on sourdough. The Garden Court is truly famous for its burgers, including one with Teleme cheese, bacon, and grilled onions at $8.95. We also like the healthy Tuscany Burger, made with turkey, fresh basil, garlic, and roasted red peppers ($7.95). The Garden Court also offers many selections with no or low fat, no refined sugar, and nonfat dairy products. Special kids stuff appears when needed, and there are great picnic baskets to go.

 Fine points: New staff T-shirts proclaim, "If you leave here hungry, it's your own fault." So there! Stacy and Rich now host monthly dinners, which are usually sold out six weeks in advance. Dogs can enjoy the new county dog park across the road.

🐾 *The Garden Court Cafe and Bakery, 13875 Sonoma Highway, Glen Ellen 95442; phone (707) 935–1565. Open 7:00 A.M.–2:00 P.M. daily. MasterCard and Visa. Not wheelchair-accessible. Definitely dog friendly, including bowls of water, dog treats, and a greeting from the house Dalmation, "Blue."*

SONOMA COUNTY REGIONAL PARK, just across the road from the Garden Court and Secret Garden (6.4 miles from Sonoma Plaza), contains acres of wild, open spaces. This is a very popular but nevertheless little-known regional park. You can walk on trails or cross country into Glen Ellen, or have a picnic under native valley oak trees. From here you have a breathtaking view looking east across Sonoma Highway at the Bouverie Audubon Preserve. There is just a $2.00 parking fee.

🐾 *Sonoma County Regional Park; phone (707) 527–2041. Open sunrise to sunset. No credit cards. Partly wheelchair-accessible; the Portapotty rest rooms are not accessible.*

(Stacy's) Granny's Chicken Fried Steak with Creamy Gravy

from Stacy and Rich Treglia, Garden Court Cafe

8–10 4–5-oz top round steaks
(have your butcher tenderize)

cooking oil (Wesson works best)

2 cups milk

For the batter:

½ cup buttermilk

6 eggs, beaten

For the flour mixture (batter):

6 cups flour

1 Tbs salt

2 Tbs pepper

For the steaks:

Preheat a deep fry pan, preferably a cast-iron skillet, filled halfway with cooking oil to medium-high heat. Season the steaks with salt and pepper.

Mix buttermilk and beaten eggs. Combine flour mixture ingredients.

In batches of 4–5, one steak at a time, cover with egg batter and then dip into flour mixture. Repeat one more time, patting steaks down to make sure flour mixture sticks to the steak (this makes the steak really crispy).

Place steaks in hot oil, turning once. When brown and crispy, remove from pan and drain on cookie sheet covered with paper towels. Repeat with rest of steaks. *Hint #1:* While cooking gravy, place steaks in oven set to 250° F to keep warm.

For the cream gravy:

Let oil cool in steak pan for a few minutes; then drain through metal strainer in metal container, saving the "crispies." To make the roux, leave a little of the oil and the browned flour drippings in bottom of pan. Sprinkle the drippings with flour from steak mixture and cook on medium heat until brown and the consistency of wet sand is achieved. *Hint #2:* I usually make extra roux and then put it aside.

Add 2 cups milk and stir frequently with wire whisk, making sure that you scrape the bottom of the pan to keep flour from burning. Bring to a boil; then lower temperature so that gravy simmers and thickens (about 15 minutes). If gravy gets too thick, add more milk; if it's too thin, add more roux. The gravy consistency depends on how you like it, thick or thin; it's up to you. Season with salt and pepper to taste. Enjoy.

When I was a kid we would have this for dinner. Mom and Granny would serve mashed potatoes, green beans, and Wonder Bread. Yes, Wonder Bread, with butter on the potatoes and gravy on the bread. At the restaurant we serve it for breakfast with eggs, potatoes, and biscuits.

Rosemary Wood's Beltane Ranch, farther down the highway, presents a classic historic California bed and breakfast with exquisite food and grounds. Both M. F. K. Fisher and Julia Child used to send friends to stay here. For details, see Chapter 6, Where to Stay in Sonoma Valley.

KENWOOD

This tour of Kenwood takes you 20 miles round-trip from Sonoma Plaza—25 miles if you visit the town of Glen Ellen. A slow drive through Kenwood will cap your experience and confirm your suspicions that Sonoma Valley is one of the most beautiful secrets in the world. You'll understand why stars of the business and entertainment worlds have flocked here to live in privacy in the last few years.

Kenwood hosts some specialized and special events, the most famous of which is the World Championship Pillow Fights (usually presided over by comedian Tommy Smothers), 3K and 10K runs, and a chili cookoff on July 4. There's a huge Easter Breakfast at the Kenwood Depot, a Father's Day Pancake Breakfast at the Fire House on Sonoma Highway, an August soccer camp, the Holiday Open House over Thanksgiving weekend, and the Festival of Lights fund-raisers to benefit local charities at all Kenwood wineries in December.

If you want to try all the wineries, plan a route in advance. It is safest if you go to those on one side of the highway, cross it once, and then tour those on the other side of the highway. Just *taste;* don't drink. Crossing Highway 12 several times is truly perilous.

Sites you should check out include the classic California Kenwood Community Church (9637 Channing Way, off Warm Springs Road), the Kenwood Community Club in the old Kenwood Depot (314 Warm Springs Road), and the park and soccer field between Shaw and Maple Streets.

Opposite Dunbar Road's intersection with Sonoma Highway, you'll see the southernmost of the Kunde Vineyards. Used as cattle grazing land for decades, the Kunde family's vineyards run for about 2 miles along the right (east) side of the highway and up the hillsides of the Mayacamas Mountains on the eastern side of the valley. About 0.8 mile north of the Dunbar intersection, you will see the Pagani ranch house, a classic California wood house and barn. One of the most photographed sites in Sonoma Valley, the Pagani grapevines put on an unequaled show of fall colors, from light yellows to deep, blood reds.

We tell you about CAFE CITTI, toward the north end of Kenwood, first and out of order, because we think you might need it for picnic supplies at Kenwood wineries. Cafe Citti is an informal, Italian-style trattoria. Its long

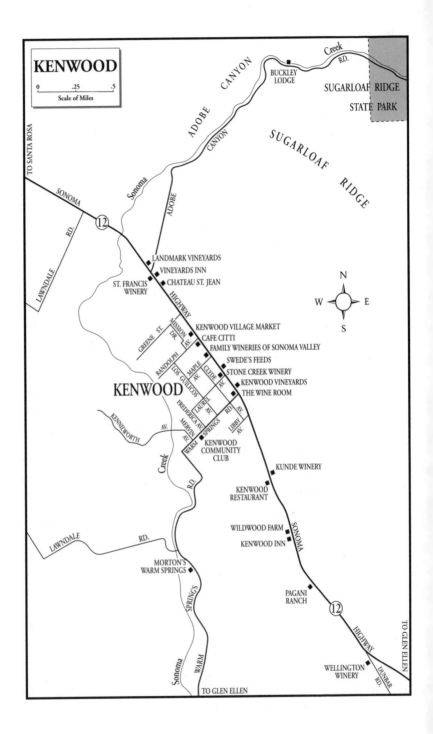

KENWOOD

0   .25   .5
Scale of Miles

TO SANTA ROSA

SONOMA RD.

LAWNDALE RD.

ADOBE CANYON

Sonoma

ADOBE CANYON

Creek RD.

BUCKLEY LODGE

SUGARLOAF RIDGE

STATE PARK

SUGARLOAF RIDGE

12

N
W   E
S

LANDMARK VINEYARDS
VINEYARDS INN
CHATEAU ST. JEAN
ST. FRANCIS WINERY

HIGHWAY

GREENE ST.
MISSION DR.
RANDOLPH AV.
LOS GUILICOS
MAPLE AV.
CLYDE AV.

KENWOOD VILLAGE MARKET
CAFE CITTI
FAMILY WINERIES OF SONOMA VALLEY
SWEDE'S FEEDS
STONE CREEK WINERY
KENWOOD VINEYARDS
THE WINE ROOM

KENWOOD

FREDERICA AV.
LAUREL AV.
MERVIN AV.
WARM SPRINGS RD.
LIBBY AV.

KENNILWORTH AV.

Creek

KENWOOD COMMUNITY CLUB

KUNDE WINERY

LAWNDALE RD.

KENWOOD RESTAURANT

WILDWOOD FARM
KENWOOD INN

SONOMA

MORTON'S WARM SPRINGS

SPRING'S RD.

PAGANI RANCH

12

HIGHWAY

TO GLEN ELLEN

Sonoma

WARM

WELLINGTON WINERY

DUNBAR RD.

TO GLEN ELLEN

tables are covered with vinyl "chintz" tablecloths and decorated with fake flowers. Thin, crisp cellophane-wrapped Italian breadsticks are on every table. Cafe Citti has black ceiling fans and indirect lighting, though, which help make this former diner a little more glamorous.

Locals crowd the place every day. We have seen the owners of local wineries and workmen here at lunch. Judges and lawyers stop by from Los Guilicos Juvenile Court up the road for a huge bowl of soup and loaves of French bread. Waiters from other restaurants come by daily. Some Sonomans plan their trips to Santa Rosa with a stop at Cafe Citti on the way home.

When you come in the front door, it's best to find a table, have a seat, put down your stuff, and then take the time to study the menu on the wall above the counter. By the time you read the fine print, your mouth will be hanging open in amazement and hunger. When you think you know what you want, take your questions and order up to the counter. The agreeable staff will bring your food to your table when it is ready or wrap it to go.

Local or Chianti wines come in short, thick Italian peasant glasses. Cafe Citti instantly became known locally for its roasted chicken Toscana ($8.99) and pasta. You select the noodle shape and size you want as well as the sauce (the choices include the basics plus clam and putanesca). At first we followed local recommendations and tried the chicken and all the pasta variations.

One day at lunch we discovered the deal of the century. Cafe Citti sandwiches are dreamy and incredibly filling. Our favorites are the tuna and egg or chicken salad. Proof of the chicken being local, Jerry discovered a whole thigh bone in his sandwich! Despite that surprise, the sandwich on sourdough was sensational. Each sandwich ($5.75–7.95) comes with your choice of a variety of pasta salads or an outstanding cabbage and carrot salad. You get to pick the dressing for the coleslaw—our favorites are pesto and sun-dried tomato, both of which are consistently memorable. All salads are available in half-pints to quarts.

 Fine points: Luca and Linda Citti also offer tiramisù ($4.28), cannoli, gelato, and almond and chocolate torte. There is an excellent selection of local wines and several Chiantis. When you order by the glass, the wine comes in short, thick Italian peasant glasses. Beer is also sold.

♣ *Cafe Citti, 9049 Sonoma Highway, Kenwood 95452; phone (707) 833–2690. Open 11:00 A.M.–3:30 P.M. and 5:30–9:00 P.M. Monday–Thursday, 11:00 A.M.–3:30 P.M. and 5:30–8:30 P.M. Friday–Saturday. MasterCard and Visa. Beer and wine. Wheelchair-accessible through the north door.*

Now, back to the wineries. First we'll take you up the east side of Sonoma Highway north of Glen Ellen and the Garden Court Cafe. At the north end of

Kenwood, we'll cross Highway 12 from Landmark Vineyards to St. Francis and come back toward Sonoma along the west side of the highway.

The KUNDE WINERY family is one of the oldest and most respected in Sonoma Valley. Founder Louis Kunde settled here in 1904, when he bought James Shaw's Wildwood Ranch, which had vines planted in 1879. For decades the Kundes ranched and raised cattle on their 2,000 acres; and the cattle undoubtedly enriched the volcanic soil for later vineyard endeavors.

When Louis died in 1922, his son Arthur ("Big Boy") Kunde kept the winery open during Prohibition, but he finally had to close the doors when his sons were drafted into service during World War II. Having been resurrected by Big Boy's sons Bob and Fred, the winery is now one of the most beautiful and technologically advanced in California.

Beside the vastness and beauty of the Kunde property, the winery has a pleasantly understated ambience meant to feel like the old, rustic ranch barn. The caves and 32,000 square feet of tunnels carved into the natural hillside behind the winery are fascinating to tour. The property includes eight lakes and the Old Dunfillan Winery—the romantic setting of many weddings, including one of movie star Geena Davis. The marriage is already defunct, but it was a great party! Enjoy the color palette in September of bright pink crape myrtle trees surrounded by pink, orange, and white impatiens, as well as the large pond and picnic tables.

 Fine points: A spacious and romantic tasting and dining room 175 feet below a Chardonnay vineyard is available for special events and tastings. Featured wines: Estate Chardonnays, Gewürz-traminer, Zinfandel, Merlot, Cabernet Sauvignon, Syrah, Pinot Noir. Owners: The Kunde family. Winemaker: David Noyes. Cases: 65,000. Acres: 750.

❧ *Kunde Winery, 10155 Sonoma Highway, Kenwood 95452; phone (707) 833–5501. Open 11:00 A.M.–5:00 P.M. daily. MasterCard, Visa, and American Express. Wheelchair-accessible.*

Come back out Kundes' driveway to the highway and turn right 0.3 mile to KENWOOD VINEYARDS. A rustic redwood building houses Kenwood Vineyards, a classic Sonoma Valley winery that was once the Pagani Brothers winery, begun in 1906. Kenwood Vineyards was founded in 1970 by longtime college pals and wine enthusiasts from the San Francisco Bay Area. Today Michael Lee, Marty Lee, and John Sheela specialize in "small lot" winemaking, handling the harvest from each vineyard separately to preserve the individuality and integrity of each lot. Kenwood is one of the few Northern California wineries that has received a "certified organic" designation (even though many wineries in the Northwest are organic). As testimony to the success of their philosophy and wines, they just bought VALLEY OF THE MOON WINERY and vineyards, which they are replanting and rebuilding.

We can attest to the informal charm, humor, and relaxed atmosphere at Kenwood. This is not a wine-snob sort of place. Whether you know a lot or absolutely nothing about wine, you will be comfortable here. The house cats, named Chardonnay and Pinot, greet you in the tasting room.

Kenwood puts on an unusual number of special events pairing food and wine, along with the Kenwood Winery Holiday Series. Samples of monthly food-and-wine pairings include January's chocolate-dipped biscotti with Artist Series wine, February's focaccia bread with Jack London Merlot, salmon puff pastry with Sonoma Valley Chardonnay, and October's marinated Kenwood mushrooms with Reserve Chardonnay. One of our favorite Kenwood events is the annual Staff Art Show in November and December. A recent theme was art made with recycled materials, to coincide with America Recycles Day.

WHOA!!! MERLOT BROWNIES
from Kenwood Vineyards

1 cup Kenwood Vineyards Merlot, reduced to $1/4$ cup

4 oz bitter chocolate

$3/4$ cup ($1 1/2$ sticks) butter

3 eggs

2 cups sugar

1 tsp vanilla

1 cup all-purpose flour

1 cup coarsely chopped pecans

Preheat oven to 350° F.

Melt chocolate and butter together in a double boiler. Combine eggs, sugar and vanilla in another double boiler and heat to 100 to 110°. Then whip in a mixer until medium peaks form.

Mix melted chocolate with Merlot and butter and then combine with the egg mixture. Fold in flour and half of the pecans.

Spread batter in a greased 9 x 13-inch pan and sprinkle remaining pecans on top. Bake at 350° F for 45 minutes or until desired texture is reached. Recipe yields 2 dozen brownies.

Fine points: Many locals buy Kenwood's table wines for everyday use. Their Kenwood White Table Wine is almost always Sauvignon Blanc. Featured wines: Sauvignon Blanc; Chardonnay; six vineyard-designate Zinfandels, including Jack London and Nuns Canyon; Cabernet Sauvignon. Owner: Gary Heck of Korbel. Winemaker: Mike Lee. Cases: 450,000. Acres: 330.

KENWOOD VINEYARDS TASTING ROOM

🌿 *Kenwood Winery, 9592 Sonoma Highway, Kenwood 95452; phone (707) 833–5891; fax (707) 833–1146. Open 10:00 A.M.–4:30 P.M. daily. MasterCard, Visa, and American Express. Wheelchair-accessible.*

As you leave Kenwood Vineyards, turn right onto Sonoma Highway. After a couple of driveways, be sure to stop at the Strawberry Fields stand if it is open. The strawberries sold here, along with those grown at Watmaugh Road and Arnold Drive west of downtown Sonoma, are the most succulent and fully flavored of any we have ever tasted.

Just north of the strawberry stand, SWEDE'S FEEDS serves the Kenwood community as a genuine old-fashioned feed and grain store. It looks like a temporary permanent or permanent temporary structure and endeavor. You can get everything you need here for your animals, tools, and gossip for the ranch or home.

🌿 *Swede's Feeds, 9140 Sonoma Highway, Kenwood 95452; phone (707) 833–5050. Open 9:00 A.M.–6:00 P.M. daily. MasterCard and Visa. Wheelchair-accessible.*

Right in the middle of Kenwood, turn right up the long driveway to CHÂTEAU ST. JEAN, which was founded in 1973 and named for owner Ken

Sheffield's sister Jean, who may or may not be a saint. The winery was sold in 1984 to Suntory International (Japan), which also owned Château Lagrange and Château Beychevelle in Bordeaux, France. Suntory, in turn, sold it in 1997 to Beringer Wine Estates Group, also known as Texas Pacific Group and Silverado Partners. Other wineries that form this "group" include Beringer, Napa Ridge, Château Souverain, St. Clément, Meridian wineries, and Stags Leap Winery.

Aiming exclusively at the premium wine market, the winery's credo is "Only the finest." Château St. Jean's 1986 Cabernet Sauvignon was served in the White House, Queen Elizabeth has enjoyed its Chardonnay, while late ambassador Pamela Harriman served its wines at the American Embassy in Paris.

As you drive up the beautifully expansive driveway to Château St. Jean and into the parking lot, you'll see a gentle, Mediterranean-style tower ahead of you. Visitors might assume that the nymphet in the courtyard fountain is St. Jean herself, but remember, she doesn't exist!

The tasting room and hospitality center are located at the western side of the courtyard in the 1920 château, which is the anchor of the property. Over the years, Château St. Jean has graciously and generously made the château and its expansive porches and lawns available for local charities to host elegant fundraisers and parties. As you walk from the courtyard to the château, you pass an elongated fish pond, which the founder's son designed to look like Lake Michigan.

To enter the hospitality center, walk between the pond and the building and around to the western porch. Once inside, you feel as if you have walked into a comfortable, well-appointed living room, with your favorite relatives as hosts. Besides selling ample pours of their best wines, Château St. Jean places generous cubes of bread on plates for you to sample grapeseed oils or simply to cleanse your palate. Reserve wine tastings are held upstairs. Don't miss the new gift shop to the left as you enter the winery, where you will find collectors' corkscrews, throw-away cameras, screen savers, oil, mayonnaises, chocolates, and colored glassware.

 Fine points: Château St. Jean hosts students from around the world every summer and has all of them sign French oak barrels. Ask to see this area. Château St. Jean also recommends that you visit in January or February to have a real conversation with the winemaker and receive individual attention in the tasting room. Featured wines: Chardonnay, Fumé Blanc, Pinot Noir, Cabernet Sauvignon, Merlot. Owner: Beringer Wine Estates. Winemaker: Steve Reeder. Cases: 250,000. Acres: 255.
❧ *Château St. Jean, 8555 Sonoma Highway, Kenwood 95452; phone (707) 833–4134. Tasting room open 10:00 A.M.–4:40 P.M., self-guided tour 10:30 A.M.–4:00 P.M. daily. MasterCard, Visa, and American Express. Wheelchair-accessible.*

Farther north of Château St. Jean, enjoy a break at VINEYARDS INN Mexican restaurant on the right. Recognizable by its blue windows facing the western afternoon sun, Vineyards Inn serves outstanding margaritas and mouth-watering Sonoma-Mex (Mexinoma? SonoMex?) food. (Do not confuse the Vineyards Inn with the Vineyard Inn Bed & Breakfast south of Sonoma.) We know lots of partial purists who hike up and down Sugarloaf Mountain just east of the restaurant to toughen up—and then collapse with a pitcher of margaritas at the Vineyards Inn.

Steven and Colleen Rose organically grow most of the produce used in the restaurant and fly in the fish from Hawaii. The Roses have enclosed what was once an outdoor patio to accommodate their growing and popular year-round clientele. With many traces of foods directly and indirectly from Spain, the Roses offer appetizers ranging from steamed clams and egg rolls with shrimp and Hawaiian dipping sauce to salmon/shrimp cakes, eggplant con queso, and lime garlic calamari. Prices range from $4.25 to $17.95.

The menu, which is dedicated to Chef Steven's father, Harry, features separate sections from Spain and Mexico, "Tio's Fajitacos," pastas, paella, and asadas. Our favorites include Enchiladas San Francisco, with Dungeness crab, mushrooms, and jack cheese ($11.95); grilled Catalan vegetables with eggplant, mushrooms, sweet peppers, and potatoes ($10.95); the Paella Valenciana ($31.00 for two); Steak Mallorca, which is top sirloin marinated for three days ($12.95); and Pollo Locito, local chicken marinated in tequila, garlic, and salsa puree ($9.95). Selections from the children's menu are $4.25.

🍃 *Vineyards Inn, 8445 Sonoma Highway, Kenwood 95452; phone (707) 833–4500. Open for lunch 11:30 A.M.–2:00 P.M., for dinner 5:00–9:30 P.M. MasterCard and Visa. Wheelchair-accessible.*

Sugarloaf State Park begins on Adobe Canyon Road. This is an excellent place for hiking, as we describe in Chapter 7.

Facing Adobe Canyon Road at Sonoma Highway, and across from Vineyards Inn Restaurant, you'll find LANDMARK VINEYARDS, 11.5 miles north of Sonoma. Proprietor Damaris Deere Ethridge moved her winery operation from Windsor to Kenwood in 1989. Sonoma architect Adrian Martinez designed the new winery with a California Spanish Mission–style exterior and a contemporary, state-of-the-art interior. The winery features an expansive interior courtyard facing dramatic Sugarloaf Mountain (many fund-raisers and weddings take place here), and the winery's tower conference room offers a 360-degree panoramic view of the northern Sonoma Valley. Sonoma artist Claudia Wagar was commissioned to paint the wall mural that has become the focal point of the hospitality center, complemented by Susan Giller's wall tapestry.

LANDMARK VINEYARDS' ROMANTIC COURTYARD

Mrs. Ethridge—the great-great-granddaughter of steel-plow inventor John Deere—asked her son, Michael Deere Colhoun, to move from the East Coast to Sonoma Valley to take over Landmark Vineyards. Michael's wife, Mary, serves as partner and public relations and hospitality director. You walk by a shiny green and yellow John Deere tractor as you enter the landmark courtyard.

Landmark specializes in producing exclusively Sonoma County Chardonnays. Its grapes come from Sonoma Valley, Russian River Valley, Alexander Valley, Sonoma Mountain, and Carneros appellations. The tasting room features Landmark wines, Lesley B. Fay Fine Foods relishes and preserves, imported crackers, local artwork, gift baskets, and Italian pillows.

Landmark also offers the Landmark Vineyards Cottage and Guest Suite, overlooking a working vineyard.

 Fine points: Try Landmark's new boccie court (open to the public daily) next to the picnic grounds, and take a ride on the new Belgian draft horse–drawn wagon. The romantic and picturesque wagon ride through the vineyards costs $5.00 for adults and includes tasting special reserve Landmark wines. It is offered from 11:00 A.M. to 2:30 P.M. on summer weekends. One child can ride free with an adult. Featured wines: Damaris Reserve Chardonnay, Overlook Chardonnay, Claret, Pinot Noir. Owners: Damans Deere Ethridge and Michael Deere Colhoun. Winemaker: Evan Bakke. Cases: 30,000. Acres: 11.

❧ Landmark Vineyards, 101 Adobe Canyon Road, Kenwood 95452; phone (707) 833–1144; fax (707) 833–1164. Web site landmarkwine.com. Open 10:00 A.M.–4:30 P.M. MasterCard, Visa, American Express, and Discover. Wheelchair-accessible.

As you leave Landmark Vineyards, turn right onto Adobe Canyon Road and stop immediately at Sonoma Highway. Across the road and slightly south is ST. FRANCIS WINERY. Cross the highway extremely carefully. Traffic moves fast here, and it's hard to see cars coming around the bend from the right (north). Turn right through St. Francis's gate, which is marked with lots of flags.

Once the Lou Behler family home and farm, St. Francis Winery is a dark redwood structure with a friendly, informal ambience and high-quality products. While the winery looks a little showy from the road, it is one of the more homey and comfortable in the Valley, and it is one of the fastest-growing wineries in Northern California, having just received county permission to expand to a 350,000-case facility.

This is a blue-jeans winery, where, if you ask, you can see some of the best historical photographs of Kenwood in a hallway. The original Behler home is a small, charming Victorian just north of the winery parking lot. It is now used for executive hospitality rooms. Somehow the exterior decorations successfully combine Disneyesque and religious motifs.

Having grown up on his family's dairy and fruit farm in Stockton, owner Joe Martin left San Francisco's corporate world in 1971 to return to his agricultural

ST. FRANCIS WINERY

roots and purchased this property. For the first eight years, Martin sold his grapes to neighboring wineries Château St. Jean, Kenwood, Ravenswood, and Jordan. Then, wanting more control of the end product, Martin built his own winery and, in 1979, christened St. Francis Winery (after Saint Francis of Assisi and San Francisco de Solano Mission in Sonoma).

St. Francis's Wine Garden patio is well situated for picnics, with tables, umbrellas, and vineyard views. Some picnic foods are sold at St. Francis, and we always taste Cuisine Perel oils, pumpkin and grapeseed oils, and chocolate sauces with little pretzels. St. Francis is one of the first California wineries to use synthetic corks to close all its wine bottles.

Be sure to check out St. Francis's new facility at Highway 12 and Pythian Road near Oakmont, just up the road.

Fine points: Featured wines: Chardonnay and Merlot. Winemaker: Thomas Mackey. Cases: 200,000. Acres: 456.

❧ *St. Francis Winery, 8450 Sonoma Highway, Kenwood 95452; phone (707) 833–4666. Open 10:00 A.M.–4:30 P.M. daily. Tasting fee $5.00 for reserve wines only, includes etched glass. MasterCard and Visa. Wheelchair-accessible.*

As you leave St. Francis Winery, the salutation on the gate overhead reads: "Gracias. Vaya con Dios." We find this a most pleasant reminder of things important, including the need for safe driving on Highway 12.

Turn right back toward Sonoma and stop at the little Kenwood Village Market shopping center.

Here you will find **MARCO DANA'S KENWOOD CAFE,** one of the most under-heralded, almost secret, affordable dining spots in Sonoma Valley. Owner Duane Margreiter runs a Kenwood-typical low-key restaurant with excellent pizzas (small for $6.00, $11.50 for extra-large, and $15.50 for the most extravagant combo), hamburgers ($4.95), pastas, and his well-known wood-smoked pork spareribs and chicken with salad and homemade bread. New salads, which Duane offers in either half or whole sizes, include blackened-chicken Caesar, Greek salad, Chinese chicken, or Warm Thai Noodle. All of these are ample and mouth-watering; they range in price from $3.95 for a half salad to $7.50 for a whole.

Most of Kenwood shows up here after soccer games (very big in Kenwood). The value is astoundingly high, with something for everyone in the family.

Fine points: Duane makes all his own hearty and chewable breads and rolls here at Marco Dana's. He no longer sells them in Sonoma, so buy some here to take along. Wine and beer.

❧ *Marco Dana's Kenwood Cafe, 8910 Sonoma Highway, Kenwood 95452; phone (707) 833–1228. Open 11:00 A.M.–9:00 P.M.*

Monday–Thursday, 11:00 A.M.–10:00 P.M. Friday–Saturday. MasterCard and Visa. Wheelchair-accessible.

Henry, Diane, and Jeff Mayo organized a small cooperative, FAMILY WINERIES OF SONOMA VALLEY, to make the superb, handcrafted wines of Sonoma Valley's family wineries available to the public. The Mayos are providing the public with an opportunity to taste and purchase some wonderful rare wines. Family wineries represented here are Mayo Family Winery, Tantalus Winery, Suncé (formerly One World), Nelson Estate, Deerfield Ranch Winery, Noel, and Sable Ridge Winery. Most of these wines are otherwise sold only in rare-wine shops, to friends, or by direct mail.

Since Henry and Diane released their estate 1994 Chardonnay, just in time for the 1995 holidays, they decided to make a charming historic building they own on Sonoma Highway available to other small wineries, and they asked a few to join them in a tasting-room venture. Now you can enjoy a visit with one of the winemakers, local art, foods, and wines in a cozy, clubby atmosphere at the Family Wineries of Sonoma Valley.

The Mayo Family Winery is the fastest growing of the wineries represented, having built their own new winery facility in 1988 and having expanded acreage into the Alexander Valley. Featured wines: Chardonnay and Zinfandel. Winemaker: Jason Bull. Cases: 3,000. Acres: 17.

➤ *Family Wineries of Sonoma Valley, 9200 Sonoma Highway, Kenwood 95452; phone (707) 833–5504. Open 10:00 A.M.–5:00 P.M. daily. MasterCard and Visa. Wheelchair-accessible.*

ROAST LEG OF SONOMA LAMB
from Diane J. Mayo, Mayo Family Winery

---

1 leg of lamb, bone removed

1 small can of tomato paste

5 cloves garlic

3 sprigs fresh rosemary

3 Tbs herbs de Provence

salt and pepper

Preheat oven to 325° F.

Chop garlic into very small pieces and mix with herbs de Provence, salt and pepper, and tomato paste. Take mixture and coat the inside of the leg of lamb where the bone was removed. Place the fresh rosemary on top, roll the lamb tightly around the rosemary, and tie with butchers' string. Place the lamb on a cooking rack in a 2-inch-deep baking pan to catch the juices.

Simply cook for about 1 hour at 325° F. Let stand for 5 minutes and slice to serve. It's that easy. For an extra bonus, place potatoes and carrots in baking pan and roast with the lamb for an easy side dish! Serves 4–6.

A KENWOOD LANDMARK: THE OLD KENWOOD DEPOT, WHICH
NOW SERVES MANY COMMUNITY FUNCTIONS

Just south of Family Wineries is JONATHAN'S FARMHOUSE, a labyrinth of collectibles supreme featuring Americana, quilts, furniture, candles, milk paint, masks, and kitchen utensils, plus garden funk in back.

Jonathan's Farmhouse, 9255 Sonoma Highway, Kenwood 95452; phone (707) 833–6532. Open 10:00 A.M.–5:30 P.M. Monday–Saturday, 11:00 A.M.–5:30 P.M. Sunday. No credit cards. Wheelchair-accessible.

STONE CREEK is actually the largest wine negotiant in California. (Stone Creek is part of Simon Levi Company of Los Angeles, which is a major national wholesale wine distributor.) The historic one-room Old Blue Schoolhouse where Stone Creek is located was built in 1872. In the 1930s it was a boardinghouse; it has also been a roller-skating rink and a hardware store.

Stone Creek blends "everyday wines for everyday occasions" that are made way over in the Napa Valley. Bottles range in price from $6.88 to $14.50.

Fine points: Winemaker: Erin Green. Cases: 200,000. Acres: none. ❧ *Stone Creek, 9380 Sonoma Highway, Kenwood 95452; phone (707) 833–5070; fax (707) 833–1355. Open 10:30 A.M.–4:30 P.M. Monday–Friday, until 5:00 P.M. Saturday–Sunday. MasterCard and Visa. Not wheelchair-accessible.*

THE WINE ROOM houses Remick Ridge Vineyards/Smothers Brothers Winery, the winery of those two funny guys and the fine wines of Adler-Fels, Moondance Cellars, Kaz Vineyards and Winery, Castle, and Cale Cellars. Two winery owners/winemakers host tasters every day, so you get to talk to them and truly find out what creating great wines is like. This is a true co-op, and everyone here has a sense of humor.

In 1972 Tommy Smothers bought 110 acres of land in Sonoma Valley. Two years later his brother Dick bought a home and thirty-acre vineyard in the Santa Cruz mountains. They combined their efforts and resources and produced their first late-harvest Gewürztraminer soon afterward. They released their first varietals in 1979 and opened the tasting room in 1985. Tom Smothers says: "Wine, like comedy, is subjective. People either like your wine—or your songs, or your comedy—or they don't. Each is a creative process and you're only as good as your last effort." In this vein, Rick Kazmier of Kaz even draws his own labels, which his wife colors.

You will also find wild Cafe Tequila chili sauces, grapeseed oil, and even Snapple. Tom Smothers's gold records hang on the walls along with a full range of wine gifts, including "Yo Yo Man" wine corks. There's a whole hilarious Yo Yo Man case of doodads and yo-yos ranging in price from $5.00 to the SmoBro collectors' yo-yo at $25.00.

 Fine points: Featured wines: Cabernet Sauvignon, Merlot, Mom's Favorite Red, Mom's Favorite White. Winemaker: Richard Arrowood. Cases: 2,000. Acres: 35.

❧ *The Wine Room, 9575 Sonoma Highway, Kenwood 95452; phone (707) 833–6131; Web site www.the-wine-room.com. Open 11:00 A.M.–5:00 P.M. daily. MasterCard, Visa, and American Express. Wheelchair-accessible.*

Up Warm Springs Road, which runs to the west off Sonoma Highway along the side of Remick Ridge Vineyards/Smothers Brothers Winery, you can enjoy the last of the natural mineral springs swimming facilities in Sonoma Valley. MORTON'S WARM SPRINGS has three sparkling pools nestled in the Sonoma Mountains on Warm Springs Road. These are all open to the public (for a fee) and are a favorite of local groups for casual gatherings.

❧ *Morton's Warm Springs, 1651 Warm Springs Road, Kenwood 95452; phone (707) 833–5511 or (800) 817–6555; fax (707) 833–5752.*

Cyd and L.T. Blackwood recently opened their LUCKY GOOSE GIFT SHOP featuring comtemporary and historic folk art and wood carvings for home and garden. They plan to add a Holiday Room and water garden in the back, along with Sonoma County gourmet specialty foods including B. R. Cohn's dipping

THE WINE ROOM

oils. In the summer you can stop by for a soda in the water garden to cool off. A fun spot for collectors.

Lucky Goose Gift Shop, 9667 Sonoma Highway, Kenwood 95452; phone (707) 833-2994. Open 11:00 A.M.–5:00 P.M., Wednesday–Sunday summer, 10:00 A.M.–7:00 P.M., November–December. MasterCard, Visa, and Discover. Not wheelchair-accessible.

Come back down Warm Springs Road and turn right onto Sonoma Highway (12) again. As you head south, you first come to KENWOOD RESTAURANT, a worthwhile destination in itself. From the first day Max and Susan Schacher reopened Kenwood Restaurant's doors in 1986, it was a popular success. Whenever our good friends, popular novelists Sue Miller and Douglas Bauer, visit Northern California, they make a reservation here. The bar is long and friendly (lots of locals eat alone at the bar), and the dining room oozes a casual elegance.

The food is supposed to be "French country," but Max also injects strong strains of California/nouvelle. The Schachers raise most of the vegetables and herbs in their own garden. Our menu favorites are the Dungeness crab cakes with herb mayonnaise ($8.95), the Bodega Bay bouillabaisse in a clear saffron broth ($15.50), the braised Sonoma rabbit with grilled polenta ($18.25), and the sweetbreads with basil, capers, tomatoes, and feta-cheese ravioli ($16.50). There is also a mixed cheese and fruit plate ($8.75), and the hamburger or Kenwood club sandwich ($7.75). Unusual side orders here ($2.50 each) include wild rice, gnocchi, vegetables, or polenta.

Classic desserts range from ice creams or sorbets, $2.25, to caramel custard, chocolate mousse with brandied cherries, tarte tatin a la mode, or walnut torte with vanilla ice cream, each $4.95. Kenwood lists its port and dessert wines along with eaux-de-vie and liqueurs on the back of the menu. It also offers the best list anywhere of wines produced in Kenwood.

Fine points: Dining on Kenwood's patio or at the tables in front just as the sun goes down presents an absolutely exquisite view of the Kunde Vineyards hills. While you sit in the shade, the sun still shines on this Provence-like Sonoma Valley landscape. Bring a sweater or jacket to dine outside. Full bar.

❧ *Kenwood Restaurant, 9900 Sonoma Highway, Kenwood 95452; phone (707) 833–6326; fax (707) 833–2238. Open 11:30 A.M.–9:00 P.M. Wednesday–Sunday. MasterCard and Visa. Wheelchair-accessible.*

Just south of Kenwood Restaurant and before Kenwood Inn and Spa is WILDWOOD FARM, a '60s-style wild and natural, always-evolving organic nursery that specializes in Japanese maples, California native plants, and drought- and deer-resistant plants. You can wander through the abstract gazebo and greenhouse among outdoor sculpture.

Wildwood's design premise makes it free from "interruptions with the hills." Because Wildwood is at the base of steep hills, sunset comes early, so it closes early, particularly in winter.

❧ *Wildwood Farm, 10300 Sonoma Highway, Kenwood 95452; phone (707) 833–1161. Open in winter 9:00 A.M.–2:00 P.M. Tuesday, 9:00 A.M.–3:00 P.M. Wednesday–Friday, 9:30 A.M.–4:00 P.M. Saturday, Sunday by appointment; in summer open until 5:00 P.M. No credit cards. Barely wheelchair-accessible.*

Next to Wildwood Farm you will find the adobe-colored stucco Kenwood Inn & Spa, which provides one of Sonoma Valley's most luxurious country experiences, from massage to exercise, exquisite foods, baths, and extravagant accommodations (see Where to Stay in Sonoma Valley, Chapter 6).

As you pass the Kenwood Inn and Spa, turn right (south) and just over the little rise in the road, the romantically beautiful Pagani Ranch will be on the right. In fall these vines turn deep orange to blood red and almost black. Unfortunately, these heart-stirring colors can mean diseased vines.

Turn right onto Dunbar Road, 1 mile south of Kenwood Inn & Spa, to

KENWOOD INN & SPA

WELLINGTON VINEYARDS. Enrico Gallo founded this vineyard in 1892, and it remained in the local Gallo family until the father-and-son team of John and Peter Wellington bought the property in 1986. This is an unglitzy, nonshowplace-type winery. Utilizing truly sustainable agricultural techniques of permanent cover crops and beneficial insects and spiders, Wellington Vineyards uses no insecticides on its seventy- to one-hundred-year-old vines. Its handcrafted wines from its own estate-grown grapes include Zinfandel, Criolla, Côtes de Sonoma (a Rhône-style blend), Noir de Noirs, and Port. Both estate-grown and purchased grapes go into the vineyard's Chardonnay, Merlot, Cabernet Sauvignon, and some Zinfandels.

Internationally famous architect George Rockrise, who now resides in Glen Ellen, designed this small, personal winery, creating an informal, homey ambience. Tables outside invite you to enjoy a picnic and wine, but you must bring your own food, as none is available here. One person who loves to hang out here is Briton Francis Ingall, who signs copies of his book *The Last of the Bengal Lancers*, which he is.

Enjoy the new gift room full of the best quality shirts and vests, not to mention lovely paintings by Michael Richie. One can find roasted-pumpkin grape-seed oil, spicy pecan vinegar, fancy mustards, and even chocolate raspberry port sauce and port-filled chocolates.

Fine points: Featured wines: Sauvignon Blanc, Chardonnay, Zinfandel, Syrah, Merlot, Cabernet Sauvignon, Port. Winemaker: Peter Wellington. Cases: 6,000. Acres: 22.

✤ *Wellington Vineyards, 11600 Dunbar Road, Glen Ellen 95442; phone (707) 939–0708; fax (707) 833–1173. Open 11:00 A.M.–5:00 P.M. daily. MasterCard, Visa, and American Express. Wheelchair-accessible.*

As you leave Wellington, turn left onto Dunbar Road and then turn right when you reach Sonoma Highway. This way you avoid disturbing local residents on Dunbar Road. Or continue along Dunbar Road and enjoy the lichen dangling from oak trees in winter or the shaded meadows in summer. Continue south on Sonoma Highway 1.8 miles, and then turn right on Arnold Drive to reach Glen Ellen.

GLEN ELLEN

While downtown Glen Ellen appears to be a teensy village, the area called Glen Ellen actually spreads for miles. Once a booming and slightly raucous lumber village, and the home of Jack London, Glen Ellen is now a quiet, slow-moving village whose residents like it that way. Wind your way for a mile past the Glen Ellen Fire Station. Around the bend you come to a romantic and elegant bed and breakfast, Gaige House. (See Where to Stay in Sonoma Valley, Chapter 6.)

On the north side of Arnold Drive, visit VILLAGE MERCANTILE, a unique collectible and antiques shop with a room dedicated to quilting and sewing classes. FINLANDIA CAFE & BAKERY offers saucy gravy and biscuits ($4.50), buttermilk Belgian waffles ($4.50), albacore tuna, Black Forest ham, and other sandwiches ($3.50–$5.50), including a special meatloaf with portobello mushroom sandwich ($4.50).

Glen Ellen has developed a mini-gourmet gulch "downtown" right along Arnold Drive. SAFFRON is the newest addition and replaced Mes Trois Filles. Saffron chef/owner Christopher Dever is bound to succeed. A graduate of San Francisco's California Culinary Academy, Chris served as chef at Bear Flag Cafe and moved along with its owners, Kristen and Peter Stewart, when they opened Deuce on Broadway in Sonoma. Chris was sous chef at Deuce, and he jumped at this opportunity to open his own place with pastry chef/owner Lindsey Ayers.

Expect a small and cheerful bistro with pale yellow walls and burgundy curtains, to say nothing of the food: delectable crab cakes, sweetbreads, and spinach salad. A real California cuisine experience with local produce and people.

While the wine list primarily features Sonoma County wines, you might also enjoy the interesting Spanish wines and sherries.

✺ *Saffron, 13648 Arnold Drive, Glen Ellen 95442; Open from 11:00 A.M.–2:30 P.M. for lunch, 5:00–9:00 P.M. for dinner. Wine and beer. MasterCard, Visa, and Discover. Wheelchair-accessible.*

Christian and Karen Bertrand bought the GLEN ELLEN INN from Bob Rice in 1993, bringing their excellent experience cooking at John Ash & Co., Kenwood Restaurant, and the Fifth Avenue Grill in New York. This is a cozy, romantic restaurant with paned windows. The kitchen is against the back wall and separated from one row of tables by a counter. There are twelve little tables inside and more outside when the weather is good. The new covered patio has allowed the restaurant to seat more diners, and the fountain and pond give the patio below a secluded, romantic feeling.

Glen Ellen Inn continues in the fine tradition of no-fat gourmet foods and offers an excellent list of exclusively Sonoma Valley wines. Chris creates "home cooking with French, Italian, Mexican and Asian influences." Some home cooking! His Sonoma Cuisine utilizes the freshest local products available; the menu changes according to the season. Karen serves your food and makes you feel extremely comfortable and at home.

GAIGE HOUSE INN

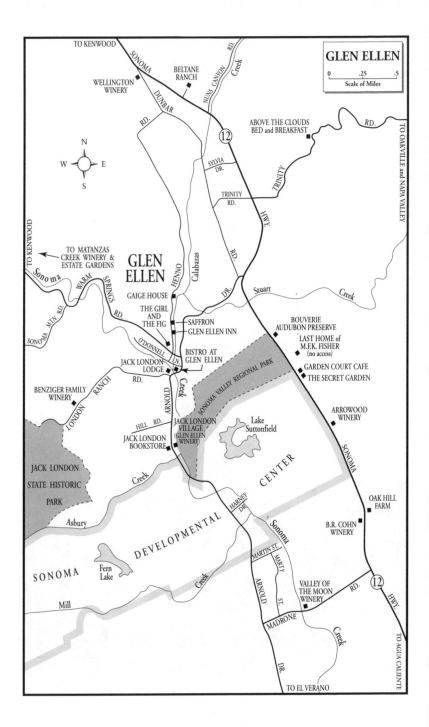

CHILLED WATERMELON-CUCUMBER SOUP
from Chef and Co-owner Christian Bertrand,
Glen Ellen Inn Restaurant

1 watermelon, seedless

6 cucumbers, seeds removed, and chopped

$\frac{1}{4}$ cup red onions, chopped

$\frac{1}{4}$ cup shallots, chopped

1 cup fresh chopped sage

$1\frac{1}{2}$ cup red wine vinegar

pinch of salt and pepper

2 cups sour cream or no-fat yogurt

Puree first six ingredients until they become liquid. Add salt and pepper to taste. Slowly whip in sour cream or yogurt until smooth. Refrigerate 6–8 hours before serving. Garnish with fresh sage. Serves 4–6.

NO SMOKE CHOCOLATE CIGARS
from Chef and Co-owner Christian Bertrand

1 lb bittersweet chocolate

$\frac{1}{2}$ lb milk chocolate

1 cup cream

$\frac{1}{2}$ cup Bailey's Irish Cream

$\frac{1}{3}$ cup cocoa powder

Melt chocolates and cream over low heat in double boiler; remove from heat. Add Bailey's and combine. Cool in refrigerator 8 hours. Scoop a large Tbs of chocolate mixture and roll into a cigar shape. Dust with cocoa powder.

Try the new Chef's Tasting Menu, featuring "whims and fancies" of the day, from $35 without wines, $50 with local wines. Dinner main courses range from homemade fusilli with grilled vegetables ($11.95), grilled Threelily Pork Tenderloin ($15.95), and grilled mango-papaya sea bass ($18.95) to a mixed grill of Ahi tuna and filet mignon ($23.95) and veal stuffed with brie ($21.95). If you are lucky, you will meet newish daughter and co-owner, Savannah Rose.

❧ *Glen Ellen Inn, 13670 Arnold Drive, Glen Ellen 95442; phone (707) 996–6409. Open for dinner from 5:30 P.M. Thursday–Tuesday. MasterCard and Visa. Wheelchair-accessible from north side of deck.*

Sondra Bernstein opened THE GIRL AND THE FIG after serving four years as Viansa Winery and Italian Marketplace's director of retail operations. Sondra expertly serves the public now with truly "country food with a French passion." You can see her French passion in her redo of the restaurant's interior, adding fabulous local art by the best local artists, Spanish tile floors, soft mustard walls, and an open kitchen where the chefs face diners across a simple counter.

Sondra, who may host in jeans or overalls and serves as Executive Chef, offers daily cheese- and wine-tasting flights that are posted on the blackboard above the counter facing the kitchen. Chef John Toulze attracts standing-room-only crowds with Pernod-steamed mussels with smoked-duck sausage, grilled figs, aromatic cheese courses under $9.00, herbed polenta with Teleme cheese and grilled vegetables ($13.95), pan-seared halibut with heirloom tomatoes ($18.95), and pork tenderloin, lamb, and steak and frites, all under $20.00. Sondra always offers a top sirloin-burger ($8.95).

Fine points: Desserts are divine, including cheese and Port, chocolate fondue, and pumpkin or lavender crème brûlée. There are outdoor tables in front, and wine and beer are served.

✢↵ *The Girl and The Fig Restaurant, 13690 Arnold Drive, Glen Ellen 95442; phone (707) 938–3634; Web site www.thegirlandthefig.com. Open for dinner from 5:30–9:00 P.M. daily. MasterCard, Visa, and American Express. Wheelchair-accessible.*

Absolutely do not miss Sondra's FIGMENTATION across the street, where you can purchase the fabulous French cheeses and sausages, local olive oils and vinegars, great books (ours!), soaps, local lavender, and whatever her imagination offers.

✢↵ *Figmentation, 13651 Arnold Drive, Glen Ellen 95442; phone (707) 939–8394. Open 2:00–10:00 P.M. Sunday–Friday, 6:00–10:00 P.M. Saturday. MasterCard, Visa, and American Express. Wheelchair-accessible.*

LONDON LODGE SALOON is the most hopping place in Glen Ellen, with good, stiff drinks at reasonable prices and unlimited popcorn that you scoop with a wooden salad bowl from the popcorn machine. Lots of local gossip and color here. Most customers live nearby.

✢↵ *London Lodge Saloon, 13740 Arnold Drive, Glen Ellen 95442; phone (707) 996–3100. Open early till late. MasterCard and Visa. Wheelchair-accessible.*

THE BISTRO AT GLEN ELLEN is the latest incarnation of this romantic, tree-shaded site beside Calabazas Creek, and this one just might stick. Combining

GRILLED FIG SALAD
from Sondra Bernstein, Executive Chef and Owner,
The Girl and The Fig

4 bunches baby arugula

4 oz pecans, roasted

4 oz goat cheese

2 oz pancetta, diced

8 figs, fresh Black Mission or Turkey

freshly ground pepper

6 oz Fig & Port Vinaigrette (see below)

Sauté diced pancetta in pan over medium heat. Cook until crisp. Reserve pancetta oil; set aside.

Cut Black Mission figs in half. Brush figs with reserved pancetta oil. Grill figs about 45 seconds on each side.

In a stainless steel bowl, toss together arugula, pecans, pancetta, and crumbled goat cheese with fig and port vinaigrette.

Place salad mixture on chilled plates and surround with grilled figs. Use peppermill to grind pepper over salad. Serves 4.

FIG & PORT VINAIGRETTE

10 dried Black Mission figs

3$\frac{1}{2}$ cups ruby port

1 cup red wine vinegar

2$\frac{1}{2}$ cups olive oil and canola oil blend

1 Tbs shallots

$\frac{1}{2}$ tsp black pepper

1 tsp salt

Rehydrate figs in $\frac{1}{2}$ cup (or enough to cover) port until figs are soft. Reduce 3 cups of port in saucepan over medium heat until it reduces by half (1$\frac{1}{2}$ cups). Puree figs with port and vinegar. Add shallots. Slowly whisk in oil. Season with salt and pepper. Refrigerate and then pour over salad when ready to serve.

impressive credentials, owner/chefs Munther and Debbie Massarweh, sous chef Paolo Neville and his wife, Jo-Jo Thomas, and Robert Radosta, bring experience that ranges from San Francisco's Tin-Pan Asian Bistro, Red Herring, McCormick's & Kuleto Seafood Restaurant, Perry's, and Betelnut, to Chicago's Pump Room and Lettuce Entertain You, the company that led many to San Francisco's Real Restaurants Corporation's Mustards, Fog City Diner, Betelnut, Bix, and Buckeye Roadhouse.

You can either dine outside with the bees overlooking crisp Calabazas Creek (we would if we weren't so appealing to yellow jackets) or enjoy the warm atmosphere of the dining room, redone with rich woods and mustard walls hung with European wine posters.

Prices are reasonable and portions are large, so enjoy. Lunch offers a stacked-high Thai chicken salad ($8.75), iceberg lettuce with great blue cheese dressing ($5.25), and mouth-watering, crispy tempura-style calamari ($8.25). Try the portobello-mushroom risotto with roasted garlic and blue cheese ($7.95) or the sesame-crusted Ahi tuna sandwich, which comes rare unless you ask to have it cooked more, as we did ($8.50).

Dinner adds a roasted vegetable stack with crispy goat cheese polenta ($13.50), steak au poivre with cognac cream sauce ($18.95), and lamb shanks, calf's liver, salmon, and trout, all under $18.00. Weekday specials range from prime rib on Monday to buttermilk fried chicken with mashed potatoes, biscuits, and gravy on Wednesday ($13.95) and Yankee pot roast for Sunday Supper ($14.95).

❧ *The Bistro at Glen Ellen, 13740 Arnold Drive, Glen Ellen 95442; phone (707) 996–4401; fax (707) 996–0850; e-mail: mybistro@yahoo.com. Open 11:00 A.M.–10:00 P.M. Sunday–Thursday, 11:00 A.M.–11:00 P.M. Friday–Saturday, brunch 10:00 A.M.–3:00 P.M. Sunday. Full bar. MasterCard, Visa, and American Express. Wheelchair-accessible.*

London Lodge Motel is a clean and inexpensive motel in downtown Glen Ellen. (See Where to Stay in Sonoma Valley, Chapter 6.) Drive up London Ranch Road, which runs west from the London Lodge. About a mile up the hill, take the driveway to the right to BENZIGER FAMILY WINERY. The sign over the gate to the winery describes and epitomizes the Benziger family's attitude toward their endeavors: EDUCATION AND GOOD TIMES. Well-groomed topiary trees line the driveway. Watch the speed bumps.

For fun and easy learning all about how wine is grown and made, Benziger is a must. Just off the parking lot, you'll find its Viticulture Discovery Center, where you can take a few steps through the entire process and touch vines and dirt. The Benzigers are known for their research and education centers. As we

THE BENZIGER FAMILY WINERY GUEST HOUSE AND OFFICES AS
SEEN FROM BRUNO'S NYMPH GARDEN

walk around the grounds here, we find ourselves taking deep breaths, sighing, and simply feeling grateful to be alive. The little educational signs planted in the garden around the "World Headquarters" always make us chuckle and force us to learn a little something. Bring a picnic—there are great picnic grounds. Even the employees are given lunch here. Be sure to walk through Bruno's Nymph Garden.

Mike Benziger founded Glen Ellen Winery. His parents, Bruno and Helen, and the rest of the Benziger clan developed it into one of the most successful in the country. After Bruno's unexpected death, Helen and her nine children eventually sold Glen Ellen to Heublein, retaining all the wonderful old grounds and buildings they treasured.

Now they produce the highly respected Benziger Sauvignon Blanc, Cabernet Sauvignon, and Merlot. Their Zinfandel won "Best Zinfandel in California" at the 1997 California State Fair.

The Benziger tasting room and shop has the best collection of wine-country books and guides around.

The sign on the gate as you leave says THANK YOU FOR VISITING OUR RANCH HOME, and the Benzigers mean it.

DOOR TO NOWHERE, BENZIGER FAMILY WINERY

Fine points: You can see the whole works on Benziger's Tram Tour, a wagon pulled by a Massey 375 tractor through the fifty-eight-acre estate. Tours take about forty-five minutes and leave the central buildings at 11:30 A.M. and 12:30, 2:00, and 3:30 P.M., delivering you at the tasting room and wine shop. How convenient! *Wine Spectator* has called this the best winery tour in the industry. You can also take yourself on a self-guided walking tour. Featured wines: Fumé Blanc, Pinot Blanc, Pinot Gris, Chardonnay, Pinot Noir, Merlot, Zinfandel, Syrah, Cabernet Sauvignon, Muscat, Sangiovese, Barbera, Canelli, and Cabernet Franc. Owners: The Benziger family. Winemaker: Joe Benziger. Cases: 170,000. Acres: 100.

🍇 *Benziger Family Winery, 1883 London Ranch Road, Glen Ellen 95442; phone (707) 935–3000 or (888) 490–2739; Web site www.benziger.com. Open 10:00 A.M.–5:00 P.M. daily. MasterCard, Visa, American Express, and Discover. Mostly wheelchair-accessible.*

MATANZAS CREEK WINERY and MATANZAS CREEK ESTATE GARDENS are an absolute must on anyone's wine and pleasure-seeking tour. Matanzas Creek is about 7 miles out Warm Springs Road and then Bennett Valley Road, but you must go. From Santa Rosa, take Farmers' Lane to Bennett Valley Road, or take the Highway 12 exit off Highway 101 and follow it to Bennett Valley Road.

The new tasting room is a peaceful and beautifully designed sanctuary, and the gardens and lavender fields, sculpted by Gary Ratway of Digging Dog Nursery to complement the surroundings, reflect owner Sandra MacIver's desire to re-create the inspiration and refuge she found in her grandmother's gardens in New Orleans, now listed on the National Register of Historical Landmarks as Longue Vue House and Gardens.

Matanzas Creek Winery respects the interdependence of its four parts: The estate vineyard helps winemakers make outstanding wines, the profit made from lavender products supports the maintenance of the elegant gardens, the gardens support the entire operation by bringing new visitors to the winery, and after the fall crush, the vineyards' grape skins, seeds, and stems are used to fertilize the vineyards, gardens, and lavender fields.

Sandra Stern, whose grandparents founded Sears Roebuck, brilliantly bought one hundred acres in the Bennett Valley in 1971, built a reservoir, planted Merlot vines in 1975, and purchased another 119 acres next door in 1976, the same year she harvested her first grapes. In 1977 Sandra hired winemaker Merry Edwards and converted an old milking shed to a small winery. In 1979 Bill MacIver joined Sandra in developing the winery, the vineyards, and their relationship, and in 1980 they married at their home on Matanzas Creek Estate. As early as 1981, their 1979 Merlot won the Sonoma County Harvest Fair's Sweepstakes Award, just the first of many commendations to come. Matanzas Creek makes only a few wines, and makes them very, very well.

Sandra and Bill MacIver have always been active advocates on behalf of social, environmental, wine-industry, and humanitarian causes, for which we respect them greatly. In 1996 the *Wine Spectator* named Sandra one of the twenty most influential people in the modern wine industry. We also enjoy seeing longtime local friends Kathy Kennett and Bill Maffei whenever we visit the tasting room.

 Fine points: Featured wines: Chardonnay, Sauvignon Blanc, Merlot under Matanzas Creek and Journey labels. Owners: Sandra and Bill MacIver. Winemakers: Bill Parker and Susan Reed. Cases: 38,000. Acres: 270.

❧ *Matanzas Creek Winery and Estate Gardens, 6097 Bennett Valley Road, Santa Rosa 95404; phone (707) 528–6464 or (800) 590–6464; fax (707) 571–0156; e-mail matcrkwine@aol.com, Web site www.matanzascreek.com. Open 10:00 A.M.–4:30 P.M. daily. MasterCard, Visa, and American Express. Wheelchair-accessible.*

JACK LONDON STATE HISTORIC PARK, the next stop on our tour, is up London Ranch Road from Benziger. Walk around Jack London's Beauty Ranch, including a forest of oak, madrone, Douglas fir, and redwood, and with open land and streams. The main focus of the ranch is the House of Happy Walls, a home and museum built by London's second wife, Charmian, after his death in 1916. Here you will see a lot of his personal stuff, such as the rolltop desk where he wrote, his piano, and trunks and clothes.

About half a mile down a gently sloping hill, you will find the remains of Wolf House, the "dream house" that Jack and Charmian built. It burned to the ground the night before they were supposed to move in. Partway back toward Happy Walls, take a cutoff to find London's ashes, but follow the trails. Be sure to get the State Parks guide so you don't get lost, and follow the trails appropriate for your abilities. (The trail guides are available here and at the State Parks Regional Office next to the Barracks on the Plaza in Sonoma.)

❧ *Jack London State Historic Park, 2400 London Ranch Road, Glen Ellen 95442; phone (707) 938–5216. Open 10:00 A.M.–5:00 P.M. daily. $6.00 per vehicle, $5.00 with one senior in car. MasterCard and Visa in shop. Museum and cottage are wheelchair-accessible.*

Now come back down London Ranch Road to downtown Glen Ellen. GLEN ELLEN VILLAGE MARKET is a good place to stop for a healthy snack or a latte. There are tables on the side of the store facing the London Lodge, but you must enter through the parking lot.

Glen Ellen Village Market is the northern branch of Sonoma Market. Formerly known as Shone's and located across the street for decades, this store carries every gourmet-type food requirement you might have. This is the best place in Glen Ellen to get picnic supplies, although you might also try the Garden Court Cafe for entire picnic meal baskets.

Many of the vegetables sold at the Village Market are locally and organically grown, the wines and juices are local, much of the meat is free range and chemical-free, and they make some of the best espresso in Sonoma Valley. The hot deli foods are more healthful and less fatty than at Sonoma Market, and the cooks even make the sandwiches more interesting.

❧ *Glen Ellen Village Market, 13751 Arnold Drive, Glen Ellen 95442; phone (707) 996–6728. Open 7:30 A.M.–9:00 P.M. daily. MasterCard and Visa. Wheelchair-accessible.*

On the right (west) side of Arnold, you might notice a large brick building, the former Hotel Chauvet, built in 1906. The building remains empty due to high costs of earthquake retrofitting.

JACK LONDON VILLAGE, on Arnold Drive south of Glen Ellen, is a romantic, rustic, dark wood complex in which it is fun to lose oneself and imagine actually hearing Jack London's "call of the wild." Hanging over and facing the creek, the

WOLF HOUSE

buildings house many small craft studios and shops, with an ever-changing tenant population.

The old stone building in the complex was built partly by General Mariano Vallejo in 1840 and was expanded in 1881 as a winery. The Pagani family bought it in 1914 and produced their prize-winning Glen Ellen wine, then abandoned the whole operation in the 1950s. Originally renovated by Sonoman Charles Beardsley, the complex is owned by the Jack London Group, which includes John Pflueger.

GLEN ELLEN WINERY, which does not make wine in Glen Ellen, has a tasting room and History Center. Once the home of Chauvet and Pagani wineries, the History Center features attractive murals by local artist Judy Williams, a Panorama Room, and—our favorite—the Train Room, with photos of trains that actually came up the valley. You will also find elegant Marcel & Henri pâtés, Rouge et Noir brie, Sonoma Cheese Factory cheeses, and cigars.

Fine points: Heublein bought the Glen Ellen label from the Benziger family in 1993. Its renovation of the old buildings has certainly helped the neighborhood and has attracted locals and visitors to see the new digs. Featured wines: Chardonnay, Sauvignon Blanc,

White Zinfandel, Gamay Beaujolais, Pinot Noir, Merlot, Cabernet Sauvignon, Grenache, Syrah, Petite Syrah, Port, Joshua Chauvet Brandy. Winemaker: Charlie Tsegeletos.

❧ *Glen Ellen Winery, 14301 Arnold Drive, Glen Ellen 95442; phone (707) 939–6277. Open 10:00 A.M.–5:00 P.M. daily. Admission to the History Center is free. MasterCard, Visa, American Express, and Discover. Wheelchair-accessible.*

Walk behind the History Center to explore more shops, galleries, and cafes.

THE RANCH STORE is the brainchild of Julie Atwood and features California ranch and agricultural heritage, from history to books, stuff with which to surround yourself, old and new photos, local arts and crafts, and historical references to Jack London's Beauty Ranch. Julie is one of those people who makes everything she touches turn to gold. It's worth a stop. Julie features local artists' furniture and large art, woodwork, ironwork, and ceramics for home and garden.

❧ *The Ranch Store, 14301 Arnold Drive, Glen Ellen 95442; phone (707) 935–2310. Not wheelchair-accessible.*

ART FOR LIVING, another of Julie Atwood's enterprises in Jack London Village, is a successful gallery that she moved "home" from Petaluma to the space previously occupied by Chandelle wines, a negotiant. Art for Living presents contemporary crafts, fine arts, and custom furniture and lighting. We are all lucky to be able to enjoy Julie's exceptional energy and design talents.

At JACK'S VILLAGE CAFE, next door to The Ranch Store, Debra DeMartini and Chef Brandon McCreight bring you the best of espressos, muffins, scones, light foods, excellent breakfasts, salads, sandwiches, and turkey- or beefburgers. Wine and beer are served. There is great outdoor seating facing the creek.

❧ *Jack's Village Cafe, 14307 Arnold Drive, Glen Ellen 95442; phone (707) 996–0755. Open 9:00 A.M.–9:00 P.M. MasterCard and Visa. Wheelchair-accessible.*

Be sure to visit Angela Casazza's Re-psyche Mosaic Art.

At the southern end of Jack London Village, check out THE OLIVE PRESS, which replaced legendary Bill's Hardware. The Olive Press is a unique cooperative olive-oil mill and retail center that allows commercial producers, growers with small harvests, and even hobbyists with one tree to make their own "estate" extra virgin olive oil. The Olive Press even opens its doors for "community pressings" in November and December, and you receive your share of the batch in proportion to the percent of the olives you bring into the batch.

Ed Stolman spent time learning in the cooperative olive-oil mills in southern France. He found the perfect press in Italy, a Pieralisi, and brought it back to Glen Ellen.

Here you can enjoy viewing the crushing process and tasting from local labels such as B. R. Cohn, Chalone, Iron Horse, Lila Jaeger, B. G. Buck, Spectrum Naturals, and Beltane Ranch. If you have one or more olive trees, The Olive Press will take you through the whole process, from picking the olives to delivering the olive oil to you. And—surprise, surprise!—you can buy olive oil here, too, wholesale or retail, as well as an exceptional collection of books about olive oil and cooking with it, Majorca olive-wood utensils and French olive-wood salad bowls, infused oils, organic Meyer lemon preserves, olives, olive-oil soaps, and even baby olive trees to start your own olive grove!
⁂ *The Olive Press, 14301 Arnold Drive, Glen Ellen 95442; phone (707) 939–8900; fax (707) 939–8999; Web site www.theolivepress.com. Open 10:00 A.M.–5:30 P.M. daily. MasterCard and Visa. Wheelchair-accessible.*

At the JACK LONDON BOOKSTORE, across Arnold Drive from Jack London Village, Winnie Kingman carries on her late husband Russ Kingman's mission of collecting and preserving London's words and work. The Kingmans began the store in 1972 and have collected a treasury of books by and about Jack London as well as London-related memorabilia.

THE OLIVE PRESS AT JACK LONDON VILLAGE

In the early 1980s they brought Jack London's youngest and only surviving daughter, Becky, to Glen Ellen to live behind the store with them. She died in 1992, and her apartment is now primarily the Jack London Research Center, which is open to anyone. It includes every book written about the author; twelve binders of photos about him; and boxes of manuscripts, theses, dissertations, cassettes of interviews, and 50,000 3-by-5 cards on him. The Jack London Foundation also meets here. This is a must stop on any trip through the Sonoma Valley.

☘ *Jack London Bookstore, 14300 Arnold Drive, Glen Ellen (707) 996–2888. Open 10:00 A.M.–5:00 P.M. daily, closed Tuesday. MasterCard, Visa, and American Express. Wheelchair-accessible.*

As you continue back toward Sonoma, south on Arnold Drive, you will pass under a "tree tunnel" through the SONOMA DEVELOPMENTAL CENTER. This is some of the most beautiful property in the Sonoma Valley.

The Tudor-style houses and large, flat buildings with bars on the windows used to be called Sonoma State Hospital. Today the Developmental Center is a state-owned facility that cares for Californians whose mental or physical impairments prevent them from living on their own. It is the largest employer in Sonoma Valley. The original brick building at the west end of the circular driveway first housed people whose families committed them as "crazy" in the early 1900s.

Lots of local softball teams play on the lush green lawns you see from Arnold Drive. The terrific Wine Festival and Liberty (bike) Ride begins and ends here the second weekend in July, and the Special Olympics run through most of August.

☘ *Sonoma Developmental Center, 15000 Arnold Drive, Eldridge 95431; phone (707) 938–6000, events (707) 938–6805.*

The next landmark on the west side of Arnold Drive is HANNA BOYS CENTER, which gives a homelike experience and educational benefits to boys from troubled families. Hanna has changed its emphasis from "troubled boys" to "boys from families with problems," a significant shift. A favorite charity of the late crooner Bing Crosby, Hanna Boys Center can always use financial help. Every year Hanna offers a tour. Call for information.

☘ *Hanna Boys Center, 17000 Arnold Drive, Sonoma 95476; phone (707) 996–6767.*

Next door and to the south of Hanna Boys Center you'll find Sonoma Mission Inn Golf & Country Club, a nationally recognized golf course praised frequently by *Golf Digest*. Maya Angelou used to live across the road.

JACK LONDON BOOKSTORE

You'll enjoy a visit to SONOMA MISSION GARDENS, a unique nursery that features and sells native and ornamental plants. Colorful and talkative peacocks in an enclosed habitat greet arrivals who stroll onto the plush lawn behind the nursery building. Colorful annuals and perennials are always available here. This is also an excellent source for bareroot trees, roses, and even wisteria. Dave Fazzio and his entire staff truly love plants. They share their vast knowledge freely. Go in just to take a stroll and talk to the birds.

🍂 *Sonoma Mission Gardens, 851 Craig Avenue (at Arnold Drive), Sonoma 95476; phone (707) 938-5775. Open 9:00 A.M.–5:30 P.M. Monday–Saturday, 10:00 A.M.–5:30 P.M. Sunday. MasterCard and Visa. Patio is wheelchair-accessible.*

ROB'S RIB SHACK, the local Mecca for barbecued-rib fans, is just a short distance south of Sonoma Mission Gardens and the driving range, or about 0.2 mile north on Arnold Drive from Verano Avenue. One side benefit of Rob's Rib Shack is that it is located next to the local golf driving range, so you can at least watch someone else get his or her exercise while you indulge in barbecued chicken and ribs that can dribble down to your elbows.

This was a funky local "patio" diner until Rob took it over after he left London Lodge in Glen Ellen. It is the ultimate in Sonoma casual, meaning that boots and jeans are just fine or expected. As signs warn, Rob has the right to refuse service to the politically correct. Strings of colored boot and chili lights line the walls. Picnic tables fill the inside dining area, and white plastic chairs and tables are most comfortable outside to watch the sunset over Sonoma's western hills.

The ribs and chicken are smoked over almond wood in a Sonoma brick smoke oven in back and are sometimes reheated when you order. While they are succulent, with one of the best sweet/sour/spicy homemade sauces around, be sure to ask that your chicken be heated thoroughly.

Rob's garlic mashed potatoes are divinely creamy and simultaneously lumpy; the killer fries are crisp; the coleslaw is tangy and makes you want more, more, more; and even the chicken-sausage sandwich and Caesar salad are worth going for. Hand-squeezed lemonade and "concrete-thick milkshakes" tempt even the strongest.

 Fine points: Rob's offers nightly specials, featuring short ribs to cioppino at $9.95, and barbecued oysters and country and blues music on Sunday afternoons. Cigar smoking is encouraged outside. Local wines and microbrews.

☙ *Rob's Rib Shack, 18709 Arnold Drive, Sonoma 95476; phone (707) 938–8520; fax (707) 938–0496. Open 11:00 A.M.–9:00 P.M. daily. MasterCard and Visa. Wheelchair-accessible.*

JUANITA JUANITA turns out more fun, sass, and better Mexi-Sonoma food than anyone else. Kathy and Jill's motto for fine dining is, "Food isn't properly seasoned unless it is painful to eat!" They line up more than thirty bottles of hot sauces on the counter from which you can choose your cure or poison, depending on your outlook.

This wonderfully eclectic, women-run Mexican joint more resembles a colorful truck stop than the addictive food haven it is. The decor is bright primary colors, all of them, and epitomizes the creative Sonoma spirit. We have to warn you that no one is treated like a stranger here; everyone is subject to light-hearted teasing—local workers, "downtown Sonoma people," and visitors alike.

If the weather is good, try the patio just outside the restaurant. The entire menu, which isn't all that long or complicated, is painted on the exterior wall; it's also on the inside wall in case you need it. There have been lots of new menu additions. Our favorite is the spinach and mushroom quesadillas. Prices range from $2.25 for a basic taco to $9.50 for a Jerk in a Blanket, which is half a roasted chicken with "Jamaican" herbs and spices, wrapped in a very big tortilla with rice and beans. There are also daily specials and "kids stuff" like kids' burritos, nachos, quesadillas, etc., for $3.00.

Every table holds a small plastic "garbage can" of dangerous chips and green salsa, which does not burn your head off. You have your choice of meats: chicken, carne asada, barbecued pork, or chorizo with every dish where meat shows up. Juanita Juanita is also vegetarian-sensitive, so you'll find no-meat burritos, and everything else is available without meat.

Fine points: Anything here with pulled pork is worth going off the old diet for. We can't even do this in our own kitchens, nor would we want to try when we can come here for it. The crowds are growing due to write-ups in a couple of national magazines, so hurry. Wine, beer, and selected microbrews on tap.

↝ *Juanita Juanita, 19114 Arnold Drive, Sonoma 95476; phone (707) 935–3981. Open 11:00 A.M.–8:00 P.M. sharp! daily. No credit cards.*

People come from all over the San Francisco Bay Area every weekend to kick up their heels and experience old-fashioned fun at LITTLE SWITZERLAND, a haven for Germanesque food, polka, and beer. The bar is lined with posters and old German feeling. You pay a $5.00 cover charge to go into the back room, which is lined with old-world German murals, for the music and dancing. To get here, turn east off Arnold Drive on Grove Street and follow it to its end at Riverside. Little Switzerland is on the left.

Newish owners Yves and Annette Casabonne have converted the menu from reliable, heavy German food to more "French–Italian," perhaps to reflect their Basque backgrounds. The best thing on the menu is the broiled New York steak ($9.50, including salad). The salmon, when they have it, is light and excellent.

But most people come here for the fun, music, dancing, and atmosphere. Some people indulge in sampling the thirty kinds of beers, while others drink nothing. Full bar.

↝ *Little Switzerland, Corner of Grove and Riverside, El Verano 95433; phone (707) 938–9990. Open 6:00–11:00 P.M. Saturday, 3:00–9:00 P.M. Sunday. MasterCard and Visa. Wheelchair-accessible.*

At AUBIN EGG FARM you can buy laid-today brown or white eggs from organically fed free-range chickens. You can get here by turning left (east) from Arnold Drive

---

JUANITA JUANITA FAMOUS
CHIPS
*a collaborative effort from
Kathy and Jill*

tortillas

oil

salt

Cut tortillas in pieces, throw in oil, add salt, and that's it. Good to go.

below Temelec or by turning west from Broadway below Wedekind's. You will know the place by the little BROWN EGGS sign in front of the house on Watmaugh Road. Mr. Aubin welcomes customers here and also sells at the Sonoma Farmers' Market. The eggs cost $1.75–$3.50 per dozen.

☘☙ *Aubin Egg Farm, 965 West Watmaugh Road, Sonoma 95476; phone (707) 938–8343. No fixed hours; just come by. No credit cards. Wheelchair-accessible.*

To get back to Sonoma Plaza from Arnold Drive, proceed east on West Watmaugh Road and turn left at Broadway. You may also get there by taking Petaluma Avenue, Verano Avenue, Boyes Boulevard, Agua Caliente, or Madrone Road to Highway 12; turn right (south), pass Maxwell Village, and then turn left (east) onto Spain Street or Napa Street (Highway 12).

CHAPTER 6

WHERE TO STAY IN SONOMA VALLEY

*S*onoma Valley is as rich with independent and creative lodging as it is with wineries and restaurants. There are no real chain hotels
here, and there are many excellent innovative places to stay that reflect
the local pace of life and values.*

We now highlight, within the narrative, our favorite inns and bed and
breakfasts. Afterward we list almost all other lodging possibilities, from the most
rudimentary to the most elegant. Because in the Sonoma Valley the travel
distances are so close, most likely you will select a place to stay by its overall
qualities rather than by its location.

While several people offer rooms or cottages at their homes, we have
decided to refer you to only those that are licensed, for your protection and
ours. We do not mean to suggest that those establishments whose brochures you
may obtain but that we don't include are inferior—sometimes they just haven't
been in business very long or are not yet serious, full-time innkeepers.

We divide this chapter by area on the same basis as the rest of this guide.
Note: If a lodging is wheelchair-accessible or accepts pets, we say so.

SOUTH SONOMA

MORNINGSONG COUNTRY LODGING is a low-tech, solid-redwood 1950s
California ranch house on seven acres of pear and apple orchards, restored in 1990
by Dan and Ann Begin. The Begins welcome guests to wander around the
orchards and pick all the wild blackberries they can eat and carry. The emphasis
here is on quiet solitude, not group living and conversation with other guests. Hot
action at Morningsong is swinging in the hammock under the big old oak tree.

Flowers surround the fully equipped one-bedroom cottage with queen bed
and futon, which can accommodate up to four people. The cottage is reached

via the grapevine-covered patio. In the main house are two guest bedrooms with private baths. Picnics and other leisurely pursuits are encouraged. Occasional light aircraft make noise approaching or leaving Sonoma Skypark during the day only.

 Fine points: Breakfast is served on table linens in the cottage or in the Mexican-tiled dining room. Fresh fruit, Danish, cheeses, and beverages. Rates $110 for room, $150 for cottage. No credit cards.

Morningsong Country Lodging, 21725 Hyde Road, Sonoma 95476; phone (707) 939–8616.

Thomas and Kathleen Anderson refurbished the SPARROW'S NEST INN in 1987. It is now a cheerful, well-appointed, early twentieth century–style inn. Located on Denmark Street, off Fifth Street East, the interior is pleasant and airy. It has Victorian decor and wicker mixed in, creating a Laura Ashley feeling. Comments in the guestbook include "cheerful, neat, English country-style cottage, feels fresh, private, hosts respect guests' privacy."

The cottage can accommodate up to four guests, with its queen bed and double sofa bed. (A crib can also be arranged.) Flowers bloom in spring and summer, and geese, chickens, blue jays, and sparrows entertain throughout the year. (The birds you hear chirping on the answering machine and in the background when you speak with Kathleen are pet cockatiels, not domesticated sparrows.) Guests receive a boxed treat on their first night and a surprise dessert on the second night.

The Andersons offer several amenities such as videos, games, books, soaps and shampoos, blow dryer, curling iron, and ironing board.

 Fine points: Continental breakfast includes baked goods from Artisan Bakers, served on linen. Romance level: great. Rates: April–October $135 Sunday–Thursday, $150 weekends and holidays; November– March $100 Sunday–Thursday, $115 weekends and holidays. Well- behaved pets welcomed by arrangement. MasterCard, Visa, American Express, and Discover. Smoking outside cottage only. RV parking.

Sparrow's Nest Inn, 424 Denmark Street, Sonoma 95476; phone (707) 996–3750; fax (707) 938–5569; e-mail SprrwsNest@aol.com. Web site www. innsandouts.com.

Poet/painter Janice Crow and her artist husband John Curry are resident owners of STARWAE INN. The cottages and octagonal home are all furnished with their original art, and Janice and John maintain their studios on the property. The four cottages of Starwae are now vacation rentals, rented by the week or month, and each has a full kitchen.

Located across from Sangiacomo Vineyards and just south of Woodworks, the cottages once housed Janice and John's extensive pottery studios. Wood, stone, and metal sculptures surprise the eye. Propped along baseboards, art books and magazines stand beside cartoon anthologies, awaiting your leisurely browsing. Many rooms feature furnishings handcrafted by John using wood, paint, and a sense of humor.

You can stroll and visit the guinea hens and peacocks that strut around the former dairy farm next door or sit and watch the wildflowers grow. All bedrooms feature queen beds and luxurious comforters. Each room has a vineyard or mountain view and private bath. Cribs are available, but rollaways are not.

A favorite of Judith and Bill Moyers and their family, Starwae's ambience is eclectic English gardens lined with lilac hedges. "Casual and unpretentious, wonderful whimsy and humor, somewhere between the Ritz-Carlton and a country inn, and why rush anywhere" are among guests' comments.

 Fine points: The weekly rates are $500–$850, depending on the cottage; monthly rates are $1,200–$2,000. MasterCard, Visa, and American Express. No smoking; no pets. Limited wheelchair-accessibility.

Starwae Inn, 21490 Broadway, Sonoma 95476; phone (707) 938-1374; e-mail: starwae@aol.com.

VINEYARD INN is a classic Mission Revival–style motor court with flamingo-pink stucco and turquoise trim on the bend where Arnold Drive intersects with Highways 12 and 121, across from the 76 station and Carneros Deli. Each small room has its own name and shower; each is furnished with Mexican furniture and antiques, in keeping with the exterior and interior decor. Golden Gate transit stops across the street, with easy transportation to Marin and San Francisco.

The Vineyard Inn attracts many repeat European travelers and visitors to Sears Point Raceway. It also offers a conference room, free to paying guests, or for just $50 a day to others. Manager Herwig Loose will also cater meetings and parties in the conference room.

 Fine points: Continental breakfast with homemade croissants, seasonal fruits, juices, and breads. There is a barbecue and picnic area in the center of the property, whose bright flowers cheer all visitors rounding what used to be called "El Bend Grande" on their way to Sonoma. Rates $79–$109 for standard rooms, $119–$149 for small two-room suites with wet bar and refrigerator, and $129–$169 for Jacuzzi rooms. MasterCard and Visa. Laundry facilities.

Vineyard Inn, 2300 Highway 121 (Carneros Highway), Sonoma 95476; phone (707) 938-2350, fax (707) 938-2353.

MACARTHUR PLACE, at Broadway and East MacArthur Street, looks like the Victorian mansion it was when the Goode family owned it. Suzanne Brangham bought the property in 1997 and restored and redecorated the home with historic sensitivity. She added some rooms; converted the century-old barn to a 4,200-square-foot conference center; added a swimming pool, pétanque courts, and horseshoe pits; all for this thirty-three-room inn and executive retreat.

Fine points: Rates: $150–$350. MasterCard, Visa, and American Express.

MacArthur Place, 29 East MacArthur, Sonoma 95476; phone (707) 938–2929; fax (707) 933–9833; e-mail info@macarthur-place.com; Website www.macarthurplace.com.

AROUND SONOMA PLAZA

All of the accommodations we list in this section are within a few short blocks of Sonoma Plaza. You can walk or ride in your wheelchair from each of these to the Plaza, thanks to sidewalk ramps at every corner.

Hotels, Motels, and Inns

SONOMA VALLEY INN is one of the best Best Westerns, just a block west of Sonoma Plaza and across Second Street West from the Marketplace shopping center. Built in 1987 to imitate California Mission–style architecture, the entire inn focuses away from the street and toward its own inner courtyard, with a womblike gazebo, spa, fountain, and heated swimming pool. Rooms are spacious and have either a fireplace or a Jacuzzi tub. A few have mini-kitchens, and most have patios or decks for outdoor privacy. Norman Krug and his son Aaron Krug, the inn's manager, recently added new suites and deluxe suites as well as a new, larger conference room. This is a great place for meetings and parties.

Sonoma Valley Inn is definitely children-friendly, allowing kids up to twelve years old to stay in the same room with adults for free.

Fine points: Continental breakfast is delivered to your room. Coffee and other refreshments are available all day, and fresh fruit and biscotti are served in the afternoon. Rooms have hair dryers and refrigerators (which hold a complimentary bottle of wine for arriving guests). There are even two washing machines and dryers for guests' convenience. Cribs and rollaways are available. Romance level: medium high. Rates $135–$375 (luxury mini-suites), AAA, senior, and group rates available.

MasterCard, Visa, American Express, and JCB. Wheelchair-accessible. Air conditioned. Non-smoking throughout.

🌿 *Sonoma Valley Inn, 550 Second Street West, Sonoma 95476; phone (707) 938–9200 or (800) 334–5784; fax (707) 938–0935.*

On the northwest corner of Sonoma Plaza, SONOMA HOTEL has been given a face-lift by new owners Tim Farfan and Craig Miller, who bought the historic building in August 1998 from John and Dorene Musilli. The Musillis had restored the hotel in 1980s. It has been called "a wonderful place close to the City but a hundred years away." The two-story building was built in 1886 as Weyl Hall, after its owner, who had arrived from Bingen on the Rhine, Germany. Originally a dry-goods store and butcher shop occupied the street level. The high-ceilinged hall on the second floor served as community center, dance hall, and general center of noise and carousing.

In the early 1900s the third floor was added to include twenty-one guest rooms, known as the Plaza Hotel in the Sebastiani Block. During the 1950s the gracious balcony was removed and all the furnishings were sold. Now you can enjoy the wood-paneled staircase; the romantic and quaint foyer with the original fireplace and stained-glass windows (guests are served breakfast here at cafe tables); and rooms furnished with Victorian, French, and English turn-of-the-century pieces. All furnishings are appropriate to the late nineteenth century.

Five of the current seventeen rooms have private baths with clawfoot tubs and water closets. Third-floor rooms share bathrooms. Each room's historic decor is in keeping with its name, such as The Bear Flag Room, Yerba Buena, or the Italian Suite. Maya Angelou wrote *Gather Together in My Name* in Room 21.

Fine points: Breakfast consists of fresh pastries, coffees, and juices served on cafe tables in the exquisite lobby overlooking Sonoma Plaza. Romance level: highest. There is wine tasting each afternoon in the lobby. No smoking and no pets. Rates $95–$235. MasterCard, Visa, and American Express.

🌿 *Sonoma Hotel, 110 West Spain Street, Sonoma 95476; phone (707) 996–2996.*

Right on the northwest corner of Sonoma Plaza, the EL DORADO HOTEL is one of the most historic and romantic small hotels in Sonoma. Re-restored by Chili Kohlenberg and then by Claude Rouas and Bob Harmon, who own PIATTI, the El Dorado's upstairs rooms have an old-world feeling of casual elegance. Some of the twenty-eight rooms face Sonoma Plaza; you can sip wine in the evening on their balconies, or, in the morning, drink coffee and watch the ducks, the birds, and even the whole town wake up. Other rooms face the El Dorado's exquisite garden courtyard, with French windows and balconies overlooking the flowers and trees. All rooms feature goose-down linens.

 Fine points: Continental breakfast for two, included in each room rate, usually consists of coffee, fruits, and freshly baked breads and pastries. Full bar during Piatti restaurant hours. Romance level: highest. Rates April–October $180 (queen), $195 (king) Friday and Saturday with two-night minimum, $150–$160 Sunday–Thursday; November–March $150–$160 Friday and Saturday, $120–$135, Sunday–Thursday. Rooms west of the swimming pool are at ground level and are wheelchair-accessible. MasterCard, Visa, and American Express.

✥ *El Dorado Hotel, 405 First Street West, Sonoma 95476; phone (707) 996–3030.*

One of Sonoma's oldest and most romantic hotels, the SWISS HOTEL is right on Sonoma Plaza in the heart of the action and history. Because of city earthquake upgrades, the entire hotel has been remodeled and restored to casual elegance. All rooms are decorated with antiques, and the floors were left slanting just to make guests feel like the old days.

The entrance to the Swiss Hotel Restaurant bar is the door to the left, and the door to the right takes you right into the hotel lobby and stairway. The five guest rooms are all upstairs. Rooms 4 and 5 open onto the front balcony overlooking Sonoma Plaza, a great spot for sipping and staring off into space. If you are a light sleeper, though, take the back rooms away from the bar.

Fine points: Continental breakfast is served in the dining room. Rates $120–$140 midweek, $140–$180 weekend, summer; $90–$110 midweek, $110–$130 weekend, winter. MasterCard and Visa. Romance level: highest. Not wheelchair-accessible.

✥ *Swiss Hotel, 18 West Spain Street, Sonoma 95476; phone (707) 938–2884.*

EL PUEBLO INN, where West Napa Street turns north as Highway 12, is a classic California motel built in 1959 by locals Lorna and Ray Bradbury. Their children, Holly Bradbury and Cal and Wendy Stewart, now run this Sonoma institution, and it may be the best accommodation deal in town, if you don't mind traffic noise. Adobe brick walls, heavy redwood post-and-beam walkways covered with wisteria, and a large heated swimming pool, lawn, and shaded garden make El Pueblo Inn a popular accommodation for families and singles alike. Several local wineries and Sears Point race crews house guests here.

Fine points: Every room has coffee, tea, cocoa, and fabulous Splendido biscotti. Rates $75 Sunday–Thursday, $90 Friday–Saturday, winter, slightly higher in summer; senior, AAA, and group discounts available. MasterCard, Visa, American Express, and Discover. Two excellent handicap rooms, each with two double beds, are available, as well as coding communication for the hearing-impaired. Telephones in rooms. Cribs and rollaways available. Air-conditioning.

❦ *El Pueblo Inn, 896 West Napa Street, Sonoma 95476; phone (707) 996–3651; fax (707) 935–5988.*

Bed and Breakfasts

Donna Lewis's VICTORIAN GARDEN INN has the most beautiful gardens and ambience of any lodging in downtown Sonoma. Nestled among valley oaks and magnolias, the 1870 Greek Revival farmhouse and pump house sit beside Nathanson Creek, 2 blocks east of Sonoma Plaza. The original renovation of this historic property was done by Marge Eliassen, an active preservationist whose son Garth sold it to Donna. She brought her substantial talents as an interior designer and host from Park City, Utah.

The Victorian Garden has lawns and paths winding through the trees and along the creek with several seating areas, each with its own outlook and feel. Behind the white, two-story Victorian home is a swimming pool and well house, which even has two guest rooms; and the Woodcutter's Cottage, with a fireplace, queen bed, and sofabed. A late 1800s pump organ and an elegant fireplace are focal points in the living room, where guests can sip a complimentary beverage from the coffee and tea cart set up at all times in the dining room on a "help yourself" basis.

Each of the four guest rooms has a private entrance, private bath, designer linens and toiletries, and electric blankets. Terry-cloth robes and down comforters attract repeat customers from all over the world. The Top O' The Tower is in Marimekko-style blue and white with wicker and overlooks the pool, gardens, and patios. The Garden Room features Laura Ashley classic rose, while the Woodcutter's Cottage is done in subtle hunter green and redwood. You can bathe in an extra large clawfoot tub and then sit in front of the used brick fireplace.

Fine points: The Inn provides a large California breakfast with Sonoma Cherry Tree juices; hardboiled eggs; piles of seasonal fresh fruit; fresh bagels with assorted cream cheeses; Celebration Baking's muffins, Danish, and cinnamon buns; local jams and famed Vella cheeses; pastries by chef Denise Elliott of the Culinary Academy, and hot beverages. All this is served in the dining room, on the patio, or on a wicker tray in your room. Guest rooms are completely free of television, telephone, and radio;

clocks are available upon request. Romance level: highest. Rates $99–$195, plus taxes. Visa, MasterCard, American Express, JCB, and Enroute.

✲↙ *Victorian Garden Inn, 316 East Napa Street, Sonoma 95476; phone (707) 996–5339 or (800) 543–5339; fax (707) 996–1689; Web site www.victorian-gardeninn.com.*

Just ½ block west of Sonoma Plaza, part of Norma and Larry Barnett's THISTLE DEW INN was built in 1869. Their new-kid-on-the-block front house was built in 1905. The Barnetts offer six guest accommodations, all tastefully decorated to give a cozy feeling of seclusion and privacy. Through the front door you walk down the hallway to an extremely comfortable living room, with velvet-covered couches, Oriental rugs, a fireplace, books, and jigsaw puzzles. Thistle Dew Inn features museum-quality Stickley and Limbert Arts and Crafts furniture from 1910.

Norma and Larry have contributed much to Sonoma since they bought the Inn in 1990. Larry serves on the Sonoma City Council and owns Healthy Planet Products (publishers of Sierra Club cards), and Norma conducts psychotherapy practices in both Sonoma and Oakland.

Larry is an avid gardener who has collected and kept alive 450 succulent plants. Don't touch! He is also an accomplished chef, having learned the arts of cooking and art collection from his mother in New York. Thistle Dew Inn guests have a special treat in store: afternoon hors d'oeuvres and morning breakfast from Larry's talented hands and heart.

 Fine points: Breakfast is always an elegant treat, varying with what Larry finds freshest in the market, and served in the dining room, whose windows look out on West Spain Street. The kitchen is small, but the Barnetts welcome guests to come on in for a snack, keep their picnic supplies in the refrigerator, and walk through to the garden and hot tub. Bicycles and helmets are available for guests. Romance level: high. Rates $115–$180, weekdays, $125–$210 weekends; winter rates a bit lower. MasterCard, Visa, and American Express.

✲↙ *Thistle Dew Inn, 171 West Spain Street, Sonoma 95476; phone (707) 938–2909 or (800) 382–7895; fax (707) 996–8413; e-mail thistledew.com; Web site www.thistledew.com.*

Located just a block east of Sonoma Plaza, THE HIDDEN OAK is a large, two-story California Craftsman bungalow framed in purple wisteria. Watch for the colorful flag in front.

Built in 1914 as a home, it housed local women teachers during World War II and later was refectory for Trinity Episcopal Church, which was then next door. Catherine Cotchett lovingly restored the house as a bed and breakfast after buying it in 1984 and gave it its present name. In February 1999 she sold it to Valerie and Don Patterson, who reopened the B&B in May 1999. The Pattersons moved from Dallas, Texas, when Don, a telecommunications specialist, was promoted and transferred to the Petaluma office of his company. He and Valerie, a nurse and "mom," determined that Sonoma was "the only place to live."

The redecorated upstairs guest rooms are all large and airy, full of antiques and plush pillows. Each room has its own bath and is named for its decor. The California Oak Room looks out on an old, mighty valley oak. The English Garden Room has a view of Sonoma's foothills of the Mayacamas Mountains. The large French Lilac Room has two queen beds covered with white comforters. Guests can lounge on the front porch in the classic wicker furniture.

 Fine points: Valerie cooks and servess a full breakfast on weekends and a cart breakfast the rest of the week. Coffee and newspapers are available in the parlor for early-morning risers. The Hidden Oak also offers complimentary bicycles for guests to ride around the town or to the nearby wineries. There are public telephones upstairs. Smoking is allowed only on the front porch. Romance level: high. Rates $120–$165. MasterCard, Visa, American Express, Discover, and Diners.

The Hidden Oak, 214 East Napa Street, Sonoma 95476; phone (707) 996–9863; Web site www.hiddenoakinn.com.

Known for years as the home of the Farrell family lumber business, TROJAN HORSE INN is a large, pleasant place right on Sonoma Highway, between Spain and Napa Streets at the west end of downtown. You can't miss the Trojan Horse, since it is freshly painted off-white with dark blue trim.

A tragic fire turned into a blessing, and the Trojan Horse is now completely rebuilt, with a French country flair. Once inside, you discover one of the most exquisite inns in town. It is decorated with English and French antiques throughout. Guests enjoy a rose garden, Jacuzzi, terraced plantings, and a fenced picnic area overlooking Sonoma Creek.

All rooms have private baths, and each has its own decor and personality, ranging from a wood-burning stove and queen brass bed to a corner room with a high, century-old oak bed; the Victorian room, with California elegance; and the Jack London, decorated in nectarine and leafy green. Their most popular room is the Grape Arbor, done in silver lavender and silver rose, with a Jacuzzi and high queen oak bed overlooking the country view toward the west.

Joe and Sandy Miccio (pronounced Mickey-o) bought the Trojan Horse in October 1997, putting to good use Joe's twenty-three years' experience at the San Francisco Hilton Hotel and Sandy's work in accounting.

Fine points: Full breakfast with entrees ranging "from country to gourmet" featuring fresh, natural local ingredients. The Miccios host a social hour every day between 5:30 and 6:30 P.M., with complimentary wine and hors d'oeuvres. Romance level: high—three smacks from "Best Places to Kiss in Bay Area." Rates $135–$165, and about 20 percent lower in winter. MasterCard, Visa, and American Express. Children over twelve welcome. Air-conditioned. Smoking outside only. Wheelchair-accessible.

🍇 *Trojan Horse Inn, 19455 Sonoma Highway, Sonoma 95476; phone (707) 996–2430 or (800) 899–1925; fax (707) 996–9185; e-mail trojaninn@AOL.com.*

A historic Italianate mansion, known as the Clewe House, built in 1876 (see page 39), CEDAR MANSION was renovated in the 1990s and turned into a bed-and-breakfast in 1998. In April 1999, Robert Kowal, a former hospital administrator from Baltimore, bought the mansion, put in new tennis courts, and installed a swimming pool, gourmet kitchen, and spa. He has also purchased all new furnishings, including four-poster beds. It is located on a quiet side street less than two blocks from the Plaza.

Fine points: There are five units and extensive well-shaded gardens and lawns. Rates $365–$445. Visa, MasterCard, and American Express.

🍇 *Cedar Mansion, 531 Second Street East, Sonoma 95476; phone (707) 938-3206, (800) 409-5496; fax (707) 935-7721; e-mail: info.@cedar-mansion; Web site www. cedarmansion.com.*

A long-time favorite with many repeat visitors, SONOMA CHALET BED AND BREAKFAST is the oldest bed and breakfast in Sonoma. Built by a Swiss family in the 1940s, it became a bed and breakfast in 1980. The Swiss-style farmhouse and country cottages, designed like chalets, are surrounded by three acres of century-old eucalyptus trees, lawns, and flower gardens. The property overlooks the 200-acre Montini ranch.

All rooms are colorfully decorated with hand-painted murals and have balconies or decks. Window boxes are filled with radiant geraniums. The Honeymoon Cottage sits across a wooden bridge and invites a perfect romantic retreat. Owner Joe Leese says, though, "There is the 'crow' of the chickens and the 'waddle' of ducks to contend with, as well as a few ornery geese." Local deer come to peer at the guests occasionally.

Fine points: Breakfast is served in the country kitchen, on the deck, or in your cottage. It includes fresh fruit, juices, hot pastries, French roast coffee, granolas, and yogurts. Romance level: highest. Listed in "Best Places to Kiss in the Bay Area." Rates $95–$180. MasterCard, Visa, and American Express. Smoking outside only. No pets.

❧ *Sonoma Chalet Bed and Breakfast, 18935 Fifth Street West, Sonoma; phone (707) 938–3129.*

Architectural designers Robert Behrens and Marga Friberg have enhanced their home to convert their studio and cottage to some of the most comfortable and private accommodations in Sonoma Valley. THE COTTAGE AND STUDIO are located in the block just north of Mission San Francisco Solano de Sonoma, and a short block from Sonoma Plaza. All rooms have fireplaces and private courtyards and are popular for extended and repeat visits.

The Cottage itself includes a skylight in the cathedral ceiling, Mexican-tile floors, a double French door, dining area, "European" kitchen, and a small private garden with a redwood deck. Guests enjoy late afternoons in the garden patio and hot tub. The Studio entrance is through a private, stucco-walled courtyard and resembles a carriage house, with massive redwood doors, fireplace, and kitchen. They have recently added three additional units.

Fine points: Rates $135–$265. Cottage and courtyard rooms are wheelchair-accessible. No credit cards.

❧ *The Cottage and Studio, 302 First Street East, Sonoma 95476; phone (707) 996–0719; e-mail RKB@aol.com.*

A pair of bed-and-breakfasts located on the east side of downtown Sonoma, and the west side of the valley, are EASTSIDE-WESTSIDE owned and operated by Karen Kardum. Each is a classic house in a residential neighborhood with beautiful warm interiors designed by architect Adrian Martinez. Eastside has a lap pool and pool house, laundry and kitchen, while Westside has a hot tub, and both include BBQ facilities. Eastside is less than a five minute stroll to the Plaza, and Westside has nearby hiking and is close to Sonoma Creek. Good tip: you can reserve all three units in each B&B for family and friends.

Fine points: $185 with two night minimum. MasterCard, Visa, and American Express.

❧ *Eastside-Westside: 836 Austin Street (Eastside); 1204$\frac{1}{2}$ Solano Avenue (Westside), Sonoma 95476; phone (707) 481–4644.*

MAGLIULO'S (pronounced "my YOU loz") PENSIONE inhabits an 1884 Victorian home next to Deuce Restaurant at Broadway and Andrieux Street, which was once Sonoma's mortuary. Magliulo's Pensione feels like a family home, with its hardwood floors, rooms in shades of rose with fresh flowers and antiques, antique quilts, ceiling fans, an outdoor cabana, a big old fireplace and hearth in the parlor, and rose bushes in the surrounding garden.

Fine points: For breakfast, fresh fruit, muffins, croissants, hot and cold cereals, fresh squeezed orange juice, and fresh coffee are served in the dining room. Full bar in restaurant. Romance level: high. Rates: $110 for rooms with shared baths, $150 for rooms with private baths. Register at the restaurant before going to the home. MasterCard, Visa, and Discover. Wheelchair-accessible.

Magliulo's Pensione, 691 Broadway, Sonoma 95476; phone (707) 996–1031; fax (707) 996–1032.

Only a half block north of the Plaza, the main building of THE BRICK HOUSE BUNGALOWS dates back to 1907 when it was built of local stone to resemble an Italian farmhouse. Over the years bungalows and lofts were added which look out on a central courtyard with a fountain and extensive gardens sheltered from the street.

Proprietors Joe Gough and B. J. Clarke have decorated each of the five units with what they call "civilized rustic" furnishings, and decorated each room with Kilim carpets and patterned fabrics.

Fine points: Each unit has a kitchen or kitchenette and a private patio. Children welcome only by arrangement, no smoking in-doors, minimum stay on holidays. Rates: $200–$250, with weekly rates $1,000–$1,200. MasterCard, Visa, and American Express.

The Brick House Bungalows, 313 First Street East, Sonoma 95476; phone (707) 996–8091; fax (707) 996–7301, Web site www.brickhousebungalows.com.

BANCROFT BED & BREAKFAST offers three guest rooms in the historic Bancroft House, for decades a nursery and home of the Roger Bancroft family. A Queen Anne stick house built in 1906, Bancroft House features accurately restored public rooms, sturdy European antiques, and generally genteel ambience. Owners Michael Woods and artist Diane Wendt Woods also own the Monet Gallery, a few doors south, and create a feeling of Monet's environment for you to enjoy. Each of the three guest rooms is named and decorated for the Impressionist reproduction that hangs on its wall. Some of the furnishings bear old Sonoma stories, and colors are used to make you feel as if you're living in an Impressionist painting.

Fine points: Full breakfasts are served on weekends and adapted from nineteenth-century French recipes featuring omelets or quiche, homemade breads, sweet butter, fresh fruit, and coffee or tea. Weekday breakfasts include homemade breads, cereal, juice, and coffee or tea. Rates $129–$149, lower rates December–March. MasterCard and Visa.

❧ *Bancroft Bed & Breakfast, 786–790 Broadway, Sonoma 95476; phone (707) 996–4863; fax (707) 996–1394.*

RAMEKINS, Suzanne Brangham's cooking school and bed and breakfast, next to her sensational GENERAL'S DAUGHTER, has several individualistic and interesting rooms available to general visitors as well as to cooking-school students. This is a great place to focus on your culinary interests during the day and evening, stay on the peaceful property, and enjoy a splendiferous breakfast prepared by the resident chef the next morning.

Fine points: Rates $125–$195. MasterCard, Visa, and American Express.

❧ *Ramekins, 450 West Spain, Sonoma 95476; phone (707) 933–0450; fax (707) 933–0451; e-mail info@ramekins.com; Web site www.ramekins.com.*

BOYES HOT SPRINGS

SONOMA MISSION INN SPA AND COUNTRY CLUB is best known as Sonoma's most elegant accommodations, but even that elegance is casual. Its foundation is one of the original spas that sprang up because of Sonoma Valley's natural hot springs. Pleasure-seekers have flocked here in large or very small, clandestine groups to the rooms in the main building for nearly two centuries.

Each new owner has brought improvements to the inn, one of the most recent of whom was RAHN Properties, of Fort Lauderdale, Florida, which added new buildings with larger rooms and the European-style spa in 1981. In 1997 RAHN sold the property to Texas's Crescent Realty, resulting in many personnel and trend changes, again. In the winter of 1999–2000 RAHN completed doubling the size of the spa to a giant 27,000 square feet and added thirty new rooms.

In 1991 the Inn finally found a source of the legendary mineral waters that originally made the resort famous. They discovered it 1,100 feet directly beneath the Inn, and the magical water is now used in the Inn's two pools and indoor and outdoor whirlpools. A true oasis, SMI provides a complete spa facility, with a coed bathhouse, including aerobic studio, sauna, steam rooms, hot mineral-water whirlpools, two gyms, and locker rooms with showers. Full-length robes and thongs are available at the Spa reception desk. Body treatments, from massage and aromatherapy to herbal wraps, seaweed wraps, and to European back treatments, beauty treatments, exercise classes, and equipment, are all offered here. Bring your tennis racquets and reserve a court.

Lest you wear yourself out just thinking about all this healthy activity, we hasten to add that many people prefer to lounge beside the pool and eat and drink, plain and simple. There may be no better place for these restful activities. The SMI Grille features healthful salads and entrees at lunch and the best of Sonoma Cuisine, from grilled vegetable Napoleon appetizer and pan-seared Sonoma foie gras to entrees of grilled Petaluma chicken breasts with creamy polenta, oak-roasted salmon, and grilled rack of Sonoma lamb and oven-roasted tomatoes. The new chef is Toni Robertson, formerly executive chef at Pan Pacific in Singapore.

Fine points: SMI will prepare picnic baskets, ranging from $16 to $30 per person. Rates range widely, from $169–$525 weekdays and, $245–$650 weekends, winter, to $235–$675 weekdays and $295–$795, summer. SMI also offers spa packages. MasterCard, Visa, and American Express. The Sonoma Mission Inn is one of the few luxury resorts in the world that is completely smoke-free.

❧ *Sonoma Mission Inn Spa and Country Club, 18140 Sonoma Highway, Boyes Hot Springs 95416; phone (707) 938–9000 or (800) 862–4945; e-mail SMISPA.com.*

If you want to hold a conference, a retreat, or just a group good time, then WESTERBEKE RANCH is ideal. Located on the way up the western hills of Sonoma Valley, there are eighteen units, but the ranch can sleep up to fifty-eight persons. Under the trees is a large pool; conference rooms available; good food cooked on the premises.

Fine points: Owned by the ecologically sensitive Westerbeke family, this is the valley's ideal moderately priced gathering place. Rates start as low as about $100 a day for a group, but $50 for each person. The rates should be discussed since they try to fit your needs to the price. Children are more than welcome.

❧ *Westerbeke Ranch and Conference Center, 2300 Grove Street, Sonoma 95476; phone (707) 996–7546. MasterCard, Visa, and American Express. Wheelchair-accessible with advance notice.*

GLEN ELLEN

Two outstanding bed and breakfasts are on the east side of Sonoma Highway (12); they have Glen Ellen addresses but actually are located between Glen Ellen and Kenwood. You should consider both of them if you want to be centrally located in this part of Sonoma Valley.

ABOVE THE CLOUDS BED AND BREAKFAST owners Claude and Betty Ganaye won the 1995 Sonoma League for Historic Preservation Award of Excellence for restoration, and for good reason. Originally built in 1850 as a mountain cabin, the building was later destroyed by fire, was rebuilt around 1900, and then fell into decay. The Ganayes bought the secluded property in 1986 and had Sonoma architect Adrian Martinez design plans for renovation, including preservation of the house's original character and stone chimney. Work was completed in 1993.

This is a fabulous place (truly above the clouds) from which to watch the sunset while sipping Sonoma Valley wines between 5:00 and 6:00 P.M. We have received rave reviews of Above the Clouds from our readers.

To get here, turn right (east) off Sonoma Highway onto Trinity Road, which is almost 8 miles from Sonoma Plaza. Continue carefully up Trinity Road for 3 miles. The driveway to Above the Clouds begins just east of the Mayacamas Volunteer Fire House. You can also approach from the Oakville Grade off Highway 29, south of Oakville in Napa Valley.

The three guest rooms are all decorated in pleasant, relaxing pale shades, from green to peach and lilac, with antique iron or brass beds and French antiques. Each has a private bath, queen bed, down comforter, lace curtains and drapes, and lots of plush pillows. Two rooms have double-size showers, and one bathroom has a tub/shower. Robes are provided. Claude and Betty recommend that you bring a swimsuit and thongs for the heated pool or Jacuzzi.

 Fine points: The full breakfast might include crepes, blintzes, quiche, fresh fruit, and baked apples, depending upon the season; it is served between 9:00 and 10:00 A.M. in the dining room, veranda, or library. (Coffee and tea are available from 8:00 A.M. in the kitchen.) The Ganayes happily serve foods appropriate to your special diet needs, including completely vegetarian breakfasts. Just let them know. Romance level: highest. Rates $175 all units, all days with a two-night minimum on weekends. MasterCard, Visa, American Express, Discover, and JCB. Wheelchair-accessible.

❧ *Above the Clouds Bed and Breakfast, 3250 Trinity Road, Glen Ellen 95442; phone (707) 996–7371; e-mail abovetheclouds@vom.com; Web site www.sonoma.com.*

BELTANE RANCH is another divine bed and breakfast. Owner Rosemary

Wood is a respected friend of many of the country's finest chefs and foodies, and for good reason. Her 1892 Southern-style, two-story house with wrap-around balconies overlooks her 1,600-acre ranch. It has been in the same family since the 1940s.

Surrounded by flowers, berries, and vegetable gardens, Beltane Ranch is only about twenty minutes (8.2 miles) from Sonoma Plaza. Turn right (east) off Sonoma Highway near the Beltane Ranch signs and drive through vineyards, fields, and old oak trees to the majestic house.

Once the retreat of a San Francisco madam who hailed from Louisiana, each room has a private entrance off the balcony/veranda, since there is no interior staircase. Each room has electric blankets, ceiling fans, and individual thermostats, but no air-conditioning. Rooms 1, 2, and 3 all have views to the west, particularly important for watching the sunset in the Valley of the Moon. Fine unpretentious and comfortable antiques complement soft colors throughout. Downstairs hardwood floors and a warm fireplace invite guests to sit for hours. The Beltane also has 8 miles of its own hiking trail, well-placed hammocks, and a tennis court and racquets are available for your exercise and pleasure.

In February 1996 Beltane Ranch was named one of the one hundred best affordable places to stay in the United States. It is often booked by entire families or groups of couples; children ages five and over preferred.

Fine points: Manager Anne Soulier takes pride in their full breakfast, which may include mouth-watering homemade scones, omelets, fruit, juices, and hot beverages. The meal is served in the garden, on your own veranda, or at a table off the kitchen in cool weather. Romance level: highest. Rates $130–$220. No credit cards.

❧ *Beltane Ranch, 11775 Sonoma Highway, Glen Ellen 95442; phone (707) 996–6501.*

Barbara and Tim Korn's RELAIS DU SOLEIL WINE COUNTRY GUEST RANCH offers an unusual guest ranch experience on Nuns Canyon Road in Glen Ellen. The turn-of-the-century farmhouse and bunkhouse on 120 acres give you a true getaway treat with champagne on arrival, occasional barrel tasting of Tim's medal-winning wines, chances to talk to the steelhead in the creek, and do a lot of communing with the Valley of the Moon and Jack London's spirit.

Fine points: Four rooms in the main house and bunkhouse range from $175 to $250, plus $50 each guest over two, and you can take the entire ranch for $1,000 per night for up to twelve guests. Don't miss the Arabian horses (Barbara says: "If you can catch 'em, you can ride 'em"), ranch kitty Theodore Roosevelt, golden eagles Mr. and Mrs. Jack London, and a wild turkey named Whiskey.

❧ *Relais du Soleil Wine Country Guest Ranch, 1210 Nuns Canyon Road, Glen*

Ellen 95442; phone (707) 833–6264; fax (707) 833–6151; e-mail Soleil@sonic.net. MasterCard and Visa. Not wheelchair-accessible. Pets by special arrangement.

Kenneth Burnet and Greg Nemrow bought GAIGE HOUSE, a large 1890 Victorian, from Ardath Rouas in 1996. Gaige House is in "downtown" Glen Ellen, and you can't miss it—it is a large, two-story beige building with darker brown trim and a picket fence and gate, right on Arnold Drive. It was recently named one of the top ten romantic getaways in the world by the A & E Channel, and has been named the "finest inn in the wine country" by Fromner's.

The new proprietors further renovated this grand house in the 1999–2000 fall and winter. They also added two rooms by the pool, reaching a total of fifteen.

The front door has intriguing beveled glass set in heavy wood, the floors are hardwood with runners, and a carved wooden banister leads guests to rooms upstairs. The Gaige Suite on the second floor is particularly spectacular, with 12-foot ceilings, a four-poster canopied king bed, a large whirlpool tub in the bathroom, and a wraparound balcony overlooking the garden and the mountains.

Several rooms face west and overlook the large swimming pool (heated May–October) and the Sonoma Mountains. The work of Valley artists is featured in every room, bathrobes are provided in all rooms, and television is available on request. Eight guest rooms have private baths, and most now have fireplaces.

Fine points: Heidi West is now the head chef, with Diane Peck, a graduate of the Tante Marie Cooking School, cooking on weekends. They serve a full breakfast, which may include classic eggs Benedict, brioche rum French toast, lemon soufflé pancakes or southwestern poached eggs, and Peet's coffees, all worth the trip. Diane is always willing to adapt to special dietary needs. The meal is served 8:30 to 10:00 A.M. in the dining area, facing the deck and swimming pool, or outside in warm weather, with seating times arranged upon check-in. You can also enjoy complimentary wine in the afternoon between 4:30 and 6:00; and cookies, cold drinks, and hot tea are always available. Rates $230–$395 April–November and $150–$395 December–March; two-night minimum on weekends and holidays. MasterCard, Visa, and American Express. Young children and pets should stay home.

❧ *Gaige House, 13540 Arnold Drive, Glen Ellen 95442; phone (707) 935–0237 or (800) 935–0237; fax (707) 935–6411; Web site www.gaige.com.*

Kristi Hallamore Jeppesen brings her Norwegian roots and inclination toward perfection and hospitality to her lovely GLENELLY INN BED & BREAKFAST. She and her late mother, Ingrid Hallamore, purchased the inn in

1990 and have redecorated it beautifully. Glenelly was originally built in 1916 by a French couple, Adolph and Anastasia Larigne, as a country resort and railroad inn. Over the years it has had several names, including Larigne Resort, Cambou's, and Rigal House. To get here, take Arnold Drive into "downtown" Glen Ellen and turn west onto Warm Springs Road. Glenelly's entrance is about ⅛ mile on right.

The grounds are lush, with 200-year-old grandfather oaks, majestic pines, and other native plants. The larger building, constructed in French Colonial style with verandas on both floors, was the original hotel. Six of the eight guest rooms and the Common Room, where country-style breakfasts and afternoon refreshments are served, are here.

The smaller stick-style building has always served as the owners' residence. One-time owner Lorraine Pasini painted most of the fruit-drying trays hanging in the inn. In 1987 the then-owners, Addie and Gray Mattox, won a commendation from the Sonoma League for Historic Preservation for restoration and preservation of the building. The Hallamores have added a spa, hammocks, dozens of flower beds, trellises and stone walkways, and have completely redone the interior.

All rooms feature down comforters imported from Norway, plush bath towels, fine linen, excellent reading lights, private baths with clawfoot tubs, and private entrances.

 Fine points: Kristi Hallamore Jeppesen presents the finest of Sonoma Cuisine, including herbs, vegetables, and fruits from Glenelly's gardens, to create a well-rounded breakfast. She makes all muffins and breads and might offer various juices, melons, kiwis, poached pears with crème fraiche, glazed apples, buttermilk scones, granola, and sometimes breakfast bread pudding. Romance level: highest. Children are definitely welcome. Rates $135–$160—an excellent value. MasterCard and Visa.

❧ *Glenelly Inn Bed & Breakfast, 5131 Warm Springs Road, Glen Ellen 95442; phone (707) 996–6720; e-mail glenelly@VOM.com; Web site www.glenelly.com.*

JACK LONDON LODGE is the least expensive okay accommodation in Glen Ellen. This is a typical, twenty-two-room motel with basic accommodations, a swimming pool, and reasonable prices nestled in the "hustle-bustle" of downtown Glen Ellen. You can enjoy the bar and restaurant next door or the many others nearby. Half the rooms have king beds, and half have queens.

Fine points: Rates $120, but as low as $65 in winter. MasterCard and Visa. The downstairs rooms are wheelchair-accessible.

❧ *Jack London Lodge, 13740 Arnold Drive, Glen Ellen 95442; phone (707) 938–8510; fax (707) 939–9642.*

KENWOOD

At THE KENWOOD INN AND SPA, Terry and Roseann Grimm have turned a historic building into an elegant and romantic Tuscan villa, with a lovely swimming pool, lawns, fountains, Jacuzzi, and fountains in the central courtyard of the buildings—and a heavenly spa. The Kenwood Inn is just 9.7 miles from Sonoma Plaza, on the west side of Sonoma Highway, just south of Kenwood and Wildwood Farm nursery.

Nestled at the bottom of the Sonoma Mountains' east side, the inn's rooms look eastward toward the vast, romantic beauty of the Kunde's rolling vineyards. Surrounded by mature rose and herb bushes, persimmon, fig, and olive trees, the original four-room main building is cloaked in ivy. The new, smaller Italianate buildings have only two to four suites. They have 10-inch-thick walls made of an experimental material composed of Styrofoam and concrete, resulting in a Mediterranean stucco texture.

The entryway and kitchen are breathtaking, with stone and tile floors. They give a genuine feeling of being in Tuscany. The former antiques store is hand-painted throughout with faux marble and trompe l'oeil.

The inn's twelve suites are among the most elegant in the Valley, with privacy and seclusion important factors in the ambience. Each suite contains European antiques, lush fabrics, featherbed and down comforter, Egyptian cotton sheets, and private bath and working fireplace. Upstairs suites have balconies, and downstairs suites have private terraces. Exquisite imported tapestries and velvets make the rooms sumptuous and cozy. A complimentary bottle of wine awaits newly arrived guests in their rooms.

Under the expert direction of Laurie Braal, Kenwood Inn's Spa provides a full range of services, including a popular couples massage. You might want to try the new Fantasy Room with a two-person soaking tub, two massage tables so that couples can enjoy body wraps and massages simultaneously, with lush pillows under a canvas canopy. Wow! The spa also features aromatherapy, body wraps and scrubs, and facials including Faccia Bella. Alternative body therapies include anticellulite massage and a two-hour East Indian Ayurvedic healing treatment.

 Fine points: Chef Charles Holmes creates possibly the most outstanding breakfast of all Sonoma Valley in a country Italian kitchen with copper counters and commercial range. Breakfasts are inspired by Mediterranean products and may include Charles's famous scones or muffins; freshly pressed carrot, apple, and celery juice with ginger root; fruit tarts; an Italian apple betty with whipped cream; special egg dishes every day with polenta, breads, or croissants; salmon quiche;

and Sicilian sausage sautéed with olives and potatoes or Tuscan white beans with stewed garlic and rosemary baby artichokes. Yogurt is usually available also. Breakfast is served in the old world–style dining room or, in good weather, at outdoor tables. Watch for weekend lunches open to the public during summer. Romance level: highest of the high. Rates $285–$325 Monday–Thursday, $325–$395 Friday–Sunday, winter; $295–$395 Monday–Thursday, $325–$425 Friday–Sunday, April 1 through summer. MasterCard and Visa. Room 1 is wheelchair-accessible.

The Kenwood Inn and Spa, *10400 Sonoma Highway, Kenwood 95452; phone (707) 833–1293.*

If you want to stay right in the middle of a working vineyard, LANDMARK VINEYARD AND COTTAGE is it. Landmark offers two accommodations near the winery. The one-bedroom guest cottage has a full kitchen, a sunny sitting room, and a bath, and overlooks the vineyard itself. The elegantly decorated guest suite has an unparalleled view of Sugar Loaf Ridge and Hood Mountain. It also features a secluded private patio and romantic fireplace.

Both the cottage and suite are furnished with two single beds. You may enjoy a complimentary bottle of Landmark's prize-winning Chardonnay on arrival. These are both homes away from home.

Fine points: Breakfast is continental-plus. Just for the fun of it, Landmark has added a boccie court adjacent to the picnic grounds; it is open to the public daily. Belgian draft horse–drawn wagon tours of the vineyards are run by Wine Country Wagons on summer weekends. Rides are free. Rates for cottage, $170 for two or more consecutive nights, $195 per night, $700 per week; for guest suite, $150 per night for two or more consecutive nights, $175 per night, $525 per week; two-night minimum on weekends. MasterCard and Visa.

Landmark Vineyard and Cottage, *101 Adobe Canyon Road, Kenwood 95452; phone (707) 833–0053 or (800) 452–6365; fax (707) 833–1164.*

THE PLACE TO STAY LIST

If you can't find a place to stay from among our favorites listed above, then this list will guide you to additional choices.

Unless we indicate otherwise, you can assume that all of the following telephone or fax numbers are in the 707 area code. If you wish to write to any of the places covered in these lists, the ZIP codes are: Sonoma, 95475; Boyes Hot Springs, 95416; Glen Ellen, 95442; and Kenwood, 95452.

Bed and Breakfasts

Around the Plaza

STONE GROVE B&B, 240 Second Street East, Sonoma; phone 939–8249; three units, $75–$145

ANDREA'S HIDDEN COTTAGE, 138 East Spain Street, Sonoma; phone 996–4180; one unit, $137.50 Friday–Saturday; $110 weekdays.

ASHLEY'S YELLOW DOOR, 153 Andrieux Street, off Broadway, Sonoma; phone 996–3286; two units, $75–$165

CEDAR MANSION, 531 Second Street East, Sonoma; phone 938–3206; five units, $365–$445; in historic Clewe house

ERICKSON'S, 851 Second Street East, Sonoma; phone 938–4654; two units, $50–$135

COTTAGE 885, 885 Second Street East, Sonoma; phone 938–3859; fax 996–1237; one unit, $100–$150

GITTI APARTMENT, 270 West Napa Street, Sonoma; phone 938–3177; two units, $100 weekdays, $150 Friday or Sunday, if both days $135 each night

EASTSIDE-WESTSIDE, 836 Austin Street (Eastside); 1204½ Solano Avenue (Westside); phone 481–4644; two restored houses; three units, each $185

THE STONE COTTAGE, 391 East Spain Street, Sonoma; phone 933–3333; a former Sebastiani house, across from Sebastiani Winery; one unit, $150–$200

Outside the Town of Sonoma

RANCHO LA CUESTA, 17000 Gehricke Road, Sonoma; phone 935–1004; two units, $145–$215

MERLOT PLACE, 1090 Castle Road, Sonoma; phone 935–7751; fax 935–9334; one unit, $125 weekends, $75 weekdays

CASTLE VINEYARDS COTTAGE, 1105 Castle Road, Sonoma; phone 996–4188; one unit, $150, must book two nights, weekends and holidays

CREEKSIDE HOUSE, 18711 Melvin Avenue, Sonoma; phone 996–5702; two units, $125–$150

WESTERBEKE RANCH AND CONFERENCE CENTER, 2300 Grove Street, Sonoma; phone 996–7546; sixteen units, $46–$109

Glen Ellen

LITTLE YELLOW HOUSE, 23450 Arnold Drive, Glen Ellen; phone 938–1983; two units; primarily for weddings, summer through October in lovely garden pavilion, capacity 200, call for rates; bed and breakfast, if available, $260 for two nights

TANGLEWOOD HOUSE, 250 Bonnie Way, Glen Ellen; phone 996–5021; one unit, $165

Kenwood

THE LITTLE HOUSE, 255 Adobe Canyon Road, Kenwood; phone 833–2536; one house, $160 for two or $200 for four

CHAPTER 7

BEYOND WINE TASTING

*S*onoma Valley is not just about eating, drinking, romancing, and sightseeing. There are many other things for visitors to do. In this chapter, we describe a variety of intriguing recreational pursuits, should you want to do something in Sonoma's clean, fresh air besides taste wine and eat. Here you find out where to fly on a trapeze or in a trick-rolling biplane, take a long walk or ride in your wheelchair, hike or bike, ride a miniature steam train, count birds, play golf or tennis, ride horses through Jack London State Park, swim, or take a guided tour.

TRAPEZE FLYING

Sam Keen's SONOMA TRAPEZE TROUPE, at his ranch on Norrbom Road, gives visitors an even greater sense of thrill and empowerment than a ropes course, with no limits or end to the artistic and physical adventure. If your fancy is tickled just a little, come on up and have a look. Don't worry—almost everyone who tries it is scared at first, just in varying degrees.

You can drop in on Sunday afternoons, watch for a while, and even try flying if you wish to. Then, if you're interested, you can take a two-hour class ($30) and explore your potential. Be sure to call ahead to be sure there's a class that day. Classes are taught by instructors from The San Francisco School of Circus Arts. This is one of the few trapeze centers that has a woman catcher.

The Sonoma Trapeze Troupe also leads processes for de-tox teenagers (who, incidentally, often get more of a high on the trapeze than they ever did on drugs), special-interest groups, and battered-women's groups. Some scholarships are available for at-risk and disadvantaged groups. Sarah Ferguson, Duchess of York, taped a segment here for her *Adventures* series, seen on ABC. Imagine the birthday party, private group, or class you could have here!

Look for Sam Keen's book on trapeze, launched in New York with The Big

Apple Circus and in San Francisco with The Flight of the Spirit, featuring the Flying Cranes at Grace Cathedral on Nob Hill.

Directions: From Sonoma Plaza, take First Street West north. It becomes Norrbom Road at the Veterans Building. Continue across cattle guards to address. Careful on one-lane road.

❧ *Sonoma Trapeze Troupe, 16331 Norrbom Road, Sonoma 95476; phone (707) 996-9010. Classes on Sunday afternoons for $30; drop by after 11:00 A.M. on Sundays to watch. No credit cards.*

FLYING WITH AN AIRPLANE

Vintage Aircraft (formerly Aeroschellville), at the Sonoma Valley Airport, offers uniquely exciting rides in biplanes and a Navy war plane. Christopher Prevost has meticulously restored and maintained several legendary planes to provide you with a once-in-a-lifetime flying experience. This is a must for thrill-seekers.

Prevost offers rides using 1940 Boeing "Stearman" biplanes and a North American–built World War II Navy SNJ-4 warplane designed and built to train pilot cadets in the World War II Air Force and Navy. Rates range from $60 to $135 for scenic, aerobatic, kamikaze, dawn patrol, war bird, or glider rides.

❧ *Sonoma Valley Airport/Vintage Aircraft, 23982 Arnold Drive (Highway 121), Sonoma 95476; phone (707) 938–2444. Open 10:00 A.M.–5:00 P.M. Saturday and Sunday. MasterCard and Visa. Wheelchair-accessible.*

HOT-AIR BALLOONING

Recent rules prohibit hot-air balloon landings and takeoffs in Sonoma, because property owners complained that they and their cattle got scared or disturbed. Hence, no balloon companies currently operate here. Other balloon companies fly by but cannot land. They are:

AEROSTAT ADVENTURES, P.O. Box 2082, Healdsburg 95448; phone (707) 433–3777 or (800) 579–0183; e-mail aerostat@sonic.net; Web site www.aerostat-adventures.com.

AIR FLAMBOYANT, 250 Pleasant Avenue, Santa Rosa, 95403; phone (707) 838–8500 or (800) 456–4711; fax (707) 838–8900.

NAPA VALLEY BALLOONS INC., P.O. Box 2860, Yountville 94599; phone (707) 944–0228 or (800) 253–2224.

WALKING AND HIKING

Sonoma Valley is a walker's paradise. Whether you walk just a little or hike obsessively, there is interesting terrain for you to explore.

Downtown Sonoma

Plan A: Follow Chapter 2 of this guide.

Plan B: Take a walking tour with MARV PARKER'S SONOMA PLAZA WALKING TOURS. Marv knows everything in the League for Historic Preservation's booklet and more. His entertaining tours last about one hour, leave from in front of the Sonoma Valley Visitors Bureau (east side of Plaza, facing Sebastiani Theatre) Friday and Saturday at 10:00 A.M., or by appointment, and cost $10 per person. He gladly takes groups by pre-arrangement.

❧ *Marv Parker's Sonoma Plaza Walking Tours, P.O. Box 15, Sonoma 95476; phone (707) 996–9112.*

Veteran winery host and guide Birgitta Sarver leads walking tours of essential historic sites, wineries, vineyards, gardens, nurseries, vegetable farms, and cheese producers; Friday–Sunday mornings and by appointment during the week.

❧ *Birgitta's Walking Vineyard Tours,* phone (707) 939–0988.

Plan C: Get a copy of the League for Historic Preservation's Walking Tour Guide at Vasquez House in El Paseo Courtyard off First Street East or from the Sonoma Valley Visitors Bureau on the east side of the Plaza.

The Bike Path in Sonoma

THE BIKE PATH, which is used more by walkers than bike riders, extends from just north of Sebastiani Winery, on Fourth Street East, all the way to Sonoma Highway at Lyon's Restaurant. The path is about 2 miles long and recommended for daylight hours. Legions of locals use it all day long, with regulars greeting one another and worrying if someone doesn't show up for a few days.

The scenery is unequaled. You pass through vineyards; The Patch organic-vegetables farm; Sonoma State Park, including the fields around Lachryma Montis, home of General Mariano G. Vallejo; and more "urban" Sonoma, which isn't very urban. It's breathtaking at any time of year, but the mist rising from the vineyards and the Vallejo home fields with the sun shining against the hills on early February mornings is our favorite.

Glen Ellen

BOUVERIE PRESERVE has free guided nature walks October–May. These docent-led walks of up to forty persons help you discover the rich natural history and beauty of this 500-acre preserve. Walks are mildly to moderately strenuous, over varied terrain. The Bouverie Preserve encompasses the Bouverie Audubon Preserve and the Bouverie Wildflower Preserve. The land has remained undisturbed since the 1930s. Former owner David Pleydell-Bouverie donated the land to the Audubon Canyon Ranch in 1979. It includes four distinct plant communities and more than 100 species of birds, 350 species of flowering plants, and large mammals such as bobcat, gray fox, coyote, and mountain lions.

Guided walking tours generally take place once a month during winter and twice a month the rest of the year, often on the first and third Saturdays. All walks start at 9:30 A.M. and end at 1:30 P.M. Reservations are required. In addition to group tours, school tours may be reserved.

✤ *Bouverie Preserve, P.O. Box 1195, Glen Ellen 95442; phone (707) 938–4554. No credit cards. Not wheelchair-accessible.*

HIKING

Locals' favorite hikes include SONOMA VALLEY REGIONAL PARK, on Sonoma Highway in Glen Ellen; THE BOUVERIE PRESERVE, across the road (described above); and SUGARLOAF RIDGE STATE PARK, up Adobe Canyon Road from Sonoma Highway (between Vineyards Inn and Landmark Winery) in Kenwood.

SUGARLOAF contains 21 miles of trail through three ecological systems: chaparral-covered ridges, oak and fir forest land along the open meadows, and redwood forest. Camping is available. Admission is $5.00 per car.

✤ *Sugarloaf Ridge State Park, 2605 Adobe Canyon Road, Kenwood 95452; phone (707) 833–5712.*

JACK LONDON STATE HISTORIC PARK affords a chance to hike and live history all at once. The park includes London's grave, the ruins of Wolf House, Charmian London's House of Happy Walls, and 500 acres of prime Sonoma Valley land. Be alert for rattlesnakes. Dogs must be kept on a leash. Hiking trails are quite steep, and no drinking water is available. An excellent map is available from the State Parks Regional Office, next to the Barracks on Sonoma Plaza or at Jack London State Park.

✤ *Jack London State Historic Park, 2400 London Ranch Road, Glen Ellen 95442; phone (707) 938–6216. Open 10:00 A.M.–5:00 P.M.*

BICYCLING

THE BIKE MAN, Doug McKesson, is the extremely popular owner of Goodtime Bicycle Company. He conducts bike tours and rents bikes (in addition to selling them, of course). Doug leads the Sonoma Mission Inn's tours and provides their guests with bikes and helmets, organizes gourmet excursions for two to forty people and rides for college buddies kicking off their fourth decade together, brings along gourmet or special diet lunches using local products, and even helps ship home your wine purchase.

 Fine points: Gourmet lunch rides leave Goodtime Bicycle Company every weekday, with excursions to Kenwood wineries every Tuesday and Thursday, and Sonoma wineries Monday, Wednesday, and Friday. Lunch rides start at 10:30 A.M. and end around 3:00 P.M. Lunch rides cost $55 per person. Regular bike rentals are $5.00 per hour, or $25.00 per day, for twenty-one-speed mountain bike, helmet, basket, map, and emergency road service.

❧ *The Bike Man, 18503 Sonoma Highway, Sonoma 95476; phone (707) 938–0453. Open 9:00 A.M.–5:00 P.M. Monday–Saturday, 10:00 A.M.–4:00 P.M. Sunday. MasterCard, Visa, and American Express.*

SONOMA VALLEY CYCLERY is across the street from Sonoma Valley High School on Broadway. This bike shop has a few more sophisticated, serious bikes for sale and rent.

❧ *Sonoma Valley Cyclery, 20079 Broadway, Sonoma 95476; phone (707) 935–3377. Open 10:00 A.M.–6:00 P.M. Monday–Saturday, 10:00 A.M.–4:00 P.M. Sunday. MasterCard, Visa, American Express, and Discover.*

GOLFING

LOS ARROYOS GOLF CLUB is the course that a lot of locals play, for several reasons: It's mostly flat, has a nine-hole course, has a pitch 'n' putt course, and is much less expensive than Sonoma National Golf Course. Los Arroyos's one drawback is that it can be very windy as fresh air blows in from the west.

 Fine points: Par 58. Handicap 1–18. Length 3,078 yards. Weekday fees: adults $10.00 for nine holes, $15.00 for eighteen; seniors and juniors $7.00 for nine holes, $10.00 for eighteen; weekend fees:

slightly higher. Twilight fees: noon–one hour before sunset: weekdays $9.00, weekends $11.00. Los Arroyos recently converted its driving range to the pitch 'n' putt course, $5.00 fee to play twice. Pull carts $2.00. Rental clubs $5.00 per set, $1.00 for pitch 'n' putt club.

❧ *Los Arroyos Golf Club, 5000 Stage Gulch Road, Sonoma 95476; phone (707) 938–8835. Open 7:00 A.M.–sunset daily. MasterCard and Visa.*

SONOMA MISSION INN GOLF & COUNTRY CLUB, formerly Sonoma National Golf Course, was designed in 1926 by Sam Whiting and Willie Watson, the same architects who designed the Olympic Club lake course in San Francisco. The Sonoma Mission Inn bought the golf course in 1999, has a new chef (Robert Champagne), and is generally molding the entire enterprise to its high standards. The course covers 177 acres and has an excellent pro shop managed by local Stephanie Monnich.

Fine points: Green fees: Monday–Thursday $70, after 1:00 P.M. $50; Friday $85 after 1:00 P.M. $65; Saturday–Sunday $100, after 1:00 P.M. $75. Special fee deal for Sonoma County residents; Monday–Thursday $55 all day. Dress code: collared shirts, no jeans. Reservations accepted two weeks in advance.

❧ *Sonoma Mission Inn Golf & Country Club, 17700 Arnold Drive, Sonoma 95476; phone (707) 996–4852 or (800) 862–4945. Open 7:00 A.M.–sunset. MasterCard, Visa, JCB, and Discover.*

HORSEBACK RIDING

SONOMA CATTLE COMPANY offers Sonoma Valley HORSEBACK RIDES at Jack London State Historic Park and Sugarloaf Ridge State Park in Sonoma Valley, and at Bothe-Napa State Park in Calistoga. These exquisite rides on usually reliable horses meander past vineyards, through forests, and across meadows, with the full gamut of colors and smells special to the natural wine country and panoramic views of Sonoma Valley and San Francisco. Sonoma Cattle Company also conducts horseback rides as Napa Valley Trail Rides in the Napa Valley and Bothe-Napa State Park.

Fine points: There are two kinds of rides: basic and special. Basic rides are 1½ hours at $40, two hours at $45. There is a Sunset Ride at $45, and a private ride at $45 per hour. Special rides may include a lunch ride at $65, western barbecue ride at $90, or a full-moon ride at $45. All riders must be at least eight years old. Reservations required.

❦ Sonoma Cattle Company, P.O. Box 877, Glen Ellen 95442; phone (707) 996–8566. Call for appointment. MasterCard and Visa.

PRODUCE AND FLOWER MARKETS

Farmers' markets and local food producers offer a gustatory and social insight into a local culture and economy. We suggest you visit these markets to learn more of Sonoma's way of life.

SONOMA FARMERS' MARKET appears from nowhere every Friday morning at the Depot Park parking lot, summer and fall Tuesday evenings in front of Sonoma City Hall, and winter Saturday mornings in front of City Hall in the Plaza. There are some extra markets a few days before holidays. Here you can find truly gourmet or boutique potatoes, squashes and tomatoes of many varieties, greens, the salad mix Paul Wirtz sells to many premier restaurants, beets, eggplant, mushrooms, plants, painted gourds, stained glass, and even bird and bat houses.

These markets are your a chance to buy Sonoma organic produce from the local and extremely independent growers who supply most of the finest restaurants in the San Francisco Bay Area. Nearly all varieties of produce grown in the country are grown in California. Nearly everything grown in California is grown in Sonoma County, and everything grown in Sonoma County is grown in Sonoma Valley. Hence, this farmers' market is the heart, soul, and origin of Sonoma Cuisine. Some of Sonoma's famous bakeries also sell here, as do local wood-carvers, jewelry makers, gourd carvers, flower arrangers, and growers of flowers and native plants.

❦ Sonoma Farmers' Market; phone (707) 938–2980.

THE PATCH is Sonoma's downtown veggie farm as well as the pride of Bette Kolstad and the Second Street East neighborhood. Just up the street from Vella's Cheese and across the Bike Path, Bette grows organic vegetables on five acres owned by the Castagnasso family. The Patch usually operates on an honor system, meaning that you read the price list, weigh your vegetables, and put your money in the locked and locked-down metal box. Locals line up for The Patch's sweetest-in-the-universe corn, which is usually available July 4 through Thanksgiving (maybe stretching it ever so slightly). Several kinds of tomatoes, squashes, onions, along with the corn, may convert you on the spot to vegetarianism.

❦ The Patch, 260 Second Street East, Sonoma 95476; phone (707) 939–9054. Open 11:00 A.M.–5:00 P.M. No credit cards.

ELLIE'S KILLER OSTRICH MEATBALLS
from Eleanor Franceschi, Sonoma Knolls Ostrich Ranch

---

1 lb ground ostrich meat
1 medium onion
4–5 cloves garlic
1 egg
seasoned bread crumbs
garlic salt, salt and pepper to taste

Put onion, garlic, and egg into a blender and blend until liquid. Mix into meat and add bread crumbs until mixture holds together. Add garlic salt, pepper, or any other spice desired. Brown in olive oil. Makes 6 servings.

Bill and Ellen Adamson grow chemical-free strawberries and make preserves, jams, pepper jellies, and ices at their increasingly known HAPPY HAVEN RANCH. Their work is especially admirable because the Adamsons began this project after Bill had a temporarily debilitating stroke. He now works the ranch with his cane, and Ellen cooks up a storm. Due to new packaging and labeling, their preserves' sales have skyrocketed recently. You can buy Adamson's goodies at the Farmers' Market, at the ranch, and at some gourmet grocery stores. Try the strawberry rhubarb, plum lemon or strawberry jam, plum nut chutney, or hot green or red pepper jams. These are top of tops.

Happy Haven Ranch, 1480 *Sperring Road, Sonoma 95476; phone (707) 996–4260. Call ahead for hours.*

At their OAK HILL FARM, Ann Teller elevates vegetable and flower growing to an elegant art. To get there follow Highway 12 north through Boyes Hot Springs. As you pass the Valley of the Moon Winery signs, begin to slow down. Turn right just past the upended eucalyptus tree stump.

Employee Teresa runs the barn, an extremely clean, large room where she uses her artistic talents to create wreaths, dried and fresh flowers, sumptuous vegetables, garlic braids, and general fun. Kathleen and a few other friends used to bring M. F. K. Fisher here to shop, since she lived just to the north. Teresa remembers Mary Frances coming in to tell her how to do things better! We think she does a beautiful job.

Oak Hill Farm, 15101 Sonoma Highway, Glen Ellen 95442; phone (707) 996–6643. Open 10:00 A.M.–3:00 or 4:00 P.M. Thursday–Sunday, June–December.

At AUBIN EGG FARM you can get laid-today brown or white eggs from organically fed, free-range chickens. You can also find the Aubins and their eggs at the Sonoma Farmers' Market. Locals save their egg cartons and return them for recycling. Eggs are $1.75–$3.50 per dozen.

❧ Aubin Egg Farm, 965 West Watmaugh Road (between Broadway and Arnold Drive), Sonoma 95476; phone (707) 938–8343. No fixed hours, just come by.

CHEESE FACTORIES

VELLA'S CHEESE, one of the finest producers in the world, makes small lots of fine cheeses and wins loads of national and international medals. Vella's cheeses are primarily sold here and in gourmet groceries.

❧ Vella's Cheese, 315 Second Street East, Sonoma 95476; phone (707) 938–3232. Open 9:00 A.M.–6:00 P.M. Monday–Saturday, 10:00 A.M.– 5:00 P.M. Sunday.

SONOMA CHEESE FACTORY, on the north side of Sonoma Plaza, produces large quantities of specialty cheeses and sells them broadly. Here you can watch cheese-making through a window in the back wall.

❧ Sonoma Cheese Factory, 2 West Spain Street, Sonoma 95476; phone (707) 996–1931. Open 8:30 A.M.–5:30 P.M. Monday–Friday, 8:30 A.M.–6:00 P.M. Saturday–Sunday.

LAURA CHENEL'S CHÈVRE, one of the finest and most respected goat cheese producers in the western United States, is located at the intersection of Highways 121 and 12 (Napa Road) in what used to be Stornetta's cow dairy. Laura Chenel does not accept visitors, much to our disappointment. You can, however, find her cheeses in Sonoma Market, Glen Ellen Village Market, and most gourmet grocery stores.

❧ Laura Chenel's Chèvre, 4310 Fremont Drive (Highway 12/121), Sonoma 95476; phone (707) 996–4477.

TRAIN RIDING

Sonoma's TRAINTOWN RAILROAD AND PETTING ZOO is the most well-developed scale railroad in the Americas. We highly recommend Traintown to bring joy to anyone of any age. It is just plain, clean fun for all ages.

You climb into a miniature steam train and wind your way through ten acres of planned landscaped park filled with thousands of native trees, animals, bridges over lakes, tunnels, waterfalls, and replicas of historic buildings. While adults may feel they have arrived in Lilliputville, you also may feel as if you would like to stay here and not go back to the real, big world.

Kermit the Engineer might be driving the train (on Fridays a diesel engine pulls the train, and on weekends a steam engine pulls it), and trips take twenty minutes. Fares are $3.75 for adults, $2.75 for children and seniors. When you get back to the station, you can pet ponies and goats and buy a snack or enjoy your own picnic on the grounds. You may also try the merry-go-round, Ferris wheel, or enjoy the mechanical exhibits. Pizzeria Capri, next door, is also a good place for lunch.

❧ *Traintown Railroad and Petting Zoo, 20264 Broadway, Sonoma 95476; phone (707) 938–3912. Open 10:00 A.M.–5:00 P.M. Friday–Sunday, plus holidays, in winter; 10:30 A.M.–5:00 P.M. daily in summer. Not wheelchair-accessible.*

SWIMMING AND GAMES

MORTON'S WARM SPRINGS is one of the last of the natural mineral-water swimming holes in Sonoma Valley. Morton's has three beautiful pools, volleyball courts, and a game room with billiards, air hockey, all the latest games, and a jukebox. You can also play in the old-style horseshoe pits, a baseball field, a regulation-size basketball court, and the traditional European boccie ball court along Sonoma Creek under ancient trees.

Morton's has acres of rolling lawns, eleven natural picnic settings and barbecues and shaded tables, water, electricity, and bathrooms. A snack bar, loaded with junk foods, is located close to the pools. Wine and beer are available. Weekday rates are $3.75 for children and seniors, $5.25 for adults; slightly higher on weekends and holidays. School, group, and exclusive-use rates are available.

Morton's is well known locally as a family gathering place and for hosting family and corporate picnics up to 2,400 people. If you reserve for a large party, Morton's will even provide the barbecue and "personal picnic attendants." Owners Maureen and Dino Bozzetto hope to make improvements and develop a full spa and health club.

❧ *Morton's Warm Springs, 1651 Warm Springs Road, Kenwood 95452; phone (707) 833–5511 or (800) 817–6555; fax (707) 833–5752. Open May– September during daylight hours, later by reservation. No credit cards. Wheelchair-accessible.*

ONE-HOUR TRIPS FROM SONOMA VALLEY

During your stay in the Sonoma Valley, you might want to make a trip outside town for a day to sample other forms of fun or entertain the kids. Each of the following destinations are just about an hour's drive in each direction, meaning that you can leave Sonoma after breakfast and be back in time for dinner.

SIX FLAGS MARINE WORLD provides a fabulous experience for kids of all ages, combining education (shh!) and entertainment. More than a zoo, Six Flags Marine World allows you to touch and experience.

Here you can wander around 160 acres of wildlife park and oceanarium. Watch the famous water-ski show, the killer-whale show, and African safari animals. Children love meeting the animal trainers. See Tiger Island, Looney Toons games and rides, Butterfly World, Elephant Encounter, the Walrus Experience, the Aquarium, and Seal Cove, and take an Australian Adventure. Try the Giraffe Feeding Dock and the Gentle Jungle. Enjoy new theme park rides if you dare.

There are food booths galore, but picnickers are welcome. There are lots of picnic areas, but groups should make reservations.

Directions: From the Sonoma Plaza take East Napa Street, and turn right onto Eighth Street East. Go to the arterial stoplight at Napa Road. Turn left on Napa Road to the stop signal at the intersection of Highways 12 and 121. Turn left toward Napa. Proceed to the stoplight and intersection of Highways 121 and 29, south of Napa. Turn right toward Vallejo and proceed 8.6 miles. Turn left onto the Marine World Parkway for 1.6 miles, and turn off at Six Flags Marine World.

Fine points: The rate for children four–twelve is $24 (under three, free), adults $34, and seniors and disabled $25. Group rates are available. Many retailers, such as Safeway Stores and Taco Bell, offer discount coupons up to 50 percent off. Schedules change, and long-term remodeling is going on, so be sure to call for the latest information before you come.

❧ *Six Flags Marine World, Marine World Parkway, Vallejo 94589; phone (707) 643–ORCA (6722). Open 10:00 A.M.–5:00 P.M., Wednesday–Sunday, in winter; 9:30–6:30 daily, Memorial Day–Labor Day. MasterCard, Visa Diners Club, Carte Blanche, and JCB–JAL. Wheelchair-accessible; wheelchairs are for rent next to the Main Gift Shop.*

The WESTERN RAILROAD MUSEUM at Rio Vista Junction is a twenty-five-acre museum with 110 pieces of historic train cars, streetcars, and the defunct Key System Route (one-time San Francisco–East Bay electric trains) collection. Also on exhibit are a 1904 wooden interurban train that used to operate between Petaluma, Santa Rosa, and Sebastopol and California's last nickel streetcar from Chico.

Directions: Take East Napa Street, turn right onto Eighth Street East, and continue to the arterial stoplight at Napa Road. Turn left on Napa Road; then turn left toward Napa at the intersection of Highways 12 and 121. At the intersection of 121 and 29 south of Napa, turn south toward Vallejo for 8.6 miles. Turn left onto Marine World Parkway and merge into Highway I-80 east. Take the Highway 12 exit (which appears soon) off I-80 east. Pass Fairfield. The Western Railroad Museum will be on the right.

Fine points: The rates (adults $5.00, children four–twelve $2.00, kids three and under $1.00) include unlimited rides on vintage trains.

❧ *Western Railroad Museum, 5848 Highway 12, Rio Vista Junction; phone (707) 374–2978. Open 11:00 A.M.–5:00 P.M. Wednesday–Sunday.*

The Sᴏɴᴏᴍᴀ Cᴏᴀsᴛ ʙᴇᴀᴄʜᴇs, including Dillon Beach and Tomales (actually Marin County), and Bodega Bay, are all off Highway 1. *Caution:* All these beaches are dangerous for swimmers, with covered rocks and a strong undertow. No lifeguards. Watch children carefully at all times.

Directions: Take Broadway south from Sonoma Plaza, turn right onto Watmaugh Road, cross Arnold Drive at the signal, and proceed to the stop sign at Highway 116. Wander through the beautiful oak-tree "tunnel" around and up the hills, down the other side, and keep right toward Petaluma. Turn right at Adobe Road. Vallejo's Petaluma Adobe is on the right. Continue past Angelo's Meats and turn left at East Washington Street. Cross Highway 101 on the bridge, pass through Petaluma (or stop for great antiques), and keep going toward west. Washington becomes Bodega Avenue (two lanes). Follow it to Dillon Beach–Valley Ford fork. If you take the road to Tomales and Dillon Beach, you'll see the picturesque Victorian farming town of Tomales, or you can wind your way down to the Pacific Ocean at Dillon Beach ($5.00 per vehicle admission charge).

You can also take Highway 1 north from Tomales, follow the signs to Bodega Bay, and still pass through Valley Ford, a charming, teensy rural town with antiques and Granucci's Italian restaurant.

There are still other things you can do on this route.

Cʜᴀɴsʟᴏʀ Hᴏʀsᴇ Sᴛᴀʙʟᴇs offers beach rides along their 700-acre working ranch near Salmon Creek, north of Bodega Bay. You can horseback-ride on the beach, through Salmon Creek Canyon, and in the Wetlands Wildlife Preserve. Chanslor also has a petting zoo, pony rides, and hay-wagon rides. Rates range from $5.00 to $40.00; the petting zoo and pony rides cost $1.50 per person.

❧ *Chanslor Horse Stables, 2660 Coast Highway 1, Bodega Bay 94923; phone (707) 875–2721. Open 8:00 A.M.–8:00 P.M. daily. MasterCard and Visa. Not wheelchair-accessible.*

Old downtown Pᴇᴛᴀʟᴜᴍᴀ has revived, preserving many old-time shops, businesses, and Victorian homes. This is a great place to hunt for antiques and good coffee.

Directions: Follow the directions to the Sonoma Coast beaches above, and turn left off Washington Street onto Petaluma Boulevard.

Tourist Center, *799 Baywood Drive, Suite 1, Petaluma 94954; phone (707) 769–0429, events line (707) 769–5640.*

PETALUMA FACTORY OUTLETS offer the works in outlet shopping, from Levi's to Ann Taylor and Brooks Brothers, Corning Revere to Le Gourmet Chef and Mikasa, Bass to Joan & David. While this might not be something the kids will appreciate, dedicated shoppers certainly will.

Directions: Get off Highway 101 at Washington Street, head west on Washington to Petaluma Boulevard, and turn north (right) onto Petaluma Boulevard. When you see the signs, turn right to the outlets.

On the PETALUMA QUEEN RIVERBOAT CRUISES, you can enjoy Dixieland jazz while sipping, dining, or just gazing on this authentic, three-decker paddlewheeler. Cruises take two hours. Full linen and china service.

Fine points: Lunch cruises run Wednesday–Friday, Champagne Brunch cruises Saturday and Sunday, Dinner cruises Wednesday–Friday, Dinner Dance cruises Saturday, and Dixieland Jazz Cruises Sunday. Rates range from $15–$25 without meal to $29–$49 with meal; children ages three–eleven half-price.

Petaluma Queen Riverboat Cruises, *255 Weller Street, Petaluma 94952; phone (707) 762–2100 or (800) 750–7501. MasterCard, Visa, American Express, and Discover. First deck is wheelchair-accessible.*

SAFARI WEST gives you a vicarious trip to Africa, in the guise of a private wildlife preserve and working ranch engaged in propagation programs to ensure conservation of endangered species of African animals, with herds of antelope, eland, gazelle, zebra, and more. Be sure to visit Safari West's brand new Wings of Africa & Beyond 15,000-square-foot, walk-through aviary.

Directions: Take Sonoma Highway (12) north and follow signs to and get on Highway 101 North. Take the River Road/Calistoga Exit off Highway 101. Turn right and follow the road for 6.7 miles to Franz Valley Road. Turn left, and you're there.

Fine points: You can contribute to new programs here by attending the annual Beastly Ball for the same price as entry to the park. ("Things just get complicated if we change the numbers," explains Safari West.) Daily tours at 8:00 and 11:30 A.M. and 3:00 P.M. Custom tours by appointment only, two and a half to three hours each. Rates for adults are $48, for children sixteen and under $24. MasterCard, Visa, and American Express.

❧ *Safari West, 3115 Porter Creek Road, Santa Rosa 95404; phone (707) 579–2551; e-mail Peterlangco@juno.com. Wheelchair-accessible (please call ahead to discuss your special needs).*

The RUSSIAN RIVER is one of our favorite short trips for a change of scenery. You may have heard of river residents' plight during floods, but they are an unusually resilient bunch who somehow pick up and start over. One reason they stay is that the Russian River and its towering redwoods and general ambience are so uniquely beautiful. Life here is at the same time simple and difficult.

As you enter the Russian River valley, you wind through vineyards, rolling hills, and the Yaka Ama Indian Reservation (great native-plant nursery here), Mark West Vineyards, Piper Sonoma, and lots of campgrounds. You then pass Fort Cook, Korbel Champagne Cellars, and Rio Nido (14.1 miles west of Highway 101). Drive slowly, because there is so much to see.

Directions: Drive north on Sonoma Highway through Kenwood and Santa Rosa and then north on Highway 101 to the River Road, Guerneville exit (just past the Luther Burbank Center for the Arts) to the Russian River. Exit left and then turn left over Highway 101 and you're on your way.

Our favorite spot (and that of most River Rats, as the locals call themselves) for a late breakfast around here is THE LAST GREAT HIDING PLACE. The Hiding Place moved to its current location in 1995 after a flood, which turned out to be a great opportunity to improve surroundings and redecorate. The dining room and bar are primarily mauve and green, and the deck faces south over the river. Service in this gay restaurant is friendly, professional, helpful, genteel, and full of local humor.

Favorites include whole-wheat pancakes with piles of fruit on top, omelets, and biscuits and gravy. Portions are large, and no one rushes you to seat the next customers. They just have to wait. There's a full bar.

Directions: Follow above directions to Russian River, passing through Forestville to Rio Nido and Guerneville. The Last Great Hiding Place is on the left going into Guerneville.

❧ *The Last Great Hiding Place, 9605 Old River Road, Forestville; phone (707) 887–9506. Open 9:00 A.M.–9:00 P.M. daily. MasterCard and Visa. Wheelchair-accessible.*

In GUERNEVILLE we suggest you park the car and just stroll around the 2-block resort town. Try Pat's Fountain and Bar, the locals' favorite coffee shop and greasy spoon; the Rainbow Cattle Co., the local favorite gay bar; the Guerneville

Five and Dime; King's Sport and Tackle; and Sweet's River Grill for breakfast, lunch, or dinner.

On Armstrong Woods Road, right off River Road, is the small Cinnebar Street Shops with a used bookstore (Twice Told Books), laundromat, and coffeehouse. The Coffee Bazarre, once quite bizarre, now offers one of the best Caesar salads around, sumptuous vegetarian chili, the best ice cream, melt-in-your-mouth scones, and decent espresso. The interior looks wonderful now, and the new owners roast coffee beans right on the spot. Love that aroma!

ARMSTRONG WOODS is a must for nature lovers. Some of the country's oldest trees are here for you to enjoy and help preserve. To get there, take Armstrong Woods Road off River Road for about 3 miles.

Guerneville's main public beach is JOHNSON'S BEACH, which has a children's roped-in area, a large snack shack with beer, and a truly diverse guest population. Johnson's beach cabins are the bargain of the Western world; they are old, but they are also no-frills clean and only $35 to $40 per night. Johnson's Beach is headquarters for California jazz lovers in September, when it hosts the Russian River Jazz Festival. To get to Johnson's Beach, turn left anywhere in downtown Guerneville 1 block from the river. Look for the beach-access sign.

Four miles west of Guerneville on River Road is Monte Rio, a small and old community with the Rio Theater, a quonset-hut moviehouse; a nursery; a convenience store; roadside jewelry merchants; and Jerry's Restaurant, the local hangout, with wholesome meals, stiff drinks, and just enough attitude. Turn right and go down under the bridge to Monte Rio beach, complete with snack shack and canoe, kayak, and umbrella rentals.

Another 4 miles west on River Road brings you to Duncans' Mills, a restored and boutiqued frontier town from which the North Shore Railroad once loaded logs inland to build California. Beside the train depot and museum is a local favorite, the Gold Coast Coffee roasters, whose coffee is sold throughout the Redwood Empire; Candy and Kites, where we buy a windsock every year; and the Blue Heron Restaurant and Bar.

Across River Road is another bunch of shops and delis whose tenants change so frequently we urge you to check them out yourselves.

Five miles west of Duncans' Mills, the road forks. Your choices are Jenner-by-the-Sea and eventually Eureka to the north on Highway 1, or Bodega Bay and Stinson Beach to the South.

North, at JENNER-BY-THE-SEA, the Russian River meets the Pacific Ocean, a sight one must experience. We have actually been convinced that we have arrived at heaven watching the sunset from our dinner table at RIVER'S END RESTAURANT, north of Jenner. It is expensive but well worth it. The food and view are exquisite, even when the fog or rain are in.

River's End Restaurant, 11051 Highway 1, Jenner-by-the-Sea; phone (707) 865–2484 or 869–3252. Open for lunch and dinner 11:00 A.M.–9:30 P.M. Friday–Monday. Lodging open daily. MasterCard and Visa.

If you turn left (or south) at the fork at Highway 1, you can visit the delights of Bodega Bay, with its fishing boats, shops, and seafood restaurants, and then follow signs across country roads to Petaluma, Sebastopol, Santa Rosa, Sonoma, or even San Francisco. Coming back through Petaluma or Sebastopol, you can arrive back in Sonoma, comfortably in time for dinner and a sound sleep.

CHAPTER 8

HISTORY OF THE SONOMA VALLEY

or 7,000 years before the first white man appeared on the scene, Sonoma Valley was the home of Native Americans. These early inhabitants of the Valley were primarily Coast Miwok, except in the Kenwood area, which was the southern border of a tribelet of the Pomo, named the Yuki (called Wappo or Guapo by the Mexicans, meaning "brave ones"). In what is now the City of Sonoma and over the hills into southern Napa County lived a clan of Miwok, who called themselves the Huichica. Farther to the southeast, around present-day Vallejo and Fairfield, was the territory of the Suisun, related to Wintun of the Sacramento Valley.

The Coast Miwok dwelt in villages of simple thatched huts from late autumn until mid-spring, and then set up camps for hunting, fishing, and enjoying the outdoors at various sites in the Valley. Most days the men and boys perspired in a sweathouse and then rinsed off in a cold stream or lake. These first peoples of the Valley were hunters and gatherers. Their food staple was acorns ground into meal by mortar and pestle and baked into a form of bread.

The first whites arrived in Sonoma Valley in 1810, when a troop of Spanish soldiers marched southeast from the coast after landing near Bodega Bay. They tramped along the route of present-day Highway 12 through Kenwood, which they considered too swampy for settlement because Sonoma Creek often over-flowed its banks.

FATHER ALTIMIRA CHOOSES SONOMA

After Mexico achieved independence from Spain in 1821, the new govern-ment was anxious to gain control of California north of Mission San Francisco de Assisi (Mission Dolores) and to protect its interests against the spread of

Russian influence from its trading post at Fort Ross. At the same time the Catholic Church wished to add to its existing chain of twenty California missions. The San Francisco Mission had proved to be unhealthful, due to cold and damp conditions. A small mission had been established in 1817 in San Rafael as a sanitarium for sick Indians and a good place to grow food. From the San Rafael hills, the padres could see the Petaluma Valley.

A young Spanish priest, Father José Altimira, was dispatched from Mission Dolores to locate a site for a new mission on the Petaluma plain. Accompanying him were Indian workers and a troop of soldiers, for this was a governmental as well as religious enterprise. On June 26, 1823, Father Altimira left Mission San Rafael, passed through present-day Novato, and headed eastward over the hills into the Petaluma Valley. Altimira was not particularly impressed, so he continued over the next range of hills, following the route of present-day Highway 116. He was delighted by his first view of Sonoma Valley below. That night they camped near what is now Arnold Drive and Stage Gulch Road.

For two days Altimira and his men explored the southern end of the Valley and then rode into Napa Valley. They soon returned to Sonoma Valley, riding as far north as what is now Warm Springs Road. Despite his instructions to place the mission on the Petaluma plain, he chose Sonoma. On July 4, 1823, Altimira set up an altar and raised a cross between Sonoma and Sears Point, at a spot on what is now the Cline Winery, north of Highway 121, before heading back to Mission Dolores.

He returned to Sonoma Valley on August 25 and began construction of the Mission, originally called New San Francisco, but soon officially named San Francisco Solano, for St. Francis of Solano, a missionary from Italy to Peru in the 1700s. The Mission's namesake was famous for performing miracles, including predicting a devastating earthquake, which spared the altar of his church. Altimira's Mission was soon referred to as San Francisco Solano de Sonoma.

The redwood-built Mission was officially dedicated on April 4, 1824, with twenty-six Miwok children baptized. An adobe brickyard was established, pastures laid out, and a small vineyard planted. Within the year the church burned down (possibly ignited by unhappy natives) and a new Mission was built, which also was damaged by fire. Finally, adobe was used to construct the Mission, and a church with a tiled roof was completed by 1829. There were quarters for the padre, houses for the soldiers and their families, and a granary.

In 1826 Father Altimira left the Mission and sailed back to Spain, unwilling to take Mexican citizenship. He left behind fields of grain, fruit trees, a herd of 2,000 cattle, thousands of sheep and pigs, as well as 3,000 grapevines, which began producing by 1828.

The Mission became home to as many as 700 natives, and some 1,300 Indians were baptized between 1823 and 1834. Many Indians learned agriculture and manufacturing, but there was discontent over the serflike system under which they lived. One padre had a difficult time explaining to his superiors his extensive use of flogging to enforce rules and punish runaways. Although not a military post, soldiers were assigned to protect the Mission personnel and to add muscle to control any wayward natives. Most important, the Sonoma Mission was the northern outpost of Mexican influence in California. To the north lay only Indian tribes and the Russians at Fort Ross.

MARIANO VALLEJO TAKES CHARGE

The role of the missions changed dramatically in 1834, when the Mexican government implemented "secularization." Control of the missions and their extensive lands was transferred to governmental authority, making these properties and land claims available for land grants to colonizers and favorites of those in power.

Striding into Sonoma's history that year came twenty-seven-year-old Lieutenant Mariano G. Vallejo, commandant of the presidio in Yerba Buena (the future San Francisco). His first assignment was to transfer the Mission's properties to civilian control. He also had to reduce its function to that of a parish church, much to the chagrin of the remaining padre, who protested in vain and departed in 1835.

Vallejo, born in Monterey, began construction of the largest adobe in northern California east of present-day Petaluma, as a headquarters for his agricultural operations, and placed the Sonoma Mission Indians under the harsh ministrations of his younger brother, Salvador. Lieutenant Vallejo also obtained from the Mexican government a gigantic land grant of 44,000 acres (later expanded to 66,000). Vallejo's grants stretched from present-day Petaluma, through most of Sonoma Valley, and over to Napa Valley; it was bordered by San Pablo Bay on the south.

In less than a year, Vallejo was ordered to create an official pueblo (town) in the area close to the Sonoma Mission and lay out surveyed streets, blocks, and lots. He promptly developed a city plan with the help of William A. Richardson, the Englishman who had founded the trading post of Yerba Buena in 1822. Sonoma was only one of six towns in California designated a pueblo. Others included Los Angeles, San Jose, San Diego, Santa Barbara, and Monterey, but not Yerba Buena. Thus, Sonoma had been mission, pueblo, and military headquarters—the only California town to be all three under Mexican rule.

General Mariano G. Vallejo

The centerpiece of the pueblo was an eight-acre plaza, diagonally across the road from the Mission chapel. The plaza was initially a dusty, treeless parade ground and would not become a verdant park until the early 1900s. A principal road (now Broadway) from the south terminated at the plaza. To this day, property descriptions often refer to the "Old Pueblo" lots and streets.

Vallejo began construction of a palatial adobe across the street from the plaza and a barracks for his soldiers. It still exists, at the corner of Spain and

First Street East. His brother Salvador also started construction of an adobe house for himself.

Mission Indians continually faded away under the civilian control. Between 1837 and 1839 a smallpox epidemic killed hundreds of natives, who lacked immunity to this old-world disease. At first the Vallejos responded to warlike threats (real or imagined) by Indian tribes with harsh military measures. When a small army of rebelling natives swept into what is now Solano County from the south, Mariano Vallejo led an attack on the Indians. More than 200 Indians were killed at a cost of only seven Mexicans. The rebellion collapsed. Soon, however, General Vallejo entered into peace treaties or alliances with various neighboring chiefs. The most valuable such arrangement was a long-term pact with Chief Solano (a name taken upon baptism in Sonoma) of the Suisun, who protected the frontiers of the Mexican settlement and joined in battle against threatening tribes. The remarkably tall (6 feet, 7 inches), charismatic Solano was something of a character (he once schemed to kidnap a Russian noblewoman from Fort Ross), but a reliable ally when trouble appeared.

In 1838 Vallejo was confirmed as "commandante general" for Alta California (all of the territory from San Diego northward). Some historians refer to him as commander only of "the northern frontier," since he headquartered in Sonoma. But it was in the north where trouble loomed, in the form of a Russian threat from Bodega Bay; and, if he had stayed in the provincial capital, Monterey, he would have had little to do. Besides, he preferred to stay aloof from the internecine disputes that plagued the government in Monterey and the governor, Vallejo's hard-drinking nephew, Juan Bautista Alvarado.

On one occasion, however, Vallejo found it necessary to make a show of military strength in Monterey. With few soldiers of his own, he enlisted Chief Solano, dressed him in a Spanish-style uniform, and they rode at the head of a hundred mounted Suisun tribesmen through the dusty streets of the capital. The people of Monterey were scared stiff, and antigovernment talk was stilled for a time. In addition to his own land grant, Vallejo secured much of what is now Kenwood, entitled Rancho Guilicos, for John Wilson, who was married to a sister of Benicia Vallejo, the commandante's wife, and a large tract for his mother-in-law, Maria Lopez de Carrillo, centered in present-day Santa Rosa. The original Carrillo adobe still stands. Vallejo's generosity with public lands included a large ranchería in the Valley of the Suisun for Chief Solano.

Across from the Mission, Vallejo built a billiard parlor and started a new Mission church at the southwestern corner of the compound, although the first chapel had been at the eastern end. The Mexican government also granted land for a Catholic cemetery east of the Plaza on Napa Street, which is still in use. Vallejo planted a vineyard of Mission grapes north of the Plaza. It was a pleasant, bucolic existence. The Russians lost interest in expanding and sold Fort Ross to John Sutter in 1841. The Indians, their ranks depleted by illness, were relatively quiescent, and houses began to dot the landscape as new colonists arrived. Vallejo's wife, Benicia, delivered thirteen babies; not all survived. His sister Rosalía married Jacob Leese, an American merchant in Yerba Buena, who traded property there for a land grant (Huichica) southeast of the Sonoma pueblo. Leese also built a large, U-shaped, two-story adobe home and store at the corner of First Street West and Napa Street, a portion of which still exists. In 1843 Vallejo turned over the administration of the pueblo to a civilian city council with his brother-in-law Leese as alcalde (a Mexican combination of mayor and judge). The council then began raising funds for a cemetery, jail, and city hall. The local census showed fifty-nine "citizens," twelve foreigners (including Americans), and six Indians. Women, children, and most Indians did not count. By 1845 the true population of Sonoma was 300 people. There were now forty-five houses.

Sir George Simpson, head of the British-owned Hudson's Bay Company, visited Sonoma in 1845. Simpson reported that the Vallejos were gracious hosts who set a magnificent dinner table. Simpson was appalled, however, at the sad condition of the Indians, who were barely sheltered in rude huts.

The Bear Flag "Revolt"

The influx of Americans into California became so significant that the Mexican government issued warnings that they were not welcome. Vallejo ignored the anti-immigrant policy and was hospitable to Americans as colonists. By 1846 some 10 percent of the residents of California were transplanted Americans.

Although unknown in California for more than two months, on May 13, 1846, the United States declared war against Mexico, supposedly as a result of clashes along the Rio Grande, the border between Mexico and Texas, which had been annexed to the United States in 1845. President James K. Polk's real aim was the acquisition of California from Mexico.

There remains some confusion as to what instructions were sent from U.S. Secretary of State James Buchanan to Thomas Larkin, the American consul in Monterey, with a copy delivered to Captain John C. Frémont ("the Pathfinder"), a U.S. Army "topographical engineer" who was "exploring" southern Oregon and northern California with a crew under his command. The secret dispatches (carried by a marine lieutenant who journeyed through Mexico posing as a merchant) apparently told them to sit tight and await events.

In May 1846, however, Frémont led his men south from Oregon and set up camp near Sutter's Fort (Sacramento), where he encountered a band of twenty Americans interested in throwing off Mexican rule. They were mountain men, adventurers, settlers, and an alleged convicted murderer. Their first order from Frémont was to intercept a herd of horses being sent by General Vallejo to General José Castro at Santa Clara, which they did on June 10. Now equipped with first-class mounts, the Americans decided to capture Sonoma, the frontier center of Mexican authority. Frémont would later say that he ordered the taking of Sonoma, but more likely his strategy was basically to cause trouble.

General Vallejo's Sonoma command consisted of his brother, a Frenchman named Victor Prudon (Vallejo's personal aide), and a handful of soldiers awaiting assignment. In the words of historian Bernard deVoto, "Sonoma was a tiny cluster of adobe houses and could have been captured by Tom Sawyer and Huck Finn."

On June 13, 1846, the band of Americans rode out from the Sutter's Fort area heading for Sonoma. They were joined by thirteen more settlers as they passed through Napa Valley. They arrived in the Plaza shortly after sunrise on June 14. General Vallejo was asleep. Awakened by whoops and hollers, and looking out upon this rough-looking troop of armed riders, he quickly donned his full-dress uniform and invited the leaders to come in.

Vallejo greeted them with "What can I do for you?" and offered them glasses of brandy or wine. He talked of having a discussion on a "friendly" basis, until he was cut short by Ezekiel Merritt, Captain Frémont's spokesman, who announced that they had not come to be entertained but, rather, "meant business." Merritt stated that the Americans intended to set up an independent government of California; he then placed General Vallejo, his brother Salvador, his brother-in-law Leese, and Victor Prudon under arrest.

Vallejo chatted with his captors and ordered wine for all the men under Merritt's command. Almost disappointed that the victory had come so easily, some of the Americans drank too much and began talking about looting. William Ide, however, a nondrinking carpenter from New England who had a ranch in what is now Tehama County, made a rousing speech, reminding the invaders that they were in Sonoma to form a republic free of Mexico. Ide's oratory was so impressive that he was thereupon elected by acclamation as the first and only president of the Republic of California.

The government of the republic needed a symbol of authority. William Todd (Mary Todd Lincoln's nephew) made a flag out of a petticoat and a chemise, drew a red star in one corner, ran a strip of red flannel along the bottom border, and painted on it a supposed grizzly bear (which more closely resembled a fat, misshapen pig). With "poke juice" he lettered in "CALIFORNIA REPUBLC," but had to blot out the last syllable to insert an "I". Shortly the Mexican flag was lowered from its pole in the Plaza and in its place was raised the California Republic's makeshift banner, the precursor of the state's bear flag.

President Ide penned a proclamation declaring the advent of the new nation and inviting "all peaceable and good citizens" to come to Sonoma to assist the so-called Bear Flaggers in establishing a republican form of government. This declaration was printed in both English and Spanish.

Meanwhile, Mariano and Salvador Vallejo, Leese, and Prudon were taken on horseback by a squad under Merritt to Sutter's Fort, 85 miles away, where Frémont ordered them imprisoned.

Ironically, Mariano Vallejo had come to the conclusion that California would be better off as part of the growing United States. His problem was how to make such a break consistent with his honor and responsibility as an official of the Mexican government. He regarded the Americans as enterprising and the U.S. government as more effective than the distant authorities in Mexico City, who ignored the needs of California. At heart he was a Californio first and Mexican citizen second.

The immediate aftermath of the Bear Flag revolt was a foray by Mexican troops from Monterey, who were chased off by Bear Flaggers north of Petaluma. A Mexican squad, however, ambushed and killed two Bear Flaggers near Santa Rosa, leaving their hacked bodies by the roadside. Near San Rafael three unarmed members of the pioneering Berryessa and DeHaro families were cornered by Frémont's Americans. In the most disreputable act of his career, Frémont ordered them shot, on the paper-thin excuse that he had no means to keep prisoners. Ben Kelsey refused Frémont's order to execute the captives, but Kit Carson carried it out. The son of the slain Berryessa was the alcalde of Sonoma. William Todd was caught by Mexican soldiers, but other Bear Flaggers, led by Henry "Fighting" Ford and Granville P. Swift, rescued him.

Frémont, many Bear Flaggers and their families, and a group of American sailors (from a U.S. warship that had just anchored in San Francisco Bay) converged on Sonoma on July 4 for a giant fiesta, attended by many of the Mexican residents of the pueblo. It was obvious that most of the local residents were reconciled to the fact that the future of California lay with the United States and not Mexico.

THE AMERICAN MILITARY TAKES OVER

On July 9, Navy Lieutenant Joseph Warren Revere, grandson of Paul Revere, rode into the Plaza with the news that Monterey had been captured by the United States Navy, and that Commodore John D. Sloat, highest-ranking American military officer in the territory, had ordered the American flag raised at Sonoma. Down came the Bear Flag, and up went the Stars and Stripes. The independent California Republic had lasted twenty-five days.

Sloat became increasingly worried that he had exceeded his authority or that rumors of war were not true, so in mid-July he turned his command over to the younger, energetic Commodore Robert F. Stockton, who was bolstered by the arrival in Monterey of Frémont and his California Battalion.

Revere had acted as if there were a war between the United States and Mexico, but he was bluffing, as were Sloat, Stockton, and Frémont, since they did not get the official declaration of war until early August—it was published in the first issue of *Californian* on August 15 in Monterey. Many Bear Flaggers were sworn into the U.S. Navy as a company of "horse marines" in August, as part of Frémont's company. Revere took the original Bear Flag and later contributed it to the Society of California Pioneers in San Francisco. It burned in the 1906 earthquake and fire. In 1911 a more artistic rendering of the flag was adopted as the official flag of California. Mariano Vallejo and his three compatriots languished in Sutter's Fort until released the first week in August by order of Commodore Sloat (his final act before sailing away), upon the urging of Thomas Larkin, the American consul in Monterey, whose half-brother was married to General Vallejo's sister.

The Mexican War ended with the Treaty of Guadalupe Hidalgo, signed on February 2, 1848, ratified by the U.S. Senate in March and the Mexican government in May. California became American, but neither a territory nor state. All Californios were granted the full benefits of American citizenship under the treaty. (As recently as 1992 the Sonoma Valley Chamber of Commerce used the treaty to challenge the right of the state highway department to ban outdoor seating on Broadway because outdoor seating was legal in 1848. The state abandoned its efforts to enforce its prohibition.) The Vallejos and the vast majority of Californios swore loyalty to the United States and became American citizens.

Lieutenant Revere and a handful of American naval and army personnel occupied Sonoma until relieved in April 1847 by an army unit called the First New York Volunteers (often referred to as Stevenson's Regiment), who were quartered in the Barracks. In the fall of 1847, the first steamship transportation was established between Yerba Buena and Sonoma, in the form of the 37-foot sidewheeler *Sitka*, purchased from Russians in Alaska. It docked at "the Embarcadero" near the mouth of Sonoma Creek, in what is now known as Schellville.

The Blue Wing Inn (called Sonoma House until the mid-1850s), an adobe building across the street from the Mission, was built in two stages around 1840. It served as a hotel, gambling joint, and saloon. It did a bustling business and was tolerant of all types of clientele, including (according to legend) the famed horse-thieves and killers Joaquin Murietta and his partner "Three-Fingers" Jack García, who drank in the bar while their men scouted the countryside for likely horses to steal. Nervous customers never challenged their presence. The place was popular with the American soldiers quartered in Sonoma and with the '49ers returning with gold dust, ready to spend and gamble.

Sonoma became the Pacific Coast headquarters of the U.S. Army in 1849, with Colonel Joseph Hooker ("Fighting Joe" in the Civil War) as second in command to General Persifer Smith, military governor of California. The handsome Joe Hooker gave his name to the slang for prostitute, since he was both tolerant of and partaking of the coterie of women who followed the soldiers. These ladies were soon known as "Hooker's girls" and finally just "Hookers." Several other future heroes of the Civil War were stationed in Sonoma, including Phil Kearny, William Tecumseh Sherman, and Philip Sheridan, while Ulysses S. Grant stopped long enough to have a few drinks at the Blue Wing.

The Gold Rush, Prosperity, and Statehood

The crucial 1848 event for Sonoma was the discovery of gold by James Marshall at John Sutter's mill, near Coloma. By 1849 the California Gold Rush was on. More than half the soldiers living at the Barracks deserted for the gold fields. As the only settlement with commercial enterprises between Sacramento and San Francisco, Sonoma made money from miners who stopped over on their way, needed supplies, or later freely spent their newfound wealth.

On February 18, 1850, Sonoma County was formed as one of the original twenty-seven counties in anticipation of California's attaining statehood. At the same time the Sonoma pueblo was incorporated as a city and named the county seat. A courthouse was established in a two-story building with a large veranda, built in 1849 across from the Plaza, where the Great Western Bank now stands. The city council's first task was to improve the Plaza, which was gouged with holes left from digging for adobe. An open ditch ran across the Plaza, which was the scene of bronco-busting contests, cattle grazing, and staged fights between dogs and raccoons on which locals would wager.

Mariano Vallejo was the most prominent Californio delegate to the convention, held in the temporary capital of Monterey, which wrote the first state constitution. Then he was elected to the temporary Senate, taking his seat on December 27, 1849. He became a member of the first State Senate when California achieved statehood, September 9, 1850, but served only one session.

In 1851 General Vallejo began the construction of an American-style

SONOMA LANDING AT LAKEVILLE, IN THE 1880S, WITH A
DONAHUE FERRY

Victorian mansion at the northern head of Third Street West in Sonoma, with extensive landscaping. Dubbed Lachryma Montis ("Tear of the Mountain") for the ample spring on the property, it was completed in 1852.

The army left Sonoma in January 1852, depriving local merchants of a major source of income.

Meanwhile, at the northern end of the Valley, John Wilson, Vallejo's brother-in-law, sold his 18,833-acre land grant to merchants William Hood and William Pettit for $13,000 rather than fight a battle over the legality of his title to land he had never occupied. Hood eventually built a large home (the Hood House, now a California Landmark), completed in 1858, and began subdividing and selling property from the Los Guilicos Rancho, stretching from south of Kenwood north almost to Santa Rosa. Transportation to the Sonoma Valley at the time of statehood included a daily stagecoach that stopped in Sonoma on its run from Sacramento, through Napa, to Petaluma. There was also a paddlewheel steamboat from San Francisco and other bay points to the Embarcadero at the mouth of Sonoma Creek, and a ferry docked at Lakeville, near Petaluma Creek (now River). Those boat trips were followed by a bumpy coach or wagon trip over primitive roads into Sonoma. Regular stage runs between Sonoma and Santa Rosa were not established for two more decades.

Sonoma pioneer Nicholas Carriger and Bear Flagger Granville Swift returned from the goldfields as rich men. Carriger, who had previously built the pueblo's first wooden (not adobe) house, purchased 1,000 acres from Vallejo west of Sonoma at $4.00 an acre. There he constructed a modest mansion. Big, handsome, and illiterate, Swift bought what is now Temelec and erected the most prestigious mansion in the Valley for his young bride, Eliza. With Indian labor he planted magnificent gardens and erected stone walls. Swift believed that the Indians should be slaves and kept them in irons like a chain gang. Not trusting banks, he buried boxes of gold under the garden, from which a dishonest gardener stole some $24,000 in ingots.

The stone edifice, completed in 1858, cost the then-stupendous figure of $250,000 (it is now the clubhouse for the Temelec Homeowners' Association). Swift's bride soon tired of lonely country life and producing babies, so she divorced him. He returned to prospecting and was killed when his horse threw him over an embankment.

Salvador Vallejo also prospected for gold, with a crew of Indians doing the heavy work. He returned to Sonoma in 1849 with a substantial profit, which he put into two buildings—what is now the El Dorado Hotel and the still-standing adobe next door on First Street West. He also added a new wing to his home on Spain Street. The profligate Salvador, however, was soon forced to sell all of his buildings to satisfy debts. By the 1880s his home's annex on Spain Street had become an inn, which eventually would take the name Swiss Hotel.

SQUATTER'S RIGHTS VERSUS THE LAND GRANTS

More significant than individual fortunes, the Gold Rush brought hundreds of new settlers into Sonoma Valley in the early 1850s. These newcomers wanted land for farms, ranches, and homes. Arriving merchants and tradesmen needed space for stores, workrooms, and businesses. For these new arrivals, the old Mexican land grants, supposed to be honored under the peace treaty, were just pieces of paper. The Mexican property descriptions were often vague and not based on surveys. To compound the confusion, the treaty had empowered the alcaldes of the existing pueblos to grant deeds to unoccupied land. Although they did not yet realize it, the Californios' way of life was doomed.

Vallejo, who had doled out land grants with such casual generosity, found his own property titles challenged in court. People who had purchased from him were in peril of losing their homesteads. Just to be sure, some new arrivals paid both the City of Sonoma and Vallejo for the same lots. With so much open territory at his command, Vallejo had been careless with the land grants; in 1846 he gave his children's piano teacher 1,000 acres as payment for five years of music lessons.

A U.S. Land Commission was created to hear title disputes, but it moved like a glacier in most cases, with hearings, evidence collection, and court appeals taking as long as thirty years. The newcomer's trick was to take possession of land based on a claim of "squatter's rights" and then challenge the legality of the property title. Then the new claimant would threaten to make the legal process so expensive for the owner who traced his title to a Mexican grant that he would either give up or sell cheap.

Vallejo's holdings were gradually reduced over the years by this process. William Hood and his family would similarly lose much of the land purchased from Juan Wilson's grant. Jacob Leese was fortunate enough to get an early ruling confirming his Huichica grant, much of which he quickly advertised and sold in lots, while retaining a cattle ranch. His experience was a rarity, but he soon squandered his wealth in bad investments.

The system of gigantic land grants to favorites had been absurd from the beginning. No single person or family could farm or ranch properties as large as Rhode Island, unless based on a feudal system of tenant farmers or serfs like the Indians under the Mission fathers. Giving all the land to a handful made no sense if towns, farms, working ranches, and homesteads were to be developed through the vitality of settlers.

SONOMA LOSES THE COUNTY SEAT TO SANTA ROSA

At the urging of leaders of the growing community of Santa Rosa, in 1853 the state legislature approved a referendum on whether the county seat should stay in Sonoma or be transferred to Santa Rosa. After a spirited election contest, in September 1854 Santa Rosa won by a narrow margin among the 600 registered voters in the county. In the wee hours of the following Friday morning, a group of Santa Rosans slipped into the Sonoma Courthouse and piled the county archives and furniture into a wagon pulled by mules. Thwarting a possible claim of vote fraud by the City of Sonoma, they made what became known as the "hundred-minute dash" to Santa Rosa. Some of the records blew off the wagon, never to be found.

The four-year record of Sonoma as a center of legal justice and peacekeeping had not been first-rate. The two elected judges were noteworthy for a total lack of knowledge of the law. On three occasions convicted prisoners awaiting hanging escaped from the dilapidated jail. Purchased by the county from one of the judges, the adobe courthouse was poorly built; "unfit for a cattleshed," declared the county grand jury. When the county government was "taken" to Santa Rosa, the pueblo's first newspaper, *The Sonoma Bulletin,* editorialized, "We are only sorry that they did not take the courthouse along...." In 1861 the building collapsed.

Like the departure of the military, the transfer of the county seat hurt Sonoma economically. Local merchants were deprived of business from county employees and lawyers who came to town to appear in court. It was also a blow to the town's prestige and doomed it to being a backwater. Like a symbol of its decline, the large bell that had hung in front of the Mission since 1829 disappeared in the mid-1850s.

With the adoption of a state public-schools law in 1857, however, four public elementary school districts were formed, including the existing Dunbar School, built in 1850. The 1857 enrollment in the Valley was eighty-nine children. Maximum teacher pay was $125 a month for a principal. The first public school in Sonoma was conducted at the Methodist Church until 1870. Various private schools were kept in homes and commercial buildings starting in the 1840s. The most prominent were St. Mary's Hall (Presbyterian) between 1852 and 1856; and the Ver Mehr Academy, directed by an Episcopalian minister and his wife (attended by the Vallejos' daughters) from the late 1840s until 1859.

Cumberland Literary College for Young Ladies and Gentlemen was founded in 1858 by the Cumberland Presbyterian Church of Virginia, with classes in the old Mariano Vallejo home on the Plaza. In 1860 Cumberland took over the northern portion of Salvador Vallejo's buildings on First Street West, which had been and would again be the El Dorado Hotel. While called a "college," Cumberland was essentially a high school, with day students from the Sonoma Valley and boarding students from throughout the West, reaching a maximum enrollment of 400. In 1866 the college moved to a new building just off Broadway, near present-day MacArthur. That structure later became the first public high school. Portions of it still remain, peeling paint and all, behind the Sonoma Auto Center car lot.

THE WINE INDUSTRY: FROM COUNT HARASZTHY TO *PHYLLOXERA*

Hungarian Agoston Haraszthy (his full last name was Haraszthy de Mokcsa) was a man with a persistent dream: to find an environment in the United States in which he could produce fine wines. He had been banished from his homeland in 1840 after an unsuccessful revolt of army officers attempting to liberalize the autocratic rule of the Hapsburgs over Austria-Hungary. Arriving in the United States claiming to be a count and a colonel, he attempted to start a town and vineyards in what became Sauk City, Wisconsin; he moved on to Illinois and then to California, first San Diego and then San Mateo County, without success. Haraszthy wrangled an appointment as the director of the Mint in San Francisco, but the count was sacked when accused of sweeping up the gold dust from the floor as a fringe benefit of the directorship.

Haraszthy visited Sonoma in 1856 to inspect the old

COUNT AGOSTON HARASZTHY

Mission vineyards (then owned by one of the Bear Flagger Kelseys) and a few acres that Vallejo had planted at Lachryma Montis. He immediately felt that this was the rich soil and proper climate for grape growing that he had been seeking. He began purchasing potential vineyard land in January 1857, acquired grape cuttings from Napa, and planted vines that produced grapes for a new varietal named Zinfandel. He called his vineyards Buena Vista, a name that lives on.

While his newly planted vines were maturing for the four years before the first harvest, Haraszthy convinced the governor of California to name him official emissary to vineyardists in Europe so that he could explore the potential of bringing new vines to make wine production a major California industry. Armed with these credentials, plus a letter of introduction from Secretary of State William Seward, the count traveled to Europe in 1861. He returned the next year with 100,000 seedlings for planting in Sonoma and distribution to other California sites. Haraszthy transformed the state's commercial winemaking from small personal holdings into big business. Indeed, Haraszthy's Zinfandel became the first California variety to gain international fame. The Haraszthy family solidified its place in Sonoma when a pair of Agoston Haraszthy's sons, Arpad and Attila, married two of Mariano Vallejo's daughters,

Natalia and Jovita, in a double wedding on June 1, 1863. The greatest social event in Sonoma's history, the marriage is reenacted at the Mission each September during the Vintage Festival, although the original was held at Vallejo's Lachryma Montis.

The "father of the commercial wine business" did not fare as well as the industry he sired. For several years his Buena Vista Vineyards prospered. He built a stone winery, dug three caves deep into the hill to provide cool cellars, and his wines regularly won prizes at competitions. Haraszthy benefited from the financial support of San Francisco banker William Ralston, but eventually the two quarreled and Ralston withdrew his backing. Then an earthquake destroyed part of the winery and the caves collapsed, burying 30,000 bottles of champagne. But the real ravager of the commercial wine industry was a little bug, the dread *phylloxera* aphid, which attacked vine roots.

Haraszthy, however, did not live to witness this predator's devastation. He turned over the winery to his son Arpad in order to pioneer a plantation in Nicaragua. One day in 1869, the count fell into an alligator-infested river there and disappeared.

The Sonoma Valley wine business that Haraszthy had spawned was being carried on by European-trained vineyardists and winemakers Jacob Gundlach, Charles Bundschu, Emil and Gustav Dresel, local rancher Nicholas Carriger, and dozens of others. By 1876—shortly after *phylloxera* was first found in Sonoma Valley—the wineries in the Valley produced 2,335,000 gallons of wine. The economy of the Valley was flourishing in a flood of Zinfandel, Tokay, Cabernet Sauvignon, and Riesling. Within three years of the infestation, however, the vineyards were withered and the wine industry crippled.

Eventually Sonomans would lead the rejuvenation of California's wine business. With the aid of a magnifying glass, Valley vineyardists Horatio Appleton and Oliver W. Craig examined the roots of affected vines and isolated the insect. University of California biologists identified the culprit as *phylloxera vestatrix*, imported as piggyback riders on French vines. Ironically, these little louses had originally come from vines grown on the East Coast of the United States, taken to France for experimentation. For years experts could not find a rootstock that was impervious to *phylloxera*, but eventually Dresel and Gundlach imported several species of vines that could withstand the insect when grafted to existing rootstock. By the turn of the century, California wineries had revived.

Meanwhile, in 1860, attorney A. A. Green of San Francisco filed a lawsuit demanding that the Sonoma City Council bring a legal action to obtain title to all lands laid out in the pueblo map of 1835—some 20 square miles. If Green's suit were successful, all titles traceable to Vallejo's and Leese's grants would be invalid. Panic swept the settlers. Vallejo responded in 1862 by sneaking a bill through the state legislature that revoked the city charter. Thus, there was no city council to be ordered to challenge the titles. While the settlers' property rights were saved, the unincorporated town was left with no authority to improve streets—muddy lanes in winter and dusty trails in summer—to develop a sewer or water system, to drain the swamplands, or to provide fire protection. In 1866 a block of Napa Street businesses burned down, and in 1867 Vallejo's former palace by the Plaza was destroyed by fire.

THE RAILROAD WARS

With the Civil War over and the construction of the transcontinental railroad under way, Sonomans realized that the Valley could be revitalized by a railroad to link them with the urban centers in the Bay Area and the rest of the world. The state legislature was willing to subsidize new railroads at the rate of $5,000 a mile.

There were two competing routes through Sonoma County seeking railroad charters from the legislature. One proposal ran from Sausalito in Marin County through Petaluma to Santa Rosa and beyond, bypassing Sonoma Valley.

THE BARRACKS, MISSION, AND PLAZA IN 1867

Sonomans backed a proposed rail line from Vallejo, through Sonoma and up the Valley to Santa Rosa, to be built by the Vallejo & Sonoma Railroad Company, headed by General Vallejo's son-in-law John Frisbie. The legislature left the route decision to Sonoma County voters, setting an election for May 12, 1868. The Petaluma line won, 2,095 to 1,586 votes, leaving Sonoma isolated from progress. Goods and people coming to Sonoma still had to rely on paddle-wheel boats, followed by a bumpy ride in coach or wagon.

The Plaza remained unimproved. The now-defunct city council had once ordered a fence that was so ugly that public outcry forced its sale, at a substantial loss. The Mission was deteriorating again. Vallejo had repaired it in 1850; and in the late 1850s, he paid to have it further remodeled with a Gothic belfry and rounded window casements. It was an unfortunate aesthetic choice, inconsistent with the Mission Colonial style, which was distinguished by deep-set square windows with exposed headers.

During this unincorporated period, with the once-booming winery business suddenly a bust and railroad tracks edging toward every major community except Sonoma, the lower Valley was neglected and the town a rural slum. Nevertheless, local merchants and ranchers often prospered during this fallow period. Cheap labor, first Indian and then Chinese, was available to do the back-breaking work of clearing land and building the network of rock walls that still crisscross much of the Valley.

In 1872 another attempt was made to improve the derelict Plaza. The Society of California Pioneers (founded by pre-statehood settlers) lobbied a bill through the legislature for a Sonoma-area election to permit sale of the Plaza to the Society. Thus, the trustees (a state-approved committee) sold the Plaza to the Society for $10, on condition the Pioneers would fence, beautify, and spend $5,000 to construct a hall on the Plaza within five years. A fence was erected, a few trees were planted, but a campaign for money to build a Pioneer "temple" was a total failure. The Pioneers' title to the Plaza was abandoned in 1880. That year a group of businessmen financed the construction on the Plaza of the Pavilion, a circular building for stores and offices. Later it would also house the city government and a two-cell jail. When the bicycle craze came along, a racing track was laid out on the Plaza. In short, it was a disorganized wasteland.

In 1876 a promoter named Joseph Kohn sold some railroad-hungry Sonoma investors on an experimental monorail called the Crew Prismoidal System, in which the cars traveled on a single, triangular wooden rail. More than 3 miles of single "track" were built from the ferry docks at the Embarcadero at Schellville toward Sonoma. The Sonoma Valley Prismoidal Railway had a splendid test run with local society on board. Then it died—victim of the slight problem that the monorail could not cross roadways.

THE PLAZA WITH THE "PAVILION," IN THE 1880S

Kohn quickly switched signals and founded the Sonoma Valley Railroad Company, which acquired a right-of-way from the Embarcadero to Sonoma, and built several miles of narrow-gauge track before running out of money. Seizing the opportunity was Peter Donahue, owner of the largest manufacturer of rails and locomotives in San Francisco, who had a sharp eye for ailing railroad companies. He also had a reputation for businesslike management and a record of successful completion of railroads in Marin and Sonoma Counties, including the main Marin to Santa Rosa route via Petaluma.

Donahue proposed to the county that he be granted the right to build a rail line from the ferry pier at Sonoma Landing, near the mouth of Petaluma Creek, to connect with the incomplete Kohn line at a swampy place called Wingo, near San Pablo Bay, where speculators had laid out city lots. There the tracks would turn north to reach Sonoma through Schellville, follow the route of present-day Eighth Street East, and then turn west toward the Plaza along East Spain Street. Much as Sonomans resented being part of this rapacious outsider's growing system, the fact was that Donahue could produce. All he asked was the right to use Spain Street in front of the Mission as the entry into the center of the city. He soon convinced the Pioneer Society, then titleholders to the Plaza, that he should be permitted to build a station and roundhouse on that sacred ground. The railroad had enemies who feared that it would take business from Sonoma or who did not like the location of the terminus at the Plaza. To avoid a confrontation, Donahue had his crew work through the night laying the last several hundred feet of track down Spain Street to the Plaza. The next morning, in December

1879, the first train, pulled by an engine with the politically correct name of *The General Vallejo*, puffed up to the Plaza. A crowd, led by the locomotive's name-sake and his family, greeted the train with floral garlands.

GROWTH OF TOURISM, AND REINCORPORATION

The arrival of the Donahue railroad (with the new corporate name of The San Francisco & North Pacific Railway Company) ushered in the growth of the tourist industry in Sonoma. Instantly Sonoma Valley was less than half a day's easy ride from San Francisco, and just an hour from Marin County. Hotels, resorts, and summer cabins rose quickly to meet the influx of travelers arriving from late spring to early autumn. At the Vineburg stop and in downtown Sonoma, buggies and coaches met the trains, or people walked to a hotel or resort.

Sonoma's first three-story building, the Garibaldi Hotel, was completed on First Street East in 1880, a few months before the trains came. The Garibaldi joined other hotels, like the Toscano, Union (dating from 1849), El Dorado, Sonoma, and Tecino (later Swiss), already on the Plaza.

In the 1870s Solomon Schocken purchased the Barracks—which was used for stores and offices—and remodeled it in Victorian style. For $3,000 in gold in 1881, he also bought the Mission from the Catholic Church, which had just recovered title after a long legal battle. One factor leading to the decision to sell was the shaking from the trains chugging by the door of the crumbling Mission. The Catholics used the money to build a new parish church on West Napa Street, and Schocken converted the Mission to a warehouse and hay barn. The early *Sonoma Bulletin* had died in 1855 after three years, when its witty and acerbic publisher, A. J. Cox, moved away. After two decades of being without a paper, Frank Merritt founded the *Tribune* in 1878, which had four owners in its first five years. A small competitor was the *Index*. In 1883, Edward J. Livernash, who was just seventeen, bought and combined the two newspapers as the *Sonoma Index-Tribune*, which was a popular journalistic success but a business failure. Young Livernash left to become a prominent newsman in San Francisco and Denver, and he served a term in Congress. To the rescue of news-paperless Sonoma came San Francisco newsman H. H. Granice, who bought the defunct newspaper (equipment and the name) and issued his first edition in December 1884. Granice published the *Index-Tribune* until his death in 1915. At that time the paper was inherited by Granice's daughter, Celeste Murphy. She and her husband, Walter Murphy, edited and published the *Index-Tribune* for the following thirty years.

After two decades of civic anarchy, several Sonoma leaders obtained authority from the state legislature to reincorporate. By better than a three-to-one margin, local voters elected to incorporate the City of Sonoma as a sixth-class municipality starting September 3, 1883. The new city, however, encompassed only 1 square mile, compared to the sprawling 20 square miles of the pueblo created in 1835 and dissolved in 1862. The new boundaries included Vallejo's home and the Mountain Cemetery (at the head of Second Street East) down to present-day MacArthur to the south, eastward to Fifth Street East, and to Sonoma Creek on the west.

THE RISE OF GLEN ELLEN, KENWOOD, BOYES HOT SPRINGS, AND EL VERANO

Eight miles northwest of Sonoma lay the settlement of Glen Ellen, which took its name from Glen Ellen Vineyards, established by Colonel Charles V. Stuart in 1860. Stuart built a substantial stone home and a winery, named for his wife, Ellen. When the community adopted the name Glen Ellen, Stuart renamed his home Glen Oaks.

Near the junction of Dunbar Road and the present Highway 12, retired sea captain Charles Justi occupied a ranch that he had purchased from General Vallejo. In the late 1860s Captain Justi built a tavern and inn there to serve travelers. Daily stage trips were under way between Sonoma and Santa Rosa by 1870. In July 1872 the Justi Inn was appointed the post office for Glen Ellen.

Donahue extended his narrow-gauge railroad to Glen Ellen in August 1882. The railway made the area an easy and attractive destination for vacationers and weekend picnickers, triggering a boom in resorts, hotels, and campgrounds. Joining Justi's Inn were a dozen hotels, including the Mervyn, the Riverside, Gordenker's, Waldruhe, and the Chauvet, which still stands, an empty relic of past glory. A cabin could be purchased for less than $300. Wells Fargo set up an agency in the village's business area near the creek in 1883. Mammy Pleasant, the infamous San Francisco "Voodoo Queen" and madam, bought a ranch on the outskirts of Glen Ellen in 1890 for weekend entertaining, now the Beltane Ranch on Highway 12.

Back in Sonoma, City Trustee Henry Weyl obtained a judgment against the Donahue railroad in 1886 under which the court canceled the right-of-way on Spain Street. It forced the relocation in 1890 of the depot and turntable to the current site of Depot Park, the same year that the railroad was converted to broad gauge. Peter Donahue died in 1885, leaving the railroad empire to his son Mervyn Donahue, who had a reputation as a playboy, but who proved to be a shrewd operator. Within two years young Donahue opened a Marin

County–to–Napa rail line, closed down the ferry to Sonoma Landing in favor of rails to a junction at Ignacio in Marin, which connected with a broad-gauge line running to a ferry in Tiburon. Sonoma and Glen Ellen were finally connected with rails to Marin County and San Francisco, but they were still not linked to the transcontinental railroad owned by the Southern Pacific. That rail giant countered Donahue's extension by laying down tracks for the Santa Rosa and Carquinez Railroad Company (an S. P. subsidiary) from a junction south of Napa, up the Sonoma Valley. This line crossed Donahue's rails at Schellville and again at Madrone Road, stopped at Glen Ellen and several other points, before terminating in Santa Rosa. With the ceremonial driving of a gold spike, a completion celebration was held in Santa Rosa on June 20, 1888.

But the town of Sonoma could not rejoice because it had been bypassed on this new line, which was connecting directly to the rest of the United States. Sonoma had only itself to blame, because in 1885 the city trustees had turned down a Southern Pacific request for a right-of-way. It was a boon for Glen Ellen because there was now a second rail line bringing more travelers.

Just four days before the Carquinez-Santa Rosa rail line's completion, a two-story depot was inaugurated for a stop called El Verano (Spanish for "summer" or warm season), just across Sonoma Creek from the town of Sonoma.

The Southern Pacific used as "front" corporations The Sonoma Valley Improvement Company, headed by Charles Crocker (one of the "Big Four" who owned the S. P.), and the Verano Land Company, incorporated by local

THE SOUTH SIDE OF NAPA STREET, EAST OF BROADWAY, IN 1892

JUNE 14, 1896, THE FIFTIETH ANNIVERSARY OF
THE BEAR FLAG REVOLT

businessman George H. Maxwell, with Crocker's secret backing. The Verano Land Company bought 700 acres from ranchers Howard Clark and Oliver Craig (who had isolated the *phylloxera* insect, which had destroyed his vineyard). Maxwell laid out a city plan, planted some trees, and built a few model houses, just in time for the railroad's arrival. Then Maxwell sold lots from $80 on up to passengers given free excursions on the new rail line. A raffle was held, with a new home the grand prize. The company built the Bellevue Hotel on Grove Street. Maxwell also founded a newspaper, *The Whistler*. In 1889 a post office was established for El Verano.

A year later the bloom was off the rose, and El Verano was a town with almost no residents, fields of weeds instead of houses, and a lawsuit that successfully challenged Maxwell's legal authority to grant the land titles he had sold, on the basis that he had a conflict of interest as a secret employee of Crocker's Sonoma Valley Improvement Company.

The insiders made a small fortune. Maxwell went away, retaining only title to his farm, but his name lives on in the Maxwell Village shopping center and Maxwell Farms Regional Park, purchased in the 1980s from his descendants.

Within a decade, however, El Verano achieved a rebirth, as people began building homes and summer cabins. Longtime residents of the Valley bought up lots from out-of-towners. Vineyards were planted. Mullen's General Merchandise opened in 1899, taking over one of the original buildings. It is now Inskeep's Inn, a tavern that retains its frontier-style wooden veranda. In the first decade of the 1900s, Danieli's Grocery, which has become Caselli's, and Danieli's boardinghouse, now McNeilly's Tavern, were open for business.

The coming of the railroad made it possible for the state to establish The California Home for the Care and Training of Feeble-Minded Children, in a farmhouse on 1,670 acres just south of Glen Ellen in 1889. The following year construction of the first institutional building started. A post office and a train stop were built for the Home, and both were named Eldridge, in honor of Oliver Eldridge, one of the state's site committee. The Home's buildings were modern for the times, and landscaping under the shade of trees gave the Home a parklike aspect, which it still retains. Twenty years later it was renamed Sonoma State Home, then Sonoma State Hospital in 1953, and most recently, in 1988, it was given the euphemistic title of Sonoma Developmental Center. Locals still call it the State Hospital. It is the largest employer in the Valley.

Mariano G. Vallejo, the man who once held title to all of the Valley, died at his home in 1890. For fifty-five years he had been the Valley's most influential citizen, even after his fortunes were reduced and he had no official powers. His daughter Louisa Emparan, the young and beautiful widow of Mexican consular official Richard Emparan, took over maintenance of the home and was a social leader of Sonoma for another fifty years. In 1933 she sold Lachryma Montis to the state, but she continued to live there until her death in 1943.

Los Guilicos Rancho, to the north of Glen Ellen on the road to Santa Rosa, drew the interest of various wealthy English families in the 1870s and 1880s who bought large parcels from William Hood, his family, and successors. Starting in 1888 with the construction of the Santa Rosa and Carquinez Railway and the building of a depot in what was called Kenwood, even more buyers were attracted. The Kenwood Station, the only stone depot built on the line, lasted longer than the railroad, serving now as the Kenwood Community Club.

The same year the railroad was completed, a new stage road with a base of rock over the swampland was built from Kenwood to Santa Rosa, along the route of today's Highway 12. Before that time the stages had to take a rough trail along the base of foothills north of Kenwood.

Starting in 1887, a band of land speculators, incorporated as the Sonoma Land & Improvement Company, surveyed and filed a map for the Town of Kenwood. This same company built Kenwood's first hotel, the forty-five-room

Kirkwood, completed in April 1888. Pedroncelli's, the Kenwood Hotel, and Petri's soon followed.

The Sonoma Land & Improvement Company also recorded a map of small lots and streets for the envisioned town of South Los Guilicos on open land between Kenwood and Glen Ellen. They sold many 25-foot-wide lots; but, as a town, South Los Guilicos never made it. The map lives on in a maze of confusing property descriptions for various larger holdings.

Boyes Hot Springs, just north of the railroad town of El Verano, takes its name from English immigrant Captain Henry E. Boyes, who developed the natural hot springs into a resort in the 1890s. The Native Americans of Sonoma Valley had enjoyed the warmth and medicinal value of the sulfurous hot water that bubbled to the surface. The developers of Los Guilicos (soon to be Kenwood) sold lots that were advertised in 1889 as bordering on "the celebrated old Indian Medicine Spring."

General Vallejo gave the name "Agua Caliente" (hot water) to his holdings northwest of Sonoma. He sold seventy-five acres of Agua Caliente to a retired physician, Episcopalian minister, and former alcalde of San Francisco, Dr. Thaddeus M. Leavenworth, who dug a well down into a hot-water spring and set up a swim tank and bathhouse. One day, in a fit of temper, Leavenworth filled in the spring with rock and burned down his bathhouse.

Years later Captain Boyes and his wife bought the property, which they named Agua Rica, and rediscovered the source of the hot water in 1895. Boyes built a pool, 150 by 75 feet, which was later enclosed, and the Boyes Hotel. Its popularity as a happy and healthy spa was immediate and lasted for more than half a century. Nearby, the Agua Caliente Springs and Fetters Hot Springs resorts also tapped into the hot aquifer. The community of Boyes Hot Springs (sometimes referred to as just Boyes Springs, or recently The Springs) sprang up around these spas, with summer cabins and tents set on wooden frames, many of which have been expanded and improved to become full-time homes on meandering shaded streets.

THE SONOMA VALLEY WINE INDUSTRY REVIVES

The comeback of the Sonoma Valley wine industry after the *phylloxera* disaster was celebrated with the first Vintage Festival in 1897, organized by the Gundlachs, Bundschus, and Dresels on their Rhine Farm. For several years the annual festival was held there, featuring pageants in costume, skits and songs written by members of their families, and free wine for all comers.

Nowadays the Vintage Festival is celebrated each September in Sonoma Plaza, and the wine is not free.

By the turn of the century, numerous Sonoma Valley wineries and vineyards were in profitable operation. At the 1900 Paris Exposition, the Cambertin vintage of Gundlach-Bundschu won a gold medal, and in 1904 the Dresel vineyards took first prize at the St. Louis World's Fair. A railroad stop and post office were established in 1897 at Vineburg (called Vineyard until 1906) to serve the wineries, vineyardists, and resorts south of Sonoma.

Father Altimira, the founder of the Sonoma Mission, had noted the fine basalt rock in his early reports. By 1880 San Francisco was in need of rock for buildings and paving streets, which were still in the cobblestone era. To meet this market demand, the first commercial quarries opened in the hills above Sonoma in 1880. Merchant Solomon Schocken leased sixty-two acres north of Sonoma, now known as Schocken's Hill, from which he started taking rock in 1886. The birth of the Sonoma basalt business attracted Italian stonemasons, the most prominent being Augustino Pinelli. He employed his talents to build the Pinelli building (now El Paseo), and the rents he received paid to buy other properties, such as the Blue Wing.

THE PLAZA COMES OF AGE

The long-neglected Plaza was finally given proper attention in 1903 by the newly formed Sonoma Valley Woman's Club (originally called the Ladies Improvement Club). Phoebe Apperson Hearst, the wife of Senator George Hearst, made a substantial donation, and tons of donated fertilizer were spread, trees and grass planted, benches placed, low spots filled in with soil, and a fountain installed.

A new Sonoma City Hall was built on the Plaza between 1906 and 1908 by the city trustees, with identical facades facing each direction so as not to favor any merchants. In 1911 the trustees applied for and received a $6,000 grant from the Carnegie Foundation to build a library, with the proviso that the city spend $600 a year to maintain it. The library was completed in 1913 and served until 1978, when a regional library was built on West Napa Street. Today it is the headquarters of the Sonoma Valley Visitors Bureau.

On July 4, 1907, the Woman's Club unveiled a rock monument in the Plaza, commemorating the Bear Flag Revolt. A larger rock, surmounted by a statue of an idealized Bear Flagger, was dedicated in 1914, thanks to the grand sum of $500 appropriated by the state legislature.

THE PINELLI BUILDING (NOW EL PASEO), ABOUT 1900

A final landscaping design for the Plaza was drawn by a University of California student, and by 1915 the Plaza's beautification was basically finished. Added over the years were a fountain facing First Street East, donated by the Sebastiani family; a new fountain in front of City Hall, funded by the Sonoma Kiwanis; a duck pond; a children's playground; more trees; and the Grinstead Amphitheater, named in honor of Judge Ray Grinstead. The Woman's Club also took an interest in restoration of the Mission, and with the help of the California Historic Landmarks League and a campaign for funds headed by the *San Francisco Examiner*, the Mission compound was bought from Solomon Schocken for $3,000 in 1903. Before reconstruction could be completed, however, the Mission was badly shaken by the April 1906 earthquake, which devastated San Francisco and collapsed the top story of the bank building at the corner of Broadway and Napa Street. Some weakened Mission walls and roofs gave way during the following three years.

As money was raised, improvements were made and finally the California legislature appropriated $5,000 so that Mission restoration could be completed

SAMUELE SEBASTIANI, FOUNDER OF SEBASTIANI VINEYARDS
1875 TO 1944

in 1913. The rebuilding of the chapel and the *convento* not only strengthened and beautified the Mission but also returned it to its Mexican Colonial–style origins. The missing Mission bell was found in 1910 in San Francisco's Sutro Museum by Kate Hill and Dora Stofen of the Sonoma Woman's Club. A celebration of the return of the bell was held in 1920, with Governor William D. Stephens performing the unveiling.

SAMUELE SEBASTIANI'S WINERY REVOLUTION

As for the recovering wine business, enter Samuele Sebastiani from Farneta, in the wine-producing Tuscany region of Italy. Arriving in San Francisco in 1895, at age twenty-one, he worked for two years on an artichoke farm, saving enough to purchase a wagon and pair of horses so that he could get into the stone-hauling business. For seven years after coming to Sonoma, Sebastiani carted rock in his wagon from Schocken's quarry to the railroad and to barges at the mouth of Sonoma Creek. In 1902 he took a second job in the Burgess Winery, which burned down less than two years later.

The year 1904 marked the modest beginning of the Sebastiani dynasty in Sonoma Valley winemaking. Samuele purchased a small Sonoma wine cellar from a relative by marriage for no money down. (He paid it off from profits within five years.) The same year he married a sixteen-year-old local girl, Elvira Eraldi. Sebastiani developed the concept of using railroad tank cars to ship volume production of wine for others to bottle under their own labels. This contrasted with the individual bottle sales that most wineries employed and was superior to loading barrels on freight cars, which Samuele had done until 1909. Using this mass-production concept, the winery's growth was phenomenal. Its building was expanded in 1913 to provide Sebastiani with a storage capacity of 300,000 gallons. This building still exists as part of the winery on Fourth Street East.

FIRE! FIRE! FIRE!

The great San Francisco earthquake in April 1906 shook Sonoma badly, causing the collapse of the top floor of the bank at Broadway and Napa Street, damaging the front wall of the Mission, and cracking walls all over town. But Sonoma's most consistent enemy was fire.

From its founding, Sonoma has been plagued by fires. Until modern times there was inadequate fire protection, low water pressure and supply, and buildings that were not fire-resistant. Flames destroyed the early Mission chapel twice, much of Napa Street's buildings opposite the Plaza in 1868, and the jail in the 1870s, killing two prisoners. St. Francis Solano Church burned to the ground on two occasions: in 1896, when the pastor let burning weeds get out of control, and again in 1922.

Sonoma's most devastating conflagration swept almost all of First Street East opposite the Plaza on September 18, 1911. The blaze spread north and south from a cobbler's shop halfway down the block, moving slowly but surely from one building to the next. Virtually every able-bodied man turned out to try to halt the fire's progress. Women and children tamped down burning cinders that threatened the Barracks and other buildings on the north side of the Plaza. Augustino Pinelli pumped 6,000 gallons of wine from his tank in the Blue Wing basement over that old adobe and on his Pinelli Building (now El Paseo). His wine saved the Blue Wing and preserved the outside shell of the Pinelli Building. The Duhring Building on the corner of Napa Street was also saved when the building to the north was torn down to form a firebreak as the flames advanced. Gone were the Garibaldi Hotel, the Poppe law office, a saloon, the City Bakery, and several shops and historic adobes.

A four-day grassfire swept down the Valley in 1964, destroying twenty-five homes in Boyes Hot Springs. Shortly thereafter the Boyes Hot Springs resort went up in smoke, ruining its pipeline into the ancient mineral springs, followed by fire loss of Fetters Hot Springs in 1975.

The first industrial building on Eighth Street East burned, putting three businesses on the street. Seven structures in El Verano were destroyed in a 1961 blaze. St. Andrew's Presbyterian Church was a recent victim of fire. The preserved Depot (in 1977) and the once-saved Duhring Building (in 1990) both met fiery fates, only to rise from the ashes like latter-day phoenixes. In 1995 a giant, persistent grassfire swept through the hills just north of many homes, destroying acres of vineyards and several outbuildings before the wind abated. Fortunately, only one large house was completely burned. In January 2000, a half dozen stores in the Marketplace burned down, due to arson.

JACK LONDON AND THE VALLEY OF THE MOON

Author Jack London purchased a 260-acre ranch in Glen Ellen in 1905 that he called Beauty Ranch. It was both a hideaway for himself and Charmian—who was his typist, his mistress, and later his wife—and a place to entertain his numerous friends (including a host of Bohemian freeloaders). With his increased literary success, he expanded his holdings to 1,400 acres.

After a disastrous sailing trip across the Pacific, London and Charmian settled on the ranch in 1909. World-famous for his novels *Call of the Wild, The Sea-Wolf, White Fang, Martin Eden,* and many others (he published some forty-nine books in all, as well as reporting on the Russo-Japanese War), London was suffering from a painful combination of uremic poisoning, nephritis, and suspected syphilis.

The most popular American writer of all time, London gave Sonoma Valley worldwide publicity and forever established its nickname with the 1913 publication of his novel *Valley of the Moon,* in which he claimed that was the Indian meaning of the word *Sonoma.* While he made Glen Ellen famous, he had a reputation in the Valley as a contentious habitué of the Valley's saloons. The late Russell Kingman, however, a noted London historian and founder of the Jack London Foundation, claimed that reports of London's hard drinking and carousing were more legend than fact.

In 1911 London put a crew of thirty artisans to work constructing his dream house, a twenty-three-room, stone- and wood-beamed mansion, to be named Wolf House, because "Wolf" was Jack's nickname. One night in 1913, as the house was in the final painting stage, it mysteriously caught fire and burned to the ground, only partially insured. Arson was suspected by the devastated

A RARE PICTURE OF JACK AND CHARMIAN LONDON

Londons, but Kingman, who studied the evidence years later, was convinced that the cause was spontaneous combustion from a pile of oily, paint-soaked rags.

For the next two years, London wrote furiously to raise funds to rebuild the house, but his health declined. His pain was only partially controlled by heavy doses of morphine. On November 22, 1916, London died of uremia, at just forty-one. He is interred in Jack London State Park, where the ruins of Wolf House and the Jack London Museum are located. The title *Valley of the Moon* is his legacy to Sonoma Valley.

With the growth of automobile travel, Sonoma needed highway access. In 1917 Sonoma and the rest of the Valley celebrated the completion of the "Black Point Cutoff" (now Highway 37) between San Rafael and Vallejo. This highway linked the Valley at Sears Point to a more direct route to the east and west to the main north/south road from Marin to Santa Rosa (Highway 101), instead of relying on circuitous country roads over the hills. It was the motor-vehicle replay of the Valley's desire for railroad linkage in the 1880s and '90s.

PROHIBITION: NATIONAL JOKE AND VALLEY DISASTER

January 16, 1920, was the blackest day in Sonoma Valley history. On that date the Valley's expanding and thriving wine industry came to a crashing halt, as Prohibition went into effect. The Eighteenth Amendment to the U.S. Constitution prohibited "the manufacture, sale or transportation of intoxicating liquors . . . for beverage purposes."

Actually winemaking had become temporarily illegal on June 30, 1919, when a wartime restriction on using grapes for alcoholic beverages was allowed to remain in force even though World War I had been over for more than six months. Attempts to exempt wine as a food, or allow "local option," had failed in the wave of political power exhibited by the Prohibitionists.

Samuele Sebastiani successfully applied for a license to produce wines for sacramental and medicinal use. The exception for church services was based on a ruling that this usage was not for a "beverage" purpose. Fewer than ten California wineries received a sacramental-wine license. The rest of the Sonoma Valley wineries were out of business. Some of the vineyardists who had supplied them converted to growing fruit.

Like much of the country, the people of Sonoma Valley treated Prohibition as a bad joke. Small home-based vineyards produced grapes that they sold nationally for home winemaking, for "personal consumption only," which was legal as long as the wine itself was not sold. The limit was 200 gallons a year—

enough to keep a family in a constant state of inebriation. Dehydrated grape mash was shipped with the warning not to add yeast, since that might cause "illegal fermentation." Stills and "speakeasies" sprang up. Restaurants and cafes kept hidden liquor bottles for special customers, which meant anyone with the price who did not look like a government agent.

Federal revenuers and sheriff's deputies, hunting for illegal booze, would swoop down on resorts and make arrests. The revenuers decided to make an early example of Emma Fetter of Fetter's Hot Springs, whom they caught serving liquor. She was sentenced to nine months in jail, which was reduced to thirty days. A $300 fine became more common. During just one week in August 1922, eleven places in El Verano were raided, including the unrepentant Fetter's.

For plumber Ted Riboni, Prohibition proved to be a bonanza. He became expert in building illegal stills, putting together more than fifty of them, scattered throughout the hills. Even the Sebastianis employed his talents. For a time, each night Riboni would hook up a pipe from the fermenting tank of Sebastiani wine meant for the altars of churches and let it flow into a secret vat. Before dawn he would return, unscrew the pipe, and remove any sign of the diversion. The government inspectors checking the level of production of sacramental wine were never the wiser.

With illegal liquor and the flaunting of the Eighteenth Amendment came a spirit of lawlessness. A former San Francisco madam known as Spanish Kitty kept a string of hookers in cottages on her property in El Verano between 1910 and 1941, when the aging Kitty was busted on a drug charge. And, for more than a year, the FBI's "Public Enemy Number One," the notorious bank robber, killer, and prison escapee "Babyface" Nelson, lived in El Verano, often having a drink at what is now McNeilly's Tavern. One night a fearless deputy sheriff named Emmett Mullen came charging through the front door of Nelson's hideout, a cottage at Parente's Villa, and Babyface ran out the back, never to be seen again in the Valley.

But the tourist business in the Valley, which had lived on overnight guests coming by railroad, fell into decline, and during the 1920s several resorts closed down.

On the positive side, wealthy San Franciscans and foreigners took an interest in buying property in the Valley. A 280-acre estate in the western hills on the way to Glen Ellen from Sonoma, known as Sobre Vista, was sold in 1896 to sugar millionaire Rudolph Spreckels. In 1915 Temelec Hall, which had fallen into disrepair, was purchased by Lolita Coblentz, who restored the mansion to its former grandeur. Senator George Hearst, father of newspaper mogul William Randolph Hearst, had long owned a ranch and vineyards in the Valley, and friends of the Hearsts followed his example.

REPEAL, DEPRESSION, AND VALLEY OPTIMISTS

Repeal of Prohibition made liquor legal again in December 1933. Sebastiani was already geared up because it had been in limited production during Prohibition. For others, however, it would take years for new vines to mature, and fruit growers had little money to spend for replanting. A pear growers' meeting would draw greater attendance than a gathering of vineyardists. During this period more milk than wine was produced in the Valley. But shortly wineries like Pagani and Valley of the Moon (on the old Hearst ranch) were producing, primarily in bulk or for San Francisco restaurants. Bars opened (or came out into the open), and restaurants, resorts, and hotels no longer had to hide the bottles.

But, while repeal gave a minor boost to Valley business, the Great Depression had already sent the national economy reeling. Throughout the 1930s Sonoma County, including the Valley, remained frozen in place, as if waiting for the world to get moving again. Exceptions included Tom Vella, Celso Viviani, Samuele Sebastiani, and George Nicholas.

Vella and Viviani launched the Sonoma Cheese Company in 1931, giving birth to the Valley's world-famous cheese industry. In 1945 they split into two companies: The Sonoma Cheese Factory, on the Plaza, which is also a deli; and the Vella Cheese Company, in the original building on Second Street East, north of the Plaza.

In the depth of the Great Depression, Samuele Sebastiani built the ornate Sebastiani Theatre, which was completed in 1934, the Sebastiani Bus Depot at West Spain and First Street West in 1936, and the Sebastiani (now Cuneo) Apartments in 1938. He also bought the original mission vineyard in 1935. His veiled offer to privately redevelop the city if it were renamed "Sebastiani" was gently rebuffed. Two years later he turned over active management of the winery to his son August, who immediately started an expansion program at the winery.

A member of the Depression generation was George Nicholas, a 1935 graduate of the University of California School of Agriculture (now UC-Davis). Young George noticed that a Sonoma Valley turkey rancher had been able to breed turkeys that produced white instead of black pin feathers. If such a cosmetic change could be achieved, he reasoned, why not breed turkeys more suited to American tastes? While he and his wife, "Johnny," lived east of town in a rural house without indoor plumbing, George began the tedious process of selective breeding of generations of turkeys with more white meat and a fuller, more meaty body. The result of his experiments was that Nicholas turkeys became the world standard, with Nicholas Turkey Breeders shipping turkey eggs and sperm to turkey growers everywhere. While the Nicholas family is no longer involved, the company's distinctive forest-green sheds and laboratories still dot the Valley both east and west of Sonoma.

When there was talk of tearing down the Barracks for a parking lot, *Index-Tribune* publishers Walter and Celeste Murphy bought the building in 1935. The Murphys renovated the old adobe, turned the second floor into an apartment for themselves, and remodeled offices and retail stores on the ground floor.

Vacationers were not using the railroad much, for it had been replaced by automobile and bus travel. By 1942 the last railroad tracks and trains north of Sonoma were abandoned. Nevertheless, the Boyes Hot Springs pool was attracting crowds. Starting in the 1920s, the San Francisco Seals and Oakland Oaks of the Pacific Coast League took spring training for the baseball season at Boyes or Agua Caliente. Locals could watch future stars like Joe and Dom DiMaggio up close.

Sonoma Valley's drivers became directly linked to San Francisco with the 1937 opening of the Golden Gate Bridge. The long lines of automobiles to and from the ferries between Sausalito and San Francisco on pleasant weekends were no more. The great bridge provided a sense of optimism for the future—a time when the economy would complete its upturn.

In 1938 David Pleydell-Bouverie, a wealthy young Englishman, bought a tract of land east of Highway 12 in Glen Ellen. It did not look like much, with piles of junked cars, no trails, and waist-high grass. But Bouverie, an architect by training, had a keen eye; he found old Indian caves behind waterfalls and used rags to hand-flag trails. It took almost three decades, but the result was a lovely home for Bouverie and his stream of guests, as well as the creation of the Bouverie Preserve and Audubon Canyon Ranch, where nowadays docents conduct nature walks and research for young students.

America's entry into World War II again put Sonoma Valley on hold. With gasoline rationing, tourism went into a further decline. August Pinelli headed the draft board that determined which sons of Sonoma would be sent off to war. There were few essential industries in the area, so almost every young man without physical problems went.

One day in 1943, United Press correspondent Frank Bartholomew, in San Francisco, spotted a legal notice of a sale of a house and acreage in Sonoma for a remarkably low asking price. On a whim, he bid on the property sight-unseen and got it. What he did not know was that this was Count Haraszthy's original Buena Vista property, which had become a home for an elderly woman who had neglected the place. Bartholomew did not even bother to visit his new purchase until the end of World War II, because he was busy reporting world events.

While her husband General H. H. "Hap" Arnold was directing the Army Air Corps (to become the U.S. Air Force) and traveling to conferences of the Allied leaders, in 1943 Eleanor ("Bea") Arnold visited Sonoma. She decided that she had found the ideal place for retirement after the war and bought forty acres with an old farmhouse in the foothills on the west

THE PARADE UP BROADWAY ON THE
100TH ANNIVERSARY OF THE BEAR
FLAG REVOLT

side of the Valley between Sonoma and Glen Ellen.

Samuele Sebastiani died on March 27, 1944. All Sonoma businesses closed their doors during his funeral.

POSTWAR RESURGENCE

The end of the war in 1945 ushered in many changes for Sonoma Valley. The national economy was upbeat, people had money to spend, and gas and liquor rationing were history.

Walter and Celeste Murphy, who did not have children, turned over the *Index-Tribune* to their young nephew Robert Lynch—son of Celeste's sister, Ramona

Granice Lynch—fresh from Navy service. Robert Lynch is still publisher, with two of his sons, William and James, serving as editor and business manager. In the 1980s the *I-T*, as the locals call it, switched from a weekly to a twice-a-week format.

GOVERNOR EARL WARREN AND
TEENAGER MARILYN PINELLI
(GALLAGHER) AT THE 100TH
ANNIVERSARY OF THE BEAR FLAG REVOLT

Gregory and Harriet Jones found a run-down adobe on West Spain Street just off the Plaza, which they purchased in

GOVERNOR PETE WILSON AND MAYOR RICHARD DORF ENJOY THE
150TH ANNIVERSARY OF THE BEAR FLAG REVOLT. *INDEX-TRIBUNE*
PUBLISHER ROBERT LYNCH AND *SANTA ROSA PRESS-DEMOCRAT*
COLUMNIST GAYE LEBARON ARE IN THE BACK ROW.

1948 and began meticulously restoring by hand. Their example led to renewed public interest in saving old adobes. After Gregory Jones's death, Mrs. Jones presented their *La Casita* to the League for Historic Preservation in 1980, with the right to live there until her death, which came in January 1996, at age ninety-eight.

Light manufacturing developed on Eighth Street East, east of Sonoma, with the old rail line providing easy freight hauling. To meet a pent-up demand for housing, middle-class homes were erected in record numbers, particularly on the west side of Sonoma, in El Verano, the east side of Boyes Hot Springs, and in Kenwood.

A centennial celebration of the Bear Flag Revolt in 1946 drew 50,000 people to Sonoma, including Governor Earl Warren. Leading a parade that followed a 3-mile course was Sonoma Valley's newest celebrity, Five-Star General Hap Arnold, creator of the modern Air Force. Arnold Drive and Arnold Field were named in his honor.

In 1947, next door to General Arnold's ranch, the Catholic Archdiocese of San Francisco founded Hanna Boys' Center for boys from broken homes, with no parents, or with other problems. It has grown in buildings and in success stories in the years since.

BARTHOLOMEW STIRS WINERY DEVELOPMENT

Discovering that his prewar impulse purchase was the birthplace of the California wine industry, Frank Bartholomew (by then vice-president of UPI) reincorporated the Buena Vista Viticulture Society. He and his wife took on the daunting task of resurrecting the Haraszthy vineyards and renovating the old stone buildings. The enthusiasm of the sophisticated Bartholomew—and the quality of his Buena Vista wine—encouraged others to believe that Sonoma Valley would bloom again as a vintner's paradise.

Symbolic of Sonoma Valley's return to the front rank of California wine producers was the revival in September 1947 of the old Vintage Festival, once held on the Gundlach-Bundschu Rhine Farm. Called the Valley of the Moon Vintage Festival, it was centered in the Plaza and became the Valley's premier annual event. The Festival includes parades, wine tasting, grape-stomping contests, reenactment of the Vallejo-Haraszthy double wedding, water fights between competing fire departments, an art show, and food concessions raising funds for schools and service clubs. San Franciscan James Zellerbach, former ambassador to Italy, planted vineyards in the hills and established Hanzell Winery. Zellerbach employed modern techniques and equipment, but he used imported French oak barrels for aging. These barrels gave Hanzell's wines a complex taste, competitive with the French. Other California premium vintners soon followed suit.

Fruit growers began pulling out trees and getting on the grapevine bandwagon. Chief among them was the Sangiacomo family, who became the leading vineyardists by volume in the Valley. Today they continue under the direction of Angelo Sangiacomo, assisted by brothers Robert and Buck. They are well known for treating their workers like family members.

In 1955 Sebastiani put out its wines under its own label and diminished bulk sales to other wineries. August Sebastiani was one of the first to respond to the jug-wine (moderate-priced blended wines) craze. This move put Sebastiani second only to Gallo Brothers in total American wine volume. It was big news in 1973 when the Gundlach-Bundschu Wine Company came back, after having closed with Prohibition. Young Jim Bundschu convinced his father Towle to replant entirely in grapes, starting in 1967. Then Towle decided to open their own winery, and by 1973 the first trickle of Gundlach-Bundschu Zinfandel was on the market. Within a decade production increased tenfold.

Ageless Frank Bartholomew sold Buena Vista in 1973, but three years later he was back with the Hacienda label, to which he brought new investors. His name continues in the new Bartholomew Park Winery, and Hacienda now belongs to Bronco Wine Company.

Mike Benziger arrived from the East in the late 1970s with a treasure of marketing concepts. He revived an old name, Glen Ellen Winery, on vineyards next to the Jack London State Park. With father Bruno Benziger's help, Glen Ellen wines soon could be found on many airlines, Amtrak, and in chain supermarkets, at moderate prices. After Bruno died, his wife, Helen, and their children managed and expanded the winery for several years. They then sold the label and production facilities to Heublein, retaining their vineyards and grounds, charm and popularity. Thus Helen and the next Benziger generation continue the Benziger Family Winery, without missing a sip.

The Kunde family, longtime major ranchers and vineyardists in Kenwood, followed the Gundlach-Bundschu example by getting into the winery business in a big way. Valley of the Moon began bottling upper-scale varietals as well as their Italian restaurant jug wines. Pagani's Kenwood Winery was sold to new owners, who modernized.

Television comedy stars (and sometime social critics) Tom and Dick Smothers opened a winery in Kenwood, with their distinctive silhouettes as a logo. Freixenet, the premier Spanish sparkling-wines vintner, built the imposing Gloria Ferrer winery, overlooking the highway south of Sonoma, and made the mansionlike premises available for meetings and parties.

The Zinfandel of Ravenswood Winery, founded in 1976, has been proclaimed the best in the world. Winemaster Dick Arrowood established a national reputation first for Château St. Jean and then for Arrowood Winery, owned by Dick and his wife, Alis. Other new wineries, often family-operated, proliferated and prospered in the 1970s and '80s, including Roche, Schug Carneros, Cline, B. R. Cohn, Carmenet, Chandelle, H. Coturri, Grand Cru, Landmark, St. Francis, Viansa, and Sonoma Creek.

August Sebastiani, an innovator who had inherited his father's place as Sonoma's leading vintner, died in 1980. The mantle had already been passed to August's elder son, Sam Sebastiani. Sam shifted toward high-grade varietals, initiated an advertising program coupling wine with food, and dominated the company's direction. Then, right after Christmas 1985, Sam was ousted as president of Sebastiani when his mother, Sylvia (who held more than 90 percent of the stock), decided that she would be more comfortable with younger son Don Sebastiani (who was completing his third and last term as state assemblyman) and son-in-law Dick Cuneo running the company.

To Sonomans, it was an earthquake. The Valley audience took sides and anguished over the split in its most prominent family. The result was that Sam sold all his personal real estate and put everything on a gut-wrenching gamble: Viansa Winery, named for wife Vicky and Sam. Built in grand Italian-villa style, the winery sits on a knoll commanding a view of the southern Valley and Sam's wetlands home of waterfowl. Viansa is now a prime tourist destination. And to show that there can be a happy ending, the Sebastiani family bound up their wounds, kissed and made up, and proved that blood is thicker than wine.

THREE DECADES OF GROWTH

Tract homes, condominium projects, and the adult community of Temelec grew rapidly in the late 1960s and early '70s. The population of the Valley, particularly in the outskirts of Sonoma, expanded apace. In the hills above Sonoma, upscale homes and large lots were developed, with names like Mission Highlands, Sobre Vista, The Ranch, Diamond A, and George Ranch.

In Glen Ellen, Vallejo's original mill (circa 1840) and the Pagani winery (1914) next door were converted into a restaurant and shops, called Jack London Village. Courtroom/council chambers and a police station were built in Sonoma under a city–county shared cost arrangement. New fire stations were erected in Sonoma, Glen Ellen, and Agua Caliente. The Barracks was replastered and spruced up by the state. The Historical Society lovingly created Depot Park, even after the original station was torched during reconstruction. The League for Historic Preservation moved the Vasquez House into the courtyard of El Paseo, which was the restored Pinelli building. The Sister Cities Association set up its headquarters in the Victorian Marcy House, dragged up Broadway to a city property next to the police station.

The past twenty years have witnessed an unprecedented growth in commercial construction, as residential building has continued unabated. Two major shopping centers were built in Sonoma and another in Kenwood, while several smaller complexes appeared and a couple of older shopping areas were expanded. In the 1980s the cost of real estate started escalating at a breathtaking rate.

More than thirty office buildings have been erected since 1975, while others have been remodeled. Under new owners, the Sonoma Hotel was redecorated and outfitted with turn-of-the-century furniture. The seedy El Dorado Hotel was gutted (taking away all but a symbolic slab of adobe wall), rebuilt to match its 1875 exterior, the rooms modernized, and a new restaurant inaugurated. New Valley restaurants have opened at the rate of at least one a year, while others have been remodeled and modernized. Marioni's Restaurant replaced what had been the school district headquarters on the Plaza. A half dozen banks, including the hometown-owned Sonoma Valley Bank, have opened their doors. Mary's Pizza moved from a funky shack in

Boyes Hot Springs to a new building, and within a few years spawned a chain. A modern library went up on West Napa Street in the late 1970s. The facade of the Sebastiani Theatre got a face-lift; in 1997 the interior was renovated with volunteer help.

Meanwhile, the Best Western Sonoma Valley Inn in downtown Sonoma joined the venerable El Pueblo and Vineyard Inn as Sonoma's motels. Victorians and farmhouses became bed and breakfasts almost overnight. New earthquake standards led to retrofitting of several downtown buildings, including the Swiss Hotel.

But the most striking change was the rejuvenation and transformation of the old queen of Valley hostelries, the Sonoma Mission Inn at Boyes Hot Springs. By the mid-1970s, despite its magnificent lobby and dining room, it was a tired, out-of-date hotel (rooms at $17 a night). The Inn went through upgradings under three successive proprietors. The current ownership spent millions to make it a prestige resort attractive to travelers, reclusive celebrities (the rule is that staff members may not make any reference to a visiting star's name), and locals alike. Finally the Inn tapped into the old hot springs and created a spa in Boyes Hot Springs for the first time in nearly forty years.

New owners also brought national prominence to Sears Point Raceway, which now attracts major auto and motorcycle races. The tens of thousands of fans create near-gridlock at the junction of Highways 37 and 121 on race days. The number of visitors to Sonoma Valley has increased each year since 1980. In addition to old favorite celebrations like the Vintage Festival, Fourth of July (in both Sonoma and Kenwood), the Ox Roast, and the Kiwanis Turkey Barbecue, the Plaza is now the scene of the Salute to the Arts, Cinco de Mayo, and the Red and White Ball. Each fall Glen Ellen hosts a charming festival.

Sonoma Valley has survived and come back with renewed enthusiasm after fires, flooding, a revolution, military occupation, insect infestation, Prohibition, railroad wars, earthquakes, pie-in-the-sky real estate speculators, and bad roads.

Father Altimira was wiser than he knew. Sonoma was the ideal site for a mission. Mariano Vallejo came as a soldier and remained as a statesman who had fallen in love with the Valley. Augoston Haraszthy needed only a week to study the soil and experience the weather to realize that he had discovered the perfect home for wine grapes. Augustino Pinelli and Samuele Sebastiani dug and carted rock from the Valley's hills to achieve the immigrant's dream of success. Jack London arrived rebellious, sick, and disillusioned and was inspired by the beauty of the Valley of the Moon.

Now it's your turn.

JACK LONDON'S CULTURAL LEGACY

Jack London, one of America's most popular writers, lived in Sonoma Valley on a permanent basis for only ten years. He had already gained fame from his works *Call of the Wild, The Sea-Wolf,* and *White Fang.* Every year thousands of high school students worldwide write book reports on these London tales.

London's Beauty Ranch, in the western hills above Glen Ellen, was his refuge. The one-time Oakland waterfront delinquent and roustabout died here in 1916, at just forty-one, and is buried at Jack London State Park. Most of his forty-nine books were gritty and hard hitting, and they extolled the struggle with nature. They were generally "West Coast" in topic, outlook, and style. His literary friends urged him to move to Carmel (and away from wife Charmian), but London was steadfast: The Valley of the Moon was his home. By example, if nothing else, he demonstrated that Sonoma Valley could be a nurturing place for writers and artists.

Nevertheless, it would be a half-century before any of them showed up. One of the first was Albert Kahn, who settled in Glen Ellen in the 1960s with his wife, Riette, and three sons. Like London, Kahn's reputation was already established. Unlike London, the product of poverty, Kahn had graduated from Ivy League Dartmouth. His *Sabotage!* was a best-selling exposé of pre–World War II, American pro-Nazi conspiracies, followed by *The Great Conspiracy* (a history of the British and American organization of a civil war in Russia in the first days of the Soviet Union).

In 1955 Kahn helped publish *False Witness,* which revealed that many of Senator Joseph McCarthy's witnesses were paid to lie to Congress about alleged Communist influence in universities, unions, and liberal organizations. Kahn was summoned before the Internal Securities Committee in 1958, where he was accused of being a Soviet spy. He boldly challenged the committee members to waive their congressional immunity so that Kahn could sue them for libel. (The senators decided that they would look elsewhere for spies.) His love for music led him to write *Days with Ulanova,* a book about a famed Russian ballerina; and *Joys and Sorrows,* with legendary cellist Pablo Casals. Kahn died of a heart attack in 1979.

M. F. K. (Mary Frances Kennedy) Fisher established herself as the outstanding American writer about the enjoyment of food with the 1937 publication of *Serve It Forth.* ("I am *not* a food writer!" she often declared sharply.) Next came *Consider the Oyster* (1941), *How to Cook a Wolf* (1942), and *The Gastronomical Me* (1943). She wrote about life as she lived and observed it, with a slight sprinkling of invention through her travels and food adventures in

France and wherever else she went. W. H. Auden called her one of the finest writers of the twentieth century.

Divorced, widowed, and divorced, Mary Frances and her daughters moved from Southern California to St. Helena in Napa County, where she lived until 1972. Then her friend David Pleydell-Bouverie offered to let her build a house on his property in Glen Ellen, with a porch facing the perfect view of exquisite sunsets over Sonoma Mountain. Her home became the Mecca for a stream of friends and devotees. She continued to write articles and edit and compile earlier stories, despite the encroachment of Parkinson's disease. Shortly before her death in 1992, Bill Moyers came to interview Mary Frances for his television series. When the camera went on, her fading voice grew vibrant for one final time.

A child prodigy, Carolyn Kizer had her poetry published in *Ladies Home Journal* at sixteen and in *The New Yorker* at seventeen. A graduate of Sarah Lawrence, she received critical acclaim and then became a critic herself for *The Washington Post, The New York Times, The Los Angeles Times,* and several journals. She served as the first literature-program director of the National Endowment for the Arts.

Shortly after moving to Sonoma with her husband, John Woodbridge, a prominent architect and architectural author, Carolyn was awarded the Pulitzer Prize for Poetry in 1985 for her volume *Yin.* Three years later she won the Theodore Roethke Prize. Her numerous books of poetry include her latest, *Harping On* (1996). She is regularly a poet-in-residence or lecturer at Columbia, Stanford, Princeton, and other universities. Her vigorous readings in the Valley always draw a crowd. Kizer's poetry often focuses on current issues and is always lively and witty, naturally involving the reader or listener in her powerful cadence. One critic says that her poems have "an irrepressible spirit of adventure.... her thoughts come on stage, alive and dancing."

Maya Angelou, famed poet and author (*I Know Why the Caged Bird Sings*), lived near Sonoma National Golf Course during the late 1970s, while her national reputation was growing.

Philosopher/psychologist/author Sam Keen is one writer who has achieved prominence *after* moving to the Valley. A regular contributor to *Psychology Today,* his books, such as *Fire in the Belly,* have created a loyal national following. His book on the world of the trapeze (yes!) has earned a hefty six-figure advance.

Valley residents today include poet-translator Stephen Mitchell; Lawrence Linderman, the *Playboy* interviewer who co-authored *Beverly,* opera singer Beverly Sills's "autobiography"; and Jungian philosopher Gil Bailie, author of *Violence Unveiled,* essays, and poetry. Lewis Perdue has published twenty-five popular slam-bang espionage and mystery novels with titles like *The Delphi Betrayal,* as well as *The French Paradox,* on the health benefits of red wine.

Several Valley painters, potters, graphic artists, and multimedia artists are making a living. Kenwood's Linus Maurer (*the* Linus of "Peanuts," by his friend the late Charles Schulz) is a successful syndicated cartoonist, gag writer, numbers puzzle creator, and serious humorous artist.

Also laboring in relative obscurity are a number of professional television and movie scriptwriters, technical writers, and hopeful novelists and poets. More than 200 poets were published in Kathleen Hill's *Sonoma Poets Collection* (1986) and *Sonoma Poets II* (1995). The second volume was composed of entries in the Sonoma Poetry Festival (sponsored by Readers' Books), named the top poetry event in the nation by Bantam, Doubleday, Dell publishers.

Community theater groups flourish; there are at least three Shakespeare productions each year. The Sonoma Valley Chorale is large and has performed throughout Europe. The Sonoma City Opera; the Children's Opera; the Town Band; jazz, rock, bluegrass, and folk groups; and individual musical performers are constantly playing at Valley venues. Musicians Norton Buffalo and Tommy Thomsen have lived here forever, as has Doobie Brothers and Night Ranger manager Bruce Cohn. Both groups participate in Cohn's annual local charity golf tournament. Various establishments present music: Murphy's Irish Pub (Irish and folk), Cucina Viansa (jazz), Little Switzerland (polka and folk dancing), Valley of the Moon Saloon, Le Bistro, La Casa among others.

Jack London would be pleased.

CHAPTER 9

THE SONOMA VALLEY LIST OF LISTS

𝒰nless we indicate otherwise, you can assume that all of the following telephone or fax numbers are in the 707 area code. If you wish to write to any of the places covered in these lists, the ZIP codes are: Sonoma, 95475; Boyes Hot Springs, 95416; Glen Ellen, 95442; and Kenwood, 95452.

𝒲INERIES

These Sonoma Valley wineries are listed in order of appearance, from south to north.

Roche Winery, 28700 Arnold Drive (Highway 121), Sonoma; 935–7115

Viansa Winery and Italian Marketplace, 25200 Arnold Drive (Highway 121), Sonoma; 935–4700

Cline Cellars, 24737 Arnold Drive (Highway 121), Sonoma; 935–4310

Gloria Ferrer Champagne Caves, 23555 Arnold Drive (Highway 121), Sonoma; 996–7256

Schug Carneros Estate Winery, 602 Bonneau Road (corner of Arnold Drive), Sonoma; 939–9363

Sonoma Creek Winery, 23555 Millerick Road, Sonoma (south off Highway 121); 938–3031; tasting on Saturday and Sunday, April–October

Sebastiani Vineyards, 989 Fourth Street East (corner of East Spain), Sonoma; 938–5532, also downtown tasting at 103 West Napa Street, Sonoma

Ravenswood Winery, 18701 Gehricke Road, Sonoma; 938–1960

Castle Vineyards, 1105 Castle Road, Sonoma; 996–1966; not open for tasting

Bartholomew Park Winery, 1000 Vineyard Lane, Sonoma; 935–9511; can taste **Gundlach-Bundschu**

Buena Vista Winery, 18000 Old Winery Road, Sonoma; 938–1266; also downtown tasting at northeast corner of First Street East and East Napa Street

Gundlach-Bundschu Winery, 2000 Denmark Street or 3775 Thornsberry Road, Sonoma; 938–5277

Hacienda Wine Cellars, 20580 Eighth Street East, Sonoma; 938–3220; tasting room only

Hanzell Vineyards, 18596 Lomita (east off Sonoma Highway), Sonoma; 996–3860; tasting by appointment only

Carmenet Vineyard, 1700 Moon Mountain Drive (east off Sonoma Highway), Sonoma; 996–5870; tasting by appointment only

Chandelle of Sonoma, 15449 Arnold Drive, Glen Ellen; 938–5862; tasting room only; historic aircraft paintings on label; order by phone or catalogue; owner Robert Arnold is grandson of both five-star General Hap Arnold and air pioneer Donald Douglas

Robert Hunter Winery, 15655 Arnold Drive, Glen Ellen; 996–0570; tours and tasting by appointment only

Cale Vineyards, 16060 Sonoma Highway, Sonoma; 939–8363; no tasting

Tantalus Cellar, 20542 Birch Road, Sonoma; fax only 996–5952; tasting only at *Family Wineries*, Kenwood

Richardson Vineyards, 2711 Knob Hill Road, Sonoma; 938–2610; no tasting

MacRostie Wines, Steve MacRostie, c/o P.O. Box 340, Sonoma; 996–4480; no tasting

B. R. Cohn Winery, 15140 Sonoma Highway, Glen Ellen; 938–4064

Arrowood Vineyards and Winery, 14347 Sonoma Highway, Glen Ellen; 938–5170

Valley of the Moon Winery, 777 Madrone Road, Glen Ellen; 996–6941

Glen Ellen Winery, 14301 Arnold Drive (Jack London Village), Glen Ellen; 939–6277; tasting room only; also *M. G. Vallejo*

Benziger Family Winery, 1883 London Ranch Road, Glen Ellen (west at Jack London Lodge); 935–3000

Wellington Vineyards, 11600 Dunbar Road, Glen Ellen (west off Sonoma Highway); 939–0708

Kunde Winery, 10155 Sonoma Highway, Kenwood; 833–5501

Kenwood Vineyards, 9592 Sonoma Highway, Kenwood (east on Kenwood Winery Road); 833–5891

Smothers Brothers Wines, 9575 Sonoma Highway, Kenwood; 833–1010

The Wine Room, 9575 Sonoma Highway, Kenwood; 833–6131, tastings of family wineries' wines, including *Smothers/Remick Ridge Vineyards, Kaz*

Vineyard & Winery, Castle Vineyards, Moondance Cellars, Adler Fels, and Cale Cellars

Stone Creek, 9380 Sonoma Highway, Kenwood; 833–1355; tasting only; blends include non–Sonoma Valley wines

Mayo Family Winery, 9200 Sonoma Highway, Kenwood; 939–2089; tasting at *Family Wineries*

Family Wineries of Sonoma Valley: Mayo Family Winery, Deerfield Ranch Winery, Sable Ridge Vineyards (formerly *One World*), *Nelson Estate Winery, Noel Wine Cellars, Tantalus Cellars,* 9200 Sonoma Highway, Kenwood; 833–5504; tasting room

Château St. Jean, 8555 Sonoma Highway, Kenwood; 833–4134

St. Francis Winery, 8450 Sonoma Highway, Kenwood; 833–6534

Landmark Vineyards, 101 Adobe Canyon Road, Kenwood (east off Sonoma Highway); 833–1144

Kaz Vineyard and Winery, 215 Adobe Canyon Road, Kenwood (east off Sonoma Highway); 833–5891; tasting at *The Wine Room*

H. Coturri and Sons, 6725 Enterprise Road, Glen Ellen (on Sonoma Mountain); 996–6247; no tasting

Laurel Glen Vineyard, on Sonoma Mountain, P.O. Box 548, Glen Ellen; unlisted number; no tasting; labels are Laurel, Counterpoint

Matanzas Creek Winery, 6097 Bennett Valley Road, Santa Rosa; (707) 528–6464 or (800) 590–6464

_R_ESTAURANTS

General

In Downtown Sonoma
(from the Plaza to city limits)

Swiss Hotel & Restaurant, 18 West Spain Street; 938–2884

Marioni's, 8 West Spain Street; 996–6866

La Casa Restaurant & Bar, 121 East Spain Street; 996–3406

Cucina Viansa, 400 First Street East; 935–5656

Zino's Restaurante, 420 First Street East; 996–4466

Mary's Pizza Shack, 452 First Street East; 938–8300

Murphy's Irish Pub, 464 First Street East; 935–0660

Maya, 101 East Napa Street, 935–3500

Café La Haye, 40 East Napa Street; 935–5994

Della Santina's Trattoria, 133 East Napa Street; 935–0576

Rin's Thai Restaurant, 599 Broadway; 938–1462
Piatti Ristorante, 405 First Street West; 996–2351
Heirloom, 110 West Spain Street; 939–6955
Depot Hotel Restaurant, 241 First Street West; 938–2980
Meritage, 522 Broadway; 938–9430
Deuce Restaurant, 691 Broadway; 996–1031
Saddles, southeast corner Broadway and East MacArthur; 938–2929
Pizzeria Capri, 1266 Broadway; 935–6805
The Ranch House, 20872 Broadway; 938–0454
Siena Red Brewery and Bistro, 529 First Street West; 938–1313
Wild Thyme, 165 West Napa Street; 996–0900
Carrow's Restaurant, 201 West Napa Street; 938–1779
Happy Garden Restaurant, 201 West Napa Street, 996–6037
Roundtable Pizza, 201 West Napa Street; 938–5564
The General's Daughter, 400 West Spain Street; 938–4004
Shanghai Restaurant, 565 Fifth Street West; 938–3346
The Winemaker Restaurant, 875 West Napa Street; 938–8489
Amigo's Grill & Cantina, 19315 Sonoma Highway; 939–0743
Gramma's Pizza & Cal-Italia Restaurant, Maxwell Village; 938–1003
Gourmet Taco Shop, Maxwell Village; 935–1945
The Breakaway Cafe, 19101 Sonoma Highway; 938–8694
Taco Bell, 19025 Sonoma Highway; 939–1706

In Boyes Hot Springs/El Verano

Little Switzerland, Grove & Riverside Drive; 938–9900
Golden Spring, 18991 Sonoma Highway; 938–1275
Denny's Restaurant, 99 Sonoma Highway; 935–0626
E-Saan Thai House, 18629 Sonoma Highway, 939–9077
Grand China Restaurant, 18350 Sonoma Highway; 996–1555
Mary's Pizza Shack, 18636 Sonoma Highway; 938–3600
LaSalete, 18625 Sonoma Highway, 938–1927
Grille at Sonoma Mission Inn; within the Inn; 938–9000
Cafe at Sonoma Mission Inn, Sonoma Highway at Boyes; 938–2410
Uncle Patty's, 15 Boyes Boulevard; 996–7979
Taqueria Los Primos, 18375 Sonoma Highway; 935–3546
Mi Buen Cafe, 17960 Sonoma Highway; 939–7601
Juanita Juanita, 19114 Arnold Drive; 939–6111
Rob's Rib Shack, 18709 Arnold Drive; 938–8520
Sonoma Golf Club, 17700 Arnold Drive; 996–3483

In Glen Ellen

Mes Trois Filles, 13648 Arnold Drive; 938–4844
Glen Ellen Inn, 13670 Arnold Drive; 996–6409
The Girl and The Fig, 13690 Arnold Drive; 938–3634
Bistro in Glen Ellen, 13740 Arnold Drive; 996–4401
Jack's Village Cafe, 14301 Arnold Drive; 939–6111

In Kenwood

Kenwood Restaurant & Bar, 9900 Sonoma Highway; 833–6326
Vineyards Inn, 8445 Sonoma Highway; 833–4500
Marco Dana's Kenwood Cafe, 8910 Sonoma Highway; 833–1228

Breakfast and Lunch

Basque Boulangerie Cafe, 460 First Street East; 935–7687
Wild Thyme, 165 West Napa Street; 996–0900
Homegrown Bagel, Market Place; 996–0166
Homegrown Bagel, Maxwell Village; 996–0177
Garden Court Café, 13875 Sonoma Highway; 935–1565
Ford's Cafe, 22900 Broadway; 938–9811
Babe's Burgers & Franks, 2660 Fremont (Highway 121); 938–9714
Cafe Citti, 9049 Sonoma Highway, Kenwood; 833–2690

Pizzas Plus

Mary's Pizza Shack, 452 First Street East; 938–8300
Swiss Hotel & Restaurant, 18 West Spain Street; 938–2884
Round Table Pizza, Market Place on Second Street West: 938–5564
Pizzeria Capri, 1266 Broadway; 935–6805
Gramma's Pizza, Maxwell Village; 938–1003
Mary's Pizza Shack, (original) 18636 Sonoma Highway; 938–3600
Domino's Pizza, 18995 Sonoma Highway; 996–2900
Marco Dana's Kenwood Café, 8910 Sonoma Highway, Kenwood; 833–1228

Delis Plus

Cucina Viansa, 400 First Street East; 935–5656
Sonoma Cheese Factory, 2 West Spain Street; 996–1931
On Trays on Broadway Deli, 603 Broadway, 938–0301

Sonoma Market Deli Counter, 520 West Napa Street; 996–3411
Moosetta's Deli Peroshki & Pastries, 18816 Sonoma Highway; 996–1313
Subway Sandwich & Salad, 18915 Sonoma Highway; 935–9035
Angelo's Wine Country Deli, 23400 Arnold Drive (Highway 121) 938–3688
Cherry Tree #2, 1901 Fremont (Highway 121); 938–3480
Carneros Deli, 23001 Arnold Drive at Highway 121; 939–1646
Glen Ellen Village Market, 13751 Arnold Drive; 996–6728

Mexican

The Ranch House, 20872 Broadway; 938–0454
La Casa Restaurant & Bar, 121 East Spain Street; 996–3406
Juanita Juanita, 19114 Arnold Drive; 939–6111
Amigo's Grill & Cantina, 19315 Sonoma Highway; 939–0743
Gourmet Taco Shop, Maxwell Village; 935–1945
Taco Bell, 19025 Sonoma Highway; 939–1706
Taqueria Los Primos, 18375 Sonoma Highway; 935–3546
Mi Buen Café, 17960 Sonoma Highway; 939–7601

Chinese

Happy Garden Restaurant, Marketplace; 996–6037
Amy's Peking Palace, 461 Fifth Street West; 938–8886
Shanghai Restaurant, 565 Fifth Street West; 938–3346
Golden Spring, 18991 Sonoma Highway; 938–1275
Grand China Restaurant, 18350 Sonoma Highway; 996–1555

Thai

Rin's Thai Restaurant, 599 Broadway, 938–1462
E-Saan Thai House, 18629 Sonoma Highway; 939–9077

Sushi

Sushinoma, 512 West Napa Street; 935–0956

Hamburgers, Hot Dogs, Sandwiches

Babe's Burgers & Franks, 2660 Fremont (Highway 121); 938–9714
Happy Dog, 18762 Sonoma Highway; 935–6211

Bill's Drive-In, 19100 Arnold Drive; 939–0130
Moosetta's, 18816 Sonoma Highway; 996–1313
McDonald's, 18988 Sonoma Highway; 938–8094
Subway Sandwich & Salad, 18915 Sonoma Highway; 935–9035
Jack in the Box Family Restaurant, 602 West Napa Street; 935–0258

Coffee

Basque Boulangerie Café, 460 First Street East; 935–7687
The Coffee Garden, 421 First Street West; 996–6645
Sonoma Valley Coffee Roasters, 464 First Street East; 996–7573
Hot Shots, (drive through) 711 Broadway, at Bancroft's Flowers
Johnny's Java, Marketplace, 201 West Napa Street; 933–3881
Brundage's Caffee Maxie, Maxwell Village; 938–3889
Barking Dog Coffee Roasters, 17999 Sonoma Highway; 939–1905
Hot Shots, 18709 Arnold Drive, at Rob's Rib Shack

ANTIQUES

Sonoma

Country Pine English Antiques, 23999 Arnold Drive (Highway 121); 938–8315
Chanticleer Books, 525 Broadway; 996–5364
Sloan & Jones, 100 West Spain Street, corner First Street West; 935–8503
Antique Center of Sonoma; 120 West Napa Street; 996–9947
Cat & The Fiddle, 153 West Napa Street; 996–5651
Margaret's Antiques of Sonoma, 472 Second Street West; 938–8026

North of Sonoma on Highway 12

Acanthus—Nothing Ordinary, 22 Boyes Boulevard, corner of Sonoma Highway; 939–9868
Curry & I Antiques, 17000 Sonoma Highway, Agua Caliente; 996–8226

Glen Ellen

Charmian's Way, 13758 Arnold Drive; 939–0215

☞RT GALLERIES

Valley of the Moon Art Association, Box 2097, Boyes Hot Springs; 996–2115

Sonoma

Artworks, 20075 Broadway; 996–2909
The Framery of Sonoma, 762 Broadway; 996–4744
Sonoma Poster & Print Company, 605 Broadway; 996–2253
Framing on the Square, 122 East Napa Street; 935–6611
J. Sumner Gallery, 111 East Napa Street, 939–8272
Arts Guild of Sonoma Gallery, 140 East Napa Street; 996–3115

Spirits in Stone (Zimbabwe Sculpture), 452 First Street East; 938–2200
Handworks, 452 First Street East; 996–2255
Milagros, 414 First Street East, El Paseo; 939–0834
Courtyard Gallery, 414 First Street East, El Paseo; 996–2994
The Fairmont Gallery, 447 First Street West; 996–2667
Art Forms, 23150 Arnold Drive; 935–0126

Glen Ellen

Arlene's Art Gallery & Studio, 15495 Arnold Drive; 996–1326
Art For Living, 14301 Arnold Drive, Jack London Village

Kenwood

D. Lundquist Fine Arts, 100 Libby Avenue; 833–6161

☞OOKSTORES

Sonoma

Readers' Books, 127 and 130 East Nappa Street; 939–1779; won national
    poetry festival contest in 1995; holds author readings
Chanticleer Books, 552 Broadway; 996–5364; used and rare books
Plaza Books, 40 West Spain Street; 996–8474; used and rare books
Sonoma Bookends Bookstore, Market Place; 938–5926; large inventory
    of current books
The Toy Shop, Market Place); 996–8474; children's books

Book Nook, 414 West Napa Streetl, 938–3280; used books, fine used paperbacks selection.

Jack London Bookstore, 14300 Arnold Drive, Glen Ellen; 996–2888; world famous collection of Jack London books and memorabilia; headquarters of Jack London Foundation.

𝓑ICYCLE SHOPS AND RENTALS

The Goodtime Bicycle Company, 18503 Sonoma Highway, Boyes Hot Springs; 938–0453; bike expert Doug McKesson leads bicycle tours

Sonoma Valley Cyclery, 1061 Broadway, Sonoma; 935–3377

𝓟ARKS

Sonoma

The Plaza, Broadway and Napa Street

Sonoma State Park (Mission and Barracks Areas), First Street East and East Spain Street

Lachryma Montis (General Mariano G. Vallejo Home), Third Street West and West Spain Street, part of State Park

Arnold Field, First Street West, 3 blocks north of West Spain Street; baseball, football, and other events

Depot Park, First Street West, 2½ blocks north of West Spain Street; Depot Museum, picnic grounds, and petanque courts (largest in U.S.)

Maxwell Farms Regional Park, Sonoma Highway and Verano Avenue (site of new Boys and Girls Club building and skate park)

Hughes Field, First Street East and Blue Wing Drive; Little League field

Teeter Field, First Street East and Blue Wing Drive; Little League field

Pinelli Park, Fourth Street East and France Street; playground

Jean K. T. Carter Park, West MacArthur and Manor Drive

Field of Dreams, First Street East, back of police station; baseball, softball, and picnic grounds

Nathanson Creek Park, Broadway, just north of Napa Road

Olsen Park, Joaquin Drive and Sherman Court, west on Linda Way (off Fifth Street West)

Eraldi Park, Fifth Street West, back of Sassarini School; playing fields

Hertenstein Park, Fifth Street West and La Quinta

Ernest Holman Dog Park, on First Street West, just northwest of police station, where you can let your dog free to play; created by donation of sue Holman in memory of her dog. Ernest.

El Verano

Ernie Smith Community Park, Arnold Drive and Craig Avenue, named for famed pioneer sportscaster Ernie Smith, who had retired to Glen Ellen.
Verano Park, Verano Avenue, 2 blocks west of Sonoma Highway
Paul's Field, Verano Avenue, 3 blocks west of Sonoma Highway; Little League

Boyes Hot Springs

Larson Park, west of Sonoma Highway; on Lichtenberg Avenue and then right on Dechene Avenue; baseball, tennis, and picnic grounds

Glen Ellen

Jack London State Historic Park, from downtown Glen Ellen west on London Ranch Road to end; includes Wolf House, House of Happy Walls, museum
Sonoma Valley Regional Park, west side of Sonoma Highway ½ mile south of Arnold Drive turnoff
Bouverie Audubon Preserve, east side of Sonoma Highway ½ mile south of Arnold Drive turnoff

𝒢OLF COURSES

Los Arroyos Golf, 5000 Stage Gulch Road, Sonoma; 938–8835; 9 holes
Sonoma Mission Inn Golf Club, 17700 Arnold Drive, Sonoma; 996–0300; 18 holes with pro shop, bar, and dining room

𝒮ERVICES

Copying

Copy Store and More, 255 West Napa Street, Sonoma; 935–1413; (also fax)
Patt's Copy World, 504 West Napa Street, Sonoma; 939–7288; (also fax)

Create! Copy It! Mail It!, 800 West Napa Street, Sonoma; 996–5679
Your Home Office, 565 Fifth Street West, Sonoma; 939–7047; (also fax)
Mail Boxes Etc., Maxwell Village, Sonoma; 935–3438; (also fax)
Sonoma Print Shop, 921 Broadway, Sonoma; 996–2218
Valley Blueprint, 18305 Sonoma Highway, Sonoma; 938–2583; (also fax)
Kenwood Connection, 8910 Sonoma Highway, Kenwood; 833–2923;
  (also fax)
None is open on Sunday.

Money Wiring

Mail Boxes Etc., Maxwell Village, Sonoma; 935–3438
Boyes Springs Food Center, 18285 Sonoma Highway, Boyes Hot Springs;
  996–0611
Or call (800) 325–6000, or try any bank.

Service Stations

South Sonoma Valley

Bonneau's 76, 23003 Arnold Drive (corner of Highway 121); 938–8133;
  has diesel
Four Corners Service, 20500 Broadway at Napa Road; 938–4176

Downtown Sonoma

Broadway Shell, 616 Broadway; 996–1611
Lambert's 76, 195 West Napa Street (corner of Second Street West); 996–0076
Redwood Gas, 455 West Napa Street; 996–3323; has diesel
Sonoma Valley Chevron, 540 West Napa Street; 996–7300
Stu's Station & carwash, 19249 Sonoma Highway
  (near Maxwell Village); 996–1122
Beacon Station, Sonoma Highway at Siesta; has diesel

Boyes Hot Springs

Cal Food & Gas, 18605 Sonoma Highway; 996–5004 (Note: Only 24-hour
  station in Sonoma Valley)

The GAS Station, 18017 Sonoma Highway; 938–3253

Arnold Drive

Derrington's Chevron, 19080 Arnold Drive at Grove Street; 996–3365;
  has diesel
Shamrock Service, 15195 Arnold Drive, Glen Ellen; 935–3605

Kenwood

Beacon, 8533 Sonoma Highway (just north of center of Kenwood); 833–1121

AUNDROMATS

Launderland, Sonoma Market Place; 935–1717
EconoWash, 188903 Sonoma Highway; 935–0577
Glen Ellen Coin Laundry, Arnold Drive and Williams Road; 939–8182

AUNDRIES/CLEANERS

Off Broadway Cleaners, 19485 Sonoma Highway at West Napa; 996–3047
Crown Cleaners & Formal Wear, 568 Broadway; 996–2626
Maxwell Village Cleaners, Maxwell Village; 996–1380
Kenwood Village Cleaners, 8910 Sonoma Highway, Kenwood; 833–2923

UBLIC TELEPHONES

Around Sonoma Plaza

In front of *Visitor's Bureau in the Plaza,* on First Street East
In front of *Plaza Book Store on West Spain Street* near First Street West
La Casa Restaurant, 121 East Spain Street

Other Sonoma Locations

Ralph's Market, Sonoma Market Place; West Napa Street and Second Street West
Sonoma Market, Sonoma Center; West Napa Street and Fifth Street West
Safeway, West Napa Street and Fifth Street West

Albertson's, Maxwell Village, Sonoma Highway north of center of town

There are other locations, but these are easy to find.

Glen Ellen/Kenwood

Glen Ellen Market, on Arnold Drive in downtown Glen Ellen
Kenwood Shopping Center, on west side of Sonoma Highway

There are also public phones at most service stations.

*R*EST ROOMS

Restrooms in Sonoma

Public

Sonoma Plaza, between City Hall and Visitors Bureau Building
Back of Toscano Hotel, on East Spain Street across from Plaza

Quasi-Public (Courtesy)

El Dorado Hotel, First Street West and West Spain Street; in lobby on left
Coffee Garden, 421 First Street West; patio in back to the left
Readers' Books, 127 East Napa Street; between rooms toward back
Zino's Restaurant, 420 First Street East; past bar on left

Otherwise, try service stations.

*O*RGANIZATIONS

Community

Sonoma Valley Chamber of Commerce, 645 Broadway; 996–1033
Sonoma Valley Visitors Bureau, east side of Plaza; 996–1090
Glen Ellen Association, P.O. Box 448, Glen Ellen; 996–1451
Kenwood Community Club, Kenwood Depot Building, 314 Warm Springs Road, Kenwood; 833–6438

Service and Fraternal Clubs

Kiwanis Club of Sonoma Plaza, Winemaker Restaurant, 875 West Napa Street or P.O. Box 1903, Sonoma; Wednesday, 12:00 noon

Kiwanis Club of Sonoma Valley, Swiss Hotel, 18 West Spain Street, Sonoma; Tuesday, 7:00 P.M.

Valley of the Moon Council of Knights of Columbus, No. 7951, St. Leo's Church, 601 West Agua Caliente Road, Agua Caliente; first and third Wednesdays, 7:30 P.M.

Knights of Columbus, St. Francis School, 342 West Napa Street, Sonoma; first Wednesday, 7:30 P.M.

Lions Club of Sonoma, Denny's Restaurant, 18999 Sonoma Highway at Verano, P.O. Box 576, Boyes Hot Springs; first and third Wednesdays, 12:00 noon

Valley of the Moon Lions Club, Grange Hall, 18627 Sonoma Highway, Sonoma; P.O. Box 90, Glen Ellen; second and fourth Tuesdays, 7:30 P.M.

Sonoma Mission Lionesses, Grange Hall, 18627 Sonoma Highway, Sonoma; second and fourth Tuesdays, 7:00 P.M.

Masons Temple, Lodge No. 14, 669 Broadway or P.O. Box 545, Sonoma; first Wednesday, 8:00 P.M.

Loyal Order of Moose, No. 2048, Moose Lodge, 20580 Broadway or P.O. Box 674, Sonoma; first and third Wednesdays, 8:00 P.M.

Sonoma Women of the Moose, Chapter #776, Moose Lodge, 20500 Broadway or P.O. Box 1696, Sonoma; first and third Thursdays, 8:00 P.M.

Native Daughters of the Golden West, Sonoma Parlor No. 209, I.O.O.F. Hall, 525 Broadway, Sonoma; second and fourth Mondays, 7:15 P.M.

Native Sons of the Golden West, Sonoma Parlor No. 111, Veterans Memorial Building, 126 First Street West, Sonoma; second Tuesday, 7:30 P.M.

Sonoma Valley Rotary Club, Sonoma Golf Club, 17700 Arnold Drive, Sonoma; Wednesday, 12:00 noon

Sons of Italy, Lodge No. 1959, Veterans Memorial Building, 126 First Street West, Sonoma; third Tuesday, 6:00 P.M. dinner, 7:30 P.M. meeting

Sonoma Valley Soroptimists, Zino's Restaurant, 420 First Street East, Sonoma; Tuesday, 12:00 noon

Veterans

American Legion, Jack London Post No. 489, Veterans Memorial Building, 126 First Street West or P.O. Box 578, Sonoma; second Thursday, 7:30 P.M.

Disabled American Veterans, Veterans Memorial Building, 126 First Street West; mail: 757 Second Street East, Sonoma; third Tuesday, 7:30 P.M.

Veterans of Foreign Wars, Veterans Memorial Building, 126 First Street West or P.O. Box 778, Sonoma; first and third Wednesdays, 7:30 P.M.

Veterans of Foreign Wars Auxiliary, Veterans Memorial Building, 126 First Street West, Sonoma; first and third Wednesdays, 7:30 P.M.

Historical and Preservation

Sonoma Valley Historical Society, Woman's Club, 574 First Street East, Sonoma or P.O. Box 861, Sonoma; first Friday (except July and August), 7:30 P.M. Headquarters: Depot Park Museum, 270 First Street West, Sonoma; 938–9765

Sonoma League for Historic Preservation, Toscano Hotel, 20 East Spain Street or P.O. Box 766, Sonoma; second Wednesday, 7:30 P.M. Headquarters: Vasquez House, El Paseo, 129 East Spain Street, Sonoma; 938–0510

Sonoma State Historic Park Association, The Barracks, First Street East and East Spain Street, Sonoma; fourth Tuesday, 4:00 P.M.

Patriotic

Daughters of the American Revolution, Veterans Memorial Building, 126 First Street West, Sonoma; second Thursday, 12:00 noon

Sons of the American Revolution, Oakmont Inn, 7025 Oakmont Drive, Oakmont, Santa Rosa; first Tuesday, 12:00 noon

Hobbies and Activities

Sonoma Valley Gardeners and Lands, Community Center, 276 East Napa Street, Sonoma; Wednesday, 7:30 P.M.

Valley of the Moon Garden Club, Community Center, 276 East Napa Street, Sonoma; first Thursday, 7:30 P.M.

Kiteflyers Club of Sonoma Valley, Maxwell Farms Regional Park, Sonoma; second Sunday, 3:30–5:30 P.M. (weather permitting)

Sonoma Valley Quilters, United Methodist Church, 109 Patten Street, Sonoma; second and fourth Thursdays, 10:00 A.M.–2:00 P.M.

Valley of the Moon Amateur Radio Club, Sonoma Police Station, 175 First Street West, Sonoma; third Wednesday, 7:30 P.M.

Women's Groups

American Association of University Women, Trinity Episcopal Church, 275 East Spain Street, Sonoma; fourth Monday, 2:00 P.M.

Daughters of the American Revolution (see "Patriotic")

Sonoma Valley Mothers Club, Vintage House, 264 First Street East, Sonoma; or P.O. Box 1256, Boyes Hot Springs; second Wednesday, 7:00 P.M.

Sonoma Valley Woman's Club, 574 First Street East, Sonoma; 938–8313; hall rental 996–9725

Venture Club of Sonoma Valley, 253 West Spain Street, Sonoma; club for business women, eighteen–forty; second and fourth Thursdays, 7:00 P.M.

Seniors

Sonoma Sons in Retirement (SIRS), Veterans Memorial Building, 126 First Street West, Sonoma; first Tuesday, 12:00 noon

Valley of the Moon Sons in Retirement (SIRS), Veterans Memorial Building, 126 First Street West, Sonoma; third Tuesday, 12:00 noon

Golden Agers Club of Sonoma, Veterans Memorial Building, 126 First Street West, Sonoma; Wednesday, 11:30 A.M.

Various seniors activities also take place at the *Jerry Casson Vintage House,* 264 First Street East, Sonoma

Social

Italian Catholic Federation, Branch 103, Veterans Memorial Building, 126 First Street West, Sonoma; second Tuesday, 7:30 P.M.

Sonoma Valley Newcomers Club, P.O. Box 776, El Verano 95433; meets third Thursday at various sites

Young People

Valley of the Moon Boys and Girls Club, 744 First Street West, Sonoma; (moving to Maxwell Farms Regional Park); supported by community contributions and run by adult board of directors; the club has many professionally supervised activities for young people, generally below high school age; 938-8544

*P*LACES OF WORSHIP

Assembly of God

New Life Assembly of God, 23109 South Central Avenue, Schellville; 935–0777; Sunday worship 10:45 A.M.

Sonoma Valley Christian Center, 700 Verano Avenue, Sonoma; 935–0922; Sunday worship 10:30 A.M. and 6:00 P.M., Spanish service 1:00 P.M.

Baptist—GARBC

Grace Baptist Church, 245 Fifth Street West; 996–2630; Sunday worship
11:00 A.M. and 6:00 P.M.

Baptist—Southern

Craig Avenue Baptist Church, corner of Craig and Railroad Avenues, El Verano;
996–9188 or 996–2393; Sunday worship 11:00 A.M. and 7:00 P.M.
First Baptist Church, 542 First Street East, Sonoma; 996–3443; Sunday
worship 11:20 A.M.

Catholic

St. Francis Solano Church, 469 Third Street West, Sonoma; 996–6759;
Saturday morning mass (first Saturday) 9:00 A.M.; Saturday vigil mass 5:00
P.M.; Saturday Spanish mass 8:00 P.M.; Sunday masses 7:30, 9:00, and
10:30 A.M., 12:00 noon; Monday–Wednesday masses 8:00 A.M.; Thursday–
Friday masses 9:00 A.M.; holy days 8:00 and 10:00 A.M., 12:00 noon, and
6:00 P.M.
St. Leo's Parish, 601 Agua Caliente Road, Boyes Hot Springs; 996–8422;
Saturday mass 5:00 P.M.; Sunday masses 7:30, 9:00, and 11:00 A.M.; week-
day masses 8:30 A.M.

Christian and Missionary Alliance

Sonoma Alliance Church of the CMA, 125 Watmaugh Road, Sonoma;
935–0724; Sunday worship 10:45 A.M. and 6:00 P.M.

Christian Science

First Church of Christ, Scientist, East Napa Street and Second Street East,
Sonoma; 938–2666; Sunday service 10:00 A.M.

Church of Christ

Church of Christ, 459 West MacArthur, Sonoma; 996–7114; Sunday worship
11:00 A.M.

Congregational

First Congregational Church (UCC), 252 West Spain Street, Sonoma;
996–1328; Sunday worship 10:30 A.M.

Episcopalian

Trinity Episcopal Church, 275 East Spain Street, Sonoma; 938–4846; Sunday services 8:00 and 10:00 A.M.

St. Patrick's Episcopal Church, 9000 Sonoma Highway, Kenwood; 833–4228; Sunday services 8:00 and 10:00 A.M.

Evangelical Free

Community Evangelical Free Church, Henno Road between Warm Springs Road and O'Donnell Lane, Glen Ellen; 996–1479, Sunday worship 11:00 A.M.

Jehovah's Witnesses

Jehovah's Witnesses, 615 Fifth Street West, Sonoma; 996–3021; Sunday worship 10:00 A.M. and 1:30 P.M.

Jesus Christ of Latter Day Saints

Church of Jesus Christ of Latter Day Saints, 16280 LaGrama Drive, Agua Caliente; 996–1497; Sunday sacrament meeting 9:00 A.M.; Sunday priesthood meeting 11:00 A.M.

Jewish

Congregation Shir Shalom, First Congregational Church, 252 West Spain Street; Shabbat service every third Friday, 7:30 P.M.

Lutheran

Faith Lutheran Church, 19355 Arnold Drive, Sonoma; 996–7365; Sunday worship 8:00 and 10:00 A.M.

Methodist

Sonoma United Methodist Church, 109 Patten Street, Sonoma; 996–2151; Sunday worship 10:00 A.M.

Nazarene

Sonoma Valley Church of the Nazarene, 18980 Arnold Drive, El Verano; 996–7578; Sunday worship 11:00 A.M.

Nondenominational

Church of the Little Flock, 276 East Napa Street, Sonoma; 938–8206; Sunday worship 9:30 A.M.

Hope Chapel in Sonoma, Sonoma Valley Woman's Club, 574 First Street East, Sonoma; 539–HOPE; Sunday celebration 9:45 A.M.

Open Door Christian Church, 1250 Lovall Valley Road, Sonoma; 996–5424; Sunday worship 10:45 A.M.

Sonoma Christian Fellowship, 170 Andrieux Street, Sonoma; 938–8371; Sunday worship 10:30 A.M.

Presbyterian

St. Andrew Presbyterian Church, 16290 Arnold Drive, Sonoma; 996–6024; Sunday worship 8:30 and 10:45 A.M.

Reformed Church in America

Sonoma Valley Community Church (RCA), Second Street East and Chase Street, Sonoma; 938–8100; Sunday worship 10:00 A.M.

Seventh Day Adventist

Sonoma Seventh Day Adventist Church, 20575 Broadway, Sonoma; 996–2008; Sabbath worship (Saturday) 11:00 A.M.

ANNUAL EVENTS

The dates of events change from year to year. Phone ahead to determine the dates and times of events. If the listed number cannot be reached, call the Visitors Bureau at 996–1090.

February

Annual Sweetheart Auction, Valley of the Moon Boys and Girls Club; 938–8544; first week

Sweethearts, Wine & Chocolate, Kenwood Winery; 833–5891; second weekend

March

Heart of the Valley Barrel Tasting, Kenwood wineries; 833–5891; third weekend

Annual B. R. Cohn Olive Oil Festival, B. R. Cohn Winery; 938–4064; third week

April in Carneros, district wineries; 996–7256; festivities and tasting; third weekend

May

Cinco de Mayo Festival, Plaza; 938–5131; May 5 or closest weekend

Annual B. R. Cohn Celebrity Golf Classic, Sonoma Golf Club; 938–4064; first weekend

Early California Days, Mission and Barracks; 996–7551; benefits St. Francis Solano School; third weekend

June

Annual Sears Point Outdoor Sports Festival, Sears Point Raceway; 938–8448; first Saturday

Annual Plaza Art and Artisan Show, Plaza; by Valley of the Moon Art Association; 996–2115; first weekend

Hit the Road Jack, starts at Plaza; 938–8544; 5K and 10K sanctioned run/walk; benefits Hospice and Valley of the Moon Boys and Girls Club; first Sunday, starts at 8 A.M.

The Annual Ox Roast, Plaza; 938–4626; benefits Sonoma Community Center; first Sunday, starts at 11:00 A.M.; includes music and art

Annual Kiwanis Turkey Barbecue, Plaza; 996–1090; second Sunday

Quilts and Cars, Barracks; 938–9535; benefits League for Historic Preservation; first Sunday

Annual Mollie Stone's Markets Wine Country Classic Vintage Race, Sears Point Raceway; 938–8448; second weekend

Vintage Race Car Festival, Sebastiani Vineyards parking lot; 938–8544; benefits Valley of the Moon Boys and Girls Club, Visitors' Bureau; second Saturday

Annual National Hot Rod Association Budweiser Festival of Fire Division 7 Race, Sears Point Raceway; 938–8448; fourth weekend; attendance over 100,000

Red and White Ball, Plaza; 938–1279; benefits local charities; wine tasting, music, food, and dancing; usually fourth Saturday evening

July

Fourth of July Parade and Old-Fashioned Celebration, Plaza; 938–4626; art show, games, evening fireworks; parade starts July 4 at 10:00 A.M.

Annual World Championship Pillow Fights and Kenwood Fourth of July Celebration, Kenwood Plaza Park; 833–2440; 3K and 10K foot races start

July 4 at 7:30 A.M.; parade at 10:00 A.M.; pillow fights from 9:00 A.M. until late afternoon

Annual IMSA California Grand Prix, Sears Point Raceway; 938–8448; second weekend

Sonoma Valley Wine Festival & Liberty Ride, Eldridge (Developmental Center); 938–6800; 100K bike ride, wine tasting, and art show; second Sunday

Salute to the Arts, Plaza; 938–1133; art, drama, music, writers, food, and wine; third weekend

Annual National Hot Rod Association (NASCAR) Autolite Nationals, Sears Point Raceway; 938–8448; fourth weekend

August

Annual AMA California Superbike Challenge, Sears Point Raceway; 938–8448; third weekend

Jazz, Art & Wine Festival, Bartholomew Park Winery; 935–9511; third weekend

Sonoma Valley Harvest Wine Auction, location to be arranged; 935–0803; last weekend

September

Glen Ellen Festival, call 996–7772 to find out date and time

Bounty of Sonoma County Celebration, Kenwood Winery; 833–5891; second weekend

Valley of the Moon Vintage Festival, Plaza and the Mission; 996–2109; blessing of the grapes, wine tasting, food, games, music, art show, historical reenactments both days; parade Sunday afternoon; last weekend

October

Sonoma Valley Film Festival, Sebastiani Theatre and parties at other venues; 996–9756 or 996–1090; second weekend

Access to the Arts, Bartholomew Park Winery, by Valley of the Moon Art Association; 996–2115; second weekend

ARTrails Open Studios, 579–2787; artists' open houses; maps available at Visitors Bureau for self-guided tours; third weekend

November

Holiday in Carneros, district wineries; 996–7256; third weekend

December

Heart of the Valley Festival of Lights, various wineries in Kenwood; 833–5891; first Thursday

Christmas Concert by Sonoma Valley Chorale, Veterans Memorial Building, Sonoma; 935–1576; second weekend

"A Christmas Carol" (or other holiday play), Andrews Hall, Sonoma Community Center; 938–4626; annual play with different scripts and local cast; three-day weekend before Christmas

*S*ERIES

Shakespeare: At various locations, particularly wineries, there are many presentations of Shakespeare by drama groups throughout the summer; 996–1090

Sonoma Valley Chorale: Throughout the year the famous Sonoma Valley Chorale conducts concerts in Sonoma; usually at Sonoma Veterans Memorial Building; 935–1576

Sonoma City Opera: Operas are presented several times during the year at the Sonoma Veterans Memorial Building; 935–1576

Concerts at Gloria Ferrer: Almost every month there is a concert at the Gloria Ferrer Champagne Caves; 996–7256

INDEX

ABOUT THE
AUTHORS

*K*athleen and Gerald Hill are native Californians who have lived in Sonoma Valley for more than two decades. The Hills have written Hill Guides *Sonoma Valley: The Secret Wine Country; Napa Valley, Land of Golden Vines; Victoria and Vancouver Island, The Almost Perfect Eden; The Northwest Wine Country; Monterey and Carmel, Eden by the Sea;* and *Santa Barbara and the Central Coast, California's Riviera.* As a team they also wrote the acclaimed exposé *The Aquino Assassination,* as well as *The Real Life Dictionary of American Politics,* and *The Real Life Dictionary of the Law,* which can be found on the Internet at Law.Com. Kathleen is the author of *Festivals USA, Festivals USA—Western States,* and numerous articles on food and travel.

The Hills have been deeply involved in national, state, and local politics and civic activities. Kathleen has served as chair of the Sonoma Cultural and Fine Arts Commission and the Sonoma Community Services Commission while Gerald was a hospital trustee and executive director of a state commission.

Kathleen earned an A.B. at the University of California at Berkeley, a degree in French from the Sorbonne in Paris, and an M.A. at Sonoma State University. Gerald holds an A.B. from Stanford University and a J.D. from Hastings College of the Law, University of California. Kathleen and Jerry have two grown children, Erin and Mack, who are, of course, perfect.